More praise for

"*New Self, New World* is an display of wisdom distilled ....wisdom traditions and the majestic individuals who have experienced them. This book is about achieving the highest dimensions of which humans are capable. Highly recommended."
—Larry Dossey, MD, author of *Healing Beyond the Body,*
 Reinventing Medicine, and *Healing Words*

"One of the most important books of the last fifty years."
—Andrew Harvey, scholar, mystic, author of *Son of Man,*
 Heart Yoga, and *The Hope*

"Shepherd has written a masterpiece. *New Self, New World* calls us back to source, artfully reminding us of the divine magnificence that we have long forgotten in our disembodied culture. As I read it, I felt my shoulders drop as my heart became more available to the moment. Read this book, and remember your self."
—Jeff Brown, author of *Soulshaping*

"[T]he rich and mind-opening ideas presented [in *New Self, New World*] deserve full understanding, and more so, to be fully experienced. At its core, this book is a cultural discourse about reconnecting to the wholeness of being human: to integrate the innate intelligence of the body into a functioning paradigm of human experience and evolution. ... To my mind, not since Ken Wilber introduced the Western world to the integral movement of East-West psycho-spirituality, has there been a catalyst for a paradigm shift that is so relevant and radically reinventive."
—Julie Clayton, *New Consciousness Review*

"Philip Shepherd presents a fascinating examination of myth, consciousness, logic, and existence as our society grows increasingly fearful and anxious. For anyone wanting a new perspective on achieving wholeness or a new sense of living a more present life, *New Self, New World* is a book worth reading. ... exceptionally well-written and insightful."
—Erin Legg, *CirclesOfLight.com*

"Shepherd's passion for adventure and exploration bear out in the broadness and humanity of his vision. Never pontifical, always accessible, Shepherd enlightens and uplifts us so that we will all try harder for a nobler and more compassionate awareness of the globe and all that is in it."
—Lois Henderson, *Bookpleasures.com*

"Shepherd challenges everything society tells us we should believe about ourselves."
—Nicole Etolen, *Prettyopinionated.com*

"*New Self, New World* is an exciting investigation of the human psyche, which is commonly male-oriented, and the deep-seated problems that result when deprived of its female counterpart."
—Juia Ann Charpentier, *Foreword Reviews*

"Shepherd believes that the culture that influences our ideas and experiences tells us the big lie day by day: 'the roots of the self do not lie in the world around us, nor even in the body, but are preserved intact within the blood-brain barrier.' This fiction of self-achieved independence comes at us from all directions when everything in science and spirituality enables us to embrace the universe as an interdependent reality."
—Frederic and Mary Ann Brussat, *Spirituality & Practice*

"Philip Shepherd has written a book which lays the foundation that could lead us humans to a much higher dimension."
—Willie Elliott, *MyShelf.com*

"Shepherd demonstrates how we come into our true humanity only when we unite with our core—the deep, innate intelligence of the body. Our consciousness is not centered in the head any more than the universe is centered around the earth... At once a spiritual handbook, a philosophical primer and a roaming inquiry into human history, *New Self, New World* cracks open the possibilities of human experience and, with clarity, inspiration and compassion, lays the groundwork for personal renewal."
—Digna, *Autumn Blues Reviews*

New Self, New World

New Self, New World

*Recovering Our Senses
in the Twenty-first Century*

Philip Shepherd

Foreword by Andrew Harvey

North Atlantic Books
Berkeley, California

Published by
North Atlantic Books
Berkeley, California

Cover and book design by Allyson Woodrooffe
Exercise photos by Jeremy Mimnaugh
Author photo by Christoph Strube
Cover dandelion photo courtesy of Julia Pepler
Exercise demonstrations by Leanne Dixon
Printed in the United States of America

New Self, New World: Recovering Our Senses in the Twenty-first Century is sponsored and published by the Society for the Study of Native Arts and Sciences (dba North Atlantic Books), an educational nonprofit based in Berkeley, California, that collaborates with partners to develop cross-cultural perspectives, nurture holistic views of art, science, the humanities, and healing, and seed personal and global transformation by publishing work on the relationship of body, spirit, and nature.

North Atlantic Books' publications are available through most bookstores. For further information, visit our website at www.northatlanticbooks.com or call 800-733-3000.

Library of Congress Cataloging-in-Publication Data

Shepherd, Philip, 1953–
New self, new world : recovering our senses in the twenty-first century /
Philip Shepherd.
     p. cm.
ISBN 978-1-55643-911-7
1. Self (Philosophy)   2. Self.   3. Consciousness.   I. Title.
BD438.5.S457 2010
128—dc22   2010002415

5 6 7 8 9 10 VERSA 21 20 19 18
Printed on recycled paper

North Atlantic Books is committed to the protection of our environment.
We partner with FSC-certified printers using soy-based inks and
print on recycled paper whenever possible.

This book is dedicated
to my mother, Jane;
to my daughters, Kate and Julia;
and to my true-hearted love, AW.

Of what use is a book that does not carry us beyond all books?

—Friedrich Nietzsche

My space chums are concerned about our evolvement because they say we're all connected. "Everything is part of everything." They started talking about a little something they call "interstellar interspecies symbiosis." To hold up my end of the conversation, I asked them to elaborate. So they brought up the Quantum Inseparability Principle. "Every particle affects every other particle everywhere." They tried to bring quantum physics down to a level I could more clearly misunderstand. Then one of them mentioned the Bootstrap Theory, and at the point they got into the Superstring Theory, frankly, I think even they were in over their heads. But here's what I got from it all: seems like there's some kind of cosmic Krazy Glue connecting everything to everything.

—Jane Wagner, *The Search for Signs of Intelligent Life in the Universe;* performed by Lily Tomlin

In order to become myself I must cease to be what I always thought I wanted to be, and in order to find myself I must go out of myself, and in order to live I have to die.

—Thomas Merton, *New Seeds of Contemplation*

Contents

Exercises

Foreword
by Andrew Harvey

The deepest meaning of the all-embracing world crisis of our time, which threatens the future of the human race and of much of nature, is that it is an evolutionary crisis. It is, at once, a death of all our agendas, illusions and fantasies of uniqueness, domination over nature, and endless growth, and a birth—whose crucible is tragedy, heartbreak and devastation—of an embodied divine humanity capable of and inspired to work directly with the Divine to transform all existing ways of being and doing everything. Seeing the crisis in this way—as an unprecedented and inescapable dark night of our species that could lead to the unprecedented birth, on a massive scale, of a new embodied divine consciousness-in-action—not only enables us to endure its necessary horrors and ordeals with faith, perseverance, and grace; it aligns us with the design of the divine intelligence of evolution itself, a design that has been made available to us, with majestic passion and precision, in the divinely inspired works of great modern evolutionary mystics such as Sri Aurobindo, Jean Gebser, Teilhard de Chardin, Father Bede Griffiths and Ken Wilber. It is the essence of our terrifying and amazing time—its central and potentially all-transforming paradox—that in our darkest hour, the most all-encompassing and transfiguring vision of what we essentially are and could be is also arising to give us the passion and the peace, the knowledge and hope and strength that we will need to rise to the full height of our evolutionary destiny.

Philip Shepherd, in his profound and original masterpiece *New Self, New World,* now adds his distinctive, elegant, fierce and tender voice to those of his distinguished evolutionary predecessors. His book—written over a decade of painstaking, grueling self-exploration, and with the highest nobility and clarity of soul—provides us all with an indispensable guide to why a radically embodied divine humanity needs to be birthed now, and birthed fast, and it also shows us how to allow this bewildering and majestic destiny to be worked out in and through us through divine grace. This is not a book to be read casually or fast; it is not a 'self-help' book with easily assimilable, facile 'practices', false promises of 'instant healing' and risibly superficial 'quick fixes'. It is that rarest of works in our age—a brave, magnificent manifesto for a new kind of divine human life, a life lived in conscious dynamic harmony of illumined mind, impassioned and tender heart and increasingly, consciously, divinized body.

Those of us who are already experiencing the rigors, demands and glories of the birth that is now taking place will find in *New Self, New World* both a brilliant forensic analysis of our current dead-end, flatland obsession with reason and the mind and all the tyrannical, matricidal and suicidal structures and actions it engenders; and a luminous, inspiring, exact and exacting description of the embodied divine human life of the birth—a life in which soul is embodied and body ensouled and the 'masculine' energies of clarity, control and forceful action dance in abandoned, perfect lucid rhythm with the restored and celebrated 'feminine' energies of adoration, tender erotic love of all creation, and wise, sustaining, humble, nourishing interrelationship. Both in the way it is structured and in the precise but richly poetic and full-breathed, almost mantric way in which it is written, *New Self, New World* not only describes this sacred marriage of transcendence and immanence, body and soul, masculine and feminine, but also embodies it with a magical power and force that is at once challenging and healing.

Philip Shepherd's book presents three ways of understanding ourselves that go so against the grain of habituated, sclerotic thinking that they can be considered revolutionary. These three radical contributions are: a new model of human consciousness; a new vision of our evolutionary history; and a new vision of the interrelated environmental, political, social and economic crises that now threaten our survival and demand a collective evolutionary leap in embodied, divine consciousness.

In the new model of human consciousness that *New Self, New World* offers, Philip Shepherd proposes a conscious 'sacred marriage' of what he calls "the two brains of the human being"—between, in other words, the intelligence we have ruthlessly and ruinously centered only in the cranium, with its obsessive and dissociated cold passion for separatist analysis, objectification and control; and the vast, free-flowing, infinitely supple and responsive intuitive intelligence of our 'second brain': that of the enteric nervous system, immune system and genetic networks, with its locus in the pelvic bowl. In this radical new model, the psyche or spirit is shown to pervade every living part and every cell of our human organism in such a way that makes the transfiguration of the human into the divine human possible. The evolutionary significance of this very grounded and precise vision cannot be overstated: it accords, in every spiritual and material detail, with the universal law of interrelationship, inter-communion and inter-responsibility that is everywhere proclaimed by both the ancient mystical systems and those of the emerging evolutionary mysticism. Our only possible release from the psychotic tyranny of a heartless and radically dissociated glorification of bodiless intelligence lies in a reclamation of the almost miraculous, sensitive awareness of all the interrelated physical and cellular systems, and in a sacred marriage of that vivid and vibrant 'feminine' body consciousness—allowed at last to speak in its own sacred language—with a purified, chastened, tenderized 'masculine' rational consciousness. It is precisely this 'sacred marriage' and the birth of the divine human it makes possible that Sri Aurobindo, in his own inimitably grand way, celebrates in his *The Life Divine*. Philip Shepherd's particular contribution to the understanding and unfolding of the birth now taking place is that it is rooted not in grand metaphysics alone, or even exclusively in a 'yogic' understanding of the mystical tantric transformation of matter, but in the latest astounding revelations of quantum mechanics and neurobiology that reveal to all those who dare to see the mystery of a material cosmos everywhere pervaded by dynamic spirit-energy. Such a vision—which fuses the highest mystical wisdom, the most advanced scientific inquiry, and the greatest and most poignant historical urgency—could only be born now. It is Philip Shepherd's peculiar grace to be its midwife.

In Philip Shepherd's second great contribution to our evolutionary crisis—that of a new vision of our history—he demonstrates how the entire 'progress' of our modern history has been severely maimed and distorted by a wholesale, ruthless, semi-demented denigration of the values and wisdom of the feminine. *New Self, New World* makes it fiercely clear that our now habitual neglect and ignorance of the center of our 'feminine intelligence'—the second brain—is part of a much larger and now blatantly lethal denigration of the feminine in all of the values that govern our rapidly more distorted and destructive relationships to each other, to Creation, and to the political, social and economic worlds we create and continue to keep going. Other major writers, of course, have pointed out, sometimes with as great an eloquence and elegance, this devaluation of the feminine and its increasingly catastrophic consequences in every domain of human life. What makes Philip Shepherd's work unique is that it demonstrates clearly and specifically how the orientation of our thinking about the body has determined and potentially aborted our evolution. In some of the greatest and most revealing pages of *New Self, New World*, Shepherd shows, definitively I believe, how the center of our thinking has risen through the body over the passing millennia, starting in the belly center of consciousness in the Paleolithic, and ascending to the isolated, tyrannical 'cranium' center in our modern era, birthing separatist belief systems, dissociated social, political, economic and scientific philosophies, and hierarchies of all kinds that enshrine division, injustice, horrible poverty and inequality, and thrive on the 'dominator delusion' that, if we continue to feed it blindly, can only now lead to the annihilation of humanity and the terrifying desecration of most of the natural world.

Once we truly dare to grasp how our own thinking is constricted and perverted by what amounts to the trained addiction of our body-thinking to predominantly masculine values and perspectives, then, Philip Shepherd suggests, we will begin to see clearly not only its horrific impact on the world around us but also—and this is crucial for our evolution and survival—the woeful superficiality, narrowness, and petty unwisdom of most of the proposed 'solutions' to the crisis we are mired in. We seem still to want to go on believing—against mounting evidence—that the interrelated crises of the death we are passing through can all be dealt with through a hyped-up, cracked-up application of the very addicted and heart-dead consciousness that created it to begin with, through technological legerdemain and wizardry, super-smart social engineering and political will radically dissociated from spiritual law or practice. This is a desperate, corrupt, bankrupt and dangerous fantasy, one whose absurdity is destined now to be exploded, and in increasingly deadly and dramatic ways, as we enter into the eye of our evolutionary perfect storm. Without the revolution that *New Self, New World* proposes—a revolution of illumined mind, sacred heart and divinized body; without entering, in fact, into the integral transformation of the birth, and acting from its healed sacred consciousness urgently in every realm of human endeavor, we will not be able even to imagine—let alone labor to construct, enshrine, embody and enact—the new ways of being and doing and creating that we now need if we are to rise to the challenge of our evolutionary destiny. What lies ahead for us if we refuse the challenge of transformation is first, unimaginable chaos and horror, and then extinction; if we accept the terrors of the challenge and submit to its rigor and demands in grateful surrender, anything is possible. The great hope that Philip Shepherd offers—and that has clearly inspired him through all the long and lonely labor of creating his masterpiece—is that the human race will wake up in time, will go on a journey into a new, vibrant, embodied wholeness of heart, mind, soul and body, and will birth in divinely-inspired sacred action, in and through divine grace, a new and far more just and harmonious world. To that hope Philip Shepherd has devoted his life, his brilliance, his energy, and all the rich and profound wisdom and analysis of *New Self, New World*. May we all be worthy of his faith.

Introduction

Bene vive ut bene vivas.
(Live well that you may live well.)

In *The Ipcress File,* an espionage movie from the sixties, there is a scene that has lingered in my memory for decades. The main character, played by Michael Caine, works for British intelligence. In the course of the film he is betrayed and taken prisoner. He knows he is going to be brainwashed, and he is also familiar with the techniques that will be used. To maintain his grip on reality, he marks the wall of his cell by scratching it each day with a bent nail. His captors systematically wear him down, but when he senses he is finally on the verge of capitulation, he smuggles the bent nail into the brainwashing chamber and, in the midst of the session, drives it deep into the flesh of his hand. Once the ordeal is over he discovers the painful gash it has left, and puzzles, and then remembers—as he looks at the mark on his hand, the full reality of his circumstances comes back to him. Because of that mark, his life is saved.

Whether or not it has actually saved my life, I have been making marks with a similar purpose for years. Less dramatically, mine have been on paper—I have scratched out notes, questions, insights, anything that might serve as a reminder of the full reality of my world. Grocery receipts have been covered, notepads have been filled, the backs of books and envelopes scribbled on—I have even typed up little cards that I could carry in my wallet. A lot of what I've written over the years was of transient value, but I kept at it as though my life depended on it. Like the open wound in Michael Caine's hand, my notes have helped to connect me with a truth that I have always found

1

difficult to name, but which sustains my life and connects me to the world. Alas, when it came to living that truth, I seemed to be chronically forgetful.

Over the years I began to understand that my forgetfulness was due not so much to my personal failings, abundant though they are; it was being triggered by something much larger: the story our culture communicates and which describes the nature of reality for us. Every culture, of course, is a construct of custom and technology and language and myth and values that, taken together, create and communicate its overarching story. The stories told by different cultures often differ radically in their particulars. In the Maori tradition food is sacred, whereas we see it as a pleasurable commodity to which our bank balance entitles us; in the Japanese tradition, the belly is the seat of truth, whereas we see it as a troublesome area prone to indigestion and weight gain; the Native American tradition understands the Great Spirit to whisper through all the events of the world, whereas we see around us a world of lifeless matter whose transformations are exclusively governed by the laws of physics.

More critically than such particular differences, though, the story upheld by each culture defines a landscape of behavior and thinking as 'normal' and then, like a chameleon, disappears within it. When that happens, the definition is mistaken for the world itself, and passes itself off as the one true reality.

Unfortunately, the camouflaged story of *our* culture represents the landscape around us as a hostile world created by chance, and indifferent to our thoughts and the events that take place within it; it describes a strictly material reality that isolates each of us in the realm of the independent self. When that description is compared to more explicit stories that have stood the tests of time and scrutiny—those of physics, say, or mythology, or art, or psychology or the world's spiritual traditions—we find that it is abrasively out of step with them. And yet our make-believe fantasy, which has all the substance of a canvas theater flat, stands between us and the world and confines us from it as surely as his concrete cell confined Michael Caine.

The single greatest harm done by the story our culture tells, though, comes from the divisions it enforces within each of us. We are assured in a million ways that the sensational intelligence of the body is not really worth paying attention to. And we find, indeed, that the more unmindful we become of our bodies, the more they appear to be mindless. And so we are persuaded to separate from the body and live in the head, assured by a culture that passes off this pathological dissociation as completely normal, natural and unavoidable. Once we are caught in the prison of our craniums, we are unable to join the world—though our hearts yearn to do so. Instead of joining it, we think about it, and analyze it, and judge it. That's just how we are, and it's what we imagine the normal human state to be. By contrast, certain other cultures tell stories about humankind's partnership with the living world, and foster an embodied sensitivity to it.

The way our culture lures us into our heads reminds me of the blown-glass wasp traps that people place in their gardens. These bottles have a hole in the bottom through which wasps can enter, drawn by the scent of a sweetened liquid inside; but once inside, the wasps cannot find their way out again. They buzz and bounce and fret inside the bottle, able to see and hear the world around them, but unable to rejoin it. So it is with us: as children we are lured up into our heads by the metaphors and values and implicit instructions of our culture and we become trapped there, unable to escape. Our thoughts buzz and bounce inside our craniums; we can see the world and hear it and think about it as our ideas go around and around in circles, but we have forgotten how to 'be' in it.

The description of 'normal' we have been raised on may be as hard to detect as a chameleon in a landscape, but it is always there, exerting its influence—and its effect can be felt in a sense of frustration or lack in our lives as we try to live a story that is at odds with reality. When we attempt to recover peace in our lives, our efforts more often resemble anxiety management than any kind of real peace. Being estranged from our bodies, we feel victimized by them—and so when they hurt or fall sick, we feel fear or annoyance or betrayal; and when we exert them or look in the mirror, we may feel guilt or vanity or anger about the shape they are in. And though we accept the fact of our essential solitude, we cannot bear the emptiness of our own company. To alleviate it, we surround ourselves with distractions: chat rooms, telephones, computer games, shopping, Web browsing, Twittering, and of course popular entertainment that wears meaning on its sleeve as an assurance to us all. We generally have neither the time nor the attention span for art that draws us into the unnamable ambiguities of life itself. When we try to improve our situation, we look about for answers that will help us connect and feel better about ourselves—yet none of the self-help prescriptions seems to work for very long. Our very impulse to self-improvement often reinforces our inner division, by which the part of the self that thinks in the isolation of the wasp trap inflicts idealized patterns of behavior on our body and feelings, all in the name of mutual benefit. Our ability to escape that divided state is hampered by our difficulty in understanding that **what holds us back are the very things we accept as the normal givens of the world.**[*]

When I was eighteen, what I wanted more than anything was to shrug off the constraints of seeing and understanding I'd grown up with, because I could feel the bricks and mortar of those 'givens' hemming me in. I left my home in Canada, went to England, bought a bicycle, and headed off on it for Japan. The bicycle seemed the ideal vehicle on which to break through the painted scrim: on a bicycle, you don't merely watch what you pass by, you belong to it. I slept in olive groves in Greece, worked in the Mediterranean on a little Arab cargo boat (the *Saint Hilarion*) with a crew of three, bedded down under the stars in the Great Syrian Desert, spent a night in an Iraqi police station as a guest of the chief of police, stayed with students in a Baghdad ghetto, toured with a Kathakali theater troupe in the south of India, and studied classical Noh theater in Japan. 'Normal' would never again be a given for me.

Through it all I wrote, committing my marks to paper lest amnesia overtake me. And slowly, over the decades, those marks began to cohere and reveal the entity I had been struggling to identify and question: the foundational story on which all the edifices of our thinking are built, the owner's manual that tells us how to relate to our own bodies and our world. It became clear that the fundamental lesion between our heads and our bodies was the prototype for all the dualities we experience in the world: between subject and object, male and female, self and world, idea and feeling, mind and matter, doing and being, man and nature, good and evil. Clear, too, that the prototype by which our heads rule our bodies establishes a tacit *hierarchy* within each duality—of head over body, subject over object, male over female, self over world, idea over feeling, mind over matter, doing over

---

[*] Throughout the book I make occasional use of both bold and italicized fonts. My hope is that the changes in font might help the reader in the way a close-up in a film helps the viewer—to pay attention differently. So please consider these fonts as an invitation to linger, to pause, to challenge, and perhaps to permit a field of implications to swarm and subside.

being, man over nature, and good (however narrowly defined) over evil. Furthermore, all of those hierarchies conform to the values of patriarchy; patriarchy itself, then, seems to be implied in the hierarchy of the idea-filled head ruling over the sensation-filled body. If that is so, then it finally becomes clear that no 'idea', however persuasive, can help us beyond our ruinous divisions. Wonderful books have already been written about *ideas* about culture and truth and freedom and responsibility and ecology and balance and what matters in life. All of those subjects are close to this book's heart—but ideas, however well-meaning, tend to feed and reinforce the dominant head; even when they moderate its tyranny, they strengthen its right to rule. A basic, rarely noticed principle extends that tyranny to all we see and do: *as we relate to the body, so we relate to the world*. The body is not, as we are encouraged to believe, a mere appendage: our relationship to it actually orients our thinking. **Simply put, as long as we remain in our heads, we will remain married to the values of the head. That in a nutshell is our culture's Achilles' heel—and by extension, the Achilles' heel of us all.** On that basis, this book attempts something else. First, to write about the lens by which we bring the world around us into focus—our head-centered consciousness; and second, to explore the appealing alternative: deepening our experience of the world by deepening our experience of the body.

In that this book is primarily about *the body* rather than about *ideas* about the body, it takes on a peculiar challenge. It does present ideas, to be sure, but those ideas are accountable first and foremost to experience; and that means that they are woven into the world rather than being tidied back into themselves. As such, the journey of this book is more akin to that of building a house than traveling to some far-off destination: just as the journey of building a house will traverse its footprint deliberately in myriad circuitous, overlapping paths as materials are woven together to create a space that enhances our living, so too with the 'footprint' of this book. Its aim is not to provide a linear argument that is logically sound and self-sufficient, per se, but to quicken readers to choices by which they can liberate themselves from the problem of our unseen normality. The book unfolds in accord with a deep organic logic; its aims and its subject matter could not be served by the structure of a more linear approach. It layers and weaves and teases out its themes, often leaning on the evidence of our senses as much as on ideas; as such it occasionally unfurls in spirals and paradox—a tendency that can frustrate a reader insistent on a thesis with a more orderly explication. But the aim of the book is not simply to present its thesis; its aim is to help readers reflect on their own experience in a way that can help deliver us all from our isolation. As a culture, we literally have to come to our senses.

The desire to look past the wall of description and clamber out of the solitary cell of the self lies at the very heart of the age-old quest of the human soul: the quest for **wholeness**—that is, to feel the world as a whole, and the self as a whole within it, and, in feeling that wholeness, to live it. In that regard, it seems to me that *the primary freedom denied us by our culture's invisible walls is the freedom to feel the unbroken wholeness of the world to which we belong*—which happens to be the world's primary reality. Other cultures, by contrast, consider the freedom to feel that wholeness to be the foremost responsibility we have as human beings. And, sure, we know intellectually that the world is more than a random assemblage of multiple and even disparate parts; but knowing that the world is ultimately a unity is not to be confused with the freedom to *feel and live* within its unity. Once we have lost our **freedom** to feel the world's unbroken wholeness, of course, we lose the freedom to feel the self as a whole. We lose the kind of **creativity** that only wholeness can support. We also, obviously, lose our ability to be **present** with the world's fundamental reality, as well as with the fundamental truth of our own lives, which lies in our relationship to that reality.

Those three issues—*freedom, creativity* and *presence*—are at the crux of our humanity, and constitute the 'footprint' of this book. Like the three legs of a garden stool, those qualities are entirely interdependent: no one of them can stand without the others. And though we may think of them merely as attributes to be desired and acquired, in the way we might seek knowledge or wealth, I believe that they are actually three different facets of the phenomenon of our natural wholeness. In turn they lead to occasions of grace, spontaneity, ease, humility and clarity, all concomitants of wholeness. And I mean wholeness in the most personal sense: the wholeness of the self that lies beyond all division; the wholeness that, when we find it, expresses its truth in each of our actions; the wholeness of a body at peace with itself and in harmony with the world around it. Our culture has so accustomed us to life in the wasp trap—in which self-tyranny, fragmentation, anxiety, alienation and stunted relationships are taken as normal—that we are in danger of mistaking as whole what is, in fact, no more than wholly normal.

Its dual concern for an understanding of the self that is holistic, and for being able to achieve an experience of the world that is holistic, aligns this book with both the ancient tradition known as the Perennial Philosophy and the newer philosophy known as Deep Ecology. Once we break free from the narrow constraints of the enclosed self, we open the door onto a sensitivity in which our union or connection with the world as a whole becomes something we clearly feel—the essence of the spiritual experience. But we are also increasingly drawn into harmony with that whole, and exposed to our responsibilities to it—the essence of Deep Ecology. To the extent that *New Self, New World* is about personal growth, it is in keeping with the Deep Ecology notion that such growth entails not just a deepening of our experience and questions and commitment, but also an expanding of our sensitivities to include all the world around us, so that the self comes to identify with the whole to which it belongs. That is true self-realization—and it literally leads us to new ways of thinking and acting and being in the world.

The book's theme of wholeness calls into question the descriptions we have literally taken into our bodies, dividing up self and world in the process. It also helps us understand the flip side of the coin: that by opening to the consciousness of our bodies we can awaken our full intelligence and come home to our wholeness, bit by bit. And to be quite clear, coming home to our own wholeness is not about establishing a private sanctuary of unity within the boundaries of our skin; it is about yielding to the radiant mystery of the felt whole that sustains us, and which we help to sustain—however it may call to us, however it may live in us, wherever it may take us. In the years it has taken to bring this book to fruition, the promise of bringing clarity to that homecoming has hung before me like a constellation, guiding its journey. And that journey has been every bit as much of an adventure for me as was that long-ago, star-crossed trip to Japan on my bike.

Part I

Do Be Do Be Do

We are literally hypnotized from infancy by the cultural milieu in which we are immersed; we see the world the way we are enculturated to see it. A prime task of adult life is to become dehypnotized, "enlightened"—to see reality as it is.

—Willis Harman, *Global Mind Change*

Creativity, in almost every area of life, is blocked by a wide range of rigidly held assumptions that are taken for granted by society as a whole.

—David Bohm, *Dialogue as a New Creative Order*

Deep ecology sees the world not as a collection of isolated objects, but as a network of phenomena that are fundamentally interconnected and interdependent ... There is another way in which Arne Naess has characterized deep ecology. "The essence of deep ecology," he says, "is to ask deeper questions." This is also the essence of a paradigm shift.

—Fritjof Capra, *The Web of Life*

1 | The Elements of Myth

The Story That Creates Reality

As a culture, and as individuals, we suffer from a case of mistaken identity. This is not just one more problem to add to our confusion—it is the central issue. Its scope is such that if you were to consider the most significant challenges that afflict us—the social problems, the environmental problems, the economic problems, the problems of alienation—and trace each of them to their origins, you would find that they all lead back to the same cultural force: the story that tells us who we are and what it means to be human. And you would find that same force exacerbating every problem we face as individuals.

Any culture is a construct of language, architecture, dress, customs, myths, values, teachings and rituals that, taken together, communicate a story that frames reality in a particular way, and so frames us too. The broad story that has been developed by the culture of the industrialized West—though it is only a story—invisibly shapes all that we do: its construct effectively takes us out of relationship with the particular life of the present, out of relationship with all-sustaining nature, out of relationship even with our own hearts and bodies, and encases our sense of self within our own skins—more specifically, within the part of us that sits above the neck. Looking out at the world around us from that vantage, we find it to be materialistic and random, shattered into its constituent bits, a world in which survival is granted only to the fittest of its specimens. We accept that version of reality because it feels right; but a shattered outer world feels right to us only because our inner world has been shattered by our culture's tacit story. A sensibility that is not whole cannot detect wholeness—and so has no reason even to believe wholeness exists in any meaningful way.

Sometimes, of course, what *feels* right to us actually *is* right. The only indication we have that our deeply felt identity may be mistaken—that there may be more to the reality of our lives than disparate parts that occasionally overlap or bump into each other—is that every other story that has actually been held accountable to questioning and research, or that has been attuned by centuries of telling and retelling, suggests that *the abiding reality of life, the abiding reality of anything, is to be found in its relationship to the whole.* That is what quantum mechanics tells us, which has been tested and challenged and retested in labs around the world; that is what the world's mystic traditions tell us, which have been shaped over aeons by countless individual journeys into the stillness that breathes through all the world's particulars; that is what works of art tell us when their significance traverses centuries and cultures with an undiminished resonance: they present truths of such relevance to the human heart that they carry us, the viewers and listeners, into renewed and vivid relationship with the world around us and with our own lives. Their ability to do that is what gives them their power to endure. Finally, we might look to the stories of myth, which have represented the human journey with a deep, living, metaphoric verity that has been refined over millennia by telling and retelling. Despite that refined verity, though, we generally find myths remote and largely irrelevant to the story to which we have dedicated ourselves. For that very reason, they promise to provoke some fruitful questions about it. Let us start, then, by asking what myths tell us about the elements of our own humanity.

Our culture likes to take a superior stance when it comes to myth. In fact, when we call something a myth, we are calling it a lie; a mythomaniac is not someone who has a mania for myths, but a chronic liar. We depict myths as harmless cartoons or view them as superstitious carryovers from our distant past—naive explanations of natural phenomena. Joseph Campbell saw something else: in his book *The Hero with a Thousand Faces,* he describes how the ageless myths are playing themselves out among us here and now—how they are *reborn within us* here and now. As he put it,

> The latest incarnation of Oedipus, the continued romance of Beauty and the Beast, stand this afternoon

on the corner of Forty-second Street and Fifth Avenue,
waiting for the traffic light to change.[1]

In the way that the dynamic of the atom is mimicked in the orbiting
of our solar system, and again in the swirl of our galaxy, the dynamic
of myth orbits through our lives and shapes them on every level—from
the personal to that of expanding civilizations. The Neoplatonic philosopher Sallustius wrote of myths, "These things never happened, but
they always are."[2] Roberto Calasso, author of *The Marriage of Cadmus and Harmony*, wrote, "The myths ... are still out there, waiting to
wake us and be seen by us."[3] The meanings in myths are multilayered
and compressed, coiled like springs, waiting to be triggered by the attentions of the human heart—which alone can unleash their timeless
vitality into the world.

The premise of Campbell's book is that through all the legends,
folktales, spiritual traditions and religions of the world, a single
myth—what Campbell called the monomyth—is being told over and
over. At its core is the journey of a single hero, answering the "call to
adventure." To be sure, that call to adventure can take many forms,
and the hero's journey may be cast in myriad eras, settings, cultures,
circumstances and adventures—but the essence of the story is fundamental to myth and, as Campbell wrote, has been "the living inspiration of whatever else may have appeared out of the activities of the
human body and mind."[4] And Campbell is as experienced a guide to
that story as we could hope for.

So what are the most basic elements of that story? The first involves the society to which the hero belongs: hunkered against the
unfamiliar, dark and shifting forces beyond its borders, the hero's society has defined its world authoritatively and shaped itself to confirm
that definition; but its very adherence to that definition compromises
its ability to transform. What cannot transform is stuck. When a symbol of redemption for the society appears in the form of a task to be
achieved or an object to be won (e.g., the search for the Holy Grail),
the hero's challenge is defined. Called to adventure, his spiritual center of gravity shifts to the landscape beyond the outer rim of what is
familiar to either him or his society. That unknown landscape may
be subterranean, distant, forested or suboceanic, but it holds terrors,
treasures and strange, often shape-shifting beings who may be possessed of supernatural powers. In answering the call to adventure, the

hero has to make a journey: he has to transgress the boundaries that society has set for itself. His society may honor him for that, or disdain him, or pay him no heed. In any event, as Campbell puts it, the hero

> cannot, indeed must not, wait for his community to cast off its slough of pride, fear, rationalized avarice, and sanctified misunderstanding. "Live," Nietzsche says, "as though the day were here." It is not society that is to guide and save the creative hero, but precisely the reverse.[5]

The hero's journey beyond what is set and known and familiar disorients and confuses and tests him. He usually has to face a grasping tyrant in the form of a king, ogre or monster who stifles the energies that feed and vitalize the universe. If the hero is successful in overcoming the tyrant, he wins a life-giving perspective, which may be symbolized as runes of wisdom, treasure, or a bride. His next task is "to return then to us, transfigured, and teach the lesson he has learned of life renewed."[6] The effect of his return is to initiate a transformation of renewal, releasing again the flow of life into the body of his society.

Myth recognizes that any society will tend to establish and enforce norms that purport to represent reality, though in truth they only represent agreed-upon customs of thinking. The definitions within which a society shelters hold the chaos of the unknown at bay, but they also stifle a society's plasticity—which means they stifle its creative ability to engage with reality. Take our own case, for example: if we could shed our mistaken identity and see the harmony of self and world for what it is, would we be able to persist in those pursuits that wreak havoc on the very air we breathe and the creatures whose planet we share? The need to transform beyond our "pride, fear, rationalized avarice, and sanctified misunderstanding" has never been more desperate, and we generally know that, but we still seem to be stuck in the very status quo that is destroying us.

The hero's task is not to threaten his society, nor to take it over tyrannically with his newfound perspective, nor to abandon it; his task is to bring his new perspective back to be integrated in such a way that the society's self-definition loosens and shifts to accommodate what it has hitherto excluded. By altering its defined 'known' to accommodate what the hero has brought back from the unknown, the society more closely harmonizes with the unseen world around it, and is newly energized in the process.

The Sacred Marriage

Myth tells us a great deal about the dynamics of a society, in particular about how its freedom, creativity and presence are affected by the ways in which it relates to both the individual citizen and the world around it; but that scale is only one of the levels on which the multivalent truths of myth operate. They also, for instance, reveal the dynamics of familial relationships, as Freud's famous treatment of the Oedipus myth made clear. For me, however, the most potent revelations of myth come about once we recognize all the players in its tales as *parts of the self*. There is a part of the self, myth tells us, that needs to venture into the unknown and bring a new perspective to bear on its own status quo, in order that it might harmonize more closely with the world's reality.

Joseph Campbell urged us to see that: "It's *you*. All of these symbols in mythology refer to you."[7] In other words, **mythic events represent the dynamics within the self that shape or thwart the transformation of our consciousness;** and *the symbols myth supplies "carry the human spirit forward, in counteraction to those constant human fantasies that tend to tie it back."*[8] The hero's role of liberator plays itself out in each of our lives, but so does the role of the grasping, controlling tyrant. By clarifying those roles, myth explicates the nature of the fantasies that tie us back, which we have called 'descriptions'; it points out the source of those fantasies within ourselves; and it offers the insights needed to free ourselves of their hold. More specifically, the various journeys made by myth's heroes navigate the disjunctures that occur between mind and body in an effort to heal them. "The ancient myths were designed to harmonize the mind and the body,"[9] as Campbell put it—they free our thoughts from the bottle so they can rejoin the lush garden of the body. As the myths show us, such a harmonization requires a soul-shaking abandonment of our craving for fantasy, that we might transcend the errors of any mere story and merge with the life of 'what is'.

But exactly how is it that the host of characters who drive the storied myths of the world can be said to represent elements of the self?

We can answer that by looking into the two primary themes of myth: one theme is represented by the polarity between *male and female,* and the other by the polarity between *hero and tyrant.* Myth explicates each theme, as well as the relationship between the themes, over and over—because together they map out the journey by which the parts of the self evolve into a whole. In a nutshell, the symbolic language of myth tells us that the self thrives as a marriage between male and female, in the harmony of which reside its fundamental strengths; that the uniting of male and female is the central concern of the hero's journey; that a failure or a refusal to find balance in that union leads to tyranny; and that the effects of that tyranny show up not just in our relationship to our own bodies, but also in our relationship to the body of the earth. Myth finally affirms that **until the inner tyrant is outed, there can be no true marriage within of the male and female elements of the self.** That event is typically represented in myth with the slaying of the tyrant and the subsequent wedding ceremony. The central importance of that union was stressed by the great modern psychologist Carl Jung, for whom, as Marion Woodman put it, "the whole process of the soul's journey is toward the inner marriage of the mature masculine and the mature feminine."[10]

The stage is set for that marriage by creation myths, which tell us that the universe began as a primordial unity of male and female and that the dividing of that unity enabled the universe to evolve. Male and female split apart at the beginning of time—commonly into sky and earth—but they continued to long for each other, as expressed by the Greek dramatist Aeschylus,

> Holy sky desires to penetrate the earth.
> Love seizes the earth with longing for this marriage.
> And rain, falling from her bedfellow the sky,
> impregnates earth; and she brings forth for men
> pasture for their flocks, and grain for them.[11]

As this imagery suggests, myths differentiate between male and female in a fundamental way. **The male element is associated with doing:** the ever-active sky brings rain and wind and thunderheads and lightning and the revolving watchfulness of the stars and planets and the blazing gaze of the sun; we are also told that the angels, who dwell in the sky and are active in the affairs of the earth, are exclusively male. **The female element is associated with being:** the earth just is; it receives the offerings of the sky in all their manifestations and integrates them to bring forth transformative life. As poet and myth scholar Robert Graves observed, "Man does; woman is." Myth tells us that these two elements of the self—doing and being—unite in us to form a unity. Neither by itself can constitute an evolving whole.

In recent decades, male/female differences have been a touchy subject—and for good reason: history warns of dire consequences for women in society whenever a difference has been acknowledged. They have been vilified, shunned, segregated and even tortured for such differences. But perhaps we are ready to honor our mutual strengths, even as they become more clearly understood. Recent advances in scanning technology, for instance, enable us to actually watch the brain at work as men and women process information and emotions, assess physical challenges, and even hear, smell and feel. The differences between them prompted feminist and psychologist JoAnn Deak to comment, "I've come to believe that the brain is the most genderized part of the body."[12] Another researcher declared, "There's not a gender gap, there's a gender chasm."[13] Their comments are based on extensive clinical evidence. Gendered brain maps show that when men are given a task, such as reading for comprehension, they are likely to use a small area in one hemisphere of the brain; when women are given the same task, they characteristically use both sides of the brain and more of the brain overall. Speaking to a predominantly female audience, JoAnn Deak characterized the differences as follows:

> We [women] are programmed to multitask; we are built to massively connect and communicate. Male brains are built to streamline and to go right to what they have to do.[14]

We use and often demand conformity to the categories 'men' and 'women' when describing ourselves, but nature pays our descriptions little heed, creating instead a range of sexual identities that express the full potential of our humanity; in the case of hermaphrodites, nature confounds the very categories of 'men' and 'women' to which we would like to hold it accountable. Unlike ours, some cultures show special respect for individuals who blur those categories, considering them to have a divine perspective: after all, if we were created in God's image, then God must include both male and female. In that regard we are all blessed with divine sensibilities, for we are all blessed with both the male element of doing and the female element of being within us.

That said, it is nonetheless true that female strengths tend to predominate in women and male strengths in men. In fact, if we look closely at the wording by which Deak characterized male and female brains, we find that it accords with what Robert Graves observed. Male brains, said Deak, are "built to streamline and to go right to *what they have to do.*" In other words, as Graves summarized it, "Man does." And again I would like to emphasize that **the male element in each of us** does, which is in strict opposition to any silliness claiming that women can't or shouldn't do.

To see how the element of Being shows up in Deak's description of the female brain asks for a subtler understanding. We might describe 'Being' as simply 'that which is' in its entirety: unfiltered, free from exclusion, replete in all its paradoxes and transformations.* Of course, the entirety of 'what is' is always in process—multitasking, to use JoAnn Deak's term: as it sustains the interaction of subatomic particles, it also sustains the formation and dissolution of galaxies and the flowering of the crocus. But despite the fact that "World is crazier and more of it than we think, / Incorrigibly plural,"[15] as poet Louis MacNeice put it, there is also a time-honored recognition, expressed in myth, spiritual traditions and the perennial philosophy, and dramatically demonstrated by quantum mechanics, that Being is a unity indissolubly bound by interrelationships; and its web of interrelationships is so finely woven that the slightest change anywhere in it affects all else that exists. As a phenomenon called entanglement demonstrates, particles can affect each other instantaneously over any distance. And so when we revisit Deak's finding that women "are programmed to multitask ... built to massively connect and communicate," we find a description that might apply to Being itself. In mythological terms, **the female element in each of us just is, at rest within the unfolding present—receiving, integrating and massively connecting and communicating with all that is.**

Male and female elements show up differently in different cultures. Some cultures are oriented in their language and art and myths and rituals to face the mystery of what is. Because they evidence a devotion to

---

* I capitalize 'Being' when used in this sense. When speaking of one's 'being', I do not capitalize it.

the female element of Being, they have been called *"goddess-centered."* I feel, though, that *it may be our own modern prejudice towards the dualism of subject/object that fosters our belief that they worshiped an **individuated** Goddess.* Being suffuses all and can be felt in all and does not stand independent, as a deity would, from the continuum of 'what is'; for that reason I prefer the term *matrifocal* to describe such cultures. Matrifocal cultures attended primarily to the female element of Being; they learned to live in accord with the rhythms and avails of nature, leaving minimal impact on the landscape, and leaving us relatively rare evidence of incursions or warfare.

Our own culture, by contrast, is oriented by its language and art and institutions and aspirations to attend primarily to the male element of doing. For that reason our culture has been called a patriarchy. But although there are ample *examples* of patriarchy throughout our culture, we are not a patriarchy: specifically, our society is no longer ruled by men. What we are, I would argue, is *patrifocal*—**focused on the fruits of the male element of doing.** That focus is rampant in our culture, and it expresses itself in both men and women. In other words, in the values it expresses, in its buildings, its idioms and its daily rituals, our culture continues to be ruled by the male element of doing and offers almost no provision for a simple, attentive appreciation of Being. Our meager efforts in that direction are exemplified by those Scenic Outlook sites on highways at which you stop the car and step out to 'do' the view and take a picture before jumping back in the car to hit the road again. When we look for guidance in orienting ourselves to the world, it is not to Being that we turn: we ask the question, "What should I do?" Our entire field of attention is attuned to the male element and the ideas by which it runs itself: doing is what we notice, it's what we think about, it's what we spend our time at, it's how we set out to solve our problems. Our enterprises of doing reshape the very landscape around us: massive concrete highways and skyscrapers reach out and up, leaving their mark; within our cities we obliterate all but the most token and closely manicured vestiges of nature; and the rural countryside is hammered into the stark, rectilinear uniformity that suits agribusiness. So entranced is our culture with the male element that we tend to justify ourselves in its terms: we commonly define ourselves by what we do and what we have to show for it, and we obsess daily over all the things we have to do or want to do—to which end we ceaselessly calculate and scheme and schematize and manage and anticipate. And so what if we are out of touch with our bodies and our breath? So what if we have forgotten how to relate to the world as it is and are almost never fully present in it? Look at what we are accomplishing, and at what we still need to get done, and at what we should be doing now.

An appreciation of Being is something of a nonissue at best for those who are addicted to doing. When we are judging ourselves or others, the ability to be present is far less important than such telling indicators as what car someone drives, for instance, or how he or she dresses. And yet despite our addiction, something nags—something seems out of place or deficient. The great ancient Greek philosopher Heraclitus left us a clue to it when he wrote of those who "are as unaware of what they do when awake as they are when they are asleep."[16] What does it mean to be truly awake? We move closer to an answer when we consider that of the hundreds of actors who may cross a stage, the handful who exhibit that magic, intangible quality of 'presence' are those who, as director Wallace Chappell put it, "seem not to be working, but just *being*."[17] Working, of course, is an expression of the male element of doing. The actors who *are* busy working are inevitably less present, less awake—but why?

Guided by Duplicates

In the same way that the male element and the female element live within each of us, so do the hero and the tyrant. If we are unaware of their pull on us, we lose our ability to make conscious choices, and we come to resemble the animated sleepers of whom Heraclitus wrote, or the actors who are so busy doing that they lack presence.

We have already identified the hero as a liberator of the human spirit, and we have considered the stages of his journey: he is called beyond the familiar sphere of his society into the unknown, to which the call has now relocated his spiritual center of gravity; his journey is strange and disorienting, and he is tested in the course of it; and if he is successful, he returns from the unknown with the seeds of renewal—the insight or perspective that his society needs for its own transformation. The success of his journey may depend on his resourcefulness, physical strength, skills or cleverness—but those qualities are less important than the hero's primary virtue: as Joseph Campbell has put it, "The hero is the man of self-achieved submission."[18] Campbell is not talking about submission to a tyrant, or to injustices, or to rule, or to the authority of any external idea. **The hero's submission is self-achieved and transformative and offered with a complete peace of mind—he chooses to die to what has been, and he finds himself reborn into the newness of the living world around him.** That is, he dies to society's *description* of Being and, in opening himself to the vibrant unknown, submits to 'what is'—which can never be fully described and which cannot be accommodated without relinquishing the norms of language, perception and sensibility, allowing them to change fundamentally. It is the restorative energy of that new knowledge that he brings back to his society. As Campbell writes,

> That is the hero's ultimate difficult task. How render back into light-world language the speech-defying pronouncements of the dark? ... How communicate to people who insist on the exclusive evidence of their senses the message of the all-generating void? Many failures attest to the difficulties of this life-affirmative threshold.[19]

What the hero risks, then, is direct contact with the voluble mystery of the unknown. In saying that it is direct, we understand that it is neither supervised nor mediated by foreknowledge or plans or interpretation. The encounter is naked, one-on-one. But if the hero stands as a symbol for some part of ourselves, how do we interpret that encounter?

Let's begin at the beginning: the hero's ordered society is a realm within which everything is objectively familiar and reassuringly defined. Campbell described it as the soul's "exile in a world of organized inadequacies":[20] a state in which the self has so closed itself to any influences that lie beyond description or control that it has lost its ability to transform. Robert Pirsig, who wrote *Zen and the Art of Motorcycle Maintenance,* coined the word *stuckness* to describe this state. Architect Christopher Alexander writes about it as our inability to "allow the forces we experience to run freely in us, to fly past each other, ... to escape the locked-in conflict which oppresses us."[21] A friend once told me, "When someone tells you they're bored, don't believe them. They're afraid." Boredom is inevitable when we shut the door on newness: preferring not to risk the unknown into which transformation would carry us, we effectively box ourselves into "a world of organized inadequacies."

That phrase of Campbell's reminds me of my first visit to New York City. The zoo in Central Park was bleak and harsh in 1971. The gorilla sat in a pool of urine on a concrete slab, and when visitors stopped by his cage to gawk, he would sweep his knuckles across the floor and send a spray arcing through the bars. The image that most haunted me, though, was that of the tiger: a rippling powerhouse of an animal, painfully and uselessly attuned to the smells and movements outside its stark cage, relentlessly pacing around and around over the same ground, ready and needing to connect with the world beyond the bars, and unable to. That image precisely evokes the exile of the soul when our living is confined to the 'known': we tread round and round in a strictly bounded, controlled, tiny realm that we ourselves have staked out, usually in compliance with the description that is issued by our culture. Like the tiger, our soul is ready to connect with the world, and needs to, but can't. The major difference is that the tiger had no choice in the matter. We do.

The nature of that choice shows up in the actor who is so busy 'working' on stage that she lacks presence. Like the tiger, she paces through the same steps and inflections and gestures night after night; but whereas the tiger's freedom has been circumscribed by others, the actor's is circumscribed by herself. Over the course of rehearsals she has made that her job: to thoroughly describe the world she is inhabiting, to look for and assign meaning to every phrase she speaks, to every gesture she makes and to every character with whom she shares the stage. Once the meaning of every moment has been established, she knows how to play it for maximum effect; she knows *what to do*. In other words, her allegiance is to the male element of doing; and that prevents the very transformations that bring a performance to life and give it 'presence'.

As Heraclitus pointed out, we know all things by their opposites. So what about the actor who is just being? Alan Alda is not only a very fine actor; he is also articulate about his process:

> The difference between listening and pretending to
> listen, I discovered, is enormous. One is fluid, the other
> is rigid. One is alive, the other is stuffed. Eventually,

I found a radical way of thinking about listening. **Real listening is a willingness to let the other person change you.** When I'm willing to let them change me, something happens between us that's more interesting than a pair of dueling monologues. Like so much of what I learned in the theater, this turned out to be how life works, too.[22]

You cannot find presence, freedom or creativity inside a world arrested by description—which is also to say you cannot find wholeness there—because any such world is a mere duplicate that has severed ties with the world it purports to represent. When you "pretend to listen," whether onstage or off, you are actually paying attention to your own ideas about how to react and are using your face and body to 'do' a duplicate of "listening" that is based on them; when you *really* listen, you abandon the foregone knowledge of how to react and, willing to 'be', you pay attention instead to 'what is'. Actor Simon Callow addressed the same issue when he advised actors to *discard all willful doing:* "the actor must be, with the totality of his being, in front of the audience *at this moment."*[23]

As Alan Alda noted, that turns out to be how life works, too. When we choose willful doing, we may pretend to listen to the world, but we are actually being guided by our ideas about it: our willfulness knows what it wants and how to get it and doesn't need to surrender to the living guidance of 'what is'. Instead, the male element of willful doing charts its course according to its duplicates of 'what is': forms of objective knowledge that are disconnected from Being and so have abandoned wholeness. But we are setting up a funny implication here: objective knowledge and wholeness seem to lie in opposing camps. How can that be? After all, knowledge is virtually the altar at which our culture worships. As Francis Bacon famously observed, "Knowledge is power." But let's leave aside what we know about knowledge for a minute and look at it afresh.

Once we acquire knowledge of something, our knowledge remains fixed and independent of the thing it represents until we choose to amend it. In other words, it exists as a duplicate. The energy of the world is in process, moving forever onwards; the duplicate is a static scheme. Such schemes are never neutral. We construct and return to our duplicates because they are meaningful to us—and in their static abstraction they preserve that meaning, the way a photograph freezes a moment. In other words, knowledge not only stands apart from any phenomenon it represents, it designates the meaning of it; so our knowledge of a phenomenon substitutes for a meaningful *experience* of it, and saves us the trouble of experiencing it repeatedly. But we should also be aware that to *designate* the *significance* of the world's phenomena is to flatten them into *signs*—and although the origin of those three words is uncertain, the great linguist and etymologist Ernest Klein suggests that they, and their ally *assign,* are all related to the Latin word *secare,* "to cut." And indeed, *when we assign meaning, we create a kind of sign for ourselves that is independent, cut away from the flux of the present.* In the way a theater flat might be painted to represent a forest, our knowledge of the world flattens it into a duplicate.

A ketchup bottle, for instance, provides such knowledge. It saves you the trouble of smelling or tasting—experiencing—in order to know what is in the bottle. The label already tells you—and the information it delivers stands independent of the fluid meaningfulness of your experience of the present, which is gathered by the senses and defies definition. As the title of a book by Lawrence Weschler puts it, *Seeing Is Forgetting the Name of the Thing One Sees.* **Like real listening, 'seeing' the present requires a willingness to be changed by it, and static knowledge forestalls the need for real seeing.** When you forget the names, forget the labels, forget the foregone assumptions and truly open to the present, its 'meaning' will dawn upon you as an unmediated response in which any vestige of a line between self and world holds no more substance than a ring of smoke. Stepping out of duplicates, you enter not only the unknown, but the suddenness of your own life, which may come upon you with such meaningfulness as to give you goose bumps or pierce you with joy; it might scrabble with claws at the heart or bring tears of gratitude and relief. If we can stretch language a little to our own purposes, we might say that only by letting go of meaning do we open ourselves to meaningfulness: the bottomless meaningfulness that lies at the intersection of our life and this transient moment.

Labels, static knowledge, foregone meaning—they are all means of convenience that effectively sidestep Being. They dismiss it. And *as long as the male element remains independent of the female, **its primary relationship will be with its own knowledge rather than with***

Being. Indeed, willful doing invariably expresses such knowledge: it expresses our known relationship to the world, our assessment of its available resources, our formulation for making those resources conform to our wishes—and it expresses, above all, how we want to be known by ourselves and the world. Willful doing is created by knowledge.

The female element, on the other hand, massively connects and communicates. This does not happen through the agency of objective knowledge; it relies instead on a sensitivity that receives 'what is' and processes it and integrates it continuously. Those capabilities are all made possible by the agency of sensation, which reminds us that the Latin word *sentire,* from which *sensation* derives, actually means both "to feel" and "to think." The sensations that enable us to 'be' constitute what we might call the thinking of being. Our sense of being is created by feeling.

The 'Known Self'

Our impatience to *assign* rather than *live* meaning is widely endorsed by our culture—but there have been dissenting voices. In *Against Interpretation* Susan Sontag addressed that impatience:

> It is the revenge of the intellect upon the world. To interpret is to impoverish, to deplete the world—in order to set up a shadow world of "meanings" ... The world, our world, is depleted, impoverished enough. Away with all duplicates of it, until we again experience more immediately what we have.[24]

To interpret a phenomenon or assign meaning to it is in a sense to solve it and thereby conquer it. The poet Rainer Maria Rilke, though, reminded us that **life is not a problem to be solved, but a mystery to be experienced.** When life is seen as a problem to be solved, it is presumed to be knowable. Furthermore, if only you can crack its riddle and grasp its meaning, then *you can win at it.* And there are countless strategies out there advising you how to do just that, from New Age pronouncements to self-help books to investment manuals to the scientifically sanctioned 'survival of the fittest'. All may help us towards certain solutions, but no solution will help us towards an experience of life's mystery. In fact, because solutions tend to stand apart from the present, they more often stand as obstacles to our experience of it. Joseph Campbell once commented,

> People say that what we're all seeking is a meaning for life. I don't think that's what we're really seeking. I think that what we're seeking is **an experience of being alive,** so that our life experiences on the purely **physical** plane will have resonances within our **innermost being and reality.**[25]

The last sentence suggests that the experience of being alive involves a harmony not just of mind and body, but also of world (the physical plane) and self (our innermost being). Campbell then tackles the fiction of 'meaning':

> There is no meaning. What's the meaning of the universe? What's the meaning of a flea? It's just there. That's it. And your own meaning is that you're there. We're so engaged in *doing things* to achieve purposes of outer value that we forget that the inner value, the rapture that is associated with *being alive,* is what it's all about.[26]

With that in mind, we might appreciate why the great myths of the world warn against seeing the self as a "problem to be solved": to whatever extent we succeed, the self will then be 'known' in a manner that isolates it, fixes it, and flattens it with foregone meaning. To solve the 'problem of the self' is to arrive at a static idea of the self—a duplicate that we use to define and identify ourselves. To the extent that we identify with that duplicate, our identity is mistaken. And in that our mistaken identity takes us out of relationship with the world, it leaves us incapable of coming into harmony with it. Confusion in all relationships is the inevitable outcome: in our relationship with the earth we walk on, with the sky we walk beneath, with the food that sustains us and the water we drink, with the people around us, and even with the genius of our own flesh.

The source of that confusion—our mistaken identity—will maintain its hold on us, supported by our culture's story in countless directives every day, until we can hold it to account. As a first step, we might haul it into the light and name it. If we were to call it the 'known self', we would remind ourselves that it is based on the presumptions of static knowledge: our duplicates. We might also note that *the realm staked out for us by the 'known self' is an example of the defined, closed society of 'organized inadequacy' beyond whose sphere of influence the hero is called to venture.* Like that society, your 'known self' is a construct that solves the problem of who you are with a set of norms defined by a repertoire of ideas, relationships and patterns of behavior that you know you want to have, that you invest with a fixed meaning, and that you dedicate yourself to maintaining. In short, **your 'known self' is the formulation of** *who you know yourself to be.*

In 1980 the physicist David Bohm participated in a seminar that was published under the beguiling title *Knowledge as Endarkenment.* In it he comments on the work of his friend and associate, the philosopher Krishnamurti, and says, "I think that Krishnamurti has been suggesting that *knowledge* is the general source of our difficulty."[27] Later in the seminar Bohm talks about

> the kind of knowledge which may produce darkness. That knowledge of what you are, who you are, what sort of person you've got to be, to whom you belong, what your desires are, what your fears are, what you can do, what you can't do.[28]

"Our difficulty" is the problem of not being present. What Bohm is describing as "the kind of knowledge which may produce darkness," we are calling the 'known self'. In order to be present you have to appreciate that **the present is an unknown**—it has never been here before, and neither have you. Presupposition cannot reveal the present to you any more than you could presuppose your response to it. **If the self is to be present—fully responsive to and participant in the here and now—then it too must remain untethered by objective knowledge.** As the present is discovered, so too is the self; and once the present is felt as a whole, so too is the self. Everything else is a form of endarkenment.

It's one thing to admit that the *present* is an unknown—but to allow that the *self* is an unknown is a bit of a kicker. We depend on our solution of the self to solve the problems of our living—and so we carry that solution around with us, like a framed picture. To the extent that we preserve that framed idea of who we are, we buffer the self from the present—the living source of creativity and freedom—and shackle it to the past, on which our knowledge of it is based. In other words, to the extent that we hold on to the idea of who we are, we are not quite awake; like the sleepers of whom Heraclitus wrote, we are living by duplicates.

Of course, the 'known self', being a duplicate, doesn't belong to the present. In fact, its static construct can only survive if it is *protected* from the unwanted vagaries of experience; and so we tend to preserve the 'known self' within the defined walls of 'me', like a framed picture, or a specimen in a jar. You cannot breathe twice into the same body, but you can breathe twice into the same 'known self'. The more you protect the idea of 'who you know yourself to be', the more it ossifies; and you accept that ossification because it seems to offer a sort of reliability. But so much comes to depend on it that you can never leave it unguarded. When we become defensive in social situations, that's exactly what is happening—we are defending 'who we know ourselves to be' from the implications of a present event. When our *self-definition* is under attack, we feel *we* are under attack. We confuse the two. And because they become confused, **we feel that when we protect the definition, we are protecting the self.** We have all met people who wear their assumptions like a bulletproof vest. That is true endarkenment. Definition, like knowledge, is endarkenment. As Lao-tzu said, "He who defines himself can't know who he really is."[29]

Who you really are is the part of you that can center itself in the energy of the present, which is and always will be unknowable in any objective way. Appreciating that, we can also appreciate that the **"all-generating void," the unknown realm into which the hero ventures, is a representation of the unknowable present**—for within its deep stillness lies the deepest unknown realm in all of reality. To open to that realm and allow your spiritual center of gravity to live there is to join the mythic hero. It is also to side with life. To remain within the boundaries of the 'known self' is to confine yourself to the endarkenment of an 'organized inadequacy'. And I stubbornly enclose the term 'known self' within quotation marks to underscore that it is a mere fiction, an abstract idea that has no substantive reality. As philosopher L. L. Whyte put it,

> To know yourself is no longer adequate, because static knowledge is not possible. You can **realize yourself** only as a developing component of the community.[30]

And yet our culture assures us that we can realize the self by knowing it, and advises us to let that static knowledge govern what we do, what we feel, how we react to new information, what we think, and also, more subtly, *how* we think—something this book ventures into in later chapters. Furthermore, we collaborate with that governance, insisting that our mistaken identity be affirmed at every turn. And so we feel horror at forgetting people's names, or calling them by the wrong names. We feel impatience at having our routines or expectations interrupted. Naturally, too, in times of national arrogance or crisis, when we most need to reinforce the image of 'who we know ourselves to be', we often elect our political leaders for their ability to answer that need. Cagey political candidates capitalize on that by crafting an image of themselves with body language and speech patterns that mirror the voter, and they assure us with paternal confidence that their intolerance of doubt is a strength, because they *know* themselves and their country. That *promise of certainty* is something our culture longs for, and at times it has proven more decisive in elections than any national policy that might actually contribute to the common welfare. Rule by those skilled in the manipulation of their own image is a natural consequence of our infatuation with the idea of 'the individual' and the fiction of the 'known self'.

Our culture clings so tenaciously to its fiction of the self as an independent and known entity that you just know something very big depends on it. I think the raw nerves of the issue lead back to our belief that **if the self can be partitioned from the seamless whole and enclosed, it can be overseen and protected.** We can control it, direct it, correct it and judge it. Enclose it sufficiently well, and we can ensure its unassailable stability in the face of life's vicissitudes.

Or so we think. In fact, something quite different happens, and it is frankly counterintuitive. For an analogy we might look to skiing or snowboarding: when you stand as a beginner on the hill, feet clamped onto a slick board or two slippery sticks that threaten to speed down the slope, carrying you with them, the natural instinct is to try to assert control by leaning back into the hill. In fact, and contrary to intuition, you learn that only by leaning forward can you achieve stability—and only stability provides choice. I'll never forget the time when learning to snowboard that I was sailing across the hill straight towards some trees, and instead of bailing out I actually leaned towards the trees I was about to hit—a pure act of faith that felt a lot like suicide at the time. To my astonishment and relief I went into what felt like a perfectly executed turn. Lesson learned. Only by leaning down the hill can you ride it freely. In the same way, and it is equally counterintuitive, stability and choice in life can only be learned by giving yourself over to the world as it is, unknown and on the move, and finding your ease within its flux. If you withdraw from that flux, you are separating yourself from the present and retreating to your duplicates.

We are told that the aphorism "Know Thyself" was inscribed at the oracle at Delphi. You might reason naturally enough that to abandon the idea of who you are—your 'known self'—is also to renounce that ageless wisdom, and *what is the point of living in self-ignorance?* Plato assured us that an unexamined life is not worth living. And, certainly, to stray from the 'known self' is as counterintuitive as leaning towards the trees you wish to avoid on your runaway snowboard. As it turns out, it is also as necessary. Just as the snowboard won't otherwise move into a turn, so too you cannot otherwise move into the world. And to move into the world is also to move into your true self—as opposed to the duplicate self that your culture instructs you to secure. That, too, is the meaning of the Delphic oracle. As Richard Tarnas writes, its advice "was seen not as the creed of an introspective subjectivist, but as a directive to universal understanding."[31] It turns out, paradoxically, that the main issue in "Knowing Thyself," one that proves as rich as it is inexhaustible, is *how to center yourself in the world of the present*—in all its mystery, its evocations, its changeable particularity.

True self-knowledge is not an entity to be possessed, but a revelation of the world itself—to be felt and explored and lived. In fact, **we could accurately say that your 'true self' is that measure of you that is continuous with the present.** To center yourself in the present is to awaken to what is most true in you. All the rest is fantasy. It's really that simple. In our culture, alas, each of us takes on so much responsibility for creating and upholding our 'known self' that only the lucky ones ever discover the relief of disclaiming that responsibility and giving over to the aliveness of the present; within its fluid ease, self-knowing is a moment-by-moment revelation of the harmonizing energies of the world to which you belong.

And that highlights a critical choice that we all face: **you can either be 'who you know yourself to be', or you can be present. One or the other. Not both.** And you can transcend the fractured divisions of self-definition only by risking the discovery of what it means to be whole.

To sum up, then, the hero within each of us is nurtured by our willingness to step beyond definition ("away with all duplicates") and into the surrender of a direct, unmediated encounter with Being. Furthermore, the 'known self' is a tool of the male element of doing: it is a construct of ideas and instructions that is intended to guide what we do and how we do it in our everyday lives; and in that it is deliberately a duplicate, it is deliberately disconnected from the living guidance of 'what is'. That state of disconnection is also, tellingly, the primary characteristic of the mythological tyrant.

The Allure of Tyranny

The central story that humanity has told itself for millennia and across cultures of the world is an explication of the forces that carry us into our wholeness as humans. If myth seems remote and irrelevant to our lives, that merely indicates how our awareness has been dulled to the interplay of those forces within us. All the more reason, then, to look anew at the countless stories of myth, for they are designed to awaken us to our innermost truths. The two primary protagonists of the monomyth are the hero and the tyrant. The polarity between them, which lives in each of us, provides myth with its second great theme—a complement to the polarity between the male and female.

Joseph Campbell has described the hero and the tyrant in terms that highlight their stark differences: **the hero, identified by his self-achieved submission, recognizes his spiritual center of gravity in the unknown present; the tyrant, identified by his self-achieved independence, seeks seclusion in the 'known self'.** Campbell describes the tyrant as "the monster avid for the greedy rights of 'my and mine'" and notes that what drives him is "an impulse to egocentric self-aggrandizement." He goes on to elaborate,

> The inflated ego of the tyrant is a curse to himself and his world—no matter how his affairs may seem to prosper. Self-terrorized, fear-haunted, alert at every hand to

meet and battle back the anticipated aggressions of his environment, **which are primarily the reflections of the uncontrollable impulses to acquisition within himself,** the giant of self-achieved independence is the world's messenger of disaster, even though, in his mind, he may entertain himself with humane intentions.[32]

There is a heck of a lot to absorb in that description—but it is laser-sharp, and I have found that it rewards a close rereading. Examples of the tyrant present themselves to us on every scale. It is easy enough to see correlates in certain leaders of government, or in the specter of most large multinational corporations, driven to acquire more for themselves and heard in the media entertaining themselves with "humane intentions." That such behavior should be sanctioned both legally and socially is only natural in a culture that gathers itself around the idol of the 'known self'. And so it is that we congratulate the self-made billionaire for what he has accumulated—and even as we call him "self-made," we ignore the fact that he depended on the whole of society as well as nature's frail resources in order to make his fortune. We also grant privileges to political leaders, appointed to serve the people but too often seduced into using that opportunity to promote the narrow interests of themselves and their friends; or to the CEO who lays off a hundred workers whose salaries, combined, do not begin to equal his own self-assigned perks; or we adulate the ego-besotted rock star, dependent on fans to sustain the fantasy of his self-aggrandizement.* Our scale of values is so skewed that our society's actions evince a deep belief that **those who acquire a lot have ipso facto demonstrated their worth, and should therefore be granted**

---

* In his compelling book, *Identity and Violence* (New York: W.W. Norton & Co., 2006), Amartya Sen argues that the more predominately someone affiliates himself with a singular identity, the more prone he will be to violence. We can all identify ourselves in numerous ways. Someone can be at the same time a father, a squash player, a brother, a Yankees fan, a churchgoer, a feminist, a neighbor, an avid pianist, a black person and the CEO of a multinational corporation. If, however, one of those identities "drowns out the rest," as Sen puts it, "the result can be homespun elemental violence or globally artful violence and terrorism." To extrapolate Sen's premise, we might also note that if one's identity as a CEO "drowns out the rest," one becomes capable of forms of violence that a father, a brother, a feminist, a neighbor, a Christian or a black person might find intolerable. One suspects that the CEO's inflated salary is in part to ensure his allegiance to that narrow, overwhelming identity. A Faustian bargain, certainly.

special privileges and opportunities to acquire more. But as Pulitzer Prize winner Jared Diamond so plainly put it, "Those people with the greatest power to make decisions in our own society today regularly make money from activities that may be bad for society as a whole and for their own children."[33] They feel entitled to do so, and our laws exonerate them in the harm they inflict. And until recent egregious excesses came to light and led to the economic collapse of 2008, the thief stealing a few thousand dollars from a bank machine has typically done more jail time than an executive who steals a few million from his shareholders.

The confusion of our values is so deep that we often respect, adulate and *ourselves aspire to* the fantasies of the tyrant. That is, we commonly yearn for the tyrant's status of pampered, self-achieved independence—yearn, like him, to be shielded by wealth and influence and fame from life's mundane inconveniences and from the need for ordinary compassion; and we are so seduced by our fantasy that we fail to appreciate the obscene cost that such wealth can exact from the soul.

The mind-numbingly disproportionate allocations of wealth within the corporate sector serve to glaze the fantasy with the special status of privilege. The idea that CEOs are a breed apart and deserving of their grossly inflated incomes was put to rest in 2008: their competence was merely mediocre, and across the board their greed and entitlement blinded them to the consequences of their actions. These people are not inventing anything to help the world, or creating anything, or even risking their own money on a venture they believe in: they are merely *the head* that tells *the corporation*—literally "the body"—what to do; and *the head,* our culture tells us in innumerable ways, is deservedly superior. Million-dollar bonuses are merely an affirmation of its superiority—one that indirectly flatters us all. And so, as we leave behind the recession of 2008–09, the bonuses are staging a quiet comeback. What is most disturbing about that is the number of studies demonstrating that the greater the pay inequities within a society, the more social unrest and the less general happiness are to be found there. So the CEO who argues for a multimillion-dollar bonus is inadvertently petitioning for a dissolution of the social cohesiveness on which he depends. The situation is further skewed when you look at the real value contributed to society by various professions, as the New Economics Foundation did in its *A Bit Rich* report. There you will find, for example, that whereas hospital cleaners create £10 of value for every £1 they earn, bankers by contrast actually destroy £7 of value for every £1 they earn.[34]

The issue we need to look at, though, isn't the inequity of a CEO's earnings, gross though they are—the problem is that most of us, in truth, would like a crack at a multimillion-dollar salary. Wealth is the primary means within our society for achieving the tyrant's independence, and we not only long for that kind of independence—we see it as a measure of personal value, freedom, security and choice. We have been raised to believe that the pursuit of personal gain is our birthright—as if the goals of the tyrant supplied our purpose for living. The seductiveness of that belief obscures our true birthright, which is harmony and the spirit of service that enables it; it is a birthright that requires a soul's journey, a transformation of consciousness. Wealth is not a catalyst for such a transformation, but a deterrent to it. The tyrannical independence made possible by wealth has as its prime goal the *avoidance* of transformation, the maintenance of the status quo of our mistaken identity. No wonder Christ compared the chance of a wealthy individual entering God's heaven to that of a camel squeezing through the eye of a needle. **Egregious wealth, let us be clear, is a measure of one thing and one thing only: your ability to ride roughshod over the world, oblivious of the inevitable damage your actions leave in their wake.** In other words, wealth measures your ability to live irresponsibly. The tyrant's dream.

Of course, personal wealth *can* be used to help the world; but experience cautions that even the determination to help out, in the hands of the wealthy, can initiate actions that are callously insensitive to their own consequences. To use the resources of wealth otherwise requires a humility and attentiveness to the world that continuously provoke transformation in us. Either way, though, wealth cannot be seen as a measure of your ability to do good. The true measure of your ability to do good is found only in the openness of your heart and in your soul's ability to transform—qualities to which personal wealth often makes us feel we should be immune. In the meantime there are people armed with no more than compassion, a sense of justice and an unswerving commitment to ease suffering who have done immeasurable good in conditions of fragile poverty.

Exercise One: **Listen to the Beat**

The chapters in this book are interlaced with exercises. Each exercise is intended as a point of departure, a bridge to newness, a form of practice to facilitate the voluntary sabotage of long-standing patterns. *Practice* comes from the Indo-European base *pra-ko-,* which means "leading over or beyond." There is no 'right' way of doing any of these exercises. They ask only the patience to feel and the willingness to move beyond the familiar and into the unknown. What does not enter the experience of the body remains bound in the realm of idea.

The shift from the closure of willful doing to the spacious energy of Being is one against which our culture has fortified us since birth. And though it can't be shepherded by idea, it can be initiated very simply—by an exercise as easy as this one, for example, which I learned from Kaoru Matsumoto, a Kyogen master. Kyogen is a classical, utterly charming and often quite hilarious form of theater from Japan. Matsumoto presented this exercise as an example of what he might do in preparing for a performance. It is simplicity itself. Lie on your back and relax until you can hear or feel your heartbeat. Count up to sixty heartbeats and then sit up.

The exercise carries you straight into the wholeness of your own sensitivity. It asks that the male element of doing grow passive to the fecund currents of life that constitute your being until finally the heartbeat surfaces into your field of attention. The first time I did it, I was astonished at how deeply I had to relax before I could clearly feel each heartbeat. And it also struck me as strange that I have lived for so many decades without ever doing just that—pausing to pay attention to the beating of my heart and to how that quiet awareness, in turn, revealed the pulse of the present. As this exercise shows, only a quiet mind can receive the present—and a quiet mind is nothing other than a quiet body.

2 | The Universal Law

The Fallacy That Confines Us

Recognizing the features of tyranny within our society isn't much of a sport; recognizing the deeper resonances of the tyrant as a part of the self is a little trickier. It is made difficult, in part, because **the tyrant's urge towards 'self-achieved independence' has so shaped our societal norms, customs and expectations that it has disappeared from view into the scenery of our lives.** Once you look at what we accept as 'normal', though, you find that it flatters our sense of 'self-achieved independence'—the essence of our mistaken identity—on every front. It shows up in the way we organize our eating (each person allotted her own bubble of space, defined by chair and placemat), our living (the scrupulously defined suburban lot with its stand-alone house, within which are our rigidly allocated bedrooms) and in our preferred modes of travel (the autonomous car, for instance, sealed as tightly as the self it carries). Communal pews are used mainly in churches and low-budget theaters—elsewhere in public we prefer any spot in which we sit to be clearly demarcated as 'mine'. Our lives used to be interwoven with our communities; now they are largely confined by the walls of our residences. We even organize nature into isolated, controlled entities whenever we can, as evidenced in the way we like to order our gardens, and keep the wild out of our cities, and bury creeks in sewers, and manage any wilderness with which we interact as if it were a threat rather than a teacher.

The way we experience the self has a profound impact on the way we describe the world around us. The brilliant medieval mystic Meister Eckhart noted that "all the images we have for God come from our understanding of ourselves."[35] We might similarly note that how we imagine nature largely arises from how we experience ourselves. The Nobel Prize–winning scientist Ilya Prigogine put it another way: "Nature is part of us as we are part of it. We can recognize ourselves in the description we give to it."[36] Since the time of ancient Greece, the description we have given to the self is of an independent, known entity. Our most basic descriptions of the natural world also had their origins in ancient Greece. Our understanding that all matter is made up of individual particles, for instance, was foreshadowed by the philosopher Melissus a few decades after 500 B.C.—which, as we shall see in later chapters, is a date of some significance in our evolving idea of the self. Democritus subsequently developed the idea that matter was made up of particles too small to be seen, but which had an independent, irreducible existence. It was theorized that all the material changes we witness are merely rearrangements of these constituents of matter, which themselves are beyond change. The Greeks called these static constituents 'atoms'; when British scientist John Dalton published *A New System of Chemical Philosophy* in 1810, in which the classic atomic model was first propounded, he was well aware of the ancient Greek predecessors to his theory.

Today most of us are familiar with the classical atomic model and hold the view that, even though the atom can be split into electrons, protons and neutrons, which themselves can be split, at some level matter is ultimately made up of tiny, independent particles that interact to create the world as we know it. What we don't always appreciate is the extent to which that classical atomic model arises from the cultural underpinnings that gave us what we might call *the classical model of the self*. In the physical model, matter is made up of molecules, which are made up of atoms, which, as the units of matter, have an independent and irreducible existence. In the other model, a society is made up of families, which are made up of individuals, which, as the units of society, have an independent and irreducible existence. When we look at *atom* and *individual* we find that though their roots come from different languages—Greek and Latin—they mean exactly the same thing, "indivisible." There is more to this than mere coincidence: we describe the world according to how we experience ourselves. **The self and the atom are both classically understood to be 'stand-alone' units that interact with other 'stand-alone' units. That understanding provides the foundation for the story by which we live—and that makes** it all the more difficult for us to recognize that it is *entirely a cultural fabrication sustained by mutual agreement.* In other societies the idea that each person enjoys a sort of independent existence is quite alien. Anthropologist Wade Davis, for example, reports that in the language of the Penan tribe of Borneo—one of the last nomadic rain-forest societies on earth—there are no words to distinguish between *he, she* or *it,* but there are six words for *we,* the pronoun that discloses relationship.[37] He also noted that "they measure wealth not by the extent of their possessions but by the strength of their relationships."[38] In a similar vein, the Butoh performer Yumiko Yoshioka explained to me that in Japanese, the word for "self," *jibun,* is written in characters that can mean "a part of nature."

We feel the essence of existence through our essential experience of the self. And we essentially experience 'who we are' as something that is as independent from the present as the meaning of a framed picture is from the wall on which it happens to hang. *That essential experience of the self leads us to see independent existence in all the particulars of the world around us, rather than seeing expressions of interrelationship.* For instance, we look inside our own cells and find the DNA molecule, and understand it to be the atom of the self, the smallest independent unit from which each of us is made. Or we look to phenomena such as words, bullies, addictions, works of art or the brain itself, and understand them all as phenomena with an existence that is independent of relationship. The lens through which we look upon the world will remain invisible until we can detect its distortions. Let us then consider some of those phenomena to see how our lens reveals them to us, as it revealed the atom, for example, to be an indivisible, stand-alone unit; and then let's test that view against the evidence to see whether it is subject to distortion.

DNA molecules first. Barry Commoner summed up our view when he wrote that DNA research has promised "to reduce inheritance, a property that only living things possess, to molecular dimensions."[39] Who we essentially are, the story goes, is contained within a molecule.

We have a similar view of *words.* The very language we speak, and on which our brains depend for their development, organizes the world into a system of static concepts represented by such words as *house, tree, sidewalk,* and so on. As philosopher L. L. Whyte observed, thought *had* to separate out static concepts in order to clarify itself. A problem arises, though, in that those concepts, "in becoming static, ceased to conform either to their organic matrix or to the forms of nature."[40] Given their relative stability, though, it seems obvious to us that the words with which we express ourselves possess a stand-alone meaning, unreliant on interdependence; and by default, they encourage us to find the same status in the objects to which they refer.

Bullies. Well, any bully has a problem, one that itself may have a variety of causes. But it is clear to us that the problem now lies within the bully—and the solution seems to require that we safely separate the bully from his victims and peers and treat him until the problem is remedied.

Drug addiction, the story goes, is a chemical dependence in the body; it is created by certain drugs, and even after rehabilitation, the dependency remains in the cells of the body and often expresses itself in a relapse. Other forms of addiction—gambling, eating, shopping— may also be ultimately explained by chemical imbalances in the body, which may in turn be corrected by pharmaceuticals.

Works of art. First of all, it is clear that a work of art means something. We generally understand that its significance is somehow captured within it by the strokes of paint, or the flow of words, and that it possesses that meaning and holds it in readiness to be discovered by an attentive audience.

The brain. We all know, and our knowledge is largely supported by the views of the scientific community, that the brain possesses a sort of stand-alone intelligence. In fact, the brain is where the true self—the mind—is thought to reside, and the body is seen as an intricate, innervated machine run by the brain. And so it is that the popular imagination accepts that if your *head* could be kept alive, your *self* would be kept alive. That this belief is a cultural artifact based on the way we experience the body we shall look at later; suffice it to say for now that this fiction is what makes it possible for us to understand—as people from cultures with different understandings of mind would not—the monster created by Dr. Frankenstein with a brain transplant; or the idiom "We can solve this problem if we put our heads together"; or the ads for cryonics that offer to freeze your head after death so that you can be brought back to life when nanosurgery is sufficiently advanced. As one such ad claims,

> medicine will eventually be able to regenerate all tissues except the brain. Therefore the objective of neuropreservation is to preserve the brain—**the seat of human identity**—as faithfully as possible. It is not possible to remove a brain from the head without injuring it. Neuropreservation therefore requires that the cephalon (head) remain intact to preserve the brain without injury. However, the definition and objective of neuropreservation is not head preservation, it is brain preservation.[41]

That is a pure expression of one of the most robust fictions by which we live, one that fathers our entire experience of world and self: the belief that **the roots of the self do not lie in the world around us, nor even in the body, but are preserved intact within the blood-brain barrier.**

But let's return to the top of the list and consider the stand-alone existence of each phenomenon in light of the available evidence.

Atoms first. For centuries science has been driven to find the thing within the thing within the thing. But the idea that the world is made up of tiny, independent building blocks has given way to the astonishing findings of quantum mechanics that show the universe itself to be a phenomenon of unbroken wholeness: the existence of everything within it is immutably reliant on everything else. As Fritjof Capra wrote in his book *The Tao of Physics,*

> The constituents of matter and the basic phenomena involving them are all interconnected, interrelated and interdependent ... they cannot be understood as isolated entities, but only as integrated parts of the whole.[42]

Every particle in the universe is under the influence of every other particle. In fact, a particle can be understood only according to the web of events to which it is linked; it has no meaning or even existence apart from those relationships. As physicist Lee Smolin has written, this is a far cry from the classical model:

> Our world cannot be understood as a collection of independent entities living in a fixed, static background of space and time. Instead, it is a network of relationships, the properties of every part of which are determined by its relationships to the other parts … the world is not made of stuff, but of processes by which things happen.[43]

David Bohm, one of the foremost theoretical physicists of the late twentieth century, views the primary job that science has chosen for itself—to understand the workings of the universe by analyzing its smallest constituent parts—to be a self-defeating exercise. The fundamental reality of the universe does not lie in tiny autonomous units from which all else is built. There *are* no tiny autonomous units. There are distinct bits, to be sure, just as the chair on which I am sitting is distinct from the floor on which it sits—but atom, chair and floor have no existence independent of the unbroken wholeness of reality: their existence is contingent on it. Bohm argues that without studying the "inseparable quantum interconnectedness of the whole universe,"[44] science cannot hope to come to terms with reality. And so it falters in its attempts to come to terms with consciousness, for example, because the phenomenon of consciousness is not reducible to constituent building blocks.

Another problem with the classical model of science is that the smaller the scale of its investigations, the less mechanically the world behaves. Eventually a point is reached where phenomena reveal an ineluctable connection between matter and consciousness.* Bohm has looked at some of the more confounding results of experimental physics and has proposed a grand-scale theory that accommodates them. He postulates an "implicate order," which he describes as an unseen realm of complete unity in which everything, *including consciousness,* is enfolded together and in contact with everything else. It is from this realm that the seemingly isolated things and events of the world

---

* For an example of this, see the Appendix.

unfold in the seen realm, which he calls the "explicate order." The explicate order is pretty much what we live with every day. The implicate order is less familiar. To explain it, Bohm uses the metaphor of a hologram. A hologram is a three-dimensional image created when a laser beam is projected through a special photographic plate. The most remarkable characteristic of a hologram—and also the trait after which it was named—is that if the photographic plate is broken, and the laser is trained onto any small, random piece of it, the whole of the three-dimensional image will still appear. In Bohm's description of the implicate order the same principle applies: the whole of the universe is implicate in each explicit part of it.

So at the atomic level the universe is an unbroken whole, and that whole inhabits each of its constituent parts, and each part is sensitized to the whole. All very well as an abstract idea, but just how sensitive is the universe to the merest of its parts? Mathematical physicist David Ruelle has given us an example that is absolutely jaw-dropping to contemplate. In his book *Chance and Chaos,* he proposes as a thought experiment going to the far end of the observable universe—ten billion light-years away—and suspending the gravitational field of a single electron. Not even of a molecule, but of an electron, which has a tiny fraction of a molecule's mass. The suspension of that tiny, remote gravitational field will be almost imperceptible on the earth. If we look at the air molecules in a room, though, and choose to follow one of them, we will find that after about fifty collisions with other molecules, the path of our air molecule has deviated from its original trajectory enough that it misses a molecule it would otherwise have hit. That happens within a fraction of a second—and from that point its path will have nothing in common with what it would originally have been. If we move outside, we will find that after only a day or so the effect of eliminating the gravitational pull of that single, far-away electron will be apparent to the eye in any turbulent part of the atmosphere, such as a storm. The effect is now "on a scale of kilometers ... the clouds have a different shape and the gusts of wind follow a different pattern."[45] When we speak of living within an interrelated, responsive universe of almost unthinkable sensitivity, Ruelle's example helps us put that statement in context. Every thought we have resonates through the universe, as does the effect of our every gesture.

What about *DNA molecules*? Well, despite the prevailing wisdom that the DNA molecule holds the complete map of who you are and will become, science has found that genetic information isn't as independent a set of instructions as was expected. As Barry Commoner explains, "Biological replication does include the precise duplication of DNA, but this is accomplished by the living cell ... genetic information arises not from DNA alone but through its essential collaboration with protein enzymes."[46] Similarly, science writer Clive Cookson tells us,

> Research into the way genes are switched on and off shows that one can almost regard them as devices for extracting experience from the environment. The "expression" of genes—their production of proteins, the chemicals that do most of the work in biology—is influenced by events going on outside your body, to an extent that would have seemed inconceivable until very recently.[47]

A relatively new science has emerged, known as epigenetics—the study of *genetic changes* that *don't* involve mutations in DNA. It was prompted in part by the observation that identical twins often become increasingly different as they age even though their DNA is identical: one woman developed breast cancer in her thirties, her identical twin didn't; another woman was afflicted with catatonic schizophrenia, and when she was admitted to the hospital, the psychiatrist on call was her identical twin. It turns out that we are not, after all, passive victims of the genes we inherit. Genes can actually be switched on and off by the choices we make, the air we breathe, the interests we pursue and the way we deal with stress in our lives. As researcher Moshe Syzf has commented, exercise may be good for more than burning calories—it may actually reprogram our genes.[48]

Let's look at *words*. Doesn't a word mean what it means, in and of itself? Ernest Fenollosa and Ezra Pound wrote that "the whole delicate substance of speech is built upon substrata of metaphor."[49] Literary critic and poet I. A. Richards similarly observed, "Thought is metaphoric, and proceeds by comparison."[50] Without analogy, without relationship, thought cannot evolve. The same is true of words, the tools of thought. The notion that "words have, or should have, proper meanings which people should recognize and stick to"[51] just doesn't hold up. It is not that words have no meanings—it is that a word has no stand-alone meaning. As Richards explains, "It is enough for our purposes to say that what a word means is the missing parts of the contexts from which it draws its delegated efficacy."[52] Eliminate those contexts, and you eliminate the word's meaning. Like a subatomic particle, a word relies on a field of interdependent relationships.

And the *bully* problem? Psychologist Debra Pepler, one of the world's foremost authorities on bullying, introduced radical new research in an effort to study it. That research has demonstrated incontrovertibly that the phenomenon of bullying relies on an array of relationships and does not exist independent of them.[53] In one study, for example, Pepler and her colleagues arbitrarily chose a ten-second window of observation and found that bullying would cease *within that brief time span* in fifty-seven percent of the cases if a peer intervened. In another study, they found a striking correlation between the number of peers watching an episode of bullying and the length of time it lasted. The problem is not isolated within the child who bullies—it permeates a complex of relationships.

Addiction is a deepening scourge in our culture, and it is convenient to think of it as something broken within an individual that needs to be fixed, or as something that can be halted with an aggressive, federally mandated drug policy. The support for that thinking traces back to the well-known Skinner box experiment. The Skinner box is, in effect, an isolation chamber for rats: a small metal cage that keeps a rat from contact with others, from nesting, from playing, from hiding or running. Hundreds of trials have been held in which rats in Skinner boxes could self-administer drugs such as heroin or cocaine: that every such rat self-administered and became an addict was taken as proof that the drugs were irresistible and ineluctably led to addiction.

Psychologist Bruce Alexander was doubtful of that logic: he thought the root problem could be the box itself. So he built Rat Park, a wooden enclosure as big as two hundred cages, replete with cedar shavings, boxes and cans for hiding and nesting in, poles for climbing, plenty of food—and company: the enclosure held sixteen to twenty rats of both sexes. To test his hypothesis Alexander provided two water bottles: one had water, the other had water laced with morphine.

The rats overwhelmingly preferred plain water. Alexander then sweetened the morphine water—but the rats still preferred plain water. Then Alexander forced the rats to become addicts, offering them only morphine-laced water for fifty-seven days. When plain water was finally available again, the overwhelming tendency was to switch back to it. That tendency is reminiscent of a 1975 survey showing that of the thousands of soldiers who became heroin addicts in the Vietnam war, eighty-eight percent simply quit when they left the war zone. So it seems clear that neither the availability of the drug, nor even its presence in the body, is the foundational cause of addiction: addiction is fostered by the user's environment. Alexander points to a sense of lost connection with one's milieu as the precursor to addiction—what he refers to as "dislocation." He believes that the sense of isolation fostered by our culture—the sense of rootlessness and spiritual impoverishment—is its own kind of Skinner box, leading to a wide range of addictive behaviors that can show up in Blackberry use, eating patterns, television habits, pornography or chat rooms, to name just a few. As Lewis Mumford observed,

> If Man had originally inhabited a world as blankly uniform as a "high rise" housing development, as featureless as a parking lot, as destitute of life as an automated factory, it is doubtful that he would have had a sufficiently varied experience to retain images, mold languages, or acquire ideas.[54]

Our cultural environment is breeding addictive tendencies in us all. And those tendencies are further exacerbated by the impoverishment of our culture's story, which takes us out of relationship and actually encourages us to experience the self as an isolated entity.

Works of art. They stand in isolation on bookshelves, or in our art galleries and our museums, and we walk up to them, and look at them, and find meaning there. And isn't that meaning contained within the independent existence of the artwork? Alden Nowlan, a Canadian poet who died in 1983, addresses that belief in his poem "An Exchange of Gifts":

> As long as you read this poem
> I will be writing it.
> I am writing it here and now
> before your eyes,
> although you can't see me.
> Perhaps you'll dismiss this
> as a verbal trick,
> the joke is you're wrong:
> the real trick
> is your pretending
> this is something
> fixed and solid,
> eternal to us both.
> I tell you better:
> I will keep on
> writing this poem for you
> even after I'm dead.

The fiction to which Nowlan refers—"pretending this is something fixed and solid, eternal to us both"—holds that an artwork is an entity of independent existence that fixes a certain meaning within its brushstrokes, or phrases, or contours. That fiction belongs to the tyrant's fantasy that informs our larger cultural fiction, which presents all parts of the world as stand-alone, knowable objects. Nowlan's view is seconded by Donald Winnicott, a gentle, down-to-earth pediatrician and psychoanalyst. Winnicott devoted himself to an understanding of creativity, because he considered it indispensable to the healthy personality. He pointed out that we tend to think of the artists as the creators and the audience as the recipients of what is created; but he observed that, for example, when the lights dim in a theater and the curtain goes up,

> each one of us will create the play that is going to be enacted, and afterwards we may even find that the overlap of what we have created, each one of us, provides material for a discussion about the play that was enacted.[55]

Winnicott's observation brings to mind the somewhat enigmatic title of Nowlan's poem: "An Exchange of Gifts." Although there is no mention in the poem of gifts given or received, we can easily understand how the poem itself is a gift by Nowlan to the reader, for any work of art becomes a gift to those who are able to receive it. But by calling the poem an *exchange* of gifts, Nowlan seems to suggest that by offering what is needed to create the poem anew, the reader, too, extends a gift; and the more generous the reader's gift, the more generous the poem's. In that context, Nowlan's title could apply to any artwork: as audience and artist bring it to life, here and now, what is happening is, specifically, an exchange of gifts. And the gifts are never the same twice.

The ability of an artwork to continually recreate itself tells us that whatever an artwork embodies, it certainly can't be a fixed, communicable truth that the rational mind can grasp—otherwise, revisiting a poem or seeing *Othello* more than once would be joyless. What an artwork embodies must be much more subtle and complex. Heidegger offers us an alternate and quite compelling view, which is elegantly summarized by philosopher Samuel Mallin in his book *Art Line Thought*. As Mallin explains, Heidegger argued that an artwork provides "entrances to the truth of the world *around* it (rather than truths that are somehow inside it like propositions in a report)."[56] As long as we are reading a poem or watching a play or looking at a painting, we are moving through those entrances into an unfolding of the world that simultaneously reveals the self. The more sensitively attuned the artwork is to its world, the more sophisticated and rich is its potential for an exchange of gifts with its audience. By understanding that an artwork opens our sensitivities to the world around it—which includes us—we are strikingly reminded of Cookson's description of genes as "devices for extracting experience from the environment." If the double helix of humanity's soul is encoded in its artworks, then it, too, is indissolubly bound to the world.

The Big Chameleon

Before we go on to reexamine the brain, let us pause to look more closely at the tyrant's fantasy of 'self-achieved independence'—a fiction our culture reads into the world around us, but which seems so far to be a fragile conceit. All of reality appears to be contingent upon relationship, including our most treasured possession—the self. We are not isolated beings in a world of independent objects; instead we belong to an unimaginably vast and sensitive interweaving of processes in flux. Rather than claim, "I think; therefore I am," we would be more ontologically accurate to say, "I relate; therefore I am." That statement would also pretty much sum up what an elementary particle might say of its existence. Or anything else, for that matter. In fact, wherever we inquire, if we inquire honestly and deeply enough, we will eventually and ineluctably be carried to an understanding that *existence is contingent upon interrelationship, and nothing exists except through its interrelationships with everything else.* We might call that the **Universal Law of Interrelationship.** Our culture bristles against that law, seeks to dispute it, and commits itself to goals and values that blithely ignore it—but a deluded determination to live in disputation of the Universal Law is powerless to refute it to even the slightest degree.

In an odd, compelling and brilliant little book called *The Chinese Written Character as a Medium for Poetry,* Ernest Fenollosa and Ezra Pound peel back the veneer of the objectified world to reveal the teeming relationships that constitute its reality, and they do so with poetic sensibility:

> Relations are more real and more important than the things which they relate. The forces which produce the branch-angles of an oak lay potent in the acorn. Similar lines of resistance, half-curbing the out-pressing vitalities, govern the branching of rivers and of nations. Thus a nerve, a wire, a roadway, and a clearing-house are only varying channels which communication forces for itself. This is more than analogy, it is identity of structure. Nature furnishes her own clues. Had the world not been full of homologies, sympathies, and identities, thought would have been starved and language chained to the obvious. There would have been no bridge whereby to cross from the minor truth of the seen to the major truth of the unseen.[57]

There is a corollary to the Universal Law that we would do well to heed: **relationship is the only reality.** If a thing exists by virtue of its interrelationships, then everything it *is,* so to speak, is expressed through relationship. It cannot express anything about itself that is independent of relationship, because it doesn't even have an existence independent of relationship. So any attempts to *understand* a thing in isolation—be it a gene, a work of art, a tree or a person—are doomed to failure. **The only reality anything can express is its capacity for relationship.** The reality of a gene, for instance, is expressed in its ability to relate to its environment—and yes, that capacity for relationship is primed and delineated by all the details of its molecular structure; but to think that a DNA molecule possesses within its independent self the stand-alone, fixed and material source of who we are is to bestow upon it the tyrant's fantasy to which we ourselves aspire.

In other times and other cultures, people have recognized relationship as the medium of reality. In the fourteenth century Meister Eckhart wrote, "Relation is the essence of everything that exists."[58] In the fifth century B.C. Alcmaeon of Croton wrote,

> No one of the things which exist in the world-order would last for any length of time were it not for all the rest. On the contrary, if a single thing were to fail, all would disappear; for all things come into existence from the same necessity and are sustained by one another.[59]

Among Native peoples in North America, there is a widespread sensibility that finds expression in the phrase "all my relations." That phrase may begin a story or speech or prayer, or may close it. It refers not just to family and relatives, nor just to the extended family to which all of humanity belongs, but to the kinship we share with all animate and inanimate forms. But even more than that, as Native Canadian writer Thomas King puts it,

> "All my relations" is an encouragement for us to accept the responsibilities we have within this universal family by living our lives in a harmonious and moral manner (a common admonishment is to say of someone that they act as if they have no relations).[60]

The reliance of existence on relationship is strikingly demonstrated by the problem of tachyons—hypothetical particles that can only travel faster than light and probably do not interact with matter as we know it. Tachyons are consistent with the mathematics and laws of physics, but if they don't *interact* with anything in our world, they simply do not exist in it. They have no relationship with it. That oddity reminds us that **any relationship involves reciprocal change; if the reality of our world resides in relationships, then it resides in a flow of reciprocal changes.**

And yet ... we still imagine a line around the self, we invest it with meaning, and often we defend it and shore it up for our entire lifetime. Our credo says: what lies inside my picture frame is me, and what lies outside it is not me—just as we think that what lies within the boundary of an atom has an existence independent from what lies outside it. We see trees the same way, and birds, and planets—we believe they all have *the quality of independent existence*. The medieval scholastic Duns Scotus drew a word from the writings of Aristotle to describe that quality and translated it into Latin as *perseitas*. That became the English word *perseity*, a philosophical term that the Oxford English Dictionary, or OED, defines as **"the quality or condition of existing independently"**; in other words, perseity refers to the idea that a thing exists in and of itself, or per se, the phrase from which perseity comes. The word has never enjoyed much currency, yet **the idea represented by perseity lies at the very heart of how our culture sees the entire world. It is our essential story and our core definition of reality. It is, we might say, the Big Chameleon:** the unseen 'norm' that tells us who we are, determining our self-image, our worldview and our actions. It is the keystone that props up the edifice of the 'known self'. It is the linchpin that binds our mistaken identity together. It is the experiential template that determines how we think. That is, we believe the brain enjoys perseity—that the brain is the sole source of our intelligence and the container of the self. That very belief—standing at the core of who we know ourselves to be—deeply affects how we experience self and world. If its effect impinges on our capacity for relationship, then it impinges on our capacity for wholeness. Reason enough to call it into question.

The Stand-Alone Brain—Not

The idea that the self is contained in the brain is one of the most robust and deeply defended fantasies of our culture. Our defense of it is an absolute necessity for us, because *the tyranny we exert over self and world **relies** on a division that withdraws our experience of thinking from the body and centers it in the cranium.* And so our culture's desperation to appoint the brain as the container of the self persists in defiance of all the evidence to the contrary, and despite the anomalies in which each of us personally experiences the self in its profoundest depths, which implicate the pit of the stomach, or the heart, or the seat of the breath.

Our culture's identification of the self with the head is so complete that it's hard to see it clearly: the trees obscure the forest. It is safe to say that not only do we experience the self in the head as we go about our daily lives—so does almost everyone we know. We also generally believe that while the brain is thinking, it does everything else too—that it alone somehow runs the heart and fights infection and regulates the bile ducts and digests our food and controls our sex drive and gives us our bodily sense of self. The prevailing orthodoxy tells us that the head *has* to command the body because the body has no innate intelligence.

The premise that the body is unthinking matter leaves the thinking self no possible refuge but the head. Our culture has been deeply and unconsciously attached to that premise for a long time. In a later chapter we'll trace the early genesis of it, but for now we might consider a single milestone in its development. Sometime shortly before 450 B.C. the Greek philosopher Parmenides expressed the idea, for the first time that we know of, that *the experience of the body is less reliable in telling us what is true than cold reason is.* If an argument of unassailable logic arrives at conclusions that do not tally with what our senses communicate, then the truth, Parmenides assures us, will be found on the side of logic. He is right that the senses can deceive us—they tell us that the earth is still and the sun moves, for example; but he also unwittingly demonstrated how much more seriously reason can do so: he and his disciples went on to prove, successfully defend and *believe in* absolute nonsense—that in reality nothing can move, for example. The folly of their reasoning, though, did nothing to detract from the status or longevity of their real legacy, which was *a dismissal of the body's experience as unreliable and a crowning of pure reason as the means to and sole arbiter of truth.* And although Gregory Palamas stood against that legacy in the fourteenth century—and was jailed for four years for his efforts—I can't find much else within European thought to directly challenge it until 1790, when William Blake, who in his day was considered mad, wrote *The Marriage of Heaven and Hell,* in which appears a passage called "The Voice of the Devil":

> All Bibles or sacred codes have been the causes of the following Errors:
> 1. That Man has two real existing principles: Viz: a Body & a Soul.
> 2. That Energy, call'd Evil, is alone from the Body, & that Reason, call'd Good, is alone from the Soul.
> 3. That God will torment Man in Eternity for following his Energies.
>
> But the following Contraries to these are True:
> 1. Man has no Body distinct from his Soul; for that call'd Body is a portion of Soul discern'd by the five Senses, the chief inlets of Soul in this age.
> 2. Energy is the only life and is from the Body and Reason is the bound or outward circumference of Energy.
> 3. Energy is Eternal Delight.[61]

There is no question that the orthodoxy against which Blake slings his truth remains a Goliath within our culture. It assures us that the energy of the body is not to be trusted and that only reason—which stands aloof from the body—can offer true guidance. That hierarchy traces back to the message of Parmenides, and it thrives today as never before, because the way we live in and see the world is more abstract—i.e., represented by reason or idea—than ever before.

Once we appreciate that we have placed the head in hierarchical supremacy over the body, we can begin to appreciate that relationship as the prototype for all other hierarchies we create. And so it is entirely natural to us that the head of the Roman Catholic Church is not called the *heart* of the church or the *belly* of the church or the *lungs* of the church—even though *spirit* literally means "breath"—because of course, rightfully, the *head* should lead and govern, even in an institution based on faith. Nor do we say "Two hearts are better than one," potent though that image might be, because when two people cooperate on a problem, their heads are naturally in charge. Similarly, our symbol for the ultimate power of kingship is a crown that sits, of course, atop the head, encircling it in metal and adorning it with jewels—a sharp contrast to karate, for instance, which symbolizes mastery with a cloth belt that is knotted just below the belly button. We might also note that *head* office would naturally choose someone who was *levelheaded* to *head up* its operations. If the company did really well, though, the success might *go to his head*, and he could end up with a *swelled head*. Such an individual is likely to *butt heads* with board members, who might then accuse his decisions of being *wrongheaded*. Eventually someone would advise the board to *keep their heads* and look around for a new leader—hopefully someone with *a good head on her shoulders* who could put corporate *headquarters* back on track and help everyone get *ahead*. Et cetera. Funny how those who are most *stuck* in the head are the most desperate to *get* ahead.

It is similarly revealing that *chief, captain* and *capital* derive from Latin words meaning "head." "Hail to the Chief" literally means "Hail to the Head"; a CFO is literally the head of finances; the captain of a team is literally its head, as is the capital of a nation; a capital offense literally means an offense against someone's head, the symbol of his life; and we might also note that the acquisitive pursuits of capitalism gratify values of the 'head' rather than those of the heart.

The head rules not just the self, then, but the hierarchies and language implemented by the self. But isn't rule by the head sort of natural and even inevitable? After all, the brain is where we do all our thinking, isn't it? And what we experience as the self is all but indistinguishable from our thinking. Why shouldn't we experience the brain as the container of the self and the seat of our identity? What other choice do we really have? How could we pretend to experience our thinking anywhere *other* than in the brain? And if our *thinking* is centered in the brain, how could *we* be centered anywhere else?

But if all the thinking we do *is* a product of activity confined within the cranium, that would ask us to reexamine the Universal Law: to wit, that there is no perseity, but only a web of unbroken wholeness in which the idea of isolation is a meaningless fantasy—so that whatever is called into existence, be it an electron, a self, a solar system or a thought, is called forth and sustained by the whole. According to those principles, the idea that the brain is a faculty that generates its thoughts independently, and interfaces with what lies outside of it through local connections, would stand as an anomaly. If that idea were true, the cryonics fans would be proven right, and the Universal Law of Inter-relationship would have to stipulate an exception: us.

What we hold to be a self-evident truth was not always so. There was a time when the self was not understood and experienced as though it were ensconced within the blood-brain barrier. For instance, the Hebrew word *sarefet* means both "diaphragm" and "thought"; similarly, the ancient Greek word *phren* means both "diaphragm" and "mind." Those examples indicate that the mind and its thinking were experienced in the diaphragm. Heraclitus, who stood at the brink of a major shift in our cultural understanding of the self at around 500 B.C., observed that "Man, who is an organic continuation of the Logos, thinks he can sever that continuity and exist apart from it."[62] As Heraclitus conceives of the Logos, it refers to the mind or thought that permeates the world and "steers all things through all things"[63]—a concept that has more than a little in common with David Bohm's concept of the implicate order. The idea that *we are part of and sustained by an all-aware, dynamic whole* has existed in many forms; it is often referred to as the Perennial Philosophy. Traditionally, that whole is understood to be hidden at all times, yet manifest in all things. The ancient Greeks called that whole the Logos; Lao-tzu famously referred to it as the Tao. Indigenous North American nations knew it as the Great Spirit, and Australian Aborigines as the Divine Oneness. It has also been called the Great Mother, Christ Consciousness, Buddha Consciousness, the One Mind, or God. As architect Christopher Alexander observed, God, described by one word or another, is a way of understanding that we are part of an unbroken whole.[64] To Heraclitus, it was absurd to think that you could draw a line around yourself and declare, "What is inside the circle is me; what is outside the circle is not me; and what lies inside the circle exists independent of what lies outside of it."

What was absurd to Heraclitus, though, is taken for granted by our fragmented, schismatized experience of the world, which hardly allows us even to accommodate the idea of an unbroken whole. And we can clearly *feel* the independence of our existence, in a way that perhaps he couldn't. When we think, for example, we can do it more effectively if we shut out the world, and sometimes if we can't shut out the world, it impairs our thinking—all of which seems to confirm that our thinking *is* independent from the world around us. The idea prevails that each of us essentially seems to have more independence from the world than the omniscient biblical God had who created it. And just as the ancient Hebrews and Christians served God and found that to be natural, we find it natural to serve the self. Serving the self, after all, is reasonable, it seems ineluctable according to the precepts of Charles Darwin, and it is the best use of our energies once they have been liberated from the shackles of religious superstition.

Or is it? If the individual *were* self-contained, that approach would make sense. If not, then by serving the self we risk serving a fantasy that may deny us access to the full scope of our own lives. There are really two issues here: **does the self have an existence independent of the world; and is what we experience as the mind or the psyche of the self contained in the brain?** First issue first.

The Self as a Skinner Box

As a young actor, I found the grip exerted on me by our story of the independent self to be the largest single impediment I faced. The line I drew around myself severed the very continuity that alone can bring truth and revelation and presence to a performance. I thought being present on stage was a matter of creating and sustaining an unshakable sense of self within me. After all, the actors I most admired seemed to be doing just that. What I didn't yet realize was that their unshakable sense of self derived from a consciousness that existed fully *in* the world, not independent of it. My willful attempts to *make* myself more present were doomed because the kind of independent existence I was trying to fulfill isn't, in fact, viable. As neurobehavioral scientist Jose Delgado explains,

> It is more or less explicitly assumed that an adult has a well-established mental capacity which functions with relative independence of the environment.... A more detailed analysis of reality, however, shows that cerebral activity is essentially dependent on sensory

inputs from the environment not only at birth but also throughout life. Normal mental functions cannot be preserved in the absence of a stream of information coming from the outside world. The mature brain, with all its wealth of past experience and acquired skills, is not capable of maintaining the thinking process or even normal awareness and reactivity in a vacuum of sensory deprivation: the individual mind is not self-sufficient.[65]

Delgado describes experiments in which subjects were placed in an isolation chamber, sort of like a human Skinner box, and studied for the effects of that isolation. Apart from the fact that the subjects lose the ability to think clearly, the most salient and seemingly inescapable effect of isolation is that *it induces hallucinations in all subjects, without exception.* Delgado describes a range of the fantasies that occurred, from sensations of movement or touch to acoustic perceptions such as "a music box playing, or a choir singing in full stereophonic sound."[66] The subjects reported that they had little control over these phenomena. Their thinking, unsupported by the world, was gradually set adrift from reality. What we can bring away from those findings is an insight of critical importance to all that follows in this book: **isolation is hallucinogenic. The greater the isolation, the more powerful the fantasies it creates.** And here we are getting closer to an understanding of the tyrant, whose dominant impulse is towards the isolation provided by his self-achieved independence, which he understands as a means of gaining control.

As long as we understand that the self is called into being by its reciprocal relationships with the world, we can refer to seity— "selfhood"—as a unique process, just as we can refer to a leaf on a tree as a unique process: each is an individual expression of a larger process on which it depends for its existence. As soon as we confuse *seity* with *perseity,* we are on the train to fantasyland, because **to think that the self has an independent existence is to understand our own cranium as a kind of isolation chamber.** A Skinner box. And the effect of isolation, remember, is ineluctably hallucinogenic. The Siren's call to that walled-in fantasyland is strong: the fiction of perseity has been seducing our culture for thousands of years. To begin to understand what that seduction has cost us we might ask, If our most advanced scientific understandings tell us that every particle is under the influence of every other particle, so that even the atom at the end of a nose hair is tuned in to the cosmos, then why is it so difficult for *us* to do the same? We can barely tune in to our own bodies, let alone into the cosmos. Virtually the same question was posed by a young student of Buddhism in a story cited by Joseph Campbell:

> The young student said to his master, "Am I in possession of Buddha consciousness?" The master said, "No." The student said, "Well, I've been told that all things are in the possession of Buddha consciousness. The rocks, the trees, the butterflies, the birds, the animals, all beings." The master said, "You are correct. All things are in possession of Buddha consciousness. The rocks, the trees, the butterflies, the bees, the birds, the animals, all beings—but not you." "Not me? Why not?" "Because you are asking this question."[67]

Now as I see it, the downfall of the young student has nothing to do with his desire to question. The Dalai Lama himself urges us to question: "Analyze. Think, think, think."[68] Questions have the power to move us forward. They open our eyes to possibility. They challenge perceptions and provide new perspectives. Where the student went astray, then, was in the specific nature of his question. It relies on a false assumption, and so reinforces it.

"Am I in possession of Buddha consciousness?" really means, "Am I awake?" *Buddha* literally means "the one who awakened." 'Being awake' is a common metaphor in spiritual traditions, and it need not be thought of as something grand or mystical—it is simply the opposite of being asleep. Heraclitus put his finger on the difference between those opposites when he observed that *when we are awake, we all share the same world; in sleep, each of us withdraws to a world of our own*: a dreamscape that only we inhabit. To be spiritually awake is to join the rocks, the trees, the butterflies, the bees, the birds, the animals, all beings. By those terms, **whoever withdraws to the isolation chamber of the self is asleep.** Heraclitus observed that most of us are asleep most of the time, and he made reference to a saying about people that was already an adage in his day: "Though present they are absent."[69] That may be true of more people today than ever before.

You have only to go downtown in any major industrialized city to see that pretty well everyone on the sidewalk is inhabiting his own exclusive world—the defining trait of sleepers. As in the Wim Wenders film *Wings of Desire,* you might imagine their internal dialogues: this man thinking about his son, angry at him for wearing baggy pants; the woman beside him gloating over a recent squash game; the woman beside her worried about facing an unhappy client; et cetera. As many worlds as there are people. Like sleepers, these people don't really notice or feel the world around them. Like commuters listening to iPods, the sounds they alone can hear—the incessant chitchat that fills their heads—drowns out the music of the world. Withdrawn and isolated, they can only hallucinate about the world, as sleepers dream.

Once in a while, though, something happens that briefly awakens people to our shared reality. After 9/11, there was a huge awakening. The lines drawn around the self started leaking profusely: people paused and noticed each other; they looked with new eyes at buildings they had walked past for years; strangers conversed with compassion. At a sports game a similar kind of awakening happens, especially when the home team is winning. The individuals who thronged into the stadium begin to merge with the energy of the event, alert to each other and to the specifics of the game on which all eyes are fastened. In theater the experience is similar again: in a really fine play, there is a sense that the whole audience is awakened to the same unfurling truth that lives before their eyes and in their hearts. Eventually, of course, 9/11 becomes a distant memory, the sports game becomes yesterday's news and the audience files out of the theater and goes home. In the terms set out by Heraclitus, people go back to sleep, back to their own worlds: "though the Logos is common to all, the many live as though their thought were private to themselves."[70]

That feels normal to us, but it is purely a cultural conceit that has embedded itself as a habit. Consider, for instance, the quantum inseparability principle—nicknamed QUIP by Nick Herbert. It tells us that any two particles that have once been in contact continue to influence each other no matter how far apart they may be. Given the 'six degrees of separation' among people, and our shared story over millions of years, we might speculate on 'the human inseparability principle'. Whomever you meet, their story is your story, in a very real sense. To take that literally and to recognize your story in everyone you see, and their story in you, is to be liberated from the solitude of your isolation chamber and from the hold of its fantasies: even as your compassion is awakened, you appreciate anew the breadth and fullness of the story you call yours and experience it in an entirely new way. To neglect that shared human truth is not only to diminish others with a convenient kind of shorthand that objectifies them—it is to impoverish your own reality.

If we return to the Buddhist master, we can see that what he was warning his young student against was *the story of the isolated self*— the very story our culture clings to and promulgates. A tree has Buddha consciousness because a tree stands in the world without prejudice, wholly open to it, seamlessly participant in it. But the student's very question, "Am I awake?" draws a line of self-consciousness around him, thereby invoking the dreamscapes of the withdrawn self. In that regard, trying to metaphorically wake up is a lot like literally trying to fall asleep. When you wake in the night, and really want to fall back to sleep, and finally start to drift into it, nothing will snap you out of that descent more quickly than the self-conscious question, "Am I asleep yet?" Similarly, when you really want a deep awakening, and after much work start to move towards it, nothing will put you to sleep more quickly than asking, "Am I awake yet?" Wakefulness is the world itself, and its all-aware unbroken harmony is enlightenment; if you are to awaken, you can only do so by joining the wakefulness of the world. Lao-tzu expressed the same thing in different terms when he wrote, "If you receive the world, the Tao will never leave you."[71] To receive the world means allowing the energy of 'what is' to touch your core; it means *liberating your capacity for relationship* so that there is enough room within you to receive 'what is' and enter the wholeness of who you are—which cannot be objectively known any more than can the present with which it is continuous.

We can see, then, that by asking, "Am I in possession of Buddha consciousness?" we interrupt the receiving with the divisions of idea and we hold the self within an imaginary line, as surely as the tiger in New York City was held within the bars of its cage.

Steinhart's Argument

What about the second issue concerning the tyrant's fantasy of self-achieved independence, an issue that actually affects how we live in our own bodies: **is what we experience as the psyche or consciousness of the self contained in the brain?**

What do the facts say? Science, that great arbiter, is largely full of confidence that the brain contains the mind. Its orthodoxy is summed up by David Papineau in his book *Thinking about Consciousness*. He assures us that "there isn't anything really mysterious" about consciousness, and he explains that all the properties of consciousness are identical with certain material properties; they are merely neural patterns in the brain.[72] When *Time* magazine published a special issue called *The Brain: A User's Guide*, it reported that the feature of consciousness that neuroscientists most agree on and find least controversial is "the idea that our thoughts, sensations, joys and aches consist entirely of physiological activity in the tissues of the brain. Consciousness does not reside in an ethereal soul that *uses* the brain like a PDA; consciousness *is* the activity of the brain."[73] That view buys into the idea of perseity as fully as the claim that the DNA molecule contains the fixed and essential self. Similarly, the journal *Scientific American Mind* claims that "mind is a set of operations carried out by the brain, much as walking is a set of operations carried out by the legs."[74] It's as if the parent journal, *Scientific American,* had never heard of the aspects of quantum mechanics that demonstrate a relationship between consciousness and the behavior of remote subatomic particles—a mystery no one can explain. If you compare the claim that "the mind is the brain" or "consciousness *is* the activity of the brain" with some of those findings, you have what amounts to cognitive dissonance.*

We could settle the issue of whether the mind is the brain once and

---

* I wish studies of consciousness would not begin with the question, "How does the brain create consciousness?" but would instead consider the observed effect of consciousness on random event generators or radioactive decay, or its ability to turn a light wave into a particle or a fractured water crystal into a symmetrical one. Then we could ask questions that are inclusive of what we know, such as, "What is the nature of consciousness, such that a thought can affect the outcome of events that are at a distance and seemingly separate from the thinker?" As Rosenblum and Kuttner state in their book *Quantum Enigma* (Oxford University Press, 2006), "There is no way to interpret quantum theory without in some way addressing consciousness" (p. 156). Why then do scientists insist on interpreting consciousness as if the findings of quantum theory didn't exist? I might refer those who are interested to the Appendix of this book, which offers a layperson's summary of one of the simplest, most elegant and most baffling experiments ever conducted: the double-slit experiment, which defies all simplistic attempts to confine the properties of consciousness within the supposed perseity of the brain.

for all if we rescued a head from the cryonics vault and conducted a whole-brain transplant. If the person who awoke after the operation was clearly the person whose brain had been inserted into the awaiting body, we could say with certainty that "where goes a brain, there goes a person," as Roland Puccetti famously argued. As it is, the technical competence to carry out that operation does not yet exist—but we have the next best thing: a surgical dissection of the physiological and psychological issues involved in a whole-brain transplant as they pertain to the preservation of the personal identity of the brain donor. This analysis was written by philosopher Eric Steinhart and published in the journal *Biology and Philosophy* under the title "Persons versus Brains: Biological Intelligence in Human Organisms." The article so singularly contravenes our deeply held orthodoxy that at the time he wrote it, and after an extensive review of the pertinent literature, Steinhart was able to write, "I am not aware of anyone who outright argues that persons do not go with brains."[75]

Again, the issue is of import to us because we define ourselves according to it, *and if we are not who we think we are, then our idea of ourselves is going to stand between us and reality,* like the wall of Michael Caine's cell. To the extent that we try to live in accord with a mistaken identity, our living will be deadened by its definition—much as the society of the mythological hero was rendered stagnant by its fixed idea of normal.

I would urge the interested reader to refer directly to Steinhart's article for the sheer pleasure of its patient, precise methodology, its thoroughness and its scope. In a mere fifteen pages it utterly demolishes a time-honored truism. I can do no more here than offer a pedestrian summary of his argument, which looks at how the memories, learning and computational processing of a psyche are realized partly in the brain, but partly also in a body's enteric nervous system, endocrine system, immune system and genetic networks; and then, to wrap up, his argument considers the psychological consequences of brain transplantation.

The Enteric Nervous System

Interlaced around the digestive organs is a nervous system that is so complex, and so neurologically similar to the brain in both structure and functioning, that it is called our 'second brain'. The idea of a single brain in the head that runs the whole show is simply false. Mechanisms in the brain that are thought to be involved in higher learning and the formation of memories are also found in the enteric brain. It perceives, processes information, and acts—and it can do so even if cut off from all communication with the cranial brain. Furthermore, it actually modulates memory and learning in the cranial brain through the secretion of peptides. Steinhart speaks of a *psychological* gut-brain axis that is sustained by the coupling of the brain and the enteric nervous system. If our 'gut feelings' are part of who we are as individuals, then we experience 'who we are' in part through an enteric brain that is unique to our own body: unique in its memories, perceptions, actions and reactions.

The Endocrine System

The endocrine system regulates some of our deepest human responses; feeding, fleeing, fighting and sex. Our personal experience of those basic responses to the world is shaped by glands like the thyroid, adrenal, testes or ovaries, which lie outside the head. Steinhart summarizes the implications of that as follows: "Endocrine glands secrete hormones that play important roles in mature brain function and that regulate many cognitive, emotional and behavioral features of adult humans. It is hard to deny the relevance of these features to personal identity."[76] If the brain goes into a new body without its endocrine system, the person cannot follow unchanged.

The Immune System

The immune system is how the body distinguishes between self and nonself, an issue central to our personhood. The immune system has more cells than the brain and is remarkably independent from its control. It can be understood as a representational system with beliefs, desires and memories; it is also able to cause cognitive and affective changes in the central nervous system, which consists of the brain and spinal cord. In other words, the state of the brain is affected by memories and cognition that lie outside of itself. The behavior of the self is largely dependent on its memories, and it has been assumed that memories are stored exclusively in the brain. But the immune system perceives, learns, recognizes, decides, acts and remembers: it contains the unique biological history of each human organism. Those memories, to be sure, are not conscious, but so much of who we are and what we experience is not conscious that it would be folly to claim that the conscious ego constitutes the person. Steinhart concludes, "If it is necessary to preserve memory to transfer the person, then whole-brain transplant fails, since it does not save the immune system."[77]

Genetic Networks

As epigenetics has demonstrated, identical twins can look and behave in radically different ways, because genes are adaptive—they switch on or off. The interaction among genes creates holistic, dynamic systems with emergent properties. Steinhart calls the genetic networks internal to cells "the mindless automata from whose interactions mind emerges."[78] If the psyche is realized physiologically, then the molecular computations at the lowest level provide its foundation: the thoughtless hardware from which the thinking software emerges. "If it is necessary to transfer the unique computational features of a person at every level, even the very lowest, in order to transfer the psyche and therefore the person, then whole-brain transplant fails, since it does not transfer the genetic regulatory networks not in the brain."[79]

Psychological Discontinuity

As the new science of neuroplasticity has shown, the brain is remarkably adaptive: it 'rewires' itself daily. When a transplanted brain is connected to a new body, it will interact with the regulatory networks of a new spinal cord, autonomic nervous system, enteric nervous system, immune system and endocrine system. As the regulatory networks of two distinct genomes are brought into chemical contact, the disruption in the activity pattern of the brain will be wholesale. The psyche, if indeed a psyche emerges at all, will not be that of either the brain donor or the body donor, but a hybrid of the two; and that hybrid is likely to be vegetative or psychotic.

Steinhart remarks that the issue of mental illness, strangely, is never mentioned in the philosophical literature on brain transplants. Studies show us, though, that even undergoing a heart transplant can profoundly disrupt the psyche, inducing psychiatric difficulties and dissociative shifts such that body image and self-concept are often significantly altered. The psychiatric disruptions induced by transplanting a whole body onto a brain are incalculable. Furthermore, as Steinhart contends, the physiological reorganizations of the brain that finds itself in a new body are sufficient to destroy the brain donor's memories and personality. Steinhart summarizes this scenario:

Suppose that Brown's bodiless brain is put into Robinson's brainless body to make Brownson. Brown's brain does not know how to regulate Robinson's body. Brownson is likely to remain in a vegetative state and to suffer violent seizures until his lower brain activity patterns reorganize into patterns compatible with the feedback from his new body. Assuming he ever wakes up, Brownson is likely to have regressed to a psychotic infantile state in which there is no coherent person. He does not know how to eat; he cannot control his bowels. He neither moves nor speaks.... Conflicts between Brownson's memories and all his sensory inputs lead to cognitive dissonance and permanent total amnesia.... Brownson is insane ... [and] suffers from the classical dissociative symptoms: seizures, headaches, blackouts. He has auditory and visual hallucinations of Brown's voice and body-image; he does not know who it is.[80]

As Steinhart succinctly concludes, "The psyche pervades every living part of the organism."[81] A telling anecdote illustrates that vividly. Paul Pearsall's book *The Heart's Code* argues persuasively that the heart is a sentient, thinking organ, one from which we have dangerously estranged ourselves. Early in the book he recounts a dramatic instance in which a young girl received the heart of a ten-year-old who had been murdered. After the transplant the girl was troubled by dreams in which she was being murdered. She described in such detail the time, place and weapon of the murder, as well as the face and clothes of the murderer, that police, acting on those details, were able to apprehend and convict the man who had slain the heart donor.

That "the psyche pervades every living part of the organism" accords with the Universal Law of Interrelationship and stands in stark contrast to the 'self-achieved independence' of the tyrant. Not only have we found that everything in the body affects everything else and as a whole sustains our experience of the self; the self exists through virtue of its relationships with the world around it, as Delgado makes clear. The tyrant is powerless to bend the Universal Law to suit his urges. Those urges are potent enough within us, though: they confine the self and kneecap our ability to recognize wholeness in the world and come into harmony with it. Let us look at how that happens.

Exercise Two: **Wakame**

When we believe that our intelligence is confined to the cranium, we interact with the body as though it were biological machinery—and it complies with that expectation, becoming rigid, stiff, patterned and mute. Its consolidations prevent us from joining the essential fluidity of the present and harden us against its guidance. This exercise, which I learned from Shintaido master Haruyoshi Ito, helps the body's intelligence to release itself into its natural, fluid sensitivity.

The exercise is called Wakame, a Japanese word for "seaweed." The soft, yielding and gentle qualities of seaweed are precisely the ones that awaken our capacity for relationship. You begin the exercise by standing in a relaxed manner, imagining and feeling your body to be a seaweed plant: your feet reach down into the seabed and are rooted there; the rest of your body floats upwards towards the unseen surface, buoyed by the sea around you. Not only that, your body also reacts as a seaweed plant would, yielding to the merest current.

Once that image is clearly felt within the body, imagine a current of water coming from behind you: without resistance you bend forward and flow with it, and then gradually float back up, buoyed by the water. Then play in the same manner with currents from the front and either side. Pay attention to any tightness the movements reveal and see if you can release it to fluidity.

The next stage requires the help of a friend. As you float up like seaweed, rooted in the ground with your eyes closed, your friend will gently push on some part of your body, as a current of water might. Like seaweed, you offer no anticipation and no resistance, but simply yield to it, then return to the upright floating position.

Your friend can adjust the speed and weight of each push, and your response should be precisely commensurate with it. To yield to fluidity in that way is also to reveal any consolidations still held in the body; once those consolidations are brought into the light, you have already brought awareness to them, which by itself will begin to change them.

When Shintaido masters practice this exercise, they are so sensitized to the movement of their partners that, though their eyes are closed, they yield to a push even before it has touched them. Similarly, when we are sensitized to the movement of the present, we yield to it and dance without need of either push or shove.

3 | Our Axial Consciousness

Mind as Sensitivity

Only as we come to see and recognize the tyrant's urges within us can we effectively move beyond them. The challenge is not an insignificant one. The need to see reality in terms of independent existence, for instance, is so 'normal' within our culture that we cease to notice it; more than that, it has so effectively compromised our sensitivity to 'what is' that we actually *feel* the stand-alone existence of everything around us, as well as of ourselves. And that feeling persists despite what we may understand about the Universal Law of Interrelationship: that there is no such thing as independent existence; that all things exist only through relationship. But how can our experience of reality be at complete odds with its actual nature? How can our sensitivity to 'what is' be so profoundly dulled that an ordinary, experiential appreciation of the unitive nature of reality is deemed an aberration, and maybe even a little flaky?

To answer those questions, it helps to realize that the very division we make between *mind* and *sensitivity* is an artificial one. It was made necessary by the essential conceit on which self-tyranny relies: the separation of our conscious reasoning from the sensitivity of our being. But consider our sensitivities to music, order, feelings, harmony, truth, rhythms of speech, arithmetic relationships, architecture, the bounce of a tennis ball, the mood of a companion or the groundswell of a social change: all are capacities of mind. Mind is sensitivity, and sensitivity is mind, just as is suggested in the Latin word *sentire*, which means both "thought" and "sensation." The idea that the mind's intelligence can be measured with an IQ test is a ridiculously narrow view that merely flatters the male element with the assertion that, as Parmenides would have it, abstract reasoning is true intelligence and the mind's sensitivities to the world are unreliable data gatherers at best. An IQ test cannot reveal who in a given group might be the most strategic hockey player, or the most brilliant composer, or the most successful entrepreneur. Whatever activity we undertake, it will be guided by our sensitivities to the world around us; but we might equally say it will be guided by our mind. And as we have seen, 'mind' is not synonymous with 'brain': an experience of the mind is an experience of the body; an experience of the body is an experience of the mind.

There remains no question that within the thinking body, the brain is a neurological center for thought, action, learning and memory; but even as we talk about 'the' brain, we betray an ancient prejudice and our deep need to live in our heads. The body's physiology shows us that our very idea of 'the brain' is false. In fact, the cranial brain is only half the story: we have two brains—one in the head and one in the gut. The fact that our second brain—which Steinhart referred to as the enteric nervous system—has only recently been recognized by medical science is a testament to long-standing prejudices that do not exist in other cultures. The Incas spoke of *qosqo*, the center in the belly that receives and digests the spiritual energies of the world. In Chinese medicine the belly is sometimes called *Shen Ch'ue* (The Mind Palace) and is considered to be the seat of learning and the repository of truth. The Japanese consider the abdomen, or *hara*, to be the place in the body where one experiences the greatest possible *presence of mind*. To ask someone in Japan to think with his belly is to ask him to ponder an issue with his whole Being and truth. In fact, the Japanese language has a broad range of expressions that use *hara* where English uses *head*. Where we would call a person *levelheaded*, they might say *hara no aru hito*, "the man with the belly"; of someone we found to be *hotheaded* they might say *hara ga tatsu*, "a person whose belly rises" (i.e., in anger); and someone who is *scatterbrained* they might call *hara no dekite inai hito*, "the man who has not developed his belly." Such parallels do not merely reflect different ways of seeing a similar issue; something more is going on: *these examples represent two different experiences of thinking itself.* And it would seem that the differences are created by culture.

In the West, the physiological basis of the brain in the belly has been discovered, forgotten, discovered, forgotten and finally rediscovered and slowly, reluctantly accepted. In 1907, for example, the American physician and anatomist Byron Robinson published an opus that summarized much of his life's extensive research: *The Abdominal and Pelvic Brain.* In it he wrote of our two brains, which he considered to be of virtually equal importance: the cranial brain and the abdominal brain.

> In the cranial brain resides the consciousness of right and wrong. Here is the seat of all progress, mental and moral, and in it lies the instinct to protect life and the fear of death. However, in the abdomen there exists a brain of wonderful power maintaining eternal, restless vigilance over its viscera.... The abdominal brain is not a mere agent of the brain and cord; it receives and generates nerve forces itself; it presides over nutrition.... It is the automatic, vegetative, the subconscious brain of physical existence. It is the center of life itself.[82]

Robinson's detailed surgical investigations mapped out the abdominal brain, including its smaller dependent, the pelvic brain, and he presented his findings in beautifully rendered anatomical drawings. More than a decade after Robinson's death, Johannis Langley published his classic work, *The Autonomic Nervous System,* which largely laid the groundwork for our current understanding of the autonomic nervous system. He classified three divisions in it: the sympathetic division, the parasympathetic division and the enteric division—which he called the enteric (or visceral) nervous system. Remarkably, and though his book was considered a classic, his discovery that the autonomic nervous system had a third division—the enteric nervous system—was virtually forgotten until the 1960s, when Michael Gershon discovered that serotonin was an enteric neurotransmitter. Even then, Gershon's research into our second brain met with such resistance that it took until 1981 before it was accepted and a new branch of study—neurogastroenterology—was officially launched. Writing of the years of resistance his ideas met with, Gershon commented,

> Neuroscientists, as a group, often tend to believe that the entire body exists just to support the brain. It is the brain that thinks, emotes, and remembers. The brain

is happy or unhappy, content or troubled. Philosophy, poetry, faith, and reason are all products of the brain. Neuroscientists, if they thought of the enteric nervous system at all, therefore considered it as a bit player, a supporting actor in a drama in which the brain was, is, and always will be the star.[83]

We could just as accurately paraphrase Gershon and observe that "Westerners as a group often tend to believe that the entire body exists just to support the brain. It is the brain that thinks," et cetera. It would seem that the neuroscientists' belief has not been entirely guided by their research; rather, their research has been guided by their culture's belief. The more general effect of that belief is to disconnect us all from our core—from our "center of life," as Robinson put it—and contract our consciousness into what we perceive to be our true center: the cranium. By withdrawing consciousness from our core, though, we inadvertently precipitate a host of imbalances. For instance, Gershon cites that forty percent of patients seen by internists have come for gastrointestinal problems. When we are out of touch with the brain in our guts, *we tend to store stress there without even being aware of it.* Researcher Candace Pert has shown that when tissues experience stress, the cells in those tissues suffer a reduced receptivity to the life-giving "information molecules," which Pert describes as "the basic units of a language used by cells throughout the organism to communicate across systems such as the endocrine, neurological, gastrointestinal, and even the immune system."[84] Eventually the receptivity to those molecules is so impaired it becomes insufficient to maintain functioning at the cellular levels—and that, as Pert explains, "is what sets up the weakened conditions that can lead to disease."[85] Pert's observations help us understand something that Eastern medicine has taught for millennia: that disease is associated with an impairment in the flow of the body's energy.

There is another imbalance created by our contraction of consciousness into the head, though, that has much graver consequences: we lose touch with our own being. To understand this larger issue, we might ask, ***What does it mean to our experience as humans that we have two brains?*** It's interesting for comparison to consider how our culture has embraced the important findings on right-brain/left-brain differences, and how that new understanding has affected the way we can pay attention to ourselves. In a way, though, right-brain/left-brain research is culturally safer for us, because it keeps the brain front and center, and so reinforces our head-centric tendencies. The clinical fact that we have two brains, though, is something we haven't even begun to accommodate. We don't even know how to entertain its implications. Architect and polymath György Doczi gives us an en-trée into the issue with his book *The Power of Limits*. The book is an extended study of the way in which *wholes are created by the union of complementary opposites,* and he notes our ancient recognition of that paradigm in such traditional polarities as Yin and Yang, earth and sky, negative and positive, east and west, moon and sun, and of course male and female. We also find expressions of that paradigm in the ancient cultures of Persia, Egypt, Greece and India. Each pair-ing holds between its poles the energetic potential for an exchange. *When complementary opposites join in such an exchange, their inter-play manifests as a generative dynamic that brings forth the forms of life.* Doczi coined the term *dinergy* to describe that dynamic, from the Greek *dia-,* meaning "through, across," and *energy.* Dinergy, Doczi explains, is no less than the source from which the creative energy of organic growth springs.[86] As such, we might also observe that dinergy is the source from which our consciousness as human beings evolves: the two brains we have been born with are the two poles of our con-sciousness, and our consciousness arises from the interplay between them. That is, the brain in our cranium and the brain in our gut are equal, opposite and complementary partners, and it is in the exchang-es between them that the creative energy of our consciousness is born. If we look at the differences between our two brains, we can begin to clarify the nature of their partnership.

Robinson associated the cranial brain with mental processes, and the visceral brain with the nonverbal consciousness of our physical existence. If these brains represent the two aspects, or poles, of our consciousness, then the findings of both physiology and our own ex-perience help us to understand that each has an essential, specialized function: **it's in the head that we can consciously think; it's in the pelvis that we can consciously 'be'.** The dissociated brain in the cranium is as little equipped to bring being into consciousness as the wordless brain in our gut is able to bring rational thinking into consciousness. Of course, the visceral brain does a great deal of thinking, just as the cranial brain is fully participant in being: it's just that ***visceral thinking*** *is empty of idea, and cranial being is insensate.* For that reason, each needs the other's strength; each finds its completion or complement through the other. Being is sensitized to the world with the help of rational thought; rational thought joins 'what is' only as it is informed by Being. We might simplify further and note that the cranial brain—the realm of will and idea—is the center of 'doing', and the abdominal brain is the center of 'being'. That contrast brings a mythic perspective to the issue, suggesting that *the cranial brain is the center of the male aspect of our consciousness and the visceral brain the center of the female aspect of our consciousness.* If we delve a little more deeply into each, we can draw those distinctions more helpfully.

The Pole of Our Conscious Thinking

Our cranial-centered consciousness has shaped our language and the hierarchy of our institutions; to examine how deeply that same hierarchy shapes our experience of life is to illuminate the nature and influence of the cranial brain. Consider, for starters, that its reasoning cannot directly *connect us* with 'what is', but can only *observe and think about* 'what is'—creating, studying and refining models of it. These models can serve us well: they help us clarify issues, analyze events, parse problems and achieve perspective. This book is an example of such models on many levels.

A difficulty arises, though, when the male pole of our consciousness seeks self-achieved independence—seeks to detach from the subtle, infinitely informed guidance of Being and run the show, perceiving life itself to be something that we can 'get our heads around', or solve—for that assumption eventually dominates our purpose and our identity, even as it robs us of life's true gifts. The powers of the cranial brain certainly excel at planning and solving—but when the exercise of those powers displaces our ability to just 'be', *so that our waking awareness is more attentive to duplicates than to reality,* then we are being seduced by the notion that, just as any experience contains information, information can somehow contain any experience. We believe that with enough bits of information you can somehow describe or represent the whole of an experience—capture it, so to speak, or pin it down. We live in the Information Age, after all, and our addiction makes the object of our longing appear disproportionately wonderful.

And yet ... if you pause to consider that belief, it collapses under the least scrutiny. As psychotherapist R. D. Laing observed,

> *Any* experience of reality is indescribable. Just look around you for a moment and see, hear, smell and feel where you are.... Your consciousness can partake of all that is in one single moment, but you will never be able to describe the experience.[87]

Experience *cannot* be described—not by words nor even by the formulas and statistics of science. A duplicate, however elaborately constructed, can never be complete. It will never have life. It will never come into relationship with the unbroken whole or answer to all that is. Yet our head-centered existence obsesses over its duplicates in its effort to represent the living world accurately and predictably—largely so that it will be able to guide us in how to react and what to anticipate. In the meantime, our obsession with duplicates resolutely distances our attention from the sensational and complementary pole of our consciousness: the mindful center of Being in the pelvis.

By isolating the cranial brain, we are restricting ourselves to a **unipolar consciousness**, one that chooses idea over sensation—as though both were not necessary. When our conscious thinking detaches from our conscious being and withdraws into the head, it is finding refuge in the one organ that is numb to sensation, one that surgeons can cut through without need of anesthetic: the brain. We are, in a literal sense, all numbskulls, and it is by retreating into the skull's numbness—by 'living in our heads'—that we enter the simpler, more orderly and predictable world of doing. But it is a desensitized, abstract world—a world, as Joseph Campbell put it, of "organized inadequacy." Fearful of Being, shielded from the energy of 'what is', the male aspect of our consciousness strives to be self-contained, provisioning itself with models of the self and its environs. The ego might spend most of its time among those duplicates, endlessly ordering them and in turn ordering us in whatever we do. That is what the private chattering in our heads is all about—but while the wasps in the bottle buzz round and round, the world carries on virtually unnoticed.

The cranium is, quite literally, our *head*quarters—*and the unipolar cranial brain serves as the model for all the corporate, governmental and organizational headquarters that exist.* Like those offspring, the head sits apart from the ordinary world, secluding itself with the equivalent of high walls and closed doors. The head is our corporate boardroom, our castle keep, our innermost stronghold, fortified and designed for impermeability; it is the source and originator of willful doing; its concern is with getting things right and issuing orders; it is our corner office, providing us with a commanding view that is safely distanced from the uncontrollable sensations of Being. **In truth, the head potentially provides each of us with our own private isolation chamber—a Skinner box for the self-achieved independence of our male consciousness.** As such, it also encloses us in a hallucinogenic environment—the source of "those constant human fantasies" that tend to tie the human spirit back, and from which it is the hero's task to deliver us. The phenomenon is self-sustaining: *once we retreat into our chamber of duplicates, we become so preoccupied and distracted that we only marginally notice the extent to which we inhabit not the wholeness of the world, but our fragmented duplicates of it.* And so it is that the numbskull-centered self eventually turns to the ultimate fantasy of cryonics to preserve itself from death, even as it insists on preserving itself from life.

That the head should rule has been an axiom of our culture since Parmenides elevated reason above the senses. **The abstract, head-centered realm of ideas is not the seat of *human identity*, as scientific orthodoxy and the cryonics ads claim; it is actually the seat of *male identity*, once the male element accomplishes its rejection of and retreat from Being.** As soon as the male element retreats to the head and raises the drawbridge that leads to the highway of feeling, it is on its own. It can sort itself out, inside its ramparts, without distraction from the flux of the sensational present—organizing its ideas about reality and inflicting them on the unfelt world. In short, **the head-centric state by which *we identify the self with the cranial brain* conforms in every respect to the mythological tyrant.**

Once we no longer feel and live "massively connected" to the world around us, we can experience the self only as a unit in isolation from the whole: trapped in our unipolar consciousness, we remain fundamentally disconnected, anxious about our future, and preoccupied with sorting and adjusting our ideas so they can better guide us. We obsess over finding ways to leverage our circumstances and improve our standing in the world. The *control of acquisitions*— of goods, money, property, status, knowledge, companies, and that trickiest possession of all, the 'known self'—becomes our substitute for a full *experience of the present*. That substitution, of course, never quite satisfies, for a full experience of the present nourishes the sensitivities of our full consciousness—the very thing from which we have barricaded ourselves. We find ourselves in the very condition against which the myths of the world warn: the tyrant within us pits the self against the self, and traps us in the detached pole of male consciousness. That is the basic effect of our cultural choice to live in the cranial brain. It is also the crux of our mistaken identity.

In the spirit of our politically enlightened age, though, we may remain suspicious of myth and wonder why the hero and the tyrant—its central figures—are conventionally depicted as men; and we would be forgiven for assuming it to be yet another outmoded expression of patriarchy. In fact, the depictions are closer to home than that: **the hero and the tyrant depict the two divergent tendencies of the male element of doing.** Since the male element is found in all men and women, the relevance of these archetypes is universal. By representing them over and over in countless stories around the world, myths are helping us to understand how the male element can evolve, sometimes very subtly, in two very different directions—towards either tyrant or hero—and that *its evolution depends on its relationship to the female element.*

The fears that have centered us in our heads are the fears that create the tyrant, and the basic fear that creates the tyrant is a fear of the female. Once the tyrant dissociates from the female, it forsakes the interplay between the two poles of our consciousness, wherein lies the source of its creative evolution; ipso facto, the cranial tyranny of our consciousness forsakes the ability to evolve. And so it is that the tyrant is stuck in trying to fortify what is 'his', intent on preserving it from a world of ceaseless change. Whenever the fantasy of what is rightfully 'his' is at odds with the world, he will seek to arrest or subjugate the world, just as he subjugates the body. The willfulness or even, indeed, a *willingness* to subjugate is the basic impulse of tyranny. That potential is alive in each of us and will spring forth whenever we heed will above world—for such an allegiance blinds us to 'what is', even as it binds us to the vanities of entitlement and to the fantasy of our personal power.

Once the male element dissociates, it lacks the foundational affirmation of 'being', so it needs to find affirmations elsewhere. Those affirmations naturally include access to possessions of special value, and they exclude precisely those things that might bring the tyrant back to 'earth'—back, that is, to the female element. And so the tyrannical male element buffers himself from contact with the ordinary, from any form of humility (which is strictly for others to feel), any questioning of or threat to his special status, any form of leveling hardship, any claims on his time but those that serve his interests, and any diminution of his control. By distancing himself from those influences, the tyrant is distancing himself from *the very experiences that might guide him towards an evolution of consciousness.* The deepest root of the word *fear* also gave rise to the words *peril* and *experience,* and it conveys the sense of "through, across, beyond." To be afraid of Being, as the tyrant singularly is, is to be afraid of experience, which is necessarily transformative. Our state of self-tyranny, then, creates a state of deprivation: it denies us the experience of living. The canker of that deprivation eats at us and gives us no rest, even as it goads us to redouble our agenda of control.

If you have any question about how deeply and unconsciously we see and identify ourselves as a unipolar consciousness that has dissociated from the female, you have only to look at the most common iconography with which we represent ourselves. I remember hearing that when icons for men's and women's washrooms were tried at Expo '67 in Montreal, they provoked a great deal of confusion. But over the years those icons have been refined to the simplest possible renderings, and today we recognize ourselves in them without any problem. They feel right to us. What is particularly noteworthy in those icons is that **they represent the head as an independent circle that hovers above, but is not attached to, the rest of the body.** That basic iconography proliferates in a variety of applications—on road signs, in ads, and in all the symbols representing Olympic sports. In other words, *the foremost cultural icon we use for ourselves and in which we most easily recognize ourselves is a picture that shows a head detached from the body.* That icon displays for all to see our most cherished and beloved fiction: the stand-alone brain, safely cut off from the sensations of Being.

The Pole of Conscious Being

The aspect of consciousness supported by the cranial brain is familiar enough to us—it's where we live. The other brain, which our male-centric culture has tacitly rejected, is less familiar: it has been variously called the enteric nervous system, the enteric brain, the brain in the gut, the abdominal brain, the second brain and the visceral brain. By-ron Robinson's book on the subject, *The Abdominal and Pelvic Brain*, looks exhaustively at it, and pays close attention to a rich concentration of neural tissue deep within it, a physiological feature of such independence that he called it 'the pelvic brain'. Its location near the foundational and sensation-rich areas of the perineum, the sacrum and the genitals places it at the experiential root of our being. The word 'pelvic' also reminds us that *as the male center of ideas is bound inside the cranium, the female center of sensational being rests in the pelvic bowl.* When we experience that brain in the gut, we can feel ourselves entering a different aspect of our consciousness: we are moving from the pole of our conscious thinking to the pole of our conscious be-ing. For reasons both experiential and associative, my preference is to depart from medical nomenclature and refer to the thinking center of the female aspect of our consciousness as 'the pelvic intelligence'. That term also makes it clear that our main interest in that mindful sensitiv-ity is not indicated by its medical classification; our primary concern is with the spiritual and mythic implications of the human journey into full consciousness.

Even in so head-centric a culture as ours, there is a vestigial aware-ness of the intelligence at work in our gut. We recognize it as a distinct mode of thinking. When we say someone "has guts," we are refer-ring to a deep resolution of mind that is able to remain steadfast and grounded in the face of great challenges. When we speak of having a "gut feeling," we are indicating a deep intuition of the mind that arises independent of the calculations of the head. When we ask for some-one's "gut reaction" to an issue, we are asking her to forego specula-tion or analysis or cleverness, and to speak from a deeper, more holis-tic mindfulness that is felt within: we are asking her to 'check in' with the thinking that rests in the pelvic bowl.

We saw that other cultures—those of China, Japan and the In-can nations—demonstrate an explicit relationship with the pelvic intelligence. The chakra system in India does as well. Chakras constitute a series of energy centers in the body—*chakra* literally means wheel or circle of energy. The first and deepest of the chakras is located on the pelvic floor, in the midst of those parts of the self that our culture is uncomfortable even naming, let alone feeling: the anus, the perineum and the genitals. That region is our 'underneath', and as such is affiliated with the chthonic, hidden life of the earth: the soft, formless dark depths of life itself. This chakra sits between the anus and the genitals, in the center of the pelvic floor, and is generally identified with the perineum, although one tradition places it just above the perineum, pretty much where the pelvic brain lies. It is associated with earth energy and groundedness, and is called *the root chakra or the base chakra, because it represents our connection to Being.* As its roots ground a tree in the earth, the root chakra grounds an individual in Being.

In practice, when we allow consciousness to suffuse the pelvic intelligence, we arrive at a place of grounded wholeness in the body—a place from which we can massively connect with the world around us, a place of conscious being that does not rely on our conscious thinking. Once you allow your awareness to descend into the pole of your pelvic intelligence, you begin to awaken to your genius for "massively connecting and communicating": conscious of your being, you find that you are at rest in the present, secure in the self and at one with the world. Whereas the cranial brain pulls to pieces and analyzes, the pelvic pole of our intelligence brings all things into relationship and enables us to feel them as a whole, which in turn imparts wholeness to the self. It is that genius that allows us to just 'be', alert to the eternal present. On the other hand, when the pelvic intelligence is shadowed in neglect and excluded from our awareness, *we lose our connection with Being: we live in a state of anxiety, and we feel alone in the world.*

The integrative power of the pelvic intelligence, long acknowledged in other cultures, has been recently discovered in a therapeutic context in the West. Paul Canali specializes in recovery from trauma. His approach recognizes and works with the body's innate intelligence, and he has developed a number of techniques to help liberate it. One of his foremost tools is called the Enteric Brain Technique, which employs various nonmechanical forms of biofeedback to increase bodily awareness and bring the autonomic nervous system into balance. The role of the enteric brain in achieving that balance is critical. As Canali has written,

The Enteric Brain is a built-in biological system to keep us on the path to health and higher consciousness or awareness. It is controlled by an innate network that tells us whether or not it is safe to become fully human and free from fear, or to stay living in fear, survival and separation.[88]

In an urban environment, anxiety dominates our emotional life, nagging at our attention and monopolizing it. When that anxiety carries us into the head, we feed it. Our pelvic intelligence holds the ultimate security that can lay all anxiety to rest, but that security does not consist of ideas. It is an experience: an experience of a bodily intelligence that is grounded in its own mindful connection to Being.

The Forgotten Corridor

The degree to which anxiety drives our culture and our daily lives indicates the distance we have traveled from the visceral center of conscious being—"the center of life itself," as Byron Robinson put it. Our culture urges us to dismiss that aspect of our consciousness every time the head is proclaimed to be our rightful ruler; every time we are assured that man is the supreme creation of the universe; with every idiom describing the body as machinery; with every suggestion that the solutions to our problems are to be found in exerting more control over the world; with every intimation that the birthright of our mind's intelligence is calculation rather than sensitivity; with every inducement to seek success through acquisition rather than service; with every description of the natural world as "resources"; with every law assuring us of our rights and entitlements while making no mention of our responsibilities; and with every new invention that gratifies our insatiable self-absorption.

Our culture's story exalts and celebrates the male assertions of doing, even as it demeans the female values of being—whether in the body, in our social institutions, or in our view of the world. Rooted in perseity, that story represents the world as a random interaction of bits that can never add up to meaningfulness, and it widely dismisses as flaky any inclination to understand ourselves as "an organic continuation of the Logos," as Heraclitus puts it. Our culture's story has been shaped by individual experience over thousands of years, but it in turn shapes the experience of every individual growing up under its influence. In fact, our culture's story actually shapes our bodies—it lives within our tissues. Recent advances in neuroplasticity have shown that the mapping of the brain is dramatically affected by the act of paying close attention to something. What we habitually neglect, on the other hand, recedes within the brain's mapping. It took me years to recover the recesses of my body from the dark cloud of neglect that had settled upon them and obscured them from view—but today they are suffused with consciousness in a way I simply wouldn't have considered possible at the outset. And I know I've only really just begun. If we wish to release ourselves from a story that is riddled with hallucination—if we wish to realize the self as "an organic continuation of the Logos" and its active partner—then we need to let go of those parts of the old story that are endarkened and endarkening fantasies and open to the reality of our true nature.

Eric Steinhart, in explicating the extent to which our "psyche pervades every living part of the organism," wrote of *the connection between the enteric brain and the cranial brain*—which we might also recognize as the conduit that lives between the female and male poles of our consciousness. He referred to that conduit as a *psychological gut-brain axis:*

> Cellular systems in the enteric nervous system and the brain are sufficiently well-coupled to form subpersonal agencies that span both systems. The result is a psychological gut-brain axis internal to the person. The enteric nervous system and brain communicate via the vagus nerve and via a variety of chemical messengers. The enteric nervous system has a high degree of autonomy within the gut-brain axis, forming an equal and often dominant partner with the brain.[89]

Our word *axis* denotes a central stem through which a reconciliation between two distinct energies or planes of existence may be achieved. In mythology the concept of an *axis mundi* (also called 'world axis' or 'cosmic axis') recurs across human cultures: it can be associated with mountains (e.g., Mt. Zion, Mt. Fuji, Mt. Kailash), places (e.g., the Garden of Eden, the Oracle at Delphi), temples or trees; it is always considered sacred; and it is generally a means by which the energies of earth and sky are brought into correspondence. The prototype for our concept of an axis mundi lives within the human body: the "psychological gut-brain axis," as Steinhart put it, is the conduit through which the two aspects of our consciousness—which we have identified with the pelvic brain and the cranial brain, earth and sky, the female and the male, or the center of being and the center of doing— are brought into correspondence and unity. **In practice, that axis is experienced as a corridor in the body though which the complementary poles of our consciousness can unite in interplay. From their interplay emerges the harmony of our full human consciousness.** When the corridor is obstructed, the poles of our consciousness remain segregated and cannot exchange—in effect, the axis disappears. When the corridor is unobstructed, our male consciousness can ground itself in our female consciousness—doing can root itself in being, to be continuously informed by it—so that we can feel the active self as a unity in exchange with the dynamic unity of the world around us. If mythology has anything to teach us, it's that a full participation of our two embodied natures is necessary to the journey into full selfhood. Our wholeness cannot emerge until the embodied corridor between the poles of our consciousness enables them to exchange and reconcile and join the dynamic, living harmony of the world—for **the true nature of our consciousness is not unipolar, but axial.** To remind us of that, we'll refer to *the energetic potential for exchange between those poles* as the **embodied axis,** and to *the interplay of consciousness that courses along it* as our **axial consciousness.**

Of the various images I have encountered that might symbolize the embodied axis, the most striking comes from the Mayan cultures of Mesoamerica. As anthropologist Brian Stross explains, those cultures uphold an understanding that

> the human body has two "skulls" (*bakeltik*)—one at the top of the spine (*bakel hol*) and one at the bottom (*bakel kub*)—and that these skulls are connected by a "serpent" (*chan*), which I take to mean the spinal cord or vertebral column. The two skulls are sacred, and ritually important because they are seen to contain the essence of a person.[90]

Stross convincingly demonstrates that the lower skull was once a core concept in parts of Mesoamerica, and he cites a range of other cultures that also regarded the bones of the pelvic girdle as sacred. One of those bones, the *sacrum*, derives its English name from the Latin *os sacrum*, or "holy bone," and Oscar Sugar has traced its origins further back to an ancient Egyptian belief that the sacrum was *the* holy bone, associated with Osiris and resurrection.[91] Some Mesoamerican Indian languages also associate the name of the sacrum with sacredness and deity. Similar associations show up in Africa and India, among others. The Mesoamerican view that the pelvis is an inverted skull joined to the cranial skull by a serpent shows up in pre-Columbian art, as well as in the Mayan myth of the Skyworld and the Celestial Monster that inhabited it: a snake with a head at each end. The rising sun is swallowed by the eastern head, progresses through the serpent's body in its daily path across the sky, and is finally discharged through the western mouth at sunset. In that cosmic image is reflected not just the path of the sun-derived energy that courses through our bodies as food, but also the integration of perception into being that courses between the poles of our consciousness. So although the body of the serpent likely refers to the spinal cord, I imagine its significance to include the experiential dimension of the inner corridor as well: we take in the aspects of the world largely through the faculties of sight, hearing, smell and taste—all located in the head—but we appreciate those perceptions as revelations of the present only by allowing them to travel the corridor within and reconcile with the center of our being. If the serpent represents the corridor, then, it includes the spine, but is centered just in front of it.

In a later chapter we'll look at how our own culture's center of consciousness began at the pelvic extreme of that corridor during the Paleolithic era of Being, then shifted along its axis during the aptly named Axial Age towards the head, to be resolutely ensconced there as the third millennium got underway. For now, though, it is enough to consider the necessity before us: to open ourselves to an integration that gives equal value to those sundered poles of our consciousness so we can grow into the sensitivity of our own undiminished awareness. Myths represent that integration in symbolic language: the hero journeys from the organized inadequacy of the head's realm of duplicates into the seething, material, disorderly center of our being in our viscera. The geography traversed by the hero's journey is that of our embodied intelligence, and the result of his journey, if successful, is to renew the world by bringing its riven elements into correspondence.

It may seem that the twentieth century has made great strides with regard to that journey of consciousness. We now know that the body is a marvel of intelligence. Or at least we think we do. But let us be on our guard enough to appreciate that *knowing* the true nature of the body—knowledge that is, after all, merely an idea—does not necessarily give us the leverage to overturn a mode of experience so deeply entrenched that it has shaped the very habits of our earthly existence: namely, the ones that reinforce the head as the superior and rightful ruler and the body as a convenience it is given to get things done. Prudence demands a closer look.

Certainly there is a lot of evidence to suggest that we are overcoming the old tyranny. Not that long ago most North Americans didn't know what yoga was, for instance; now there is a proliferation of yoga books and videos and classes. In most North American cities in the 1950s you would rarely see anyone over sixteen riding a bicycle because they had graduated to cars; now people of all ages are found pedaling along streets and bike paths. And they often share those paths with joggers. People are finding a real joy in breaking away from the numbing fatigue of a sedentary existence—in working out, taking classes in spinning, aerobics, or Pilates, playing tennis, or meeting weekly with a personal trainer. The bottom line, the thing more and more individuals are discovering, is *how good it feels to use your body*.

Our language, though, reveals the old tenacious paradigm still in charge: when we talk about *using* our bodies, we are still conceiving of the body as something we operate, as we might *use* a tool or a machine. It *does* feel good to use your body, no question about it, but we speak about it in the same way that we might remark on the sensuality of driving a well-appointed luxury sedan—which also undoubtedly feels good. And just as the current wisdom says that you should take good care of your car—changing the oil, checking the radiator and the air pressure—it also says that you have to take care of the thing that is your body: giving it the right supplements and stretches and cardio and a million other forms of maintenance. The phrases with which that current wisdom encourages us towards sensitivity—directing us to "feel your body" or "listen to your body" or "get in touch with your body"—present a paradigm by which the thinking self and the body are subtly identified as distinct and separated entities: the thinking self, which is accustomed to telling the body what to do, is being urged to open lines of communication in the other direction as well, so its supervision can be more sensitive. All well and good as far as intentions go—but *that solution actually reinforces our mistaken identity and the division at its core.* When we listen to our bodies to get information so we can make better decisions, we are better equipping the decision maker in the head: "I was gardening all day, but then I listened to my body and realized I should stop." That expression of virtue tells us that the male element is maturing into a kinder, gentler tyrant, but that it remains resolutely in charge: there is no indication that the inner tyrant might relinquish his hold and dissolve his identity of separateness in the universe of sensations in which the body dwells, and which dwells within the body; no indication that the thinking self might realize its true identity as the felt whole.

Every time our culture insists that the thinking self *has* a body, it identifies the self with the cranial brain—an identification that dooms us to self-conflict, self-tyranny, self-delusion and a stunted exchange of energies with the world, which also means a stunted possibility for self-discovery. **To move from the *head*quarters of the 'known self' to an axial consciousness that is informed by and grounded in the felt present means moving from an experience in which *the thinking self has a body* to one in which *the thinking of the body as a whole reveals the unified self.*** Even then, though, the idea of perseity holds us in such thrall that I would be remiss not to reiterate: the marriage of the female and the male within us is a matter not of learning to 'check in' with your body at occasional intervals, but of dissolving your identity of separateness in its vividly connected presence. And even more crucial to understand: nor is it about overthrowing the tyranny of the head, uniting the poles of your own consciousness, and forging of yourself a harmonious whole. That is the solution to which perseity would guide us—as though we could concentrate on the self and make ourselves whole, independent of the world. However unified the body might be, the issue of living in wholeness cannot be solved within the borders of its perceived perseity, for there's no such thing; the issue of our wholeness necessarily implicates the world that calls us into Being. And *we can't learn how to grow into that unity by taking hold of a new idea; we literally need to allow for a different experience of the self.*

Beginning to move into that different experience of the self relies, more than anything, on an awareness of the embodied axis within. **In** our culture, we generally don't experience the space between the cranial skull and the pelvic skull as an open corridor in which the confluence of self and world takes place; we experience it as a room of many chambers: the flow and exchanges of energy through that room are confounded by the variety of its inner partitions. Such partitions are typically found in the throat, chest, back, belly, organs or pelvis. Some may be obvious to us; others are too subtle for a cursory visitation of our awareness to notice; but all of them feel familiar, rather 'normal', and even necessary. And indeed, they are necessary to the 'known self', for that partitioning is what maintains it. If you pay close attention to that inner realm, you are likely to discover that some areas within it are virtually sectioned off from your consciousness, as though Restricted Access signs were posted; that different passageways through it might feel congested; that some regions might be subject to a "lights out" policy; and that nooks and crannies within it might be filled with lumps of consolidated will. In fact, you are likely to find that the baffles partitioning the natural spaciousness between the two poles of your embodied consciousness mirror the divisions, segregations and regimentations of your cranial thinking.

Those inner baffles, we should note, are the primary means by which we estrange ourselves from our being. The "different experience of the self" that a journey to unity requires is one that brings attention to the space within, discovers the baffles, and reintegrates them with our being. Once the many-chambered room is relieved of all partitions, shadows and divisions, it becomes a corridor, allowing male and female to join in interplay within us; and then self and world can come into interplay as well. As the corridor of the self opens wide, it dissolves the artificial boundary of our "self-achieved independence" and makes room within for all of existence—which, as the Universal Law of Interrelationship tells us, already lives through us, though usually unnoticed. The many-chambered room cannot accommodate the unbroken whole. *Ultimately, to be present in the world means making room for the world to be present in you.*

What keeps us from that new experience of the self, and the new world to which it opens us, is the 'normal' to which we have so deeply habituated. Our baseline consciousness is so preoccupied with doing—with its aims, its abstractions, its drives and anxieties and values—that we have organized our awareness of the body and the world according to metaphors borrowed from machinery. The body is something with which we *do*—its intelligence muted, obscured, trammeled. As a result, *the foremost experience in our lives is not of the world, but of the supervisor in the head lobbying and managing on behalf of its construct, the 'known self'*. We can feel sensation coming to us from regions of the body's machinery, but not intelligence—just as we can feel sensations coming to us from the matter of the world, but not intelligence. At best, we experience the body as a sensory feedback system that reports to our true center of intelligence in the head. What the endarkened body has become—unconscious matter—is something the self is no longer able to identify with. And why should we relinquish control in order to do so? In effect, we have created a catch-22 for ourselves: until we can experience the body's intelligence, we won't be able to identify with the body; but until we can identify with the body, we won't be able to feel its intelligence.

In my experience, the surest escape from that dilemma is with a journey made of small steps: steps buoyed by the findings of Gershon and others that we are born with two brains; steps buoyed by the findings of other cultures that recognize the two poles of a unified consciousness; and steps buoyed by our 'gut feeling' that there is more to life than the constrained, anxious self-absorption to which we have become accustomed. As we learn to let the consciousness of the pelvic skull awaken to match that of the cranial skull, we will feel again the psyche pervading "every living part of the organism." Once that happens, and the corridor within us brings male and female into correspondence and opens to make room for all the world, then we will enter an entirely different experience of the self—one that we might call the *felt self*.

The Felt Self

Until your awareness can journey to and merge with the mindful pole in the body that enables you to consciously 'be', the self will not be able to unify; and as long as your self is not unified, *you will literally not be able to feel it*. That is, you may be able to feel bodily parts and sensations; you may feel your emotions, your doubts and questions and moods and ideas and rules and entitlements and needs and confusion; and if you *attempt* to feel the self, your attention might flit back and forth among all those various structures and pieces of the 'self you know'—but you will not be able to come to rest in being and enter the living, unbroken whole of the self as it is, here and now. The fact is, as long as you continue to live in your head, the self will not even *exist* as an unbroken whole: when conscious thinking is independent of being, the male element is deliberately fracturing self and world. It is only when the pelvic center of your being is sensitized and fully participant in your consciousness—massively connecting and communicating—that the various and divergent aspects of the self will be *able* to reconcile into a whole. And it is only then that the shards and scaffolding of the 'known self' can fall away and the grounded, abiding presence of the felt self can blossom in your core, connected to all that is. Quite simply, **the felt self is the sum of what your being reveals to you—in all its manifold dimensions—through the mind's sensitivity.** It cannot be assembled or supervised in your consciousness by what you know; it can only be felt, here and now, fully informed by the indescribable present. As such, the felt self represents a surrender that enables us to live a profound and liberating truth: that the true identity of the thinking self is actually the felt whole.

That brings us to an important distinction: *when we allow the male element of doing to dominate our consciousness, the 'known self' is activated; when the female element of being comes first, the felt self is activated.* There is a big difference between the two. Our male intelligence dominates when it is activated by a fear of the female, which it then seeks to exclude; but when the female element of being comes first, it includes all: it brings all the objects of the mind's sensitivity into relationship with each other and into an exchange with the present. Only when the pelvic consciousness is given prominence in our awareness, then, and the male element forgoes the need to control or dominate, and makes peace with being, and joins it, will our axial consciousness open to self and world; for **only when being comes first can we dwell in the self and the world at the same time.** That is why the male element must learn to achieve submission. I see that universal, mythic message, "First, Being," as one of the rich veins of symbolic meaning that run through the story of Christ's crucifixion on Calvary or Golgotha. Both of those names trace back to the Aramaic *gulgultha*, which means "skull." On one level, then, Christ's death on the cross represents the surrender of the skull above to the skull below—the cross an axis between them—in order that resurrection might be possible; and with it, life in the eternal present.

When being comes first, "massively connecting" us to the vibrancy of reality, it achieves a wordless clarity that stands beyond all our made-up agendas: a clarity of being that can guide and inform all our sensitivities, even the most abstract processes of reasoning. Einstein gave us a sense of that when he wrote,

> The scientist's religious feeling takes the form of a rapturous amazement at the harmony of natural law, which reveals an intelligence of such superiority that, in comparison with it, all the systematic thinking of human beings is an utterly insignificant reflection. This feeling is the guiding principle of his life and work.[92]

The realm of the felt self is limited only by the restrictions we impose on our own sensitivity. If we begin to relax those restrictions and avail that sensitivity of the reality on which our very existence depends, its first reconciliation is with the body itself, the medium of intelligence through which all else is felt. Abandoning all expectations and simply paying attention to the body can be a revelation: so many currents and incipient forms and impulses of energy blossom within it and move and fade—like particles in a cloud chamber—and each minute stirring is part of the felt self; it belongs to our wholeness and reveals it. But there is a multitude of dimensions that intersect with those currents of energy: emotional, intellectual and spiritual dimensions, as well as all the sensations of 'now' that allow the self to rest in the present and feel it as a unity. Our being will also reveal to us the dimension of mythic archetypes or dreams that live within us, if only we can recognize them in relation to the world and unlock their energy; and finally, we might attune our sensitivity to the dimension of consciousness itself. All those stirrings within us cohere into the unity we can *feel* as the self, and they give rise to a completely different experience of self than is either tolerated by or available to the 'known self'. As our sensitivity begins to "massively connect and communicate" with the world around us, our compassion for the world will begin to reveal kinship there: the world in which the self lives, lives within the self—so that what we feel as the self dilates beyond the boundary of our skin to include the present to which we belong.

The contrasts between felt self and 'known self' are instructive. **The felt self identifies with Being and centers itself in wholeness: it** brings all that is felt into relationship with the core of our being, which is informed by what passes through the holographic corridor within us, awakening us to the manifold dimensions to which we belong. As the fractured parts of ourselves are acknowledged and brought into relationship, self-conflicts resolve, and we are able to arrive in the perfect present. **The 'known self', by contrast, identifies itself with the dissociated male aspect of consciousness, and centers itself in a realm of duplicates;** it deliberately estranges itself from the sensations of Being, and it takes charge of its duplicates through the agency of *analysis*—a word that actually means "a separation of a whole into its component parts." We can see in its self-achieved independence the foundational assertion of the 'known self': *that our thinking should be separated from our being, which is not to be trusted.* It is the assumption Parmenides foisted upon us all those centuries ago. Once thinking cuts itself loose from being, it can do what it wants. It can prove that nothing moves, as Parmenides did. It can gain the upper hand on Being, dismembering it into mere parts and reducing everything to mechanics. Posited on disunity, the 'known self' will promote disunity: driven by the tyrant's fear of the female, it can do no other than express its mistrust of wholeness.

The differences between the felt self and the 'known self' are succinctly illustrated in one of my favorite stories from the lore of Japanese Noh theater, as related by Ernest Fenollosa: one day an eighty-year-old woman noticed that she was being stalked by a young man. She turned on him in alarm and asked what he wanted. He said that he was interested in her. She replied that she was too old for him. Embarrassed, he explained that he was a Noh actor, and he was studying her in order to play the part of an elderly woman. She then berated him, saying that he would debase Noh with such practices—literal imitation was acceptable for the common theater, "But for Noh, *you must feel the thing as a whole, from the inside. You won't get it copying facts point by point.*"[93] She was right, of course. He was trying to solve the problem of portraying an old woman by observing her from a distance and amassing enough facts to assemble a reliable duplicate. Once that duplicate was clear in his head, he could direct his body to present it—the basic premise of self-tyranny. She, on the other hand, was directing him to venture beyond the familiar realm of mere facts and into the living realm of Being; she was directing him to the hidden harmony, *which belongs to the whole, not the parts, and is understood by feeling, not analysis.*

As Joseph Campbell made clear, when thinking is separated from being, the One is broken into the many, which then battle each other and can be governed only by force. Such is the state of the 'known self'—but it also characterizes a much larger theme. **The rupture between thinking and Being is the primary wound of our culture:** it segregates the poles of our consciousness and marries us to the male aspect; it foments division and conflict and hierarchies in our lives and businesses and governments; it impairs our relationship to our own community; it skews how we see our natural environment and what we expect from it; and it makes palatable certain forms of entertainment we would otherwise find woefully inadequate. In short, that rupture causes us to organize, partition and supervise the embodied corridor, rather than live its receptivity to 'what is'. If we wish to heal that wound in ourselves and in our culture, we literally have to embark on the hero's journey, which overthrows the tyrant, discovers the embodied axis mundi within, journeys to the pole of female being and grounds us in it.

Falling into the Universe

Arriving at an *idea* of the felt self is one thing; arriving at an *experience* of the felt self is something else. How do we go about "feeling the thing as a whole," as the old lady put it? How do we unlock the mind's sensitivity to that task? How do we unite it with 'what is'? How do we unlock the spaciousness of the corridor and awaken to the female aspect of our consciousness? In our culture we have so attuned the mind to the recognition of meaning and significance and have so burdened it with our *need to know* that its plasticity has shaped to accommodate those tasks, even as its ability to open to its inner awareness or sense of the self as a whole has become enfeebled. Ironically, too, the more that ability wanes, the more confident we grow in dismissing its worth or relevance. Eventually the very physiology of our mind's patterns is shaped to uphold a tyranny that relentlessly watches 'the self' in everything it does: at the ready to correct its progress, vigilant for threats, the inner supervisor flatters 'the self', warns it, chides, smoothes the way and berates, determined to achieve success for itself. This monster within us—which is characterized by supervisory self-consciousness in all we do—is activated, as we have said, by its fear of the female.

Our task as individuals, then, is to clear out the many-chambered room within, lay down its inner partitions and recover the felt whole of our being, which is our most intimate experience of reality; but that task is made monumental by the long-standing habits that reinforce the supervisory role of the male element in any task we undertake. The more active we are in trying to connect with the felt whole of our being—the more 'in charge' we are—the more we will be directing ourselves based on mere duplicates of what should be, what should be done and how it should be done. When the male element directs us like that, it pits one part of the self against the knowing, consolidated authority of another. Of all the pressures we face in our lives, the greatest ones each of us struggles with issue from the 'known self', which we have personally created. Its demands preempt the unknown present with a sense of divine entitlement and fill our isolation with the distractions of ceaseless chatter and commands. What so readily buys our compliance in that is the conceit that *we can plan beforehand what our best response to the unknowable present will be.* And so we seek to know, and we plan and act according to that knowledge. But once we decide to trust in the solutions of the tyrant, we accept division as our normal state: the many-chambered room.

The reason for that division, of course, is to exercise control—the only recourse of a male element fearful of the female: divided, those fears tell us, we can conquer and run the show. In fact, once you create that inner partitioning, you *have* to run the show: when you have closed yourself to the one means by which the *world* can call you to action—Being speaks only to being—you have to goad *yourself* to action. The exercise of such control depends on two conditions: a knowledge of what *should* be done (which is provided by our duplicates) and a way to compare that ideal with what *is* being done (which is provided by our self-consciousness). That intertwined relationship between duplicates and self-consciousness is tacitly enshrined in the roots of the word *control,* which traces back to a bookkeeping practice developed in medieval Europe whereby accounts were copied onto a duplicate register, or roll, against which they could be checked. The word derives from Old French *contre* (against) *role* (roll).

To exercise its control, then, the male element assembles a filing system of duplicates that stands apart from the fluid intelligence of the body and is at the ready to take charge of any situation—ready, specifically, to prevent Being from carrying us into a fresh, uncontrolled experience. **At the brink of any exchange with the world, the disembodied intelligence of the head wants to intervene and take over— wants the exchange to mean a certain thing, wants it to happen a certain way, wants it to secure certain results.** It can deploy its duplicates consciously, but most of them are inserted between the self and Being habitually, with a familiarity that starts to feel personal. Some examples? The supervisor in the head knows how to feel about stepping out of a warm house into the rain, and braces itself against the experience. It knows how to react to a molten-red sunset, and is ready to exclaim "Beautiful" before the moment can touch our core and quietly take us someplace wordless and new. It knows the routine when you meet an acquaintance, and is ready to jump into it—"Hi, how are you?"— before a real exchange has had a chance to begin between you. The tyrant in the head has a million solutions and is ready to supervise every single exchange according to our ideas of what 'should be'—much as medieval monks compared their accounts.

That every willful solution carries us into a self-achieved isolation is true even when the decision 'to do' is of the most commonplace variety. That was demonstrated to me on a short ferry ride with a friend. As I sat chatting with him, I ate my way through a banana. When it was finished I was left with the skin and thought, naturally enough, "I have to throw this out." I knew where the garbage cans on the ferry were and planned to pass one as I disembarked. A minute or two later, I realized that though I continued sitting and chatting, one part of me was somewhere else, waiting to throw out the peel. That's all it took: so trivial a plan as that was enough to compromise my ability to be present. Once I realized that, I was able to return to the simple pleasure of sitting on the boat, talking with a friend, and holding a banana peel in my hand. I returned to the wakefulness of the pelvic intelligence. As it says in the Tao, "Know the male, yet keep to the female."[94] When we keep to the male supervisor, we become mired in the abstractions of self-consciousness.

The wholeness of the felt self cannot coexist with self-consciousness: as soon as the male intelligence becomes the watchful supervisor, even when it merely supervises the fate of our banana peel, our felt wholeness virtually blinks out of existence—although we are not likely to notice, because we can still feel our bodies and emotions. It is a mistake, though, to think that a 'felt body' is the same as the 'felt self'. As we have seen, we can 'get in touch' with our bodies and feel them and notice many things about them without ever needing to expose ourselves to a self-achieved submission into the 'being' that they represent. The state of the felt self is not about being 'in touch' with your body. **The felt self is a consciousness so deeply grounded in the body that it recognizes the mindful, somatic self as a universe into which it has fallen, and the present as its most intimate companion; and we can enter that universe and that companionship only when we become utterly passive to them.** Passive beyond judgment or interference; passive beyond any idea or expectation of what 'should' be felt; passive beyond any wish to achieve a particular end. Bringing consciousness into the spaciousness of the body and down through it to rest in the pelvic bowl and discover 'what is'—*that is the heroic submission of the male element as represented by the myths of the world; it is the essential submission to Being.* It requires a passivity that leaves every fantasy of separation at the door and deeply attends to all that the mindfulness of the body reveals, and it is made possible by a willingness to yield to what is here now. So when spiritual traditions speak of the need to 'kill the ego', they are reminding us that until we kill *what we know the self to be,* we can't liberate ourselves from the presumptions and fears of the 'known self' and come into relationship with the spaciousness of 'what is'.

The tyrant's perspectives have so clouded our understanding of what passivity means that we need a fresh look at it. The passivity that provides our entrée to the felt self is not some sleepy, semiengaged state of withdrawal—it is exactly the opposite: an alert, fully attentive state of heightened sensitivity. **Becoming passive to 'what is' is the only means we have of coming into relationship with it.** It is the only way we can feel it. Nor, it should be said, is passivity under the purview of the female element—despite the long-standing and endarkened male view to the contrary. Passivity is what the *male* element needs in order to avoid tyranny and come into relationship with Being, carrying us into a consciousness of the whole. That is why the hero can be identified by his "self-achieved submission." But passivity is simply not an option for the female element: in order to 'Be', in order to massively connect and communicate with 'what is', the female element must be fully activated—continuously processing everything the sensibilities of the felt self are aware of, everything that courses through the wide corridor within; and that requires wakefulness, lucid receptivity, and ceaseless integration. The male element, present to all of that, remains passive to it; but as the self comes into relationship with 'what is' and responds to it, a necessity is born within—a clear imperative that calls the self into action. Calls the self to adventure. It is only through passivity, then, that the male element awakens to the necessity that will engage its strengths and ground its actions in being.

The universe of being to which passivity opens us lies so far beyond the realm of idea, and so deep within the realm of the unnamed, that it cannot be described with any pretense of accuracy. It can only be experienced. In our culture, the mind's true sensitivity has been so contracted by our need to flatten things into ideas and take charge of them that such an experience is likely to happen in incremental awakenings of consciousness facilitated by a mind that is learning to ground itself in being and pay close attention to 'what is'. If you sit quietly, for instance, and become passive to every single sensation and stirring of energy in the body, and give it your attention because it is, after all, part of you at this moment, you will find that the more passive you can become to what is happening, the more deeply you will fall into the universe that is your being. And it does indeed feel like falling, because when the scaffolding of the 'known self' is allowed to drop away and your awareness opens to the living interplay between the two skulls, there is nothing to hold on to and only the flowering companionship of the present in which to rest. Your willingness to drop into the unfurling present is what enables you to find your way to the core necessity of your being: you are lost and found all at once, informed by the sensational stirrings of the eternal moment.

In that light, we might revisit the idea of 'listening to the body'. When something ails the body, our culture encourages us to take an active role to fix it—whether that involves medication, or stretching and ice packs, or an assortment of therapies, all of which are likely to be of benefit. I have found, though, that injury or illness in the body is often a sign that we have dissociated from it to some extent—often for the purpose of not having to acknowledge a buried and uncomfortable emotional truth. If that is true, then the first, most obvious step to take is *to listen to the body and, in effect, ask it what it needs.* Ask it what burdens it harbors. By allowing those burdens to come into the light, the body, too, comes into the light. Such listening is not a supervisory activity, nor is it self-consciousness, nor does it stand apart from the body's intelligence, nor is it a solution. It is a surrender in ignorance that waits to listen and learn; it is a willingness to be changed, the opening of a door to transformation and self-awareness; it is another form of passivity by the male towards the female that will carry us towards wholeness with a wordless wisdom we can neither anticipate nor analyze, but only feel and yield to.

As we have noted, any time the male element becomes an activated supervisor, the female element disappears. That effect—as well as the entire journey through the sensitivity of the inner corridor—is represented by the story of Orpheus. A musician of divine gifts, Orpheus fell deeply in love with the nymph Eurydice, and she with him; but on the day they were to be married, she was killed and borne to the underworld. Distraught at his separation from her, and knowing her to be in Hades, Orpheus set out to find and confront the Lord of the Underworld. He ventured deep into the underworld armed only with the soothing harmonies of his music, met many dark terrors along the way, and finally stood before the Lord of Death. After listening to Orpheus's tale, the king of the underworld allowed Eurydice to follow Orpheus to the upper world—but he set one proviso: that Orpheus not look back at her until they had both emerged into daylight. Unable to hear or see her, Orpheus fought his desire to glance back until he was out, but then he turned around too soon, before Eurydice was out, and she faded before his eyes.

The journey of Orpheus represents the self-achieved submission of the male element, which enables the dissociated male aspect of consciousness to descend from the organized inadequacy of the head into the many-chambered room, restoring awareness to the universe of the sensational, dark body—just as Orpheus sought to bring life back to his female partner. Orpheus reunites with Eurydice in the lowest chamber of the underworld—the pelvic bowl—and then together they venture back up to greet the light of day. **When the male and female aspects of consciousness are reunited, then the awareness of the self as a whole, grounded in being, can rejoin the enlightened world. The gateway that opens our sensitivity to the world is the heart:** it is through the opening of the heart that the awareness of the self as a whole can sensitize to the world and come into relationship with it. In the myth, alas, Orpheus turns back to look for Eurydice too early; that is, he 'checks up' on her. He needs to know if she—his female being—is there, and how she's doing; but as soon as his gaze finds her, she vanishes without a trace. By warning the male element not to check up on female being, the myth is warning us against self-consciousness. But if we can allow our male sensitivities to journey down the corridor to the crucible of the pelvis and ground themselves in female being, so that our healed consciousness might greet the world through the opening of the heart as one sensitivity greets another—then we will experience the felt self and step into its limitless awareness.

To make that journey, then, requires not willfulness, but a deliberate and unqualified submission. It requires that you disengage your need to 'be in charge', so that you can simply pay close attention to the coursing sensitivity of 'what is' and, by feeling it, bring consciousness to it. "Paying close attention" is an opening of the mind to present experience—the female complement to the male 'need to know'; paying close attention is also the single condition that most effectively promotes the neuroplasticity of your evolving awareness.* By fostering an alert sensitivity to all the changes and exchanges precipitated by your breathing, and to the orchestrations of energy as it waxes and wanes through the scalp and jaw and throat and shoulders and torso and pelvis and legs and ankles—by simply receiving all of those sensations of the flesh and paying close attention to them, you will release endarkening tensions, open the body's mindfulness, and eventually settle into a sense of being sensationally present. You may even feel your consciousness sift down to the core of your being and *come to rest in the pelvic bowl*—inspiring the simple, joyous recognition, "Here I am." At that point what you are feeling is not just the body, but the self; you are feeling the coursing resolution of who you are, clear and grounded and at ease in the transforming present; you are "feeling the thing as a whole." And then it becomes clear: **the felt self and the present are so closely intermingled that you cannot truly feel one without the other;** by fully entering your being—which has no independent existence—you enter Being itself. The 'known self', virtually alone in its own ideas, has only them to guide it; the felt self, being fully present, is fully informed by the present, and so is truly and deeply guided in all it does.

The Nine Spheres

At the core of this book is the belief that **the individual and collective**

---

* In Norman Doidge's book on the subject, *The Brain That Changes Itself* (New York: Viking, 2007), the phrase "paying close attention" occurs over and over, and its measurable effect on brain mapping is truly astonishing.

challenge of our age is to allow the mind to identify with its true sensitivity. The interplay of consciousness along the embodied axis is the foundation of that sensitivity: through that exchange, the sensitivities of male and female conjoin, so that doing and being and heart come into relationship as a dynamic unity, and come into relationship with the dynamic unity of the world. Unfortunately, our fear of the female, so subtly and aggressively promoted by our culture, virtually disables the functioning of the axis and so contracts the mind's sensitivity. In its most collapsed state, our sensitivity is bottled inside the cranium, and we can think of little beyond our own anxious concerns; in its most dilated state, the journey to wholeness unites the poles of our consciousness and grounds our sensitivity in the limitless, unbroken whole.

The journey to wholeness is the central theme of this book—but it is much more than that: it is the foundational activity of the human mind, and the drive behind all of our major endeavors. As essayist and artist Guy Davenport noted,

> Art is the attention we pay to the wholeness of the world. Ancient intuition went foraging after consistency. Religion, science and art are alike rooted in the faith that the world/ is of a piece, that something is common to all its diversity, and that if we knew enough we could see and give a name to its harmony.[95]

Religion, science and art all grapple with the issue of the world's wholeness. But art differs from the other two in a respect that merits our attention: religion and science, in their own ways, offer *explanations* of wholeness; art offers an *experience* of wholeness, without any explanation. If we are to acquire the art of living in accord with the whole, we too have to be willing to give ourselves to an experience of the whole beyond all explanation. Even so, an attempt to bring clarity to some of the stages through which that journey passes, and to the changes it in turn asks of us, may help to bring clarity and courage to our efforts in persevering along it.

The journey is one whereby our sensitivity opens to accommodate more and more of the world around us, as it increasingly learns to attune to and come into dialogue with the mindful present. Our journey towards wholeness is often imagined as a winding path on which we forge our way ahead, but I tend to see it as one of outward expansion, much as the rays of the sun fan out to include the orbits of the planets, one by one, and the spiraling galaxy that is our home, and beyond to the limitless fringes of the universe. And although no two people embark on the same journey, we can nonetheless distinguish quantum jumps in the sensitivity of the mind as it opens to Being through ever-widening spheres. There is nothing hard or fast about the progress through those spheres: depending on someone's innate sensitivities, for instance, certain spheres may be bypassed altogether, to be explored later. Even so, we can see that our sensitivity generally expands through a first group of spheres that belong to the dissociated male aspect of consciousness (the 'known self'), then through a group in which the poles of our consciousness unite (the felt self), and finally into a sphere that unifies with the sensitivities of Being.

The first four of the nine spheres constitute the group that belongs to the 'known self'. The consciousness of the 'known self' is characteristically unipolar—steadfast in withholding awareness from the pelvic intelligence and in hailing the head as the undisputed center of the self: the Authority on high that issues commands to protect the self from the vagaries of female being. Each of these spheres, then, is marked by self-consciousness. In the course of a day our awareness might contract and dilate through the full range of these spheres many times over.

The Spheres of the 'Known Self'

First Sphere: The Realm of Abstraction
This is the most disembodied state we experience, and it is usually underpinned with anxiety. It is a realm in which our entire awareness is confined within the cranial pole of our consciousness. It is so absorbed with the assessment and sorting and ordering of its own ideas that any remembrance that we even have a body is eclipsed. In this realm, all we have to think about is our own thoughts.

Second Sphere: The Window on the World
The second sphere opens to include the world around us, but we regard it as though through a window: we recognize what we see and name it without being touched by it. As far as we are concerned, whatever we notice or encounter is represented sufficiently well by the labels we accord it, labels to which the sensations of smell, taste, touch, real

listening or fresh seeing have nothing much to add. Our main concern is to be able to identify what is seen through the glass, and we pay attention to it only as directed by the willful values of the 'known self'.

Third Sphere: The Material Body

This sphere opens into the realm of the felt matter of the body. Any action of will on the body renders our flesh as a mechanical problem. The sensitivities of this sphere sit hierarchically above the body, and take note of it, and perhaps even befriend it—actively 'listening to it' or 'getting in touch with it'. We also tell it what to do, notice it when it complains, feed it when it is hungry, try to fix it when it is broken, make it breathe slowly and deeply to calm it down, and exercise it so it will perform better and look better. In the long run, though, we are likely to feel somewhat victimized by our codependent relationship with it.

Fourth Sphere: The Emotional Body

The sensitivities of this sphere open to the energy of emotions coursing through the body: we notice them and direct them, justify them, harbor them, suppress them, resent them, and even celebrate them; but the dissociated male aspect of consciousness is not able to process them. Its fearful, controlling nature cannot allow their energy to descend through the corridor of consciousness and ground itself in being. And so we find ourselves stuck in our emotions, even as they remain stuck in us. Such emotions do not carry us into the embrace of the vivid present, but wall us within ourselves. And again, we may feel victimized by the roller-coaster rides they take us on, reliving their patterns in endless repetitions.

In this sphere, too, we feel certain ideas passionately—*more passionately, very often, than we can feel the present.* **When our passion for an idea or set of beliefs overwhelms our sensitivity to the present, our relationship to those ideas becomes our fundamental relationship.** If we can broadly understand *patriarchy* to be "rule by the male element," then *such a reality-obscuring allegiance to ideas is the essence and the defining trait of patriarchy everywhere, and on every level*—from the patriarchy that lives in the self to one that possesses whole societies. The more passionately we feel our ideas, the more deeply patriarchy runs within us and the less access we have—or permit ourselves—to the guidance of the living present. Such fundamentalism is found in many forms and in many activities, from social activism to religious extremism to the tactics of corporate boardrooms—even, ironically, to radicals within the feminist movement, whose aim was to overthrow patriarchy. All the more crucial, then, for us to understand that *any* emotional attachment to idea that eclipses the present will institute an inner patriarchy.

The next group of spheres widens our sensitivities into the axial consciousness of the felt self. The transition into these spheres carries us from a worldview posited on perseity to one that feels relationship, and from a cloaked but tenacious fear of the female to a loving appreciation of all that being is. The gap between the 'known self' and the felt self is a quantum jump that has to overleap assumptions and habits and will be hampered by unresolved trauma: such trauma binds the body in the past so that it cannot be released into the present, and it often requires naked honesty, deep-rooted dedication and years of personal work to come to a resolution. As the work is done, though, and a surrender to 'what is' increasingly takes place, consciousness seeps through the embodied axis, allowing its male and female poles to exchange and harmonize, and allowing our own being to come into relationship with Being itself. We might say that the threshold for entering the spheres of the felt *self* occurs at the point that we recognize and accord with the felt *present;* and when we not only accord with the felt present, but recognize that what we feel as its whole *is* the thinking self, we have crossed into the dilated sensitivities of the eighth sphere.

Crossing the threshold into the felt self marks a triumph of mind over matter: that is, the paradigm of head-consciousness that deadens us to the body and persuades us that all the world is mere matter loses its hold on us, and another experience takes over: our sensitivities awaken to the presence of mind suffusing all things. The body is rescued from its material limitations and is felt as mind, and the world in which we live is revealed to be limitless and intimate—one that we look upon as mind looks with love upon mind.

The foremost practical change that carries us from the realm of the 'known self' into that of the felt self is the one whereby the many-chambered room, which keeps the body's mindful energy cordoned off and divided up, dissolves to reveal the corridor by which the poles of our consciousness convene in their natural interplay. There is, in fact, nothing we do that will not be enriched by that interplay—for there is no activity in which our full consciousness is not an asset. And yet a million times a day our male-inflected view of expediency suggests to us that we don't really require the participation of our pelvic intelligence—for it seems so much easier to just 'do' what we know needs doing if we don't have to 'be' at the same time. Experience, of course, shows us otherwise: whatever we are doing, it will be empowered and informed if it is rooted in being.

Our difficulty in accepting the wakeful participation of the pelvic intelligence comes down to the huge importance the supervisor in the head places on being able to anticipate things before they happen—not just events in the world around us, but our own responses to those events as well. The duplicates and patterns and structures of the supervisor are all formulated towards that end. As you increasingly ground yourself in being, though, its energy will carry you someplace new and unexpected: you will be carried out of structure and into the present. You *cannot* anticipate where it will take you; you cannot control where it will take you. The sensitivity of the embodied axis cannot be supervised, only lived. But as you surrender to your own sensitivity, you learn, slowly, that it feels better to live in an expanded state of wakefulness to the world than to be pent up in your own ideas of it. And that in itself makes the demands of the journey preferable to not taking it at all.

The Spheres of the Felt Self

Fifth Sphere: The Body as Energy

The transition between the 'known self' and the felt self shows up above all in a shift in our sensitivity to the body. The 'known self' experiences the body as a material thing we can feel; the felt self discovers it as embodied mindfulness—a mindfulness that lives hand in hand with the sensitivities of the mindful world. The body's energy is the energy of the felt, thinking self. It shapes and reshapes matter at a staggering pace. That thinking is not secondary to the self: it *is* the self. It is secondary only to the aims of the 'known self'. To become passive to that energy and to feel it is to feel the thinking that constitutes our experience of the present: it is to feel 'what is', beyond all ideas of what the self 'should be'. To make peace with 'what is' and welcome it living within you now is to come home to yourself, healing the age-old wound between your thinking and your being. When your thinking is your being, and your being is your thinking, the mind's sensitivity can be said to reside in the fifth sphere.

Sixth Sphere: The World as Energy

As our sensitivities free up the corridor within and unite the pole of our conscious thinking with that of our conscious being, the newly harmonized self looks to the world and finds it to be changed as well. The labels that have held it at a distance have lost their relevance. The windowpane of separation has fallen away. Liberated, the world's particulars escape the confines of 'the known' and burst into the present realm of Being—where they reveal themselves to be not lumps of objective matter, but distinct embodiments of energy that can be felt from within. That is, each particular of the world naturally comes into relationship with the core of your being, and touches it vividly, and lives there, so that from the wholeness of your energy you feel the wholeness of its energy. Each particular, then, reveals the world itself to be a concourse of energy flowing and intermingling in its continuous transformations of matter. That energy lives within us even as it exists outside of us; similarly, even as we exist inside our skin, we live beyond it.

This dissolution of boundaries will sound like a flight of fantasy or a dangerous fiction to the closely guarded, reasoning tyrant of the 'known self'; in fact, it is neither. It is a submission to 'what is' that directly manifests the ultimate reality of our existence, granting us a direct and personal experience of the Universal Law of Interrelationship: that we exist only by virtue of interrelationship. That is also the foundational theme of the world's mystic traditions. As the particularity of where you are and what is around you permeates the body's intelligence, the self comes to rest in the peace of the felt present, alert to its boundless dance.

Seventh Sphere: The Heart's Energy

As our awareness descends into the body, our conscious thinking can ground itself in our conscious being; and then the opening of the heart can enable the awareness of the self as a whole to greet the world as a whole, and welcome all that it asks of us. In other words, the exchanges made possible by the open corridor within mirror the journey of Orpheus in all its particulars: just as he descends into the under-world, soothing its various, bound-up terrors with his music, our male sensitivity can descend from the head into the many-chambered room, calming its fear-bound divisions and manifesting a corridor of consciousness and harmony. That journey eventually carries our conscious thinking into the hub of our conscious being. *As Orpheus joins Eurydice in the underworld, our male element joins the female in the pelvic bowl.* The healing of their union creates a new sensitivity, a new energy, that opens our gateway to the world: the heart.

Our 'heart energy' is the energy that opens us to the world and reveals our relationship with it. When we speak of the 'heart's path', we are referring to a journey that brings the inner world as a whole into relationship with the outer. When you do something 'with your whole heart', the impulse behind your actions is called forth by the world—by its joyous, summoning necessity—and arises from your full being; at the same time, that impulse illuminates your being and expresses it through the actions called forth from you. It is through the heart that the union of Being and doing is achieved—a union that unites us with the world and releases our sensitivities into the realm of the felt self.

When polymath György Doczi considers the way in which 'wholes' are created by the union of complementary opposites, he notes how that principle expresses itself in the whorl of the daisy, the harmonies of music, the proportions of a Chinese vase, the vertebrae of the allosaurus and the spiraling of galaxies. On every level of our existence, the curves and patterns that express life express the harmony of that principle in action. More than that, though, the curves and patterns of that harmony express themselves over and over in what might be called *the ratio of universal harmony*: the golden ratio of 0.618. It is a ratio that recurs in nature, art and architecture, and what distinguishes it from all others is that **the golden ratio uniquely brings a whole and its parts into harmonious relationship, while preserving the distinct identity of each.** For instance, to create the golden ratio on a line, you divide the line into two parts such that the ratio of the smaller part to the larger is the same as the ratio of the larger part to the entire line. This harmony—by which parts are joined in relationship to the whole—reminds us that the word *ratio* comes from the Indo-European base -*ar*, which means "to join."

It is of more than a little interest to us, then, that if you draw a line from the center of the pelvic intelligence (roughly where the pelvic brain is located, a couple of inches above the perineum) and extend it up through the embodied axis to the center of the head (traditionally taken as the eyes), you will find that the point at which the center of the heart is located along that line divides it into the proportions of the golden ratio.* In other words, when the two complementary opposites of male and female unite in the pelvic bowl, and their newborn sensitivity opens the heart to bring the self into relationship with the world, that sensitivity greets the world from a point that expresses the embodied axis in the ratio of universal harmony.

If we wished to look more deeply into the larger harmony that resonates through all of creation as well as through us, we might begin to recognize the harmony of the heart's energy as an expression of the love that gives birth on a cosmic scale. Jung described that love with the phrase "cosmogonic love." Marion Woodman and Elinor Dickson write about it as

> a love that transcends our human experience of love and opens us to an unknowable reality we cannot embrace, though it embraces us. Seeing becomes a matter of perceptually seeing through, until at last we know only that we are seen. Knowing that we are seen, "if we possess a grain of wisdom," Jung writes, "we will completely surrender to this unknowable who embraces in love all the opposites."[96]

Love, Woodman and Dickson note, experiences the unknowable in opposites that work together without ceasing to be opposites. It becomes evident, then, that love is not just a feeling or emotion on an equal footing with other emotions such as anger or fear or happiness: in its essence, **love is a form of intelligence that liquefies the world even as it blurs the edges of the self:** the divisions on which the enclosed thinking of the 'known self' depends fall utterly away, and whatever your love's genius embraces, there is a sense, as you look upon it, of "life confronting life," in the phrase of Henri and H. A. Frankfort.[97] In

---

* I have compared measurements from Leonardo da Vinci's Vitruvian man, from scale drawings based on measurements for average Americans, and from myself. The results are remarkably consistent. On my own body, for instance, the two distances are 18 inches and 11 inches. The ratio of 11 to 18 is 0.611. The golden ratio is 0.618.

that sense, love is at the same time both knowing and being known. In fact, we might call love the supreme intelligence—it reveals the world to us as no other faculty can: it reveals the world in wholeness, it reveals the world in kinship, it reveals the world in ravishing specificity, and it reveals in the world a mindfulness that lives invisibly through all that is. In revealing the true and full relationship of all things to all things, and of us to the unbroken whole, love shows us, as physicist David Bohm put it, that "everything material is also mental and everything mental is also material. The separation of the two—matter and spirit—is an abstraction."[98]

The most insightful account of the nature of love's genius that I have found is provided by George Washington Carver, a botanist and inventor born into slavery in America in 1864. He was recognized from a young age for his ability to heal sick plants, and for his ability to discern which plants could heal sick animals. Speaking of his abilities, Carver once said,

> All the flowers talk to me and so do hundreds of little living things in the woods. I learn what I know by watching and loving everything.[99]

When love opens us to the world, we recognize the aliveness of whatever love shows us and are brought into dialogue with it. In summarizing that effect, Carver made an observation that, in its implications, lays the foundation for our journey to wholeness: **"If you love it enough, anything will talk to you."**[100] Consider this: the mythic figures of tyrant and hero represent two forms of dialogue: one is the chattering that occurs in the head between the divided parts of ourselves; the other opens wordlessly to the world, recognizes the living essence of it, and listens, and responds. The genius of love abandons expectations and attends to the livingness of the world's particulars, allowing them to permeate the body's mindfulness and touch its core. As that core resonates in response, the dialogue begins. *It is love, then, that liberates the thinking of the world into a dialogue with the self.* If we cannot listen to the world with our hearts, and be present to that listening with the conscious core of our being, we will never come into harmony with the world; and then the heedless self-chattering of the tyrant will doom us all.

Eighth Sphere: The Thou of the Present
As love opens us to all relationships, it opens us, too, to the one relationship that shines through all the world's particulars; and as that
happens, our consciousness expands into the eighth sphere. As Rumi
noted,

> Love will initiate you into the Universal Intellect, and
> teach you by stages how to drown your reason in its
> fire-eyed wonder and precision.[101]

The seventh sphere liquefies the material present and brings us
into relation with its living specifics; the eighth sphere brings us into
relation with the living specificity of the present as a whole. That unbroken whole has gone by many names, though it remains nameless;
it can be heard in every wave and tree, though its voice can never be
located; it can be seen in the stars of the night sky, and in a crystal of
sand, though it remains hidden. And yet, if we can but grow passive to
the felt present in our adoration of it, it waits to greet us and guide us.
The 'I' of the self confronts the 'Thou' of the present, and recognizes
itself. The thinking self confronts the felt whole and discovers its true
identity.

Heraclitus wrote, "The gods' presence in the world goes unnoticed by men who do not believe in the gods."[102] Similarly, the living
One of the present goes unnoticed by people who, because they divide
thinking from being, have no basis for believing in the world's mindful
aliveness. Aliveness and sensation go together, and they are the first
qualities we sacrifice in any retreat from the female. A retreat from the
female is a retreat from the present; but all the aliveness in the world
is to be found only in the present moment, and always will be. That
suggests a simple equation: to connect with the world's aliveness as
a whole is to connect with the present; but also, I believe, *to connect
with the present as a whole is to awaken to its mindfulness.* Any such
connection, of course, relies on the center in which we can consciously
'be'.

If the Universal Law shows us anything, it is that the *foremost* reality of our world lies in the whole, not in the supposed perseity of its
parts. We would do well to bear in mind the words of Rumi: *"The nature of reality is this: it is hidden, and it is hidden, and it is hidden."*[103]
Our culture's *names* for the unbroken wholeness of Being have been

formalized and institutionalized beyond recognition, and that leads us to dismiss the *reality* of that wholeness—whereupon we lose ourselves in existential angst over the alienating indifference and fragmentation of the world around us; but what we are actually losing ourselves in is our own willfully created isolation. As Heraclitus noted, "The most beautiful order of the world is still a random gathering of things *insignificant in themselves.*"[104] The only significance, and indeed the only *reality* to be found in any fragment, any part of Being, is in its mysterious revelation of the whole—and that applies equally to humans: in ourselves we have no significance; our living grows into relevance as it attunes to the whole and expresses it. But because that whole can never be satisfactorily analyzed, we remain suspicious of it. And because our fear of the female has desensitized us to the pelvic intelligence—the one faculty that can bring our being into consciousness—the unity of *Being* consistently escapes our notice, even as it upholds us in all we do.

The eighth sphere of our mind's sensitivity opens us to that unity and steeps us in its grace. By doing so, it eliminates the question over which the 'known self' agonizes interminably: "What should I do?" When the energy of the present is felt as a whole, the aliveness of the present is felt; when you come to rest in the living present and feel the moment around you in all its specificity, you are already entering the present necessity to which the world is calling you. The Thou of the present feels you even as you feel it; it lives within you even as you live within it; and as you begin to sense its harmony, that harmony will guide you—even as you in turn guide it.

And that brings us to the other meaning of 'felt self': *it is the self that is felt by the Thou of the world and feels itself being felt.* We often speak of this state as that of 'fully awakened consciousness': the invisible Mind makes itself known to you by moving you. Such an experience returns us forcibly to the original meaning of our word *consciousness*: it comes from the Latin *con-*, "with, together," and *scire*, "to know." Now *scire* by itself gave us our word *science*, which is indeed knowledge that stands alone; but *con*sciousness is something else. Its Latin and Greek roots literally mean "knowledge shared with another," and **the Latin verb from which *consciousness* comes, *conscire*, means "to be mutually aware."** The implication—one that this book takes seriously—is that whoever remains in the unipolar state of the 'known self' and lacks the sensitivity of mutual awareness with the world is not fully conscious.

The Universal Law tells us that there is no such thing as a stand-alone consciousness—it is merely an illusion necessary to the tyrant. If we can begin to loosen the self-tyranny we wield over the self and awaken our faculty for mutual awareness, then we will begin to heal all the artificial divisions we have imagined between self and self, and between self and world. The world is as aware of you as you are of it; to feel that mutual awareness is to land with both feet in the living present: at one with yourself, at one with the world. It is to be delivered from the stronghold of self-consciousness into the ease of true consciousness. And the essential closure of self-consciousness becomes clear once we see that the literal meaning of *self-consciousness* is "the self mutually aware of the self": a closed system trapped in its own divisions. Whereas such self-consciousness characterizes the spheres of the 'known self', the spheres of the felt self are characterized by the world-consciousness of mutual awareness.

In leaving the realms of the felt self, we might note its particular strength: the opening of the heart to our partnership with the world is supported by a deep rootedness of being in the pelvic intelligence. In fact, that is where the deepest source of our integrated energy resides: in the place where male and female unite and our sensitivities are new-born. Many Eastern traditions recognize it as the center of the energy of life—an energy known variously as *qi, ki, prana* or *chi*. Experientially, then, the felt self is a union of sensitivities by which we **rest in the pelvis and act from the heart.**

The Felt One

Ninth Sphere: The Seamless, Coursing Whole
When the mind's sensitivity opens into the realm of the ninth sphere, it enters a state that many of the world's traditions describe as 'enlightenment'. This is a state in which the hero's self-achieved passivity finally carries him into an undivided union with Being: the One Mind of the world lives within his mind and reveals the world to him. This union lies so far beyond duality that it can no longer be thought of as the felt self, for the very concepts of self and nonself are blurred. We might rather call it the felt One—a whole to which the mind's sensitivities have unlimited access. Of this state, Plotinus wrote,

Each being contains in itself the whole intelligible world. Therefore All is everywhere. Each is All and All is each. Man as he now is has ceased to be the All. But when he ceases to be an individual, he raises himself again and penetrates the whole world.[105]

As Aldous Huxley put it, "I live, yet not I; for it is the Logos who *lives me.*"[106] In a final reconciliation with Being, all resistance by the self towards the reality of 'what is' is abandoned; the mistaken identity that renders the self independent from world is abandoned; and you recognize that what most deeply moves through you is the One Mind seeking to know itself fully from your unique perspective. Thomas Merton wrote,

Zen insight is not *our* awareness, but Being's awareness of itself in us. This is not … a loss of self in 'nature' or 'the One'. It is not a withdrawal into one's spiritual essence and a denial of matter and of the world. On the contrary, it is a recognition that the whole world is aware of itself in me, and that 'I' am no longer my individual and limited self, still less a disembodied soul, but that my 'identity' is to be sought not in that *separation* from all that is, but in oneness (indeed, 'convergence'?) with all that is. This identity is not the denial of my own personal reality but its highest affirmation.[107]

The whole world is aware of itself in everyone, and in every tree and puddle and breeze. We might further understand that *you are the womb within which the intelligence of the world awakens and finds out about itself.* As Rilke wrote, "The god wants to know himself in you."[108] Such a state of heightened intelligence, of course, is also a state of heightened love. Marion Woodman described her sense of suddenly 'being known' by the maternal love of Being at the crux of a personal crisis. It came upon her with a sensuality to which every cell in her body responded, bringing harmony and wholeness in its wake; and in that newfound wholeness lay healing: "In *being known*, I knew myself as part of the one."[109]

Reflecting on the spheres of our mind's sensitivity, we might note that the widening of our consciousness through those spheres progresses hand in hand with a deepening remembrance of the body. In other words, the more deeply your consciousness can ground itself in the being of the body, the more spaciously it can open to the Being of the world; the more deeply you relax into the whole that guides you, the more you are sensitized to it.

We might sum up by comparing the four spheres of the 'known self', the four of the felt self and the one of the felt One to the three phases water goes through as it gains energy from the world around it. Ice, like the 'known self', is the most consolidated of the three and remains stubbornly rigid even when subjected to pressure—preferring to shatter rather than yield. Water, like the felt self, accommodates the energies of the world and resonates to them so that they pass through it and are revealed by it. The gaseous state—water vapor—"penetrates the whole world," as Plotinus put it, and responds effortlessly to its slightest stirrings.

The unipolar consciousness of the 'known self' is where our culture directs us to remain; but the axial consciousness of the felt self is where our wholeness waits—and it is accessible to anyone, for the ability to join the reality of the present is intrinsic to our human nature. It is what our sensitivities seek to move us towards. Nor are the nine stages of those sensitivities like a staircase that is ascended one step at a time, ever onward. I think most people play up and down the staircase—but they often do so without the awareness or context to recognize what is happening. In fact, any time they might step out of the 'known self' into the subtle realms of feeling 'what is', their upbringing would urge them to explain all they experience in terms of a world bound by the fantasy of perseity, to which they then inevitably return. Stepping into those subtle realms can feel like an accident, a moment that catches you by surprise with a sudden sense of ease and spaciousness and clarity, a sense that the energy of the world is suddenly running through you freely, revealing your connection with all that is. Thomas Merton called this achievement "self-forgetfulness in the existential *present* of life here and now."[110] In the rich simplicity of that statement we find that **self-forgetfulness is associated with a remembrance of the world around you.** As Stephen Mitchell wrote, "When we step out of self-consciousness, we step into the Tao."[111]

As we have noted, some people with particular gifts of sensitivity can skip steps along the staircase; and extraordinary circumstances, usually involving great stress, can create the same effect in almost anyone. That is, they can jump straight into the sensitivity of a much vaster sphere, bypassing intermediary ones. When such jumps happen, though, it is much more difficult for the individual to integrate the experience.

Before embarking on a journey, it helps to look around to see where you actually are now, independent of where your assumptions say you are; to have a clear sense of *how* you got there; and to learn from those with experience about the traps and challenges that lie ahead—for what would a real journey be without such things? The same diligence is equally valuable on the journey towards wholeness in our lives. It is to those issues that the remainder of this book is dedicated. In the next chapter we will assess where we are now—for until we appreciate both how deep our fear of the female element is and how subtly that fear is the 'normal' for us in almost all we do, we will be ill equipped to forge a reconciliation with it.

Exercise Three: **Floor Yourself**

Every undercurrent of our headist culture denies the existence of our second brain and directs our attention away from it. By doing so, it shepherds our experience and understanding of ourselves into a framework that effectively boxes us into our mistaken identity. Even some of the important steps we have made towards a reconciliation of our male and female elements inadvertently reinforce that identity: the work that has been done on the lateral integration of right-brain/left-brain differences, for instance, has helped us explore a certain kind of balance, but at the same time tends to deepen our cultural precept that the self is enclosed in the head. Until we face the task of vertical integration, uniting the poles of our conscious thinking and conscious being, we will be kept from the true scope of our mind's sensitivity by the mere force of habit.

The vertical integration of the self requires a clearing out of the many-chambered room within us, and it retraces the journey of Orpheus to reunite with Eurydice. The place where Eurydice waits within us is on the pelvic floor, deep within the pelvic bowl. Anyone raised in a Western culture is at a huge disadvantage when it comes to any awareness of the pelvic floor. You can begin to restore that long-lost sensitivity with a simple exercise that was shown to me by the late Gerald Fujisawa, a truly gifted doctor of traditional Chinese medicine. You start the exercise by standing with your feet a little more than your shoulders' width apart, knees soft, and a sense that the hips are floating and your breath is effortless. Bring your attention to your tailbone, and then allow the tailbone to drop straight down, the rest of the body following, until you are in a flat-footed squatting position: your head is relaxed forward, and your spine is curved and lengthened down so that your tailbone is as low as your dropped hips will let it go.

Some people are unable to keep their balance in this position. If that's the case, hold on to a table or post or countertop to help balance yourself. Either way, if you can bring your attention to the breath and relax it into the body, you will not only feel the pelvic floor moving with it, but you will also feel the entire pelvic bowl—including hips, sacrum and lower abdomen—open with the in-breath and release on the out-breath. If you can allow yourself to come completely to rest in this position, you will also experience a sensational wakefulness to your being, and to the present.

Coming up from this position is made easier by your awareness of the pelvic floor. Rather than muscling the body up through the knees, bring your attention to the center of the pelvic floor and lift from there. It's surprisingly easy.

The flat-footed squat opens up the pelvic floor to the breath and to sensation in general. But going up and down in this fashion is also healthy for the lower back, the hips, the knees and the legs. We who sit on toilets lose strength, flexibility and pelvic awareness as a result. How people in the Middle East, for instance, can wait patiently for buses in this position seems incredible to us. But in reality it is an entirely natural position, one that our species has relied on since its inception, and one that helps keep us healthy. So I try to do this at least once a day, up and down a few times. With a bit of practice you'll find that you can retain your awareness of the pelvic floor, in all its sensitivity, even while sitting or standing. Once that sensitivity has been restored, you can begin to pay attention to the consciousness of your being that rests within it and that will carry you into the newness of the present. And then the journey of vertical integration is underway.

4 | Divided Self, Divided World

> The greatest danger, that of losing one's own self, may pass off quietly as if it were nothing; every other loss, that of an arm, a leg, five dollars, etc., is sure to be noticed.
>
> —Søren Kierkegaard[112]

We have habituated ourselves to the unipolar consciousness of tyranny. The symptoms are all there: they manifest in the way we live bottled inside our heads; in the hierarchies we construct; in our denial of the visceral brain and our disconnection from the pelvic center of being; in the sheer energy we devote to activities such as acquisition and planning and consolidation; in the level of our self-absorption, which is sanctioned and encouraged to the point that we notice the world only as though through a window; and in what we see there, which is shattered and without a center. None of those aspects of our 'normal' is a given—all are consequences of the self-achieved independence that our culture guides us towards each day that we live. All are also ways of escaping the responsibilities of our own wholeness.

Given the scope of our self-tyranny, we would expect to see a widespread and profound fear of the female expressed in what we do, what we notice, what we avoid and what we gravitate to; but we would also expect to be as blind to those expressions as we are to all other aspects we take as the givens of reality—the harness that keeps us from moving towards wholeness. The aim of this chapter, then, is to draw some of those normalized expressions of our fear into the light, and to take their measure, that the loss of our wholeness might not "pass off quietly as if it were nothing."

Logos and Perplexity

The massively connected, dark, generative phenomenon of female Being was central to the writings of Heraclitus: he attended to the mystery of nature and the Logos, never seeking to master or tame that mystery, only to learn from it. His writings come down to us only in fragments and anecdotes—but even in scraps, they have been a continuing source of inspiration, especially in the twentieth century. The fragments come from a book that Heraclitus wrote, dedicated to the goddess Artemis and deposited—or perhaps hid—in her temple at Ephesus, which was one of the eight wonders of the ancient world. In most of Greece, Artemis was known as a fiercely proud virgin huntress. In Ephesus, though, where Heraclitus lived, Artemis was altogether different: an earth goddess who nurtured men, nature and the growing fields, she was depicted with multiple breasts filled with ready milk. Far from being chaste, she gave herself to love with a willing abandon: fecund, sensuous and all-sustaining.

When Heraclitus stood in the presence of its unbroken wholeness, the Logos offered him guidance, *revealing truth without losing mystery*. Our word *guidance* shares the same root as *wisdom* and *guise*: **Logos is wisdom in the guise of the world.** It opened his eyes and heart to the secret processes of becoming, which are always in evidence around us and within us: "The force that drives the water through the rocks drives my red blood,"[113] as Dylan Thomas wrote. Richard Tarnas explains that the ancient Greeks considered the Logos to be "a supreme rational-spiritual principle that both ordered and revealed," and he stresses that the highest quest of philosophers was "to grasp and be grasped"[114] by it: *to know and be known by what moves all the world.*

We can more fully understand what the reality of Logos represented to Heraclitus by considering that in his experience

- Its unknowable mystery is not an absence but a presence.

- This presence cannot be partitioned or analyzed, but it can be felt as a unity.

- The unity is not static, and its dynamic is such that it rests by changing, and changes by resting.

- Its dynamic unity includes the totality of mind and thought; it "steers all things through all things," as Heraclitus put it.

- The mystery of the whole, when felt directly, illuminates more the more deeply its mystery is experienced.

- Not only is our existence contingent upon the whole—our relationship to the whole, once we allow it to reveal itself, is as personal as that of a child to its mother.

In its limitless embrace, Being accommodates chaos and paradox: it creates all things, sustains all things, transmutes all things and destroys all things—and it does so with a capacity for awareness, or information sharing, for which we have no explanation. It is complex beyond imagining, and it is One. Reality is and ever will be a perplexity. It offers us not answers, but a predicament spiced with obstacles, wonders, revelations and adventures. Poet, musician and sometime–Zen monk Leonard Cohen once said, "These problems exist prior to us, and we gather ourselves, almost molecularly, we gather ourselves around these perplexities. That's what a human is: a gathering around a perplexity."[115]

Life by its very nature is a manifold revelation of seeming contradictions. When we ask our lives to resolve into a logical meaning that transcends perplexity, we ask the impossible, and we ask for impoverishment: the rich meaningfulness of our lives is found not outside of that perplexity, but deep in the heart of it. To accept the perplexity of the living moment without flinching is to be informed by nerve-ways that unite the present as a whole. You cannot comprehend the perplexity, or name it, or solve it, any more than you can the present. You can only feel it. And when you do feel it, you will recognize it as the doorway to your most profound experiences—the source of life's beauty and wonder and tenderness and grief and gratitude.

With that in mind, it is sobering to consider the attitude towards perplexity displayed by our culture at large. For instance, with a few luminous exceptions—President Barack Obama comes to mind—the political candidates we seem to turn to are the ones who hammer perplexity into reassuring sound bites, so we tend to elect leaders for whom reality is as unambiguous as a polished idea. Similarly, our mass media resemble a vast feeding mechanism for the 'known self'—able to take on the most complex and fraught situation and flatten it for our consumption into a story that is reassuring in its finite containment, its message and its moral implications. Above all, let's not leave our viewers perplexed. Nor, to be fair, do viewers want perplexity: products of their culture, they want authority and clear knowledge; they want the world crushed into a simple sign. The very qualities that enable someone to recognize a deep perplexity—patience and humility—are not what viewers generally offer to the little screens in their living rooms. If they did, of course, their offering would not be well rewarded. The syndrome self-perpetuates.

Our squeamishness over perplexity is ultimately an intolerance for Being, and so promotes a reliance on duplicates. When that squeamishness begins to undermine our understanding and appreciation of art—the most vital means we have for unleashing our culture's creativity—the consequences for the health of our culture are grim. Remarkably, it is not uncommon nowadays for arts funding to be contingent on a "positive message," as if harmony could be harnessed by the right message rather than the living song. And to be sure, our media generally feed our appetite for message over perplexity. When they turn their attention to the artist's song, it is almost invariably to determine *what it means*, as Susan Sontag observed. Artists are not immune either, and can be heard eagerly packaging the meaning of their work into digestible sound bites. Eventually this tendency becomes a kind of canker that eats its way into the creative process itself. And when the creativity of our arts is impaired, we are all affected.

In myth, the perplexity of Being is represented by the fabled Gordian knot: neither can be unraveled. Legend tells us that the Gordian knot was so subtly tied that the two ends were invisible, defeating all attempts to undo it. Many tried, for it was predicted that whoever could untie the knot would become lord of all Asia. Eventually Alexander the Great tried, failed, and then sliced the knot in half with his sword. This foretells the ascendant solutions of science, which, by Alexander's day in 334 B.C., were well underway: **if you can't solve the** perplexity in all its wholeness, just slice it into manageable bits, which themselves can neither reveal the mystery nor any longer contain it. With a stroke of his sword, Alexander reduced an elusive entirety to mere bits and pieces. At the same time, as Robert Graves wrote, "Alexander's brutal cutting of the knot ... ended an ancient dispensation by placing the power of the sword above that of religious mystery."[116] Over the centuries, religious *mystery* was eclipsed by religious *orthodoxy,* a word that literally means "having the right opinion." The purpose of any orthodoxy is to solve life by imposing order; in the course of religious history a fundamental dedication to orthodoxy has frequently enforced its "right opinion" with a sword.

The scientific bias of our culture creates a mood that tends to regard any discussion of mystery as a sign of intellectual flaccidity and any intrusion of perplexity into our daily lives as an inconvenience, if not an indignity. Wild nature is the most intimate mystery available to us, and we treat it not as our teacher, but as a storehouse to be plundered, a danger to be avoided or a form of entertainment to be managed for our enjoyment. We have so protected ourselves from unmanaged phenomena that we want *everything* to be managed. We don't want sound; we want sound bites. We don't want food for thought; we want predigested information. We don't just want the world on a platter; *we want it to come with instructions.* In short, we don't want perplexity; we want solutions.

So singularly is our culture dedicated to male values that *we actually see solutions as a way of tying the world together and helping us understand it as a whole.* A perplexity, on the other hand, we regard as something that requires a solution: it is a momentary flaw in our grasp of reality, an impediment to getting a reliable hold on it, an illusion that distances us from the world. The etymology of the words tells a different story. *Perplexity* comes from a Latin root that means "to intertwine, to braid"; our word *solution,* on the other hand, comes from a Latin word meaning "to untie," which itself traces back to the Indo-European base *leu-,* meaning "to cut off, untie, separate." A solution appeals to us precisely because it unties itself from the world and offers us something reassuringly independent and fixed—the hallucinogen perseity in another of its guises. We sort of know that a solution isn't reality itself, but, as with the fiction of the 'known self', we accept it as a reliable stand-in. We conveniently forget what we lose with that acceptance—and yes, our words *lose* and *solution* share the same root.

To my way of thinking, the etymology of the words is nearer the mark than what we have made of them. To be present in the world is to be present with the intertwining perplexity of its Gordian-knot entirety. And to be present with that perplexity to the point at which you can feel it as a whole is to discover it as a dynamic unity in which every part yields to every other part—in other words, *such a perplexity is a whole in harmony*. It is in the intertwining perplexity of such a whole that we sense the underlying harmony of the Logos of Heraclitus, or the Tao of Lao-tzu, or the implicate order of David Bohm. Paradoxically, then, the perplexity of the world turns out to be not confounding, but revelatory.

Yet our culture insists that to possess answers is to come closer to truth: that answers help us connect with reality by solving it. And so we look for the answers to everything. Artworks are critiqued, and praised or condemned, for the answers they are found to embody. Television seduces us with its ability to provide a stream of answers on a 24-7 basis. Religion is praised by some as a source of answers and rejected by others for the answers it provides. Science has acquired more authority than religion, because it is seen to provide more authoritative answers—answers that, like the classical descriptions of the atom, the self and the artwork, are commonly accepted as fixed, independent and eternal to us all.

Our culture is so in thrall to solutions that a question is understood to acquire value only by virtue of the answer to which it leads. Similarly, it is hard for us to understand that, far from helping us to connect with reality, *answers actually make us less attentive to it*. An answer consolidates a perspective; as soon as you have an answer, there is no further need to really pay attention to 'what is'. You already know what the front door to your house looks like, so you don't really see it when you come home. And to the extent that you already 'know' what your partner or children or parents look like, you don't really see them either. As Susan Sontag put it, answers "deplete the world." That is something Shakespeare understood well. As Stephen Greenblatt pointed out in his book *Will in the World*, Shakespeare doesn't tell us *why* Iago seeks to destroy Othello, for instance, or why Lear, having divided his kingdom, suddenly decides to grant each portion in exchange for flattery. If Shakespeare had given us those answers, his plays would have lost some of their perplexing resonance.

In our culture a question such as, "What does your front door look like?" would typically be addressed by the dissociated pole of male consciousness, so the answer would have very little relationship with present experience. ("It's black, and it has a brass handle.") No surprises there. And that is exactly the point. The assumption that keeps you from taking the time to imagine the door and discover it with an innocent eye is fair enough, but it exacts a toll that we too rarely appreciate. Specifically, that assumption ambushes experience and directs you to the consolidations of the past. By doing so it shields you from newness, from your present relationships, from what holds surprise in the world and the self. And **every instance in which you disconnect from the present indicates a more primary allegiance to the 'known self'.**

My aim is not to denounce answers—they can give you something concrete to question, something specific to reflect upon. But it is a slippery slope, because if an answer stands independent from the world's flux—something fixed, solid and eternal, to borrow Alden Nowlan's phrase—it will have the same effect on you, keeping you in your head and casting its shadow across 'what is', obscuring the particular truth of the present, its intimate life. A stand-alone answer does not sensitize you to Being, but dulls you to it; it does not move you forward, but stops you; it does not illuminate the world's unity, but endarkens it; it does not help you to learn, but flatters you with having learned. In short, a static concept is divorced from Being and cannot reveal it. As Meister Eckhart wrote,

> No idea represents or signifies itself. It always points to something else, of which it is a symbol. And since man has no ideas, except those abstracted from external things through the senses, he cannot be blessed by an idea.[117]

In our culture ready answers are taken as a sign of competence; they drive the rhythms of our social conversations, of our television chat shows, and of much of our thinking. And indeed, without answers to guide us, how could we choose what was best? Or decide what we should do next? And how else should we respond to a question except with the right answer? A friend of mine worked close to a Native community in Northern Ontario when he was a young man. He often visited a certain elder there whom he enjoyed talking to.

One day the elder looked at him and said, "You know, you are much smarter than I am." My friend, dumbfounded, asked what he meant. "Well," continued the elder, "when I ask you a question, you have the answer right away. But when you ask me a question, I have to wait for a while before I know what to say." My friend felt duly chastened. And he realized that he came up with answers to almost every question like a reflex, without pausing to feel a thing. Thanks to the elder, his reflex was put to rest, and his life more deeply blessed.

Because the native elder *felt* a question, it could come into relationship with the center of his being, thereby revealing self and world in a new light. Any question that opens doorways to Being blesses us; but opening them requires on our part, first and foremost, *a self-confessed ignorance*—no command of information, no encyclopedic knowledge could ever jimmy them open. In fact, as novelist Robert Pirsig observed, "If you have a high evaluation of yourself then your ability to recognize new facts is weakened."[118] In the sense in which the term is used here, **'self-confessed ignorance' is not a place of refuge; it is a place of encounter.** It is a state of unknowing passivity that allows you be present with 'what is', and to feel it feeling you: the state of mutual awareness. That is the stance of the Zen archer, who releases the arrow so that the shot falls "from the archer like snow falls from a bamboo leaf"[119] and comments that *he* did not make the shot; he merely waited until "It" shot the arrow. In a similar way the world calls forth ink from the brush of the master calligrapher, or the pivot from the aikido master. By letting go of what is known, you are free to encounter the living present, in all its perplexity and revelation. Just as silence is the possibility of sound, self-confessed ignorance is the possibility of encounter. As Arthur Koestler reminds us, "Every creative act—in science, art or religion—involves ... a new innocence of perception, liberated from the cataract of accepted belief."[120]

There are examples even in our own culture in which we can sense the willingness to allow a question to provoke "a new innocence of perception" rather than a ready answer. I once read an interview with the playwright Eugene Ionesco in which his first words were, "If I don't answer your questions right away, you mustn't mind me."[121] Heraclitus commented that "men have talked about the world without paying attention to the world."[122] The question/integration mode also forms the basis of the Zen koan, typified by the well-known example, "What is the sound of one hand clapping?" The value of that question does not lie in any answer, for you cannot solve a koan with ideas; its only value is as an awakener, a springboard into the perplexing wholeness of Being. As John Tarrant noted, "Koans unravel the world that we have thought up, and it is this unraveling that makes it possible for a different world to appear."[123] Socrates is another who did not let answers get in his way—he denied having any set of doctrines, and he was completely at ease with his own ignorance. Meanwhile, the questions that were born of that ignorance made many a clever man squirm.

And then there is the artist. I've read speculative articles about the lack of enduring works of art in the past decades. It seems to me that there may be some basis to the claim, and I have no simple answer to it. I do know this much, though: an artist who creates out of ideas rather than from his or her felt relationships with the world—in all its unknowability—tends to date quickly. Artworks that are created in compliance with ideas are concerned with solving problems or presenting meaning or even supplanting meaning. That's what ideas are for. Such works tend to represent a world that is mechanical, one that not only refuses to be guided by sensuality, but presents a triumph over it: art without heart—the modern infatuation. However meaningful or earnest or disturbing it may be at the time, such art has a way of appearing quaint as the years go by. Answers come and go. Only the great mysteries endure, shaping all that is. And when an artist primarily shapes his work by idea, he evicts mystery.

The Pure Obsession

The tendencies discussed above—our retreat from the all-aware whole and its deep perplexity, and our grasping at solutions—are all promoted by our culture as ways of remaining in touch with reality, when they are actually ways of keeping the male pole of consciousness dissociated from the female, which preserves what is fractured and 'known' within us. Like the tyrant, we mistake the illusions of division and control for security. To those dark tendencies we can add another, which is equally camouflaged: our wish for purity. We view that wish as a completely natural and healthy one, but to see it otherwise you need only consider that **purity is by its very nature exclusive**: pure *anything*—whether a thought, a deed or a substance—generally means the exclusion of everything else. The equation of 'purity' with 'holiness' is a travesty: exclusion and isolation are antithetical to the state of being whole, which is the literal meaning of *holy*. Similarly, to talk about the 'purity' of white light is to overlook its true nature: white light is an inclusive blend of every color of the spectrum.

Typically the urge towards purity is the desire to wall out all unwanted influences, making what is inside the wall good and clean, and holding on the outside all that is tainted and unclean. In those terms we can see that purity divides up the world and isolates a select part of it: **to crave purity, then, is—like the tyrant—to seek our redemption in isolation.** We find that craving expressed in religion, in science, in racism, in political ideologies and in every other limited view of the world's goodness. What could be better for us than pure water, for instance? Well, impure water, actually, as it occurs naturally. Pure water is deprived of all minerals, so its effect is to deplete the body. Water that has been processed by the earth, in contrast, is impure—rich in trace minerals that nourish the body. For a more extreme example we might look to the natural tendency of children to eat mud, the ultimate impurity, which has been found to strengthen their immune systems.

The notion of purity is seductively attractive to our patrifocal culture. In fact, the very nature of thinking in the typical male brain is found to be 'purer' than that of the typical female: as JoAnn Deak noted, "Male brains are built to streamline and to go right to what they have to do." In other words, they apply themselves purely to a problem, unencumbered—and uninformed—by wider relationships. They simply exclude them. Pure reason is a male ideal, and a unipolar consciousness is its natural fulfillment. Carl Jung recognized its limitations. As Marion Woodman and Elinor Dickson explain, Jung argued that

> pure reason was a pure abstraction from reality rather than an encounter with it. Not only is objectivity, as it has been traditionally defined, not attainable, but it gives us a false picture of reality by virtue of what it excludes.[124]

The pure reason of the male element relies on two supposed virtues: objectivity and the ability to discern cause. That both of those old standbys are idealized distortions has been amply demonstrated by quantum mechanics, which shows us a universe in which objectivity is an impossible fantasy and chaos and chance are commonplace. In the meantime, the number of ways in which all things female have been denounced by cultures around the world as impure and unclean is staggering. If purity were an ultimate good, then the connected, menstrual, intuitive, bodily, generative, sensitive female would *have* to rank well below the male; in fact, the underlying raison d'être of purity is to stand against the unseen, all-nurturing and transforming processes of Being. Purity is not an ultimate good; it is a tyranny. Even the supposed purity attained by 'killing the ego' is a form of tyranny. As Andrew Harvey has pointed out, you *can't* kill the ego—it always waits, ready to remind you of work still to be done. To feel you should try to kill it is to govern yourself with an impossible demand. To feel you *have* done so is to flatter that which you claim does not exist.

In this context it is revealing to consider the purity of science—for we are all held in its thrall on one level or another. As a culture, we more or less accept science as the arbiter of reality, even as we recognize it to be a predominantly male view. Its allure is not surprising, though, when you consider how readily science feeds the needs of the 'known self': it has purified its findings of any misleading intuition of the senses; it promises to answer every question concerning what is and what is not; and it promises to tell us *exactly* what makes up our reality. As such, science makes hay from a larger implication of perseity that provides the raw material for our most rampant fantasies: that is, **perseity assures us that the world is finally knowable**. To wit: if a thing has independent existence, then what is contained within it is all that need be or can be known about it; it contains its own self-sufficient explanation. Pull it to pieces and itemize those pieces and their relationships to each other, and you will create a knowledge of that thing that is complete. *Complete knowledge is the first step towards complete control, whether of a gene, a forest, a nation or the self.* In other words, our aspirations of control are given credibility by our belief in perseity; and science, more than any other discipline, enables us to exercise those aspirations.

In leaning so heavily on science, we express a certain complacency: we rely on science to tell us what is real, and the technology of science multiplies our ability to affect the world ten-thousand-fold; but we don't often call into question the terms of science—and it is the *terms* of science that determine its findings. As Werner Heisenberg noted, what scientists observe "is not nature itself, but nature exposed to our method of questioning."[125] David Bohm expressed it somewhat more pointedly when he observed that *the great accomplishment of modern science is its reliance on fact, and its failing is that only certain kinds of facts are permitted.* Kevin Dunbar, director of the Laboratory for Complex Thinking and Reasoning, conducted an extensive review of the scientific process in practice and found that researchers consistently look for evidence that confirms the theories they rely on, and inhibit evidence that contradicts them.[126]

So what are the terms to which pure science adheres in judging what is real? The most basic terms were set by Galileo, for whom *only what could be measured and quantified could be admitted as scientific*—which is acceptable enough, in that he was merely setting the terms for a tightly disciplined method of inquiry. But in time those terms became the basis for a general belief that stands as the bedrock of what we accept as true, a belief that says, **"Whatever cannot be measured and quantified is not real."** Of course, as the writer Margaret Visser astutely pointed out, this belief itself cannot be measured. Nonetheless, immune to its own criteria, it assails all other kinds of knowing. The view it espouses was famously summed up by Lord Kelvin at the end of the nineteenth century:

> When you can measure what you are speaking about, and express it in numbers, you know something about it; but when you cannot measure it, when you cannot express it in numbers, your knowledge is of a meager and unsatisfying kind: it may be the beginning of knowledge, but you have scarcely, in your thoughts, advanced to the stage of *science*.[127]

A toddler runs laughing towards his mother, who bends down, scoops him up and gives him a hug and a kiss. She has measured nothing about her toddler and has no way of expressing her knowledge of him in numbers; by Kelvin's standards her knowledge of him is "of a meager and unsatisfying kind." Kelvin, on the other hand, could pull out a thermometer calibrated in the scale that bears his name, measure the toddler's temperature, and obtain something truly satisfying—some *real* knowledge about him ("Three hundred and ten degrees!"). Those are the terms of pure science as applied to life. And increasingly, we do apply them. As Anand Giridharadas reported in the *New York Times*, parents are not only encouraged to enter data on their infant's life so that they can make number-based decisions on their child's sleeping, eating and diaper-changing patterns; in fact, self-quantification

> ... is everywhere now. *Bedposted.com* quantifies your sexual encounters. *Kibotzer.com* quantifies your progress toward goals like losing weight. Withings, a French firm, makes a Wi-Fi-enabled weighing scale that sends readings to your computer to be graphed. There are tools to measure and analyze the steps you take in a day; the abundance and ideological orientation of your friends; the influence of your Twitter utterances; what you eat; the words you most use; your happiness; your success in spurning cigarettes. Welcome to the Age of Metrics.[128]

As Giridharadas observed, "what we know instinctively, data can make us forget." Eventually, the built-in exclusions of science assure us that the ultimate reality can only be expressed by subatomic interactions; and then, of course, we turn to them to tell us who *we* really are, exactly as we used to turn to religion. But insofar as our measurements are made by tools and machines, *our view of reality is a product of the machines we build*. **We do not observe reality, but rather its effects on our measuring apparatus.** No machine can detect or measure spirit, so any belief in spirit is seen as a crutch for those who can't accept reality. Gifted individuals who heal according to 'auras' or 'energies' undetectable by machines are dismissed as charlatans. Prayer cannot be measured, love cannot be measured, sacredness cannot be measured, harmony cannot be measured, mystery cannot be measured, gratitude cannot be measured; they have all been called crutches and illusions. More critically, *the unbroken wholeness of Being—the very foundation of reality—cannot be measured*; and because our measuring machines can't record that wholeness, our language no longer has an acceptable word for it. The one thing our measuring machines *can* describe is inanimate matter, which scientists then assure us is the reality of life itself: the mechanical inevitabilities of molecular interactions—no more.*

---

* Many writers have set out to debunk the belief that life is no more than a product of random molecular interactions. Of all the examinations of that belief I have

When our faith in measuring machines leaves us doubting our own experience, we try to compensate by assigning meanings to our experience, which enable us to quantify it; or we turn to our machines to tell us what in our experience is real and what is not. But our machines can only report that the world of the self and the world of nature to which it belongs are mechanical worlds ruled by the laws of physics and chemistry. Shoehorned by our own terms of inquiry into an existence that is life-deprived and solitary, we grow self-centered and find purpose only in manipulating the world around us to our own perceived advantage.

Pure science does more than exclude from reality what cannot be measured; it also excludes everything that cannot be measured *yet*. But whether intangibles have a role to play in our world, it can neither prove nor disprove. It just lets that possibility wither from neglect as it proceeds in its pure quest to measure bits and pieces of the tangible in order to secure the real knowledge so esteemed by Lord Kelvin. As we have seen, *science* comes from the Latin *scire*, "to know," and is related to *scindere*, "to cut, split, cleave." What science excels at is splitting the Gordian knot of the world apart, measuring its broken bits and pieces, and then using those measurements to elucidate the mechanical and mathematical relationships between them. The ingenuity of science in solving those relationships is often breathtaking: consider the Atlas detector at the Large Hadron Collider—600 million times every second, it is able to take 90 million measurements.[129] The findings made by science are an honest and provocative revelation of our world; but the self-imposed limits of its inquiry ensure the limited applicability of its revelations. In the meantime, the effect of its accomplishments—*which always promise but can never arrive at a self-sufficient explanation for everything*—is classically to depict a world of discrete parts that interact according to fixed, eternal laws.

When we consider the extent to which that depiction aligns with the unipolar experience of the 'known self', it raises certain questions. And those questions, if pursued honestly, show that science is a faith-based endeavor: in short, **science is driven by the faith that the entire enterprise of nature should conform to the shattered, life-deprived, mechanical view of the tyrannical male element.** Science offers no

come across, the most astute and thorough is found in *Embryos, Galaxies and Sentient Beings: How the Universe Makes Life* by Richard Grossinger, (Berkeley: North Atlantic Books, 2003).

testable hypothesis that shows why the universe should conform to the tyrant's view; it neither names its faith nor calls it to account; it merely maintains that its view is 'neutral'. In the name of that neutrality, it dismisses revelations showing that Being is deeply interrelated through nonlocal phenomena, that life is more mysterious than mechanics can account for, and that mind and matter are so deeply intertwined as to continually express each other. The Universal Law of Interrelationship, which scientists keep bumping into, is never recognized in its full dimensionality because to do so would be to assent to a view that is quite frankly female. In my experience, the most benighted of all the sciences, ironically, is neuroscience, which seems to have manfully taken on the task of proving to us all that the brain *is* the mind, and which, as we have seen, seems to be undaunted by the abundant and incontrovertible evidence to the contrary. In other contexts, such resolute efforts in the face of insurmountable odds might be called 'courageous'.

The strength of pure science lies in exposing what is not true—but as for proving what *is* true, the best it can do is construct plausible models. As scientist and philosopher Gregory Bateson put it, "Science *probes*; it does not prove."[130] By claiming a rightful independence from the wholeness of Being, the models of science, like all pure duplicates, tacitly deny it. "Away with all duplicates," as Sontag urged. But **the stranglehold of those duplicates will not ease until we can overcome our addiction to our ultimate attempt at purity: the 'known self'.** In the *Phaedo* Plato laid out the terms for that purity quite clearly:

> It seems that so long as we are alive, we shall continue closest to knowledge if we avoid as much as we can all contact and association with the body, except when they are absolutely necessary; and instead of allowing ourselves to become infected with its nature, purify ourselves from it until God himself gives us deliverance.[131]

The Neutron-Bomb Parlor Trick

To what extent does our culture normalize its fear of the female? Consider that the true nature of Being is obscured for us by a sort of parlor trick we play on ourselves. We segregate our conscious thinking from contact with the intelligence of our conscious being, bottling it inside the head, and we extol the truths divined from that prospect as ultimate and pure. Having withdrawn into our senseless headquarters, we look upon the world and find it changed, and we bask in the truth of what is revealed to us. As though by an accomplished act of prestidigitation, the One Mind, the Living Spirit that had hitherto suffused all the forms of the world, has been made to vanish: the triumph of matter over mind.

The effect is like that of a neutron bomb, which empties buildings of all life but leaves the structures intact. Similarly, when we implode our consciousness into the head, the structures of the world are rendered lifeless, but otherwise remain intact. The body, now so distant from us, feels like an organized system of dull, unthinking matter, and we know that we are witnessing a pure truth. The self we have so isolated feels like a fundamentally independent entity—and we know that to be its essential nature. Our planet appears to be a random, multifarious happenstance floating through the inky indifference of space, and we unsentimentally accept that it is. We experience consciousness as a local, self-generated phenomenon—something each individual produces biochemically within the cranium—and we see and know its limits. True consciousness is not something in which stones or trees or planets or worms could share—so we know them to lack it. In fact, it becomes obvious that nothing is really capable of full consciousness save for the solitary specimens of humanity, trapped within their heads. Once consciousness disappears from the world around us, it appears to be no more than a mere accident of evolution unique to *Homo sapiens*. Presto!

We may deeply yearn to connect with the world from which we have separated ourselves—to undo the parlor trick—but the solutions that appeal to us, the ones that seem most promising, are those that appeal to the thinker in the head. The 'known self' doesn't like the status quo to be threatened, doesn't understand death as rebirth, and puts its faith in new ideas rather than in any newness that might be found in the unknown terrain of a direct experience. And so we are seduced by messages assuring us that the challenge and risk and heartbreak and confusion that any evolution of consciousness necessarily entails can be circumvented with the right attitude, the right ideas, the right thinking, the right actions, or the right secret. We are buoyed by a widespread hope that if we can just *believe* enough in our connection with the world, that connection will come back to life for us all by itself, without our having to bother with the structural disintegration of a descent from the fortified head into the assimilating center of conscious being.

The Forgotten Dimension

When the hero steps beyond the sphere of his known society, the whole focus of his attention is on the unknown landscape. He does not look back at what he has left, but is sensitized and alert to the shifting realm of Being stretching out beyond, from which his spiritual center of gravity calls to him. In mythic terms, the realm of Being is understood as the world of divinity, a kingdom inhabited by the gods, and symbolically situated in a land distant from the hero's commonplace human kingdom. As Campbell says, though,

> Nevertheless—and here is a great key to the understanding of myth and symbol—the two kingdoms are actually one. The realm of the gods is a forgotten dimension of the world we know. And the exploration of that dimension, either willingly or unwillingly, is the whole sense of the deed of the hero. The values and distinctions that in normal life seem important disappear within the terrifying assimilation of the self into what formerly was only otherness.[132]

Recalling Krishnamurti's assertion that knowledge is endarkenment raises a question: if, as Campbell states, "The realm of the gods is a forgotten dimension of the world we know," might what we *know* of the world be endarkening its full dimensionality? Basic science tells us our reality consists of four dimensions: three of space and one of time. We are to understand that within those four dimensions matter moves and interacts, occasionally in a way that creates consciousness— in your brain, for instance. The mystic tradition holds a very different view: the primary reality of the world is consciousness, and all within the world is a manifestation of that consciousness. The scientific and mystic views have been succinctly summarized by Wendell Berry as, respectively, "Life is a machine" and "Life is a miracle."

Our culture largely subscribes to the "Life is a machine" metaphor of science, but the paradigm in which it seeks to contain the world is a leaky one. For instance, the findings of the double-slit experiment, which are summarized in the Appendix of this book, are not understood by anyone—but they cannot even be described without reference to a conscious observer, so deeply implicated is the observer in the outcome of the experiment. In fact, the effect of consciousness on the subatomic world has been demonstrated spectacularly in a range of contexts: when someone observes radioactive decay or the path of a photon, that act can suppress the decay or make the photon behave like a particle; studies have shown that that beans grow measurably faster when prayed for;* Masaru Emoto has graphically demonstrated the effect thought can have on the formation of ice crystals; and Robert Jahn at Princeton University has shown that human intention can create greater coherence within the random generation of numbers by a computer.

Jahn's work, pioneered in the late 1970s, was further developed by Roger Nelson in a series of intriguing experiments. The most dramatic of them is the Global Consciousness Project, which uses random-event generators to output high-quality sequences of random numbers. Random-event generators run nonstop in over sixty countries, sending their results over the Internet to be correlated in a graph. Most of the time, the graph looks more or less like a straight line. But Nelson noticed that on September 6, 1997, the graph shot upwards, recording a massive deviation from the norm; that was also the day of Princess Diana's funeral. Similar effects were observed on September 11, 2001, and on the day of the tsunami that devastated Southeast Asia, and every year on New Year's Day. Summarizing the significance of his work, Nelson explained,

> We're taught to be individualistic monsters. We're driven by society to separate ourselves from each other. That's not right. We may be connected together far more intimately than we realize.[133]

---

* Larry Dossey has written extensively and soberly on the experimentally significant effects of prayer on cells, fungi, bacteria and people, among others. His examination of the trials run by the Spindrift organization is particularly illuminating. His book *Healing Words* (San Francisco: HarperSanFrancisco, 1993) is a classic on the subject.

Nelson's work raises profound questions about the nature of reality, suggesting as it does that human consciousness on a global scale can significantly affect events on the atomic scale. But as Bohm noted, there are certain facts that pure science doesn't permit—the idea, for instance, which still thrives in most aboriginal societies, that our thoughts actually matter to the world. And so it is that physics finds itself in something of a double bind: it cannot explain certain findings without reference to consciousness, yet it cannot explain consciousness.

Some physicists brave enough to address such anomalous findings have described what sounds a lot like the presence of Logos. The renowned physicist Sir James Jeans, for instance, wrote in *The Mysterious Universe*,

> Today there is a wide measure of agreement, which on the physical side of science approaches almost to unanimity, that the stream of knowledge is heading towards a nonmechanical reality; the universe begins to look more like a great thought than a great machine. Mind no longer appears as an accidental intruder into the realm of matter; we are beginning to suspect that we ought rather to hail it as the creator and governor of the realm of matter.[134]

To look at the world and see a great thought is not just mysticism; it is to witness the full dimensionality of our world: a unity in which all things are in process, and all processes are part of a single weaving. David Bohm came to understand that mind and matter cannot be understood as separate entities. Carl Jung stated, "It is not only possible but fairly probable, even, that psyche and matter are two different aspects of one and the same thing."[135] My favorite quip comes from the great physicist Erwin Schrödinger, who wrote, "Mind by its nature is a *singulare tantum*. I should say: **the overall number of minds is just one**."[136] The ancient Mesopotamian who looked at a stalk of wheat and felt the mystery of the goddess Nidaba within it may have been nearer to reality than the contemporary scientist who sees only the mechanics of molecular biology at work.

The tyrant's basic agenda of control requires a fractured world of independent bits; his fantasies are upheld by his illusion of perseity, which is provided by a unipolar perspective that has detached from the faculty of conscious being. We are so deeply wedded to such modeling that our head-centric scientists reject any description of nature in which they cannot recognize the outlines of that cherished matrimony. That rejection shows us the obverse effect of our tendency to describe the world according to our experience of the self: *we resist descriptions of nature that don't reflect our self-image.*

Thus it is, too, that in describing our own nature we reflexively turn to the self-contained, enclosed, stand-alone computer as our metaphor for consciousness. In reality, a computer records ones and zeroes and organizes and reorganizes them at lightning speed. That isn't thinking; it's programming. But the computer's efficiency at that digital systemization, its ability to go right to what it has to do in perfect disregard of any larger relationship, represents the male ideal towards which our inner tyrant strives. And so we embrace the metaphor, and with it the message that *there can be no new thoughts, only recombinations of the thoughts that have been inputted.* That fiction is a comfort to the 'known self', for which *newness,* like its etymological cousin *nowness,* can only represent a threat: both are beyond control.

In his book *Elemental Mind,* physicist Nick Herbert departs from conventional limits of inquiry to consider the nature of mind in light of the findings of quantum theory. He proposes that

> far from being a rare occurrence in complex biological or computational systems, mind is a fundamental process in its own right, as widespread and deeply embedded in nature as light or electricity.[137]

He also suggests that consciousness itself arises from

> a kind of "quantum animism" in which mind permeates the world at every level. I propose that consciousness is a fundamental force that enters into necessary cooperation with matter to bring about the fine details of our everyday world.[138]

The evidence suggests that science has formalized a fundamental oversight in enumerating the dimensions of our reality: the three dimensions of space (length, width and height) and the one of time, though sufficient to describe a reality of dead matter ruled by mechanics, are impotent to accommodate the role consciousness plays in our world—and so by themselves tacitly deny that role. We are able to assess events only according to the a priori provisions established by the dimensions we ascribe to reality. If we look at the consequences of our four-dimensional framework, we can begin to see how profoundly it affects what we see and how we behave.

For example, no two people can occupy the same space at the same time. That is an entirely obvious statement to us only because we have acquiesced in a description of reality that denies the female and so denies us the full scope of the mind's sensitivity. Just as obvious to us are the corollaries that the space you occupy is *your* space and is separated from everyone else's by the boundary of your skin; that the physical, intellectual or spiritual strength you wield is *your* strength; and even that the love that courses through you into the world is *your* love. In general, our relationships with the world are so bluntly interrupted by spatial and temporal divisions that we can bestow meaning only in bits and pieces. The whole can no longer cohere, because the whole cannot be located in the blasted particularities revealed by the isolating boundaries of space and time. Those particularities have been bequeathed to us by the assumptions and methodologies of science. The poverty of those assumptions in reading the life of the world around us is poignantly illustrated in an analogy Nick Herbert presents in *Elemental Mind:*

> If one examines the text in this book, for instance, one will find that spaces between words occur about 17 percent of the time, the letter e occurs about 11 percent of the time, and t makes an appearance 8 percent of the time, making up a distribution of letter frequencies that is surprisingly stable and independent of the content that these words express. A person analyzing this text with the tools of a statistician will end up with tables of statistical data that in some sense completely describe the way the letters are used in this book. But no matter how exhaustive the statistician's letter counts, they entirely fail to grasp the book's main purpose: **the coding of meaningful information in nonstatistical ways.**[139]

The reality described for us by the four dimensions of space and time—a reality insistent on separateness, sterilized of meaning and biased towards perseity—gives the dissociated male aspect of consciousness just what it needs for describing its world. Its dimensions are of no use in describing 'mind', though—just how big is mind? when does it start? when does it end?—or in accommodating the revelations of our subjective human experience, or even our findings at the atomic level in which consciousness is implicated. We imagine atomic collisions in terms of billiard balls—bouncing off each other to go their separate ways. In fact, as the quantum inseparability principle shows us, when colliding atoms part company, they carry a timeless, internal connection to each other: in that sense, each is partially present in the other, occupying the other's space. Our attempts to imagine the structure of the atom in four dimensions—which inevitably conjure images of a miniature solar system—are as profoundly inaccurate as was Thompson's original model of a muffin with blueberries in it. As Nick Herbert put it, "For an atom the sum of all attributes observable in all possible contexts exceeds the number and variety of attributes that a single ordinary object could possess."[140] The atom's existence is not contained by four dimensions, and so it will confound all such four-dimensional models. In fact, the efforts to determine with certainty any event within the sterility of four dimensions are doomed to fall short: we can only circle such an event with the wagons of statistical probability and announce that it is in there somewhere.

On a quantum scale, then, the four dimensions of space-time are inadequate to the tasks of description, prediction or determining causality. But that inadequacy is also evident when we consider human events. On a grand scale, we have seen that human consciousness affects local events, as in the Global Consciousness Project; but even in everyday human relationships we all know what it is to share someone else's 'space' through the consciousness of compassion, of empathy, or of love, or through meditation or prayer. Furthermore, the stories of mothers sharing their children's consciousness when a child is distressed or in danger, even over vast distances, are legion. The fact that our culture demeans such 'female' experiences ought not blind us to their vivid reality.

The anomalies found on both the quantum scale and the human scale raise a question: if the continuum of reality leaks out beyond the framework described by four dimensions, what's missing from the framework? In pondering the issue, it seems that what is missing is the same thing that is eliminated with the neutron-bomb parlor trick: **reality is five-dimensional, and the fifth dimension is that of consciousness, or mind.** It is a dimension with a reach as limitless as those of time and space. Of course, unlike those other dimensions, consciousness cannot be calibrated—just as the achievements of male doing are conducive to measurement, while female being is not. In that regard, consciousness does not measure up to Galileo's criteria for science; but without it there can be no life, and within it everything that is participates in life. Include mind as the fifth dimension, and the traditional scientific separation of matter and consciousness becomes impossible. We are brought back to Campbell's observation:

> The realm of the gods is a forgotten dimension of the world we know. And the exploration of that dimension, either willingly or unwillingly, is the whole sense of the deed of the hero.[141]

As long as we remain forgetful of the dimension to which Campbell alludes, we are left in a schismatized abstraction. It is within the isolation of that abstraction that we raise our children, do our shopping and forge our careers. It is within the impoverishment of its biochemical materialism that we stake out our successes, struggle to find meaning, and look in the mirror and seek to know ourselves. And it is from within the self-tyranny that such a blind and mindless world necessitates that we try to determine how best to save the planet.

For me, **the tragic flaw of our culture is that it looks upon a world of five dimensions and sees only four.** As such, our culture *requires* that we live from abstraction rather than relationship—for it denies the very dimension in which all is united, and it declares the subtlety that enables us to feel that dimension to be superfluous and unreliable. If the sensitivities of the felt self are realized only as we come into relationship with the living present—only as we open to our own conscious being—then our insistence on a four-dimensional reality will lock us up in the abstractions of the 'known self'. Like the tragic flaws that doom characters in Greek or Shakespearean tragedies, our insistence on four dimensions ensures our downfall if not recognized and reversed.

A declension of the five dimensions of reality is quite straightforward.

The first three dimensions are those of space; the fourth is time; and the fifth is consciousness.

- A world of zero dimensions provides for the creation of a point.
- A world of one dimension provides for the creation of a line.
- A world of two dimensions provides for the creation of a plane.
- A world of three dimensions provides for the creation of an object.
- A world of four dimensions provides for the creation of an event.
- A world of five dimensions provides for the creation of life.

That declension shows us why science is at a loss to box up life and explain it. Science can only attempt to account for it by reducing it to a set of four-dimensional molecular events—reminding us of the character from Edwin Abbott's classic book *Flatland* who tries to understand an event from three-dimensional Spaceland as it intersects his own two-dimensional world.

As with so much else in our culture, the contraction of our perceived reality from the living world of five dimensions to the material world of four reflects our patrifocal obsessions. Male doing is preoccupied with four-dimensional events: with understanding them, categorizing them, preventing them, anticipating them, or orchestrating them in a series towards a predetermined outcome. Female 'being', on the other hand, turns its attentions to five-dimensional life: yielding to its all-informing currents, celebrating it, joining in its consciousness and Energy and in the unity of its unbroken whole. In its refusal to integrate the expressions of consciousness all about us, pure science remains steadfastly purified of the female.

The recognition that consciousness is a dimension on a par with space and time is an ancient one: it is what we have described as the mystic view of reality, and it is also the tacit view of the perennial philosophy. For most of human history, societies have lived in five dimensions and have recognized that *the world's reality is most intimately experienced in terms of its aliveness.* As Sioux chief Luther Standing Bear wrote,

> From Wakan Tanka there came a great unifying life force that flowed in and through all things—the flowers of the plains, blowing winds, rocks, trees, birds, animals—and was the same force that had been breathed into the first man. Thus all things were kindred, and were brought together by the same Great Mystery.[142]

Our mind's sensitivity, being born into five dimensions, is attuned to five dimensions. And yes, "the mind can play tricks," as they say—but it can also enter the mutual awareness of 'what is' and find guidance there that is richer than words could testify to. That adventure is your birthright. The unity of the present, though, can only address a commensurate unity of the self, and the self cannot come into unity until the corridor opens within to allow our conscious thinking to ground itself in our conscious being.

The Dynamic Unity of the Present

Ultimately, 'to be whole' and 'to be present' are the same thing: either way, a unity finds its complement in a unity; the dual nature of our consciousness—being and doing—harmonizes as a whole with the present as a whole. In fact, the dual nature of our consciousness is what *enables* us to harmonize with the present—because the nature of the present is also a duality. And just as we suppress the female aspect of consciousness within ourselves, we suppress it in what we perceive of the present.

The true duality of the present was summed up by Heraclitus in a simple phrase: **"Changing, it rests."**[143] He knew that the wild changing of the world is its only constant—in fact, in order for the world to stop changing, it would have to put on the brakes, just as we brace ourselves against change by putting tension in the body. But Being does not brook divisions—it is a perfect unity that changes as it needs to, to be always at rest: by resting, it changes; by changing, it rests. The world is forever new because it is forever yielding to newness.

Echoing the terms of myth, we might observe: the present is always doing; the present is always just being. It is a perfect generative unity of male and female, the same generative unity that moves the Tao, the Logos, the artist, the mother and the hero. If we were to describe that dynamic unity, we might say that **the precise nature of the present is that of a *wild peace*.** Despite all our efforts to subdue the world's energy or harness it or impose order on its subtle chaos, the world remains wild because the present flows on unstoppably and unpredictably at every scale: from subatomic to galactic, it is a dance of burgeoning transformations of the utmost sensitivity, utterly beyond the reach of any imposed structures of control—an improvised celebration that no one can tame, and to which we all belong. But similarly, and despite all our consternations about the unknown, the wild present is also completely at peace: the One Mind rests in perfect wholeness even as it moves through every trembling leaf, burning star and floating snowflake. It is natural, then, that we should feel closest to Being when we are 'out in the wild'—for in the midst of nature's untamed abundance we are closest to the wildness of Being and the peace of it all at once, and *we can tangibly feel that seeming paradox as a unity.* And though all of nature is wild, it tells us with every dewdrop and brook and change of season exactly what grace is. Grace expresses what is wild and cannot be shown through anything tamed by idea—yet it also arises from and reveals a profound peace.

The paradox of wild peace, then, is the fundamental nature of the world in which we live. You cannot liberate yourself into the dynamic of wholeness—the present cannot live in you and through you—until you liberate yourself to its spirit of wild peace, such that you know that wild peace as a unity *and ultimately discover that unity in yourself.* To feel peace within is one thing; to feel wildness within is another; to feel your own spirit of wild peace within is to open your heart to the unity of self and world. And then you can celebrate the present in all you do.

Thomas Merton gave us a way of understanding that unity when he expressed the idea that **the way of Tao is the way of supreme spontaneity: it is at once perfect activity and perfect rest.**[144] Those two states are immutably conjoined: perfect activity is 'doing' that is nourished by the perfect rest of Being. In fact, when your doing disconnects from Being, the surest sign of that is found in your lack of perfect rest.

Understanding perfect rest is more challenging for us. It belongs to the female pole of consciousness that we have largely dismissed, so there is a popular misconception that it resides in some private, inner sanctuary to which we retreat—a haven of calm secured from the world around it. On the contrary, perfect rest is born in us by a porous acceptance of the world in all its abiding stillness and flux. To be perfectly at rest, then, is to be perfectly informed. No one who is hoarding his precious inner peace against the world's assault is informed; he is living under siege, fortified against the present, essentially afraid. Perfect rest, in its perfect acceptance, is beyond all fear.

Our culture is so obsessed with the values of male doing that we lose touch with the profound stillness of the present that underlies all things. By disconnecting from it, we deplete the present of the very foundation on which its wholeness rests. As Meister Eckhart observed, "Nothing in all creation is so like God as stillness."[145] To diminish our sense of the present, of course, is to diminish our own ability to be present: it is only in the felt stillness of the present that the self can come fully to rest. And that rest is not just an idea, nor is it some ethereal, rarified state: **perfect rest is recognized first and foremost by what is happening in the body.** Sogyal Rinpoche compared the sensation of dropping into perfect rest to the action of "pouring a handful of sand onto a flat surface; each grain settles of its own accord."[146] It is a wonderful metaphor: as the chambers within the room of the body soften, its parts yield to one another and come to rest on the ground of Being, like grains of sand on a glass tabletop.

The ground of Being within us is associated with the pelvic floor—the place where the brain in our gut rests. We should be cautious once more, though, not to be seduced by our culture's idea that the peace of the female element of Being is 'passive'—a word that makes it seem inert, phlegmatic, indifferent or sluggish. That popular view reveals more about the self-affirming values of the 'known self' than about Being. The female aspect of consciousness is not passive, but *receptive*—the very quality against which our inner tyranny defends itself. And although its receptivity might seem dormant from the sensation-deprived perspective of the 'known self', it is anything but. True, there is a sort of passivity to just receiving 'what is'—but the nature of female receptivity carries us back to the roots of the word *passive*: it comes from the Latin *passivus,* "capable of suffering," which traces back to the same Indo-European root as our words *patient* and *compassion.* **You**

cannot receive all without suffering all. An awareness of divine female Being was central to the cultures of Old Europe, and it has traveled down to us in the image of Mary who, as Joseph Campbell writes, has inherited the "names and forms, sorrows, joys and consolations of the Goddess-Mother in the Western world."[147] Andrew Harvey has written about Mary's stillness of Being and all-enduring love, which kept her eyes and heart receptive to her profoundest truths, even in the midst of horror. As Harvey points out in *The Return of the Mother,* Mary had the strength to raise her son in a life of exile, wandering, danger and poverty; she had the strength to let him leave on his own when he needed to; and finally

> she had the strength to accompany him throughout the agony of his death. I see her at the crucifixion not wringing her hands but *witnessing* her son's pain and standing in it, standing at the core of his and her suffering, so that as he writhes in agony and dies she can feed him her peace, her strength, her faith, her never-failing trust.[148]

The still peace within which female Being rests and burns and transforms is heroic—born of a self-achieved submission and sustained by a perfect receptivity that enables it to be present with what is, and with whatever is.

Perfect receptivity is found in the stillness of Being, and it marks the foundational difference between the self-consciousness of the 'known self' and the mutual awareness of the felt self. The place of perfect receptivity in the body is the pelvic bowl. The word *pelvis* actually derives from an Indo-European base meaning "bowl": the pelvis is the original begging bowl, receiving into its emptiness the gifts of the world. It is the original Holy Grail, accepting the fluid intelligence of the sacred present. It is the inverted skull, into which pour all the perceptions of the cranial skull. When we see with the eyes only, hear with the ears only or taste with the tongue only, we reinforce the many-chambered room and never discover our personal relationship with what is seen, heard or tasted. Only when the corridor is wide enough to receive the present into the 'begging bowl'—when we allow it to 'be' within the stillness at our core—can we rest in the subtle unity of its mutual awareness; and only then can it speak to us. It is to that heroic passivity that we are directed by the luminous power of the simple sentence, "Be still, and know that I am God."[149]

Our male-inflected consciousness is naturally attuned to the *activity* of the present—to its *doing*. In *Four Quartets*, T. S. Eliot directed our attention to its equal, opposite and complementary pole—"the still point of the turning world":

> at the still point, there the dance is,
> But neither arrest nor movement. And do not call it
> fixity,
> Where past and future are gathered. Neither
> movement from nor towards,
> Neither ascent nor decline. Except for the point, the
> still point,
> There would be no dance, and there is only the
> dance.[150]

As Marion Woodman said, "The still point is the point where you can *be*."[151] All great artists—dancers, poets, singers, painters—have discovered the still resting point within their conscious being that makes their art possible. It is only from that place of stillness that we can truly feel the world: **the still point is the point from which our wholeness can be informed by the world's wholeness.** It is in the stillness of the 'begging bowl' that our consciousness is made whole—ready to receive the world and answer its call through the gateway of the heart. It is in the body's stillness of being that the Thou of the world first makes itself felt. And just as Heraclitus noted that "only movement can know movement,"[152] we might also say that **only stillness can know stillness.** Joining the mindful present begins by joining the stillness of Being that permeates it. We can understand the journey of Orpheus in those terms: from the visible effects of the present into the deep, invisible stillness at its core. If the actions of the tyrant arise from the anxieties of enclosure, the actions of the hero arise from the stillness of perfect receptivity. In that resting place of Being, your life is still: your life is on fire. World and self are interfused: in the womblike stillness at the body's core resides the empty serenity of Being itself.

Returning to the phrase, "Changing, it rests," we might appreciate that in the changing that is born of rest, we find perfect activity; in the serenity that yields to changing, we find perfect rest. *The ability to rest and change is what enables us to abide within the continuously transforming now, and allows it to abide within us.* Hugh Brody, writing of hunter-gatherer societies, noted that "the possibility for transformation is a metaphor for complete knowledge."[153] That ability to join the transforming world is also found in the practice of meditation. In meditation you rest and change, and by changing you rest more deeply—by joining the way of the world you join the world, dropping into the life of the uncrystallized moment; it is a process of deep and continuous integration. When you are at one with the energy of the present, you are at one with your own life. Meditation is a way of paying attention to that energy—though some would call it heresy to say it had a purpose at all.

The grounded still point of your Being is your truest ally, the integrating genius from which spontaneous, perfect action arises. As we noted earlier, "First, being." When your body yields first to the stillness of the present, and then to its currents, you will find that *the timelessness of the still point creates timeliness in all of your activities, imparting them with felicity and ease.* When the Zen archery master executes the perfect shot and acknowledges that not he, but 'It', made the shot, he is referring to the all-informing stillness of 'Being' out of which the shot arose. To say, "First, stillness," is to submit to a revelation of our most personal relationships with the present. By unlocking our capacity for relationship, we enter an exchange with the world that invites us to develop even as it supports us in that development. And when we say, "First, stillness," we are returning to the one state the 'known self' can neither abide nor sustain itself in: in that perfect, grounded passivity, the tyrant vaporizes, and we can begin to heal the cultural wound that, for thousands of years, has been infecting our natural love of life with rule, will, strife and isolation.

It is worth remembering, I think, that perfect receptivity is made possible by the supreme intelligence of love. As Uyeshiba noted, "There is no discord in love. There is no enemy of love."[154] Love alone is ready to celebrate what self and world are becoming. And because love knows neither opposition nor discord, because it doesn't work against the world, it doesn't seek to take charge or possess or avoid or hurry or judge or *do*. Love, in that sense, is as close as we might come to an expression of conscious being, just as it is as close as we might come to an expression of conscious doing. And so it happens that from the love-sustained emptiness of the still point you see the present and understand it as a gift; and you live the present because it is all you have—and because it is more than you could ever know.

Inside the Many-Chambered Room

The entire journey of the hero can be understood as a descent into the perplexing depths of the body to reunite with the center of intelligence that enables us to 'be'. We have already seen that the 'known self' disconnects from that center and retreats to the head, forsaking our axial consciousness. But up to now we have been discussing the 'known self' almost as if it were a theoretical construct of ideas, like an imaginary rule book or map that sets the limits within which we live. In fact, it is quite a bit more substantial than that: **the structure of the 'known self' actually resides in the body and is always manifest as tension.** Where our body is blocked, the muscular tensions that create those blocks are at the same time the building blocks of our own perceived perseity: what is tense endures; it resists change—it even resists sensation, the harbinger of change. Tension squeezes consciousness from our flesh as a cider press sends juice from an apple.

Habitual tension is tension you inhabit. The mythic choice between the 'known self' and the felt self is also a choice between inhabiting the tension or inhabiting the world. The choices are mutually exclusive: by inhabiting the 'known self', you inhabit a clenched cage of flesh that can never truly belong to what is here right now. To undo that clenched construct, it helps to identify the deeper purpose of the 'known self': *it is designed, implemented and maintained specifically to prevent the wild peace of the unknowable present from touching your core.* We achieve that by buffering ourselves from the world's sensations—installing our consolidated knowledge as a mediating shield—and by dividing up the corridor of space within us, so that the body's natural currents of intelligence are thwarted, arrested, segregated and contained. That effect within us is what we have called the many-chambered room: no longer able to feel the axis of our own consciousness as a single, open corridor, we experience it as a sort of catacomb, in which the various energies of the self are boxed up in their various galleries—unable to live through us, meet each other, reconcile, and leave room within for the present. Once the sensitivity of our core is endarkened with layers of tension that themselves lie within the tensions of the body as a whole, *the core itself cannot be found—not even by the world seeking to touch it*. And then we take refuge in a sort of diversionary tactic that lets us believe that when we are bestirred by ideas, our core has been activated. But no: until the living present passes into our core, it passes us by—even as we occupy ourselves busily consolidating our ideas into tensions held in the flesh.

To grasp how an abstract idea can be consolidated into the flesh of the 'known self', we need to appreciate the nature of abstraction. The word *abstract* comes from a Latin word that means "to remove" and is made of compounds meaning "away from, by pulling." Abstraction is a form of purification; our *idea* of something purifies it by extracting it from its living context and obliterating most of the relationships that call it into being. The reason for doing so is straightforward: no idea can present a complete knowledge or definition of a thing—you cannot explicate all of its relationships, because it relates to everything that is, so your only choice is to isolate it from almost all of the relationships that actually constitute its reality; once you have separated it from those relationships, you are left with a two-dimensional idea that stands for the whole. Houses, for instance, come in a countless variety of shapes, materials and sizes, and in differing relationships to their surroundings—some blend seamlessly in, others stand out as if deposited there from some cinematic fantasyland. Yet our single word *house* is shorn of all those particulars and stands as a static concept that represents them all—which is fine and useful, except that we confuse the duplicate with reality. As Alan Watts noted, "To define has come to mean almost the same thing as to understand."[155]

Abstraction involves cutting away from reality whatever must be lost if we are to create a static concept of it. The British philosopher Cecil D. Burns took stock of abstraction when he observed that **abstraction is basically the art of forgetting.** He further commented that the Achilles' heel of most philosophers is that they forget to take into account *what* they have forgotten and even *that* they have forgotten. Parmenides used a philosophical cleaver to cut reason free from any remembrance of the body—a purification that Plato and those to follow wholly endorsed. Then, voluntarily exiled to a chamber of insensate closure, philosophers were reduced to arguing over their perspectives on their ideas, in which discussions they became increasingly mired as the centuries passed, so that by the twentieth they were largely prepared to declare life to be without meaning and man to be incapable of knowing anything but his own thoughts. And so it was that much of philosophy, which had long had helping us live better as its express aim, charged ever deeper into a self-induced amnesia concerning life—and pretty much lost any relevance to its real problems.

The *forgetfulness of abstraction* achieves a kind of reverse symmetry with the *wakefulness of the ordinary:* in spiritual terms, it is to the kinship of the ordinary that we awaken, as is suggested by the saying, "Zen is the ordinary mind." The tension between forgetfulness and wakefulness lies at the heart of the strain that appears in each of us between male doing and female Being. **In fact, the entire path of our personal journey is shaped by a tug-of-war between our desire to forget and our desire to remember.** Our desire for remembering moves us forward into being, and our desire for forgetfulness mires us in dissociated ideas, unprocessed emotions, and an endarkened core. That desire shows up as a need to withdraw into isolation and join the sleepers of whom Heraclitus wrote. Maintaining forgetfulness requires a steady drip-feed of sheer distraction, and our culture devotes itself to that. Money can't buy happiness, but it can buy distraction—whether in the form of the latest electronics and fashions, or food, drugs and alcohol, or escapist television and magazines, or self-improvement advice that offers new solutions for managing our lives rather than doorways into the newness of being. Absorbed by the self, we lessen the pain of our confinement with distraction; and to offset staleness, the newer the distraction, the better. Consumption is the opiate of the masses. We seek to gratify 'me', and we assiduously avoid a remembrance of the world.

The remembering is crucial, though. It is what feeds the soul. To remember the world is at the same time to remember your felt self. To remember is to move closer to truth. The Greek word for truth, *aletheia,* actually means "not forgetful" and comes from *a-,* "without," and *lethe,* "forgetfulness." The river Lethe in the underworld of Greek mythology, then, is literally the River of Forgetfulness—which, with a nod to C. D. Burns, we might also call the River of Abstraction. *Aletheia* is also sometimes translated as "reality." In this Greek word, then, we find the qualities of *remembering, truth* and *reality* grouped together in contradistinction to those of *forgetfulness, hell* and *abstraction.* It is a telling correlation.

Aletheia shares the same origins as the words *lethargy* (which results from forgetfulness) and *alethiology,* "the science of truth," which sounds like a pretty dull pursuit until we translate it literally as "the science of not forgetting"—and then it suddenly sounds like an apt description of any number of spiritual traditions, some of which have described enlightenment as "remembering your true nature" or "remembering your original face." It also reminds us of Michael Caine gouging his hand with the bent nail.

When we remember the world and move forward, we unite with Being and are guided by it. When our desire to forget disconnects us from Being, we retreat into idea, and then our actions can only be driven willfully, guided by an *idea* of what should be. Any such idea is abstract, and enclosed from the present; it is heedful of the known, and dismissive of the unknown. Even more critically, though, **when you give authority to an idea, you consolidate it; the consolidation of an idea is effected through a consolidation of the body; a consolidated body is a body silenced by forgetfulness.** When we forget the body, we no longer experience it as a field of intelligence, but as mere matter, run by the thinker in the head. As such, you expect it to behave the way the boat obeys the helmsman. But if you are divided from your body, you are also divided from the body of the world—which then appears to be other than you, or separate from you, rather than the living continuum to which you belong. Exiled from its divine guidance, you become marooned in the headquarters to which you have retreated. The more pronounced the abstraction, the greater the forgetfulness—and the greater the isolation.

Of course, the abstraction that carries the greatest authority for us is our construct of ideas that, together, represent 'who you know yourself to be'—which is quite distinct from the self-discovery that is made possible by the whisperings of the present moment. To really listen to the present requires a willingness to be changed by it—which is precisely why the 'known self' stands apart: it has a status quo to maintain, which keeps us from feeling certain things and assures us in feeling other things. It is a world that we are commandingly in charge of: we can shut things out of that world and choose for ourselves what to admit. The impulse to do so is natural enough: you turn away from something you would rather not feel; you pretend not to notice or choose not to see something else, because you know full well where it would lead. But natural though such filtering may be, it helps to recognize its specific purpose: to hold back the energy of maternal Being, the wisdom of Logos, and forget. Furthermore, *the world you thereby* *create and live in is no longer **this** world, but **your** world—a privately screened world that is overseen by the obsessive meddling of the inner supervisor.*

To set up and maintain the private catacomb of the 'known self', then, is to take on the task of holding back the energy and perplexity of Being with the effort of your doing. And be apprised: effort *is* required for the task—*the effort of active neglect.* We tend to think of neglect as simply a lack of attention, but it is actually a *withholding* of attention and works something like an isometric exercise.* Each little thing we neglect—a feeling, someone we find irritating, the wet of the rain on our face, a personal criticism, an unwanted bit of news—requires a little effort to stall it on the periphery of our attention. *Physical* effort. Since the sensitivity of the embodied mind is what joins us to the world—belonging as naturally to its all-aware continuum as everything else—it is with that sensitivity that our willful neglect has to contend. Our most common recourse is to diminish that sensitivity with tension: we stifle the body's intelligence so that we experience our conscious flesh as unconscious matter. The felt self becomes the felt body. **The work of neglect to which we commit ourselves, then, is what compresses the mind's sensitivity into increasingly smaller spheres.** The 'known self' simply does not exist independent of the willful doing that constricts the body with tension to keep the energy of the present from interfering with it.

Of course, we all experience tensions that come and go—muscles contract to move the body, for instance; but the private tyranny of the 'known self' relies on a habitual or chronic tension that actually starts to create adhesions in the connective tissue—compromising flexibility and responsiveness in the muscles. Equally inimical, such tension locks up emotions and memories to keep them from being acknowledged or expressed, perpetuating self-division. The more of the world we hold back, the more isometrics of neglect we require, and the more we hem in our own living, until eventually our world feels cramped, pressured and riddled with stress fractures. The many-chambered room begets the many-chambered world.

---

* As a kid I did isometric exercises in gym class in high school. In an isometric exercise the body pushes against itself with equal pressure, so that nothing moves, however hard you push. For instance, you might put both palms together in front of the chest, and push them as hard as possible against each other. If the force from each side is the same, the hands stay still. But it is exhausting.

When your *world* feels fragmented, stressed and deprived of oxygen, it's because your *body* is. The task of preserving the 'known self' by holding certain energies of the world at bay is hard work; in fact, neglect is exhausting, because it requires the body to work against itself all the time. More than a little wisdom is found in the words of dancer and teacher Willy Blok Hanson: "There is no old age, only neglect."[156] Of course, we are all human, and neglect is as inevitable as taxes. But even so, her perspective helps: a tight body is closed to the river of the world's energy; the world doesn't wear us down so much as we wear ourselves down. Over the years the toll of neglect on the body—habitual and hardening—is beyond calculation. Furthermore, that toll is compounded by the ability of the unconscious mind to express as physical symptoms what our conscious mind refuses to acknowledge. The work of John Sarno and colleagues in elucidating that ability, and in helping patients overcome chronic conditions by acknowledging issues that have long been buried in neglect, is not just remarkable—it is also remarkably neglected by the medical profession. But more on that later.

Neglect also leads us to think that the compromises of old age are inevitable, because as the tensions of neglect squeeze consciousness out of the body, we begin to experience it as biological machinery—and because all machines wear out and break down, we expect the body to as well. That misapprehension fulfills its own prophecy: the more we adhere to the machine model of the body, the more we isolate it from the sensibilities of the world and consolidate it within its own skin. It becomes heavy, rigid, and stuck—at war with itself and more *likely* to suffer injury and 'breakdowns'.

The pace at which the body actually renews itself is wondrous. It has been determined that in the space of a few years every molecule in your body is replaced. In that regard, the oldest part of it has been with you about four years, while the newest part is more recent than your last breath. In his most famous dictum, Heraclitus points out that "one cannot step twice into the same river, for the water into which you first stepped has flowed on."[157] By the same token you literally cannot breathe twice into the same body, for the body into which you last breathed has flowed on: some of the breath you took in has become part of your body, and former parts of your body are released into the world on your out-breath. The molecular processes of the body join with the world to create cells, eliminate cells, process nutrients and toxins, and reflect your every thought. In fact, thought continuously transforms matter inside the body and can even, on the quantum level, transform matter outside the body. In ways we may not even imagine, the self and the world continuously transform together.

The young children in our society, in their innocent experience of the world's energy, know no kinship with the machine and have to be systematically taught by adults to see their bodies that way. They increasingly learn to create a world that is abstract rather than ordinary, confined rather than expansive; they learn how to achieve a fixed independence from the world, and how to monitor and shore up that independence; they learn to dismiss the unknown rather than attend to it; and they learn to understand tiredness—which makes you feel worn down like a machine—as a stage on the way to exhaustion. In teaching them that, we do our children a disservice. Exhaustion—the aftermath of an unfettered exchange of energies with the world—has been called, accurately I think, the ultimate bliss. It imparts a clarity to body, mind and world. By contrast, tiredness is a woolly state that prevents you from connecting clearly with the world or yourself; it results from the attrition of holding back or trying to control the exchange of energies with the world. It betokens a diminished capacity for relationship. In fact, if we instead described tiredness as a state in which you *cannot* exhaust yourself, we would be describing it accurately. When that kind of tiredness sets in, it usually signals that you are worn down by the braking actions of your own neglect and deafened to the calling of the world. I think we unconsciously hold on to such tiredness, because it serves as an excuse, or justifies a fear. In my experience, once we recognize that subtle, unconscious mode of storytelling we can simply let go of our tiredness—and when we do so, it feels a lot like taking your foot off the brake pedal.

Such instances of deep neglect lead to a body so divided against itself that it has baffled the sensitivity of its own inner corridor: cloaked in forgetfulness, numbed to its own consciousness and consolidated against the world, the desensitized body becomes our fortified castle, guarding the private world within. That private world underscores another by-product of our intentioned forgetfulness: **any instance of neglect diminishes our capacity for relationship.** That point was succinctly made by Zen poet Paul Reps when he observed, "When we see someone we like we are in heaven. When we see someone we dislike we are in hell."[158] Seeing someone we dislike, we rein in our capacity for relationship, compressing it with the isometrics of neglect; but that compression diminishes more than our potential for exchange with that other person: our capacity for relationship with the world in general is diminished. And of course your capacity for relationship *is* your capacity for Being. "I relate; therefore I am" has as its corollary "I partially relate; therefore I partially am." By deliberately stunting our capacity for relationship, we stunt our very Being. We choke it. The more we withdraw into the privacy of our world, the more we constrict it. That is the nature of our self-made hell.

The etymology of *private* reminds us of the privations of our self-made perdition. Its roots go back to the Latin word *privus*, which literally meant "that which stands by itself"; *privus* later evolved into the verb *privare*, the primary meaning of which is "to rob, deprive, bereave." By retracting into a unipolar consciousness, we rob ourselves of our own sensational life, deprive ourselves of the divine present, and bereave ourselves of conscious being. Thus robbed, the body feels abandoned, and our lives, at their core, feel a persistent sense of lack. The more earnestly we seek a clear *idea* of what we lack, and a clear *solution* to it, the farther we turn from the endarkened chambers of our neglected body—and, too, from the life that we seek.

That is not to say that when we are lost to ourselves, we need only to look within the body's depths, as though our true self were somehow contained there. As we have seen, our Being is entirely contingent on the world around us. The roots of our truth, the roots that nourish us, don't reach down inside the body, but out into the world that sustains us. It's true that your truths register in the resonance of the body—but as with Heidegger's view of an artwork, the truths do not reside there; **the body doesn't *possess* the truths of your Being; they are not isolated from the world—they reside in it, waiting to be embraced.** In fact, 'what you are' is held by the world, just as 'what the world is' is held by you: your relationship to it is akin to the relationship between the fragment of a hologram and the whole. Look to it and there you are, if only you could recognize yourself.

We can understand the mind's sensitivity, then, in much the way that Heidegger helped us to understand the sensitivity of an artwork: each provides entrances to the truth of the world around it, which are the deepest truths of your being. As your sensitivity dilates through one sphere after another, you shed the constraints of the 'known self' the way you might shed a suit of clothes, until **your intelligence steps** out of *who* you are and into *where* you are, naked to the unknown present. When you feel *where* you are, you are feeling the weave of interrelationships that constitutes the wholeness of the self and extends continuously and without limit through all that is. When we seek to be *whole*, when we seek *health*, when we seek to be fully *integrated*—and each of those words derives from roots meaning "whole" or "to make whole"—we will be chasing phantoms if we look to find them within some presumed 'unity' of the body/mind, as though they were inner strengths, and as though the perplexities and inconveniences of the world outside were impediments to be faced down. When we really look to the world, we find that we are bone of its bone, flesh of its flesh, and blood of its blood. Wholeness of the self discounts nothing, for it belongs to all; **the wholeness we seek, and the qualities of presence, creativity and freedom that bespeak it, lie not in a putative unity of the body/mind, but in the unity of the body/world: the unity of our dual nature with the world's.** And that is the very unity that every instance of our neglect seeks to disrupt.

The body/world is the shared present that awaits beyond all the privations of the 'known' world we inhabit; it is the maternal continuum of Being that cradles each of our lives in the arms of its all-aware intelligence. The consciousness into which the hero journeys—the mutual awareness to which he submits—is just a story, of course, until it awakens something in you. Suppose that in the hectic pace of day-to-day living your male element has been running independent of your female element to the extent that the part of you that is able to 'just be' has been exiled. When that happens, we carry an invisible hell within us: that hell is the dark catacomb within the body that has been deprived of consciousness by our willful neglect; it is the mindless, biological machinery of our flesh, which we drive ever onward, pushing it through the frictions and abrasions of our self-conflicts; it is the consolidation of our flesh that has been sequestered from the light of the world by our incarnated 'shoulds' and 'shouldn'ts'. As a culture we have shouted down the subtle, all-informing song of the female element, buried her in the shadows, and pronounced that accomplishment a triumph of personal freedom. When the shadows of abstraction in the body stunt its living thought, they dull us to perplexity and corrode our capacity for exchange. 'Hell' is being trapped in a body that your own neglect has turned into idiotic, lifeless flesh.

Orpheus shows us what we face in the descent into our neglected bodies; and the particulars of his journey will be familiar to all those who have done extensive bodywork, for they will have discovered how many checks and blocks and restraints we commonly place on our bodies—especially where the breath is concerned—and they will have realized how unthinkingly we judge and direct and arrest and neglect the very energies that naturally course through the welcoming corridor and draw us into wholeness. They will also have experienced how many little deaths must be faced in order to restore Being to our doing. Descending into the body of the earth, Orpheus is accompanied only by the art of his music, which soothes all who hear it and brings them into harmony with the world. With that skill alone, he must countenance the successive images of tyranny and fear and death that dwell in the realm of Hades: he crosses Styx, the river of death; faces Cerberus, the three-headed dog at death's door; passes by the flitting Shades; passes numerous images of death; and finally meets face-to-face the Lord of Death, whose hard visage softens to the pull of the music until he weeps tears of iron. At every step of the way Orpheus encounters the tyranny of the 'known self'—"self-terrorized, fear-haunted"—and *dissolves* it (i.e., "undoes its solutions") with the harmonies of his art. In doing that, Orpheus confronted the death of the isolated doer in all its varied guises.

Restoring consciousness to the body may seem redundant to some people: after all, we can all consciously feel the body. Similarly, we might protest that the ability to *do* anything actually presupposes *being*. Renowned author and translator Stephen Mitchell addresses the same issue in yet a third way: if the Tao is in and through all things, how can you lose it? Mitchell answers, "You can never lose the Tao. But you can find it."[159] We might similarly understand that you can never lose Being, but you can find it, exactly as *you can never lose your body, but you can find it.*

When you do find the body, when you recover the pelvic intelligence and once again connect with the bottomless stillness of your being, the many-chambered room softens and opens to reveal the spaciousness of the corridor, which welcomes the light of the world and joins you to 'what is'. According to Lao-tzu, as we soften into the body, as we soften into the present, we are allowing ourselves to soften into life itself:

Men are born soft and supple;
dead, they are stiff and hard.
Plants are born tender and pliant;
dead, they are brittle and dry.

Thus whoever is stiff and inflexible
is a disciple of death.
Whoever is soft and yielding
is a disciple of life.[160]

Softness, in yielding to the world, comes into harmony with it and is *informed* by it. We might also note that *harmony reveals itself in grace:* the grace in the flight of the barn swallow is an ever-moving resolution of the give-and-take between gravity and aerodynamic lift, and it evinces the larger harmony by which we all live. It evinces that harmony because the swallow's flight is informed by all that is: by the waft of the breeze, the insects that fly on it, the disturbances in the breeze created by trees and buildings and hills, and the other swallows flying in its vicinity. All of those inform its flight and so are revealed in it.

Grace, of course, is associated with the female element: it is even used as a girl's name. The essence of grace lies in its transformations, which are made possible by its essential, yielding softness. What is not soft cannot be informed, and so cannot harmonize—and it is of more than a little interest to us that the OED describes *informed* as "enlightened" and lists as a meaning of *uninformed* "not showing animation; lifeless, mechanical." What cannot be *in*formed cannot be *trans*formed. And life depends on transformations.

Of course, the softness that opens the body to the light of consciousness and enables it to be informed also leaves us exposed; but our choice between exposure or neglect is also the choice between transformation or the stagnations of our "organized inadequacy." As Larry Dossey explains in his book *Space, Time and Medicine,*

> It is the quality of fragility, the capacity for being "shaken up," that paradoxically is the key to growth. Structures that are insulated from disturbance are protected from change. They are stagnant and never evolve towards a more complex form.[161]

What finally enables us to permit fragility within ourselves is the hard-won wisdom that finds itself informed and sustained by the deeper harmony of the world around it. "If you receive the world, the Tao will never leave you." Receptivity is the beginning of the mutual awareness between self and world, which itself is the essence of self-awareness: "Experience this; let this experience you,"[162] as Paul Reps wrote. When the shadows of neglect dissipate from your body, and the hard edges of division within it and around it disappear, you open profoundly to the world, allowing it to experience the whole of you, even as you experience the whole of it. In that body/world continuum, colors and movements and shapes and vibrations pass into you and touch your core and inform it. And the still point of that core, that life-affirming center of being in the pelvic bowl, far from being dormant, responds to the world, resonates with the present, and awakens you to it. Such an experience allows the present to lay its hands on the innermost awareness of your felt self and speak to you wordlessly. **Ultimately, the act of surrendering the corridor within to the present, so that it can come to rest in your very core—that act *is* the heroic submission to 'what is': it opens you to yourself, and to the felt present that knows you and calls you by name.** To allow the present to touch your core is to choose life over self-tyranny and awaken to an intelligence that you do not possess, but belong to. We might call it the intelligence of Being: the five-dimensional energy of the continuum that sustains our lives and urges us to risk a surrender to wholeness. Taking that risk will threaten our very identity, for it will reveal the thinking self to be no other than the felt whole.

The Ordinary Hero

Myth shows us that the hero is the one who steps beyond the realm of stasis and habit, leaves the idea-bound structures that stand like battlements against Being, and softens to 'what is'. The tyrant, activated by a fear of the female, tries to lock his world down against the transforming currents of Being. Of course, as Lao-tzu pointed out, "whoever is stiff and inflexible is a disciple of death." Whoever seeks to stand apart from the changing world cannot harmonize with it and so—wittingly or otherwise—will sow disharmony. In the long run, to seek independence from the world is to destroy and be destroyed.

Unfortunately, the default option of our society is that of tyranny: over the self, first and foremost, and over the world around us as a natural extension of that.

It's not hard to see why tyranny is the default option for us: Being has no interest in stasis, no investment in self-importance, no special exceptions for those who would rather sit out the dance; the great, mindful swirl of Becoming is all there is, and all that is exists only by virtue of it. The Universal Law places us in relationship to the process of revelation around us, not to some fixed reality. To fully abandon yourself to Being—to open your heart to it and join it with all your heart—is to abandon yourself to the mysteries of necessity through which Being will shape your growth and transformations and awakenings. It is a journey without seat belts or air bags—it offers only companionship and self-revelation and the love that sustains all things, and it knows you as a mother her child. It is not for nothing, then, that myth represents that journey to reunite with Being as the 'hero's' journey. It cannot be made without heroic courage, heroic honesty, heroic sacrifice. What our abstract-loving culture grossly distorts, though, is the nature of the hero, who is popularly understood to 'stand apart' from the ordinary world, with his lofty aims and transcendent abilities. All such ideas try to situate the hero in a sphere of "self-achieved independence" and are clearly products of the tyrant's fantasy: an achieving male, splendidly elevated above the realm of the merely mundane.

No, no, no: heroic courage is what *joins* us to the ordinary. It is what enables us to recognize the felt self within the felt whole, and it cherishes the companionship of the mundane particulars of the world—such things as might delight a child. Heroic courage accepts the slights of the world with equanimity and stands against injustice with simplicity. And it forsakes the master-slave relationships of self-tyranny, by which the self commands the self, and learns instead what it is to attend to Being. That learning curve is a subtle process, involving a million ordinary acts that each, in its way, is its own heroic journey.

When you run into someone you would rather not talk to, do you disconnect from Being and fragment yourself, or deepen your connection to Being to find guidance there? To pause and connect with the guidance of Being, even for a moment, is to take the hero's journey. Or you drop something on the floor and bend down to pick it up. Simple enough—but the habits of tyranny run deep. Do you pick it up in response to a command from the head that leaves you disconnected from being? If so, then the way in which you bend down will likely constrict and suffocate feeling in the pelvic bowl, rather than allowing it to open you to the moment. The felt self morphs into the dumb and obedient 'felt body' in the blink of an eye, so deep are the ruts that lead to it. To pick something up from the floor with the core of your being fully available to the wild peace of the present—feeling the thing as a whole—is an act of ordinary heroism: in its particulars it, too, constitutes the mythic journey of the hero. Similarly, to allow the teacup in the fulsomeness of its specificity to touch your core as you reach for it, pick it up and take a sip is an act of ordinary heroism that entails a momentary excursion into the uncharted realm of being. We might say that to take a moment to become completely passive to all the sensations of the body, so that you merge with 'what is' and acknowledge it with the full depth of your sensitivity, is at the same time the journey of Orpheus to the underworld and an opening of the soul into the sensitivities of the felt self. To allow the present to touch your core and to enter the mutual awareness of awakened consciousness is to relive the moment in which Odysseus awakens to the guiding presence of Athena.

It is with such acts of ordinary heroism that we defeat tyranny. It is with such simple excursions that we marry our doing and our being, enabling each to fulfill the other—for it is only in the union of those complementary opposites that the strength inherent in each comes fully into its own. To more fully appreciate the nature of that union, though, it would help to understand what the male strength is, what the female strength is, and how necessary both are for the evolution of our consciousness into the felt mystery of the wide world. It is to that issue that the next chapter is devoted.

Exercise Four: **Ordinary Heroism**

There is a pencil on the floor. You pick it up. What could be simpler? But try it, and pay attention, questioningly. Are you *deciding* to pick it up and then executing the order? If you don't *will* yourself to pick it up, then how *can* you? Is it possible to pick it up as an act of self-achieved submission? And if so, how does that happen? If you submit, where does the impulse to pick it up come from? As you bend down or rise, is there a sense of effort? Does that effort open you to the world or focus you on the self? Can you trace the roots of that effort back to willfulness? Are the processes of your thinking and Being happening in separate realms? If so, that's pretty interesting. Can you allow the energies of your thinking to course down the corridor and merge with your being? Can you release the awareness of the self as a whole into the heart and let it greet the mindful present? Can you "feel the thing as a whole" without willing yourself to do so—without trying? Can you feel the companionship of the present feeling you?

Being is relationship. When willfulness asserts its "self-achieved independence," it displaces relationship. What then is your relationship with the pencil? Do you feel a "self-achieved independence" from it? Is your relationship with it one of subject/object? If so, you are looking at the pencil as though through a windowpane—which places your sensitivity in the second sphere. When you start to bend towards it, does the body feel like levers and pistons working to achieve a task? If so, your sensitivity has shifted into the third sphere. But how can we transcend division and unify duality and still pick up the pencil? How can we integrate what we know so that it does not exile us from where we are? Such questions help us pay attention; they help us expose the chameleon

of 'normal' in our thinking and actions. The co-
nundrum of our self-achieved divisions cannot be
solved by any answer, though. It can only be made
unnecessary by branching into new experience.

The journey of the hero shows us what is necessary to do that: surrender, surrender, surrender—to
your life, now, which is shared with all that surrounds you and is shared with the ordinariness to
which we indissolubly belong. When the present permeates the deliberate forgetfulness that makes up the 'known self'—when the present comes to rest in our core—then we can feel the pencil as a whole
within the whole to which we ourselves belong. That kinship reveals it
to be no longer a dead thing on the nondescript floor, but a living revelation of the self. From that starting point of mutual awareness, we
undertake a journey in which *we surrender to what we might discover
in picking up the pencil*; and so we are carried out of our agenda of
doing and into the experience of being. The journey into the unknown
present always requires the spirit of discovery. Even in so simple a task
as picking up a pencil.

Two Axes, One Purpose

Nature longs for opposites and effects her harmony from them.

—Aristotle

What can we gain by sailing to the moon if we are not able to cross the abyss that separates us from ourselves?

—Thomas Merton

When the body's intelligence declines,
cleverness and knowledge step forth.

—*Tao Te Ching,* Chapter 18

5 | A Perspective on Perspective

The Male and Female Strengths

The history of Western culture over the last eight thousand years follows a broad exponential curve—beginning with the Neolithic Revolution and accelerating precipitously into and through the twentieth century—in which man increasingly stepped back from the world of nature, acquired technological mastery over it, and gained specific knowledge of it that enabled him to evict wonder and kinship from every pine needle and worm and drop of rain, until now he finally stands alone: a world unto himself, superior to all he surveys, without peer, he also finds himself lacking spiritual relevance, purpose and affinity for his world—lacking even the assuring sense that his own experience is real. Of course, reality is fulfilled only through relationship—and how can any of us relate to a world to which we believe our lives are fundamentally irrelevant? That is the problem we have created for ourselves. The trajectory of the arc that brought us here has been driven by the urge within the male element to assert itself and refute its dependence on anything feminine. As we have seen, that urge has uprooted us from our own sensitivity, and our diminished sensitivity has in turn numbed us to the body, to the earth, to its wisdom, and to the guiding imagery and intuitions of conscious being. As the child individuates and separates from its mother, so too has modern man individuated and separated from maternal Being.

Today we are witnessing a slow and reluctant awakening to the crisis to which our separation from Being has brought both us and our planet. As a species that prides itself on reason, you might think we could have anticipated that being without Being would be a problem.

But in fairness, the evolution of human consciousness requires the mature participation of both its female and male aspects—it cannot happen otherwise. The male aspect had some catching up to do, and if it has been a little overzealous in acting out the teenage-hood of its individuation—charging with self-infatuation straight into the self-glorification of the tyrant's grasping independence—it has certainly gotten the job done. And now humanity faces a choice: we can either integrate or disintegrate.

If we are to take on the task of integration—if as a culture we are to extricate ourselves from our adolescent self-centeredness and mature into grounded and aware adulthood—we need to better appreciate the distinctiveness of our male and female strengths, and how each is necessary to the evolution of our consciousness. Their unity is not just a sum of their parts; it creates a generative dynamic so specific that it actually indicates the work we were born to do—the purpose of our humanity here on earth.

The revelations of male and female differences that come to us from myth, and brain-scanning technologies, and prehistoric art all point to their distinct strengths; and so do such polarities as 'earth and sky', 'being and doing', 'yin and yang', 'belly and cranium' or 'immanent and transcendent'. What they all, in their way, suggest with regard to the female aspect of our consciousness is that **the female strength lies in its ability to dwell within phenomena and integrate them.** Being, of course, is not a thing or a state—it is a process of continuous integration. So it is with female consciousness: it is endlessly transformative because it "massively connects and communicates," bending to accommodate all that is—just as Alan Alda risked being changed by true listening. Dwelling within phenomena, it "feels the thing as a whole, from the inside"—reminding us that *integrate* comes from the Latin word *integrare*, "to make whole." The challenge of achieving integration presents particular demands: you can't take in the wholeness of something objectively—you have to feel it as a whole "from the inside"; in other words, *integration requires immanence*. But appreciating a thing in its wholeness also requires that you yourself be whole: a diminished capacity for relationship cannot relate wholly. We should note, too, that if the female principle is integration, then it must integrate paradox and perplexity, feeling the unity that expresses itself through all the seeming contradictions of the present.

If Being is all-inclusive, the work of the *male* aspect of our consciousness is by inclination selectively *ex*clusive: pure male doing dedicates its attention to narrowly defined ends and the means of achieving them. What drives it, then, is the *idea* of what needs doing and how to do it. Such ideas are abstracted from the undivided whole of being. To formulate them, the male element must first abstract *itself* from an aspect of Being and achieve an outside, objective vantage point on it; from that vantage point it can gain the perspective that will birth the idea. The male aspect of consciousness shows up very differently in the hero and the tyrant. The hero leaves the familiar terrain of his community to acquire an understanding that, brought back, releases new life into it; but throughout his journey he never turns his back on the guidance of Being, or suffers a setback if he does. By contrast, the tyrant occludes the guidance of Being by withdrawing into his "self-achieved independence," and from that prospect he gains perspectives by which he can accumulate power and consolidate his position. Despite their differences, though, both hero and tyrant show us that **the strength of the male aspect of our consciousness lies in its ability to stand apart from phenomena and gain perspective on them.** Such perspective enables analysis and reveals both sequence and consequence; those elucidate possible paths for action; the path that is chosen becomes the vision that requires the doing. Whereas female Being seeks an active integration of the transforming present, male doing seeks an active transformation of the world according to its newfound perspectives. The hero, of course, seeks that transformation from a place of self-achieved submission, the tyrant from his position of self-achieved independence.

Acquiring perspective on something, whether literal or metaphoric, necessarily involves a basic differentiation between 'I' and 'it': **we pull away from a phenomenon, stand apart from it, and look at it objectively.** In "pulling away from" it we are reminded of the root meaning of *abstraction;* and in "looking at" it we find the root meaning of *perspective.* Perspective not only creates the fundamental duality of subject/object—it also grants the subject a single and empowering view of the object. That view may reveal several of its *aspects* (a word that is related to *perspective*), but it can never disclose the whole—for, like the far side of the moon, parts will be hidden from sight and therefore subject to neglect. The perspective that initiates male doing, then, can never reveal the whole. The aspects that do come into view, though, will help formulate an idea of the nature of the phenomenon—which reminds us that *idea* literally means "the look of something." The young Noh actor was achieving perspective on the old lady precisely to present his 'idea' of her: male perspective formulates duplicates.

There is a reason, of course, that we were all born with both male and female aspects of consciousness. All-inclusive, all-aware Being just is, and feels all and integrates all, but has no perspective because it neither narrows its awareness nor steps outside itself to have a look. Its multitudinous aspects are felt as relationships within a whole, and are not manifest objectively. Pure Being, then, lacks analysis and the tolerance for exclusion necessary for perspective on itself; but analysis and exclusion are what bring certain features into consciousness—and **only what is brought into consciousness can be integrated into consciousness, stimulating its evolution.**

The thinking of the male element, on the other hand, amasses perspectives on everything, and catalogs those perspectives, and systemizes those perspectives, and assigns them relative values, all the while discerning cause and effect. All of that is brought into consciousness; as such, it awakens us to certain possibilities of choice. But however many perspectives are accumulated, they can never be integrated into a whole by the ideas of the unipolar, detached male view—at most they can merely supply some *perspectives* on wholeness. The act of integration—of "making a whole"—can only be the function of a whole; in us, that whole is the embodied axis of our consciousness, through which abstract perspective reconciles with present being, and is rendered as sensitivity. That integration is the foundational act of ordinary heroism. By contrast, a perspective that remains unintegrated stands resolutely apart from being and insists on its authoritative tyranny. The heroic and the tyrannical are the two choices available to the male element, and both concern perspective. Since the 'normal' of our culture is the consciousness of tyranny, it makes sense to look first at the consequences of the tyrant's choice.

The Unintegrated Perspective

Both the hero and the tyrant transcend the familiar "organized inadequacy" of the known world. The hero leaves because his spiritual center of gravity has shifted into the unknown landscape of Being, and he yields to its pull and follows. Something altogether different happens with the tyrant: fearful of Being, he has no inclination to venture into it; **instead, the tyrant withdraws his spiritual center of gravity from the world and consolidates it *within himself*.** By that act he separates himself from his community without having to leave it: the modern syndrome. Even so, *his act of self-achieved independence gives him a new perspective on his community that reveals it as a transformed entity: it now appears objectified and exploitable.* Though familiar to him, it has no claim on his gratitude or his heart, and it is no longer felt as the living whole to which he belongs. The One has broken into the many, and the many are found not to be a manifold revelation of Being, but individual components of a system. Because his concerns are now self-centered, his perspective on that system reveals value only where it can work to his advantage.

The tyrant's fear, then, births in him an addiction to perspective, and leaves him "alert at every hand to meet and battle back the anticipated aggressions of his environment," as Joseph Campbell put it. By keeping him at a fearful distance from the world, his addiction cuts him off from its spiritual life, persuades him the world's center is within himself, and reveals around him only threat or expedients for his personal advantage. The tyrant's addiction to perspective, then, is the mechanism behind the neutron bomb parlor trick, and it gives us a useful benchmark: to the extent that you feel your spiritual center to be *within yourself*, to the extent that the life of the world around you looks like a grand functioning system rather than an expression of the One Presence, to the extent that you feel your community to be irrelevant, you are looking from the perspective of the mythological tyrant. And that means that your perspectives, which would otherwise be a strength necessary to the evolution of your consciousness, are instead arresting that evolution. As we said earlier, it is the 'normal givens' of our world that hold us back. Nor is the arrest of that evolution unintentional: the tyrant within us fears experience—the words *fear, peril* and *experience* share the same root, remember—and he will defend his status quo without reservation, even if doing so should threaten the world around him. Because the tyrant's perspectives are unintegrated, they are unencumbered by responsibility; and so they encourage him to use his life to build his 'empire' and secure his future by working to his own narrow advantage whenever he can. As long as we ourselves are stuck in the consciousness of the tyrant, that's exactly how we will use our lives. I know that only because I have explored that terrain so fully in my own life, and can still occasionally feel its seductive pull.

What we have outlined here, of course, is a basic working model of tyranny that applies across the board, from self-tyranny to political totalitarianism; and the model tells us that the more perspectives the tyrant has on the community from which he has set himself apart, the more that knowledge will serve him in the manipulation and control of its resources. As such, we would also do well to recognize in our model the outlines of unregulated capitalism. In the values it upholds, capitalism encourages a perspective that breaks the One living mother that is our Earth into a diversity of raw materials, concentrates on defending individual rights rather than on gathering around collective responsibilities, rewards power and its consolidation, and places economic considerations before all others. Its emphasis on acquisition makes capitalism not the natural ally of democracy, but its ever-present foil. We have already noted that *capitalism* comes from a Latin word meaning "head"—it literally means "headism"—and that it systematically gratifies the values of the head rather than those of the heart. Because those values encourage isolation, they foment hallucinations in all we do—hallucinations that tell us, for example, that the cyclist riding in the rain at the side of the road is less successful than the commuter driving by in the Mercedes sedan. Hallucinations that persuade us that we are entitled to find bananas at the grocery store if we've got them on our list. Hallucinations that convince us that the elderly, whose ability to contribute to the bottom line is diminished, are an inconvenience. Hallucinations that persuade us to define 'the natural world' as everything other than ourselves, and to see in the plants and animals around us not companionship and teachings, but resources or inconveniences or mere decoration. Hallucinations that persuade us that the imbalances we inflict on the natural world are problems best solved by technology, thereby sparing us any need to question who we are or to consider the parallel imbalances we inflict on our own bodies and minds.

When our needs and emotions become entangled with our hallucinations, and both are estranged from the whole that sustains us, the damage we inflict can show up like a bleeding wound for all to see. Caught in our amnesiac fantasy, we can so completely detach from "feeling the thing as a whole" that it loses its ability to bring perspective to our isolated imaginings. The moral restraint afforded us by the whole has nothing to do with abiding by certain 'shoulds' or 'shouldn'ts' and has everything to do with the mythic "self-achieved submission" by which the hero devotedly surrenders to the coursing intelligence of Being—which is inclusive of all and brings all into relationship with the whole. Without that surrender, our actions cannot arise from the grace of Being, and so pose a direct threat to it. When we awaken from our hallucinations, it is often to find our lives in tatters, and what we hold most dear to be imperiled. Extreme examples are familiar enough: Tiger Woods, Bernie Madoff and Bill Clinton have all faced the cost of such isolated imaginings very publicly. Whether our fantasies mislead us into blind entitlement or to actions of ruinous discord, they are all a direct outcome of the **unintegrated perspectives** to which we as a society have devoted ourselves.

Our 'headist' attachment to perspective is so normal for us that it almost stands beyond the reach of our ability to question it. But consider, for a moment, how much of your waking awareness is dominated by the voice in your head: advising you endlessly, supervising you, commenting on what you just did or should be doing, and obsessing over endless perspectives on the various broken pieces of your life—perspectives that have been locked up and systemized into your 'known self' and your 'known world'; perspectives that continue to promise redemption from any problems, if only you can accumulate enough of them. In general we have so lost touch with our conscious being that we make no effort to integrate those perspectives: we can no longer, like the hero, bring them home to the pelvic intelligence so that thinking and Being can evolve together. And so we remain in our heads, and rely on our unintegrated perspectives to supervise the 'many' of our shattered body/world. And that reliance is absolute: without those unintegrated perspectives, there could be no tyranny of the self or of the world.

Our self-tyranny, then, interrupts and organizes our lives and thinking from the detached perspective of a *supervisor,* which literally means "overseer." The identification of that supervisor with the head is reinforced by the fact that we literally see from the eyes—the center of the cranial pole of consciousness. All the authority figures of our culture are based on that supervisor in the head, placed on high and set apart—like the judge who presides over a court, looking down dispassionately on its various warring factions and using the power of his position to make a ruling and administer justice. This model is radically at odds with, for instance, an aboriginal healing circle. Other such authority figures include the general on the hill overlooking the battle, or the manager in the office above the factory floor, or the helmsman overseeing the journey of the tall-masted ship. That supervisory model seems natural to us, because it is how we relate to the self.

Every resource marshaled by the supervisor in our heads—every duplicate we construct, every rule we create for ourselves or others, every map of how things 'should be'—issues from the unintegrated perspectives we gather and systemize into models of the world: we judge the world's particulars and divide them into schemes of good/bad, useful/irrelevant, mine/theirs. Such value judgments are implicitly embedded in any perspective that is not integrated, and they advise us tyrannically in all we do. Unintegrated perspectives are so deeply bound to judgment that we could also refer to them as *judicative perspectives*. When Parmenides warned that the senses can deceive us, and when Plato praised "the man who pursues truth by applying his pure and unadulterated thought to the pure and unadulterated object, cutting himself off as much as possible from his eyes and ears and virtually all the rest of his body"[163]—they were saying, in effect, that *only* an unintegrated perspective can judge the pure truth of a thing, and that *only while a perspective remains unintegrated does its judgment remain reliably pure.* That view represents the unipolar outlook of our entire culture: moving into the head, we become forgetful of the whole, and are left with only our judicative perspectives to rely on; and so we argue over them, and defend them, and compare them, and refine them, and support them with data, and hold them to represent the truth and to refute the truth of other perspectives—but we do not integrate them. As a culture we do not even know how to any more.

So deeply committed are we to perspectives, and so unaware even of what it means to integrate perspectives, that we can only stand resolutely apart from the world, impotent to join it. As Cistercian monk and writer Thomas Merton observed, we

> have been "turned around," and we are always aware of ourselves as spectators. This spectatorship is a wound in our nature, a kind of original sin ... for which "healing" is urgently required. Yet we refuse healing because we insist on preserving our status as spectators. This is the only identity we understand.[164]

And, as Merton understood, it is a mistaken identity—one to which we have so deeply habituated that it's hard even to imagine what it might feel like to allow our male perspectives to travel down the embodied axis and come to rest in the integrating center of our female being: the pelvic intelligence. But until that happens, *our consciousness will be stuck in the "original sin" of spectatorship, ceaselessly amending and arranging our unintegrated perspectives.*

The Self-Consciousness of Tyranny

The ultimate trophy for the tyrant within, of course, is the self: the more perspectives we can accumulate on the self, the more we will be able to direct it, judge it, correct it, praise it, blame it, encourage it, warn it and generally control it. And so in the same way that the tyrant stands apart from his community and gains perspective on it, we stand apart from the 'self' and watch it, and gain perspective on it, forgetful of the journey home. Standing in exile from the self, of course, means that we can no longer *feel* it as a whole, from the inside—at best we can 'know' the self and feel the body; but that's okay, because that place of exile enables us to supervise everything.

Of course, any time we are supervising the self rather than feeling it, the self is literally observing the self; and that, by definition, is *self-consciousness*: a defining characteristic of the 'known self'. As Alan Watts writes,

> The self-conscious brain, like the self-conscious heart, is a disorder, and manifests itself in the acute feeling of separation between "I" and my experience. The brain can only assume its proper behavior when consciousness is doing what it is designed for: not writhing and whirling to get out of present experience, but being effortlessly aware of it.[165]

In the twentieth century a great deal of scientific thought and debate was dedicated to determining that you cannot observe an event without affecting it. That is the Universal Law of Interrelationship at work, and it is the inescapable reality of living in the world. Every time you hear it, smell it, or even *think* about it, you are affecting it, even as it affects you: when you feel the skin of an apple with your finger, that exchange leaves both of you changed. If you have ever felt yourself being watched, you will have felt the effects of *being* observed. If you knew your phone was tapped, for instance, your conversation would be radically altered. Even as simple an event as standing at a bus stop can be complicated if you feel someone's eyes on you: how you stand, where you put your hands, and what you look at and when may all be called into question. Reality TV is painful in its unreality for that reason: conscious of being monitored by cameras and crew, participants exude self-consciousness in all they do.

If we observe *ourselves*, a similar effect takes hold; and when nothing in the world is more important than the gravitational center of your self-centered, isolated 'I', nothing else can command your attention as urgently—not even the intimate whispering of the world around you. And so the self-consciousness of self-tyranny soon leads to self-absorption—a sort of black hole of awareness. Once the whispered guidance of the world is obscured, the authoritative supervisor of the 'known self' takes over and drags you into a sort of cybernetic nightmare: to observe anything is to change it; when you observe yourself doing, it changes what you do, which you observe, which changes what you do, which you observe, et cetera. It is a self-made isolation chamber in which you cannot receive guidance from the outside world because what you mainly see is your doing and what you mainly hear are the directives of the inner helmsman. As self-consciousness grows, the white noise in your head buzzes louder and louder, overwhelming the signal of Being. Obsessing over your own cybernetics, trying to steer what you do and how you do it, you eventually forget the world. The narcissism of our culture is drawing us towards the fate of Narcissus, who was so self-absorbed that he forgot the world and perished.

The prison of self-consciousness is a stale, anxious environment. It is existentially painful to be isolated—constrained and judged in all you do. It leads to fretfulness, frustration, boredom and disappointment. Of course, those feelings themselves are an inducement to pay attention and question and grow. But rather than directing us to face those shadows and process them, our culture provides a variety of distractions to anesthetize their pain. These distractions are our *antephialtics*—drugs concocted by apothecaries to ward off nightmares. Most consumerism, for example, is of a self-congratulatory nature, promoted by ads assuring us that we deserve the best, the biggest, the fastest, the newest: "Feel better about yourself—buy something."

Television offers distraction of a different sort, one that occupies the mind just enough to deliver it from self-consciousness—although at times it seems to deliver us from consciousness of any sort. Alcohol and drugs offer another kind of escape—a high that, in its unself-conscious meanderings, seems to liberate us to just *be*, whereas, in fact, the discipline required to 'just be' is as compromised by that high as is the tyrant of self-consciousness. Nor are fitness classes generally designed to let us 'be' with the experience they offer, or to encourage a surrender of the many-chambered room to the spaciousness of the felt self; rather, we tolerate that strained experience so that when we look in the mirror, our self-consciousness will be less painful. We might also note that the time-gobbling, isolated, Internet-enabled 'socializing' we do also largely sidesteps the issue of self-consciousness by excusing us from actually having to be present with anyone except our own reflection, staring back at us from the screen. Antephialtics, all.

Insofar as the obsession with such distractions succeeds in dulling the pain of your self-consciousness, they keep you in a state of bondage: distracted from the energy of your own life calling out, you miss the summons to unite with your deepest truth and live the sheer adventure of it. Sipping at your antephialtics, you numb yourself to the soul's true hunger, and so never initiate the transformation necessary to move you beyond self-consciousness.

Oddly, that transformation depends more than anything on a reconciliation with your own ignorance, for only once you confess that you do not have the answers about what you should be doing and when you should be doing it can the tyrant be silenced and the grace of the world begin to suggest itself. Once you confess that you do not know the present, you can open your eyes to discover it; once you confess that you cannot know the world, you can begin to feel it. Such a reconciliation with your own ignorance imparts not doubt, but certainty: the certainty of being in the truth of the present, here and now. That certainty is always close at hand, if only we could keep ourselves from reaching to find it instead in what we know. As Stephen Mitchell wrote, "Insight into the Tao has nothing to do with the intellect and its abstractions. When we step out of self-consciousness, we step into the Tao."[166] That is, when we abandon our unintegrated perspectives and the self-consciousness to which they bind us, the chattering in the skull will subside, and we can walk through the door of uncluttered ignorance into the self that can be felt here and now: when you 'know' nothing, there is nothing to talk to yourself about. And there is everything to experience.

When the courage behind the mythological hero-deed is understood, we see it is precisely the courage that carries us out of self-consciousness into an openhearted reconciliation with 'what is'. By contrast, the path of self-absorption is the natural outcome of our head-centered existence, and it is the foremost poverty afflicting not just our age, but our personal lives as well. Stephen Mitchell noted that the teaching of the Tao Te Ching "doesn't see evil as a force to resist, but simply as an opaqueness, a state of self-absorption which is in disharmony with the universal process, so that, as with a dirty window, the light can't shine through."[167] When our self-absorption creates baffles and shadows within the corridor of the embodied axis, we can feel its opaqueness; when we "step out of self-consciousness," the corridor loses its opaqueness, and *we achieve a clarity of being that uniquely leads to clarity of action.* The great pianist Glenn Gould illustrated that with a story about a millipede: one day an ant watched the millipede approach, his countless legs moving in a blur of precise coordination. Excited and amazed, the ant flagged the millipede down, expressed admiration for his astonishing ability to move all those legs together in perfect unison, and asked him, "Tell me, when you start walking, how do you know which leg to move first?" "Let me see," replied the millipede—and he stumbled around for five minutes before he could get underway again. Like the millipede's legs, Gould's fingers moved in "a blur of precise coordination"—and, as the story tells us, the rich, life-infused harmony they expressed belongs to the "universal process," in Mitchell's words, and could never have been achieved with orders issued by the helmsman.

Gould's story brings to mind a provocative observation made by Jerzy Grotowski, the renowned and innovative Polish theater director. Addressing the problem of an actor's expressiveness, Grotowski commented,

True expression, one could say, is that of a tree.[168]

Every tree is expressive—from the birch sapling to the gnarled oak to the towering pine. What a tree expresses is the essence of its very Being, shining through all its living relationships with the world: the universal process, again. Nothing that is expressed by the tree results from a *decision* to express. That is what separates the tree from most performers, and it is precisely Grotowski's point:

> If the performer expresses, it is because he *wants* to express. And so, division once again arises. There is a part of the performer which orders, and a part which executes the orders.[169]

The part of the performer that orders is the knowing inner supervisor, the prototype for all our authority figures. The part of the performer that is *being* ordered, of course, is any part of the self that can be bullied—often the body, but including as well the heart, our faculties of reason and our emotions. The exercise of such authority is the basis of our self-tyranny: our frozen perspectives guide us in what should be done; to follow them, we override our own Being and overlook the myriad cues found in the nourishment of the breath, the spaciousness of the moment, the aliveness of the world and the deep harmony of the whole. Whenever we 'make ourselves do things', we segregate our thinking from our being and undertake the self-conscious task of executing what we know. Our inner supervisor then *manhandles* the body according to the endarkenment of that knowledge. This is essentially a *corruption* of the self—a word that is related to our word *rupture*, which means "to break or burst." Corruption, of course, has long been associated with tyranny, but it is actually endemic to self-tyranny. **Self-tyranny, being posited on a rupture of the self, always indicates that we have denied ourselves permission to integrate.** And what's that about? Why would we withhold from ourselves permission to be whole?

The dilemma is actually a deep one. Whatever problem we face—acting a role on stage, playing a better tennis game, closing a deal—*it helps to know going into it what you should do.* That is precisely why the young actor was scrutinizing the old lady. If you can gain an idea of what to do, you will want to secure that knowledge and use it. And if you can't get perspective on what to do, then how can you proceed? The dilemma seems to suggest that the female element of Being is utterly dependent on the male element to get anything done. But as soon as the male element takes initiative, "division once again arises," as Grotowski noted—and that empowers our isolated, judicative perspectives to override the present and frog-march us through the fantasyland of dead duplicates.

It is critical to appreciate that this division, this corruption, this ascendancy of the male element over the female is a form of self-conflict; and when we are fighting ourselves, our actions will lack grace, harmony, ease and efficiency, just for starters. In fact, they become mechanical, because they are being controlled by the cybernetics of stop-go-stop-go commands. One of the most delightful stories to illustrate that is found in *The Paper Canoe,* by Eugenio Barba, and concerns Nobel Prize winner Niels Bohr and an experiment with water pistols. Apart from being one of the world's preeminent physicists, Bohr was also a fan of movies, particularly Westerns. Given his native curiosity, he began to wonder about the typical movie showdown: the bad guy and the good guy face off on the main street, the bad guy goes for his gun first—but the good guy still beats him to the draw. One afternoon Bohr handed out water pistols to his lab workers, and they put the scenario to the test: facing off in pairs, waiting for someone to draw first, and then squirting. Empirical, scientific methodology. Sure enough, the person who drew first was consistently the slower one; like the millipede, he had to order the body to perform the action and then oversee its synchronization in executing it. The second one to draw, by contrast, didn't need to issue an order from one part of himself to another.[170] The One was not broken into the many, and could just react, guided by the world, unhampered by self-consciousness. Like the true expression of a tree.

There is an irony to all of this. In the same spirit as youths will paradoxically take up smoking as a way of showing their independence, when in fact every cigarette they light affirms their bondage, we willfully assert ourselves in the belief that any triumph of the will is a triumph for personal freedom. The truth is more complicated than that, and also less flattering. Willfulness *is* a form of mastery, but it exacts its price: **to achieve mastery over the self is also, by definition, to enslave the self;** willfulness is a form of self-bullying, and it initiates endless cycles of self-judgment, self-flattery, self-hatred and self-doubt. Like smoking, those cycles are addictive; and in the way that the culture of smoking was once endorsed by society, society currently endorses the culture of self-tyranny—without really questioning the destructive patterns it sets in motion. *In fact, our culture mistakes compliance for mastery, isolation for control, self-consciousness for self-awareness, and the exercise of power for an experience of freedom. In a similar vein, we also mistake the conceit of perseity for our* true reality, blind to the Universal Law. All of those misapprehensions ultimately issue from our devotion to unintegrated perspectives: if we hold ourselves apart from the world to maintain perspective on it, we will never find guidance within it; so we will have to guide ourselves, willfully and self-consciously.

The actions spawned by our culture of self-tyranny are as damaging to the world as they are to the self. When you define self in terms that grant it an independent existence, and create values and laws that enforce that illusion, then the world can go up in smoke as long as personal acquisition continues. *The culture of self creates a tyranny over the world, and it can have no other outcome.* A triumph of the will is the triumph of a personal fantasy, riding roughshod over what is real in search of personal gain. But freedom cannot be found in hallucinogenic isolation. It can be found, experienced and understood only when we return to the mutual awareness of the mindful present.

When mythology warns us against the tyrant, it is warning us first and foremost against the tyranny of the self. The reasons for that warning are clear: self-tyranny clouds every living moment with abstract idea, isolates the self from the world that gives it life, creates an addictive dependence on doing, and dominates our awareness with its incessant directives and judgments and anxieties and comparisons, so that our remembrance of the all-nourishing female element of Being is reduced to a mere shadow. More crucially, the closure of self-tyranny obscures our choices for escaping it—like the glass wasp trap. Consider, for example, the time-honored sentiment expressed by Publilius Syrus around 50 B.C.: "A wise man rules his passions, a fool obeys them."[171] Sage advice indeed, until we realize that the only options Publilius offers us are forms of self-tyranny: the wise man decides what he's going to feel and what he's not going to feel, and makes it so, and the fool holds on to his emotions and obeys them. States of enclosure both—and Publilius and his sympathetic readers are likely not even aware of any alternative to it.

The Story or the Sensitivity

The habits of self-consciousness have so thoroughly seeped into the very neurology of our bodies that the task of undoing them can at first glance seem overwhelming. The task is simplified once we note that

Grotowski's example of the "true expression of a tree" alerts us to the difference between 'showing' and 'integrating'. When we "decide to express," we are showing; more specifically, we are showing a version of the story of the 'known self'. In fact, if we reflect honestly, we will realize that any time our doing dissociates from our being, it does so to uphold and embellish that story. And of all the aspects of the self we enlist to play supporting roles in that fantasy, the face usually takes center stage. A poster in my daughter's school informs students, "Of all the things you wear, the most important is your expression." The visage, disengaged from the core, is arranged and paraded like a fashion accessory—and it can remain disengaged for hours, days, or even years, as we swap one expression for another, wearing the moods of our story for all to see. When *we* get stuck in doing, so does the *face*. When the *face* is stuck in doing, *we* are stuck in the head. So critical is the face to the fictions we rely on that it is increasingly popular to select the 'known self' we wish to present to the world and have our faces cut open so that idea can be surgically constructed.

Such phenomena suggest that we have found more than just a coincidence when we discover that our word *face* comes to us from the Latin word *facere*, "to do or make," and that our words *do* and *face* have the same Indo-European parent: the base *dho-*, also meaning "to do or make." Our language has lots of expressions in which *face* is used, and what is common to all of them is the sense of willfulness or opposition: we find this in the idea of a face-off, and in the idea that when there is a problem you should face up to it or you might lose face, and then someone would be more likely to face you down in the future—that is, if you were ever prepared to show your face again. And without wishing to push the metaphor too hard, we might notice that setting the face or wearing expressions on it is the first choice of those wishing to 'mask' an uncertain sense of Being. But it turns into a kind of hell, being caught in the face, so busy arranging its different expressions that one can neither know nor make peace with one's own truth; fitting, then, that the Indo-European base *dho-* also gives us our word *perdition*.

We generally imagine that we use the face to communicate a certain message to the world, but I think the truth more often lies elsewhere: the *primary* function for all the subtle and overt arrangements we impose on the face is to supervise the story that *the self is selling to the self*. A small example: one night I was alone doing some push-ups, and the more I did, of course, the more difficult they became, and the more my face expressed that difficulty. But at a certain point I realized that my face was expressing that difficulty to *me,* saying things like, "This is really hard; you might have to stop; how many more?" When I disengaged the facial muscles, I shifted almost immediately from the self-conflicts of divided doing into the simplicity of being—and the push-ups became much easier. That occasion marked the point at which I began to understand exercise as thanksgiving or prayer. The other lesson it taught me, though—to become aware of the story I was needing to tell myself—was also a lesson about the depth of our 'original sin', as Thomas Merton called it: our spectatorship. Any time we display the story of the 'known self', the main audience for that narrative is the watching self. There is a time for living your story, and a time for telling it, and both have value; but *if the story you are telling is an interpretation of the present moment which you haven't even lived yet,* then your living tumbles headfirst out of life and into a world of duplicates. And the purpose of any such world is to stave off integration and preserve the status quo.

To step out of the story, of course, you need to step out of the face. In that regard, it's interesting to note that the Venus figurines from the matrifocal cultures of Paleolithic Europe, as Campbell commented, "are all of essentially the same type. There is no action on the face at all."[172] In Noh theater, too, Zeami covered the faces—the ego doings—of most leading Noh actors with masks, and he advised those who did not wear masks to relax their faces into the stillness of a mask. He knew that when the doing is masked, Being is more likely to shine through. This holds equally true for us: sometimes simply by disengaging the facial muscles we can disengage from our doing—efface it, so to speak—and return to Being, which is the single source of play, discovery, wholeness, trust; in short, of all the elements of a creative life.

Our species seems to be hardwired to attend to the expressiveness of the face in social interactions; but consider for a moment that when we meet someone we love dearly, we forget about our face and will likely experience an expression of love that reaches out from our heart: the true expression of a tree. When conversing with someone we know intimately, we tend to look with our heart into her heart. We feel her story living in us: the human inseparability principle. If you converse with a less intimate acquaintance, it is sometimes more difficult to "rest in the pelvis and act from the heart." Should your attention latch onto the other person's face—the envoy of his 'known self'—he will often sense that and in return attend to *your* 'known self', which puts it on alert, and before you know it you are both sitting in the face rather than in the moment. When that happens, the only thing your conversation can really work out is the relationship between the fiction of your 'known self' and his.

Of course, that is precisely the agreement on which most of our social interactions are based: "I'll take care of your fantasy if you take care of mine, and both of our 'known selves' will feel better for it." It is the natural outcome of a culture that declares the world to be dead matter, the unbroken whole to be uninformed chaos, and the spirit of consciousness to be a personal possession. Hoarding our spiritual center of gravity inside of us, we endarken the world and focus on the self-serving voice of the inner tyrant—so that even on a bus full of people, you can feel alone and hear only your internal monologue as you vaguely try to uphold the story of "who you know yourself to be" for the strangers surrounding you. There is no inclination to feel the present as a whole; you merely flit back and forth between different perspectives on the people around you, perceiving them in isolation, and objectifying yourself in isolation among them. Almost invariably, **such a sense of isolation induces a low-grade anxiety that needs to judge everything**; and with that we enter our self-inflicted perdition, for any time you judge someone or something, you create a division in yourself. As Rumi so eloquently expressed it,

> Define and narrow me, you starve yourself
> of yourself.
> Nail me down in a box of cold words, that box
> is your coffin.[173]

A return to Being is made easier by remembering that the sensitivity that carries you into the felt self is one that recognizes your body, your self, your thoughts and the world as energy to be integrated. If you feel alienated, or isolated, or stuck, it is a symptom that you are resisting the world's energy and binding up your own; that is, your body puts the brakes on its consciousness by putting the brakes on its ability to exchange energy. But to look at someone's face is already to initiate an exchange of energy; to look at her from the core of your being is to open further to that exchange; to release the energy of your heart to her is to maximize the sensitivity of your exchange with her. As the energy of the exchange passes between you, it repudiates enclosure; and *once you dismantle enclosure, all that's left is the present—* the moment-by-moment perplexity that sustains you both. Beyond enclosure, you no longer look *at* the world with the face; you no longer look at the world from a fixed perspective: Being is immanent and integrative and *has no perspective.* But we might also say it looks from *all* perspectives, which amounts to the same thing. As Thomas Merton wrote, the consciousness of Being is beyond

> self-consciousness, separateness, and spectatorship. The pure consciousness ... does not look *at* things, and does not ignore them, annihilate them, negate them. It accepts them fully, in complete oneness with them. It looks 'out of them', as though fulfilling the role of consciousness not for itself only but *for them also.*[174]

The consciousness of Being, we might say, fulfills the reality of *mutual awareness.* To enter that consciousness is to undertake a journey from the 'known' to the felt; from separateness into unlimited relationship; from the constructed story to the living present; from showing to integrating. And what you are integrating, when you get right down to it, is your own sensitivity—which is rooted in your body, in the present, and in the mysterious love that is Being.

Rules versus Principles

The tyrant governs according to his unintegrated perspectives, which become his rules. To the extent that we internalize and operate by rules for ourselves, we are exercising self-tyranny. Rules underwrite the duplicates by which we try to live and solidify within us the divisions of self-consciousness. Every *should* or *shouldn't* we internalize, every *must* or *mustn't* we enforce, and every self-definition we live by is a rule that intervenes to keep us from contact with the pelvic intelligence; it preempts any need to attend to Being. Our desire to be told 'what to do when' is deep, and shows up in the popularity of various self-help initiatives that peddle different rules for how to live—redemption will be ours, we are assured, if only we can implement the solutions they propose.

That promise exploits the vanity of the male element and feeds our persistent feeling that, "If only I could get the right perspective on my situation, I could fix my problems and get free." But as soon as you question the idea of finding greater freedom by finding the right rules to live by, the absurdity becomes obvious: whoever seeks rules to live by is actually seeking to be ruled—which is the opposite of freedom. Rules exert conformity over behavior, instill compliance and stunt our natural responses; they limit questioning and learning and activity and the unruly joy of play; they separate us not only from ourselves, but from each other as well. To recognize the dehumanizing effect of rules is to gain some insight into the puzzling, well-known Zen motto:

> If you meet a Buddha, kill him.
> If you meet a patriarch of the law, kill him.[175]

A patriarch of the law is the one who upholds the rules; a Buddha is the one who holds the answers. An answer will bind you as quickly as a rule, for both stand in isolation from the energetic truth of the present. The motto shockingly reminds us how vital it is to break the corrupting hold that rules, and indeed answers, have on us. They always plant themselves between us and the world.

And yet the deep trust we place in the guidance of unintegrated perspectives leads us to gather them and harden them into rules and enlist them to solve all our encounters—not only with the world around us, but with ourselves as well. It is precisely those hardened perspectives that stake out a private world that only we can inhabit: the cage that shelters our "organized inadequacy."

If a tyrant lives by the rules of his unintegrated perspectives, the hero lives by the integrated perspectives of his principles. Whereas rules separate us from Being and forestall transformation, principles incite transformation. For example, people dreamed for centuries of taking flight. They watched beetles buzzing through the air, and butterflies fluttering by, and the aerial careening of swallows and hawks and eagles, and the solution seemed obvious: in order to fly, we would have to put together a big set of wings and flap them. More than a few disasters were engineered by that logic. Then, in the mid-eighteenth century, a Swiss physicist gave us something that would free us from flapping—he gave us a principle. In his honor it came to be known as Bernoulli's principle. With it to guide them, people could design an airplane wing that would achieve lift at a certain speed, and a propeller to help them attain that speed. A short 150 years later, the Wright brothers made history.

What a principle does, ultimately, is to *illuminate the dynamic that lies at the heart of a harmonious relationship.* Whether a principle addresses the relationships involved in aerodynamics, theater, or personal freedom, it points to the essential dynamic that enables the complementary opposites within that field to achieve harmony. What we call the Golden Rule, for instance—"do unto others as you would have them do unto you"—is actually a principle: it points to a key for unlocking the harmony of human relationships—a key so simple, powerful and essential to the fulfillment of our humanity that the principle is expressed in one form or another by all the great faiths of the world. Like any principle, it returns us to the guidance of Being and can lead to results as diverse as the people whose energy it liberates. By contrast, "an eye for an eye, a tooth for a tooth, a hand for a hand," is a rule. In the specific instance of injury, it corrals all the possible diversity of human circumstances towards a preordained result (e.g., "you caused him to lose a foot, so you have to lose a foot"); and that result is taken to represent goodness, or fairness.

Rules encourage us to act from our heads, like the tyrant; principles encourage us, like the ordinary hero, to act from our creative hearts. Developing either rules or principles requires perspective; but whereas a rule endarkens and keeps us from evolving, a principle illuminates a doorway and invites our evolution. The boundary distinguishing them is occasionally a little blurred, but that shouldn't keep us from outlining some other basic differences:

> • A rule is concerned with upholding order (as in 'law and order'); a principle is concerned with a deepening of harmony.

> • A rule seeks first and foremost to limit behavior in a given circumstance in order to ensure a specific result. In prescribing those limits, a rule has the effect of a funnel: it gathers all the varieties of human drive and hope and insight (imagine a throng of pedestrians on

a busy sidewalk) and channels them to a common point (e.g., waiting at a red light). A rule is enforced in the name of a perceived good, and so relies on a scheme of good and bad. Those who follow the rule are upholding the good and may even feel some entitlement for doing so.

• A principle points to the heart of a dynamic: the relationship that brings its parts into harmony. Understanding that essential relationship provides a starting gate for exploration, learning and play: as theater director Eugenio Barba pointed out, a knowledge of principles enables us to learn to learn.[176] The Latin word from which *principle* derives literally means "beginning." A principle does not aim at a specific result. In fact, its effect is precisely the opposite of a funnel: it starts from a common point of understanding (imagine a dozen engineers, each with their different temperaments and interests and insights, being handed Bernoulli's principle); and that understanding acts as a springboard into limitless forms of integration (the principle might generate eight different airplane designs, two hydrofoils, a valve and a Frisbee).

• A rule can be written in a flash. As soon as an authority wants a certain result, it can issue a rule to enforce it. But a rule can never be as complex as the human behavior it is trying to govern, so it will tend to precipitate unforeseen results, which in turn require more rules, which in turn precipitate unforeseen results, and so on. Rules tend to grow in complexity. George Orwell's *Animal Farm* comes to mind.

• A principle is uncovered only after someone has so thoroughly immersed himself in the dynamics of some form of exchange (human, mechanical or otherwise) and so thoroughly integrated all his perspectives that he gains insight into the heart that harmonizes it. The articulation of a principle often happens in stages, and it moves towards simplicity. The simpler a principle is, the more helpful it is likely to be.

• A rule can be broken, and when that happens, it threatens the order of the perceived good and the entitlement of those who uphold it.

• A principle can be used or discarded. There is no such thing as 'breaking a principle', for it constitutes a point of departure, not a barrier.

• We might also note that a rule reinforces an existing story, whereas a principle initiates a new one.

• Finally, as we have said, rules thwart transformation; principles promote it.

Of course, we all appreciate that rules are necessary in certain circumstances. Can you imagine the chaos that would engulf a busy intersection if we eliminated the signs, the speed limits, the traffic lights and the sidewalks—without even a traffic cop to help things along? In fact, that's exactly what has been done in some cities in Denmark, Holland and Germany in an urban planning movement begun by visionary traffic engineer Hans Monderman and dubbed 'naked streets'. The results are puzzling: traffic accidents are fewer, trip times for drivers are lower, and businesses lining the road thrive. When Christiansfeld, Denmark, took an intersection with a troubled history of traffic jams and accidents involving pedestrians and decided to go naked, the number of fatal accidents dropped from three per year to zero. But why? Well, once you take away the little green or red dot of light that orders people to go or stop, drivers and pedestrians have to notice what's happening around them, and make eye contact, and cooperate and come into relationship with *each other* rather than merely with a *set of rules*; suddenly no one using the street is granted entitlement. Because the intersection is stripped of the dissociated governance of law, drivers are no longer upheld in their *own* dissociation, and they discover and take on responsibility. Taking away rules, then, actually necessitates an evolution of consciousness away from the presuppositions of entitlement and into relationship with 'what is'. **In effect, rules take you out of relationship with the present; principles bring you into relationship with it.**

Principles activate thought in every walk of life. It is on the basis of principles that laws are written, challenged, amended—and sometimes removed, leaving a busy intersection naked. Principles of house design enable us to question and reconfigure living spaces. Principles of body-work enable us to experience our own bodies anew. And the liberating power of principles sustains the hope expressed by the writing of this book: the hope that, by looking into the grace of living in wholeness—by looking at it from as many illuminating perspectives as possible, and by allowing all those perspectives to come into relationship with each other and yield and integrate—we can find for ourselves not a solution for our own wholeness, but a principle to guide us towards it: a starting point at which we might abandon the internalized road signs and traffic lights that govern what we see and do, and 'go naked' into the world as it is, free to join its sacred unity and discover ourselves there.

To sum up our look at the dark side of the male element, then: its latent tendency towards tyranny is secured by perspectives that are segregated from Being and is fulfilled by the interventions these perspectives suggest. But what about the other side of the coin—the hero? How can the male element integrate its perspectives into the unity of the body/world? What does that mean in practice? To begin to answer that, it helps to assess the idea of 'normal' in which we have invested so much. For instance, how deeply resistant to integration is the 'normal' we have accepted?

We might begin that assessment by appreciating that the ultimate position of judicative perspective is the one that is held by the traditional Judeo-Christian-Islamic image of God: our Father who lives in heaven, far above us all, looking down from on high and judging; He is the Authority, the Overseer and Rule-maker, and He commands an all-knowing perspective. Of more critical import, though, is the fact that because He is placed at such a remote distance from us, *we* have perspective on *Him*. We consider Him and pray to Him from the perspective of distance, and that absolves us from any need to integrate His divinity into the world around us: into the ground we walk on, the people we walk with, the trees we walk among; *it absolves us, above all, of having to find His Divinity within ourselves, alive in our own hearts.* How could we possibly integrate what stands at so unattainable a distance from us? We can't—so we are off the hook in that regard, as long as we obey His rules.

How resistant are we to integration? Every idea of the world that is based on perseity—every notion that atoms or genes or thoughts have an independent existence; every conviction that the cranial brain is a stand-alone, self-sustaining and self-generating originator of consciousness; every feeling that we are all basically alone in what we do; and every fact of knowledge that we consider to be a stand-alone absolute—every such idea is a perspective that repudiates integration. Part of the Big Chameleon. As is every idea that is hardened into a 'should'. For instance, if you were to realize how many 'shoulds' you live with, and make a decision to integrate them, that in itself would constitute a *resistance* to integration, for you would merely be creating another 'should' that renders the guidance of the world unnecessary, providing as it does its own directive and goal and measure of success. Like any other 'should' we accept, such a decision does nothing to return us to the intelligence of the body: the slightest reliance on any unintegrated perspective, even one that seeks to return us to Being, is actually a barrier to that return.

Similarly, then, if you decide that you should be more sensitive and compassionate, you are committing to an idea that requires a division of the self into a part that orders, and a part that executes the order. So by directing yourself to be more sensitive and compassionate, you risk diminishing your sensitivity as you preoccupy yourself with instructions on achieving the right results; you diminish your compassion by diminishing the capacity for relationship on which it depends; and you diminish your ability to be *present* with people—which is the source of sensitivity and compassion—because you diminish your need to find guidance in the present. Any 'should' we take on that dedicates itself to a given result—even one directing us towards compassion—leads us away from the hero's love of Being, and his adventure to discover 'what is', and carries us into a scheme of duplicates.

How resistant are we to integration? Our 'shoulds' apply not just to ourselves, but to all the world: someone should pick up this garbage; she should have stopped at that yellow light; he shouldn't wear that color; it shouldn't be so cold this time of year. And so the disconnected chatter runs its course in our heads, heedless of the fact that perspective without integration is disintegration: the One broken into the many.

Some of the most transformative work you can do for yourself is to acknowledge the tacit rules you create for the world to live by, and then recognize the need within yourself to maintain that kind of judicative distance from the world, from those around you, and from your true self. You might also reflect on the extent to which *all male aggression is rooted in the sense that one's perspective is right and should prevail.* The tyrant insists on his perspective, and will not tolerate any other, even as he commits road rage, or bullies subordinates, or perpetrates war crimes on a dehumanized populace, or judges his neighbor. If any tendency, ultimately, is going to destroy us all, it will be the insistence on an unintegrated perspective that announces it is right even as it charges towards its own demise. By that measure, the most important lesson we have to learn is the one the mythic hero came to show us: the lesson of a self-achieved submission that enfolds a perspective back into the whole, and brings new life in its wake.

Exercise Five: **The Naked Tyrant**

We have described the 'headism' by which our culture organizes itself, and by which the enclosed male element rules the self. But description, as Alan Watts warned us, is not understanding. If we are to truly face and depose the tyrant we have ensconced within, we need to remove the benevolent guises behind which he takes refuge and nakedly confront him. That is what this exercise does: it pulls back the curtain on the little ruler in the head as it struggles to maintain control. It offers you direct information about the way you may have segregated your conscious thinking from your conscious being and enables you, with practice, to address that broken state, topple the partitions of the many-chambered room, and reveal the corridor within. This exercise requires the help of a friend.

To begin, sit in a chair with your torso upright and your shoulders and neck relaxed. Your friend places one hand on your forehead and one on the occipital bone at the back of your head. You then give over control of your head to your friend, so that your head becomes a completely relaxed appendage, like an arm or a leg. Your friend will then **slowly and gently** move your head in a **random fashion**. In doing so, your friend has to understand that a patient and understanding touch is needed from him to earn your trust, and that the exercise cannot happen without such trust. It is not necessary for your friend to go very far in any direction—subtle movements are best. The main thing is that your friend be aware of the slightest resistance or anticipation from you.

A few people find this exercise relatively easy. Most do not, and they are the ones for whom the exercise will precipitate a vast amount of information about patterns of control, of calculation, of needing to achieve the right results, and of the thinking bottled in the head, like wasps in a trap.

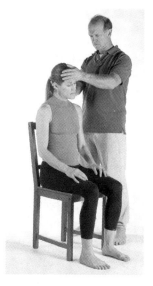

Such patterns, when first encountered, may seem to be structural elements of your very being. For that reason, only your friend can really tell you when you are taking over control of the head and when you are relinquishing it. I remember once standing for more than a minute holding my hands still in the air a couple of inches to the front and back of a young man's head, watching his head move slowly forward, touch my left hand, and then start back slowly to touch my right hand, and then start forward again. He was reading signals from my hands—actually, taking orders from them—and was doing the work himself without being aware in the least that it was he and not I moving the head. So one of the jobs of your friend is to provide occasional feedback during the course of the exercise to help you understand when you have dropped out of the authoritative control center of the head and into the fluid consciousness of being within the pelvic bowl.

You may find the exercise confusing and frustrating, and it may at some points seem almost insurmountably difficult. It may even feel at times as though you were being jostled around inside the dome of your cranium, faced with the ridiculous task of trying to concentrate while your control center is being moved erratically off-balance.

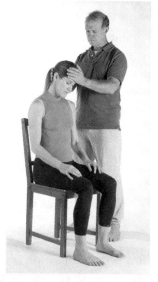

In fact, all such experiences comprise a huge information feed. The exercise is a little like an MRI for the inner tyrant, revealing its hidden structures. And although it may initially be discouraging to gain such insights into structures that seem to be so deeply a part of you, it is my experience that as soon as you bring an unseen habit into the light of your awareness, you have already begun to change it.

Culturally we are so used to with-drawing *into* the head that to attempt to withdraw *from* it may feel like trying to swim against the tide—or it may feel as if there is no way out. For me, that is all the more reason to go there. To help with that, here are a few suggestions that I have found useful.

Try thinking of the head as a bowl-ing ball, with the kind of dead weight that that implies. In fact, your friend should ideally feel at all times that you have en-trusted him with the complete weight of your head.

Your breath is also key: allow it to drop freely into the pelvic floor and release out. Be aware of any and all attempts to interfere with it, or manipulate it, or constrict it: the many-chambered room asserting itself. Part of your vigilance, too, is to keep the torso upright and open, and to keep the chest from collapsing. Be aware, also, that your as-similating center of wholeness lies in the pelvic intelligence—the more clearly you can rest there, the more readily you will process what is happening. Above all, bear in mind that the exercise is a gentle one and asks that you be gentle and patient with yourself and the discov-eries you make. It is all about leaving the 'stronghold' of the self and coming home—and as with most things, the more often you return to the exercise, the easier it becomes.

6 | The Journey Home

The One Presence

The hero's journey takes him away from the organized comfort of the 'known' to explore the mystery of 'what is'—and his insights will bring new life to his world once they have been integrated. With each generation, what the world requires in the way of 'life-giving perspectives' changes—and so the specific nature of the hero's task changes as well. Speaking of the nature of that task half a millennium ago, Joseph Campbell noted,

> Where then there was darkness, now there is light; but also, where light was, there now is darkness. The modern hero-deed must be that of questing to bring to light again the lost Atlantis of the co-ordinated soul ... the problem is nothing if not that of rendering the world spiritually significant.[177]

By hoarding his spiritual center of gravity within himself, the tyrant drains spiritual relevance from the world. The contemporary challenge of reopening our hearts to the living grace of the world around us is made both more difficult *and more likely* by the perspectives we have gathered in our far-flung explorations of space, matter, life and humankind. Half a millennium ago most people could look to the star-pierced sky and know that God had placed each twinkling jewel there for our eyes only, and that our Earth was the still center around which all else revolved. The scientific advancements that on the one hand disabused us of those presumptions have, on the other, led us to recognize an even deeper affinity with those far-flung heavenly furnaces: the matter from which we are made, and from which all life on earth is constituted, was forged in such furnaces. Staring into the night sky, we behold our light-suffused origins; and through the limitlessly refined web of the quantum mechanical world, we are still bound to them, as they are to us. By individuating from Being we have gathered perspectives that demonstrate our indissoluble connection to Being. But such perspectives by themselves, however earnestly we acknowledge and affirm them, will serve only to direct us tyrannically; until an idea is integrated, it will remain judicative and authoritative. The real issue, then, is how to regain our axial consciousness, that those perspectives might journey to the center of our being and join it, changing it and being changed in turn—birthing new responses and new responsibilities. And that raises the question: what does it even mean to integrate a perspective?

We might address that question by considering an example of the mythic journey of the hero from our own day: the NASA moon landing. That mission exemplifies the hero's journey in its simplest form: when the astronauts took flight, they executed an ultimate defection from the status quo—departing from Mother Earth and leaving her familiar terrain far behind. They sailed to an unknown landscape and walked upon it, impressing upon its face the first footprints ever recorded there. Their boon secured, they returned—changed by their experience, which itself in turn changed their community. Jean Houston was assigned to work with the astronauts to help them remember what they saw as they walked on the moon, but despite hypnosis, meditation and active imagination exercises, they didn't recall a whole lot. Finally, one of them told Jean she was asking the wrong question—what really mattered wasn't what they saw on the moon, it was what they saw as they were coming back to earth; the black and utter dark of the universe all around, punctuated by numberless pinpricks of white light—and floating within that infinity was this anomaly, this pastel orb revolving slowly through space. Looking closely, as a later astronaut Ulf Merbold described it, you could see that the curved horizon

> was accentuated by a thin seam of dark blue light—our atmosphere. Obviously this was not the ocean of air I had been told it was so many times in my life. I was terrified by its fragile appearance.[178]

Cosmonaut Boris Volynon explained,

> During a space flight, the psyche of each astronaut is reshaped. Having seen the sun, the stars, and our planet, you become more full of life, softer. You begin to look at all living things with greater trepidation and you begin to be more kind and patient with the people around you.[179]

Cosmonaut Yuri Gagarin noted,

> Looking at the Earth from afar you realize it is too small for conflict and just big enough for cooperation.[180]

These men may have left to conquer, but the perspectives they achieved awakened in them a hero's submission to 'what is', in all its fragile mystery, and rendered the world spiritually significant. On his way back from the moon, Edgar Mitchell gazed out the window and "suddenly experienced the universe as intelligent, loving, harmonious"; and the Earth itself as "a glimpse of divinity."[181]

The Earth as photographed from space was the most powerful single image of the twentieth century—and, I have heard, the most commonly published image in all of history. It gave us a perspective of 'what is' that has transformed our consciousness, though we have only begun to integrate it—for seen from space, the Earth is a living, dynamic sphere in constant flux, with no sign of national boundaries or ethnic conflicts, no evidence of ownership of its resources, no endorsement for any one of its ideologies. Having once seen the Earth from space and fully integrated that perspective, you could not return to walk its meadows and feel its rain in quite the same way ever again. And that brings us to another marked difference between a perspective that is integrated and one that is not. **An unintegrated perspective carries no responsibility:** segregated from Being, it lacks the *ability to respond to it*—the first condition of any *responsibility*. **An integrated perspective, on the other hand, cannot *but* confer new responsibility:** it is not just connected to Being; it has been fully accommodated into it, so that the newness of its vision augments the unhesitating and unthinkably sensitive responsiveness of Being itself.

To resist such responsibilities is common enough, because

responsibilities carry consequences; but any such resistance impairs our ability to respond in general: it is a form of neglect that leaves us dulled. When we seek to 'know the thing in part', as the young student of Noh was attempting to do, we are discounting the body's intelligence, which is the source of our wholeness, and of the compassion that accompanies it. The hero's task of integration, then, requires that we liberate the body's intelligence from the artifices of isolation, and open it to the one shared and ordinary present. When Joseph Campbell said that the hero-deed our age faces is that of rendering the "modern world spiritually significant," that is what he was referring to: retrieving the felt self from the shattered world of the 'known self'; retrieving the One from the shattered world of the many. That was the hero-deed of the astronauts: they carried back to us evidence of the One, refuting all our attachments to the fractured many. So although we can understand the hero as an agent of the cycle, helping to bring the season of spring to the frozen community, the *ultimate* calling of the hero is of greater moment. As Campbell writes,

> The supreme hero, however, is not the one who merely continues the dynamics of the cosmogonic round, but he who re-opens the eye—so that through all the comings and goings, delights and agonies of the world panorama, the One Presence will be seen again.[182]

As we look over the comments made by returning astronauts, that is precisely what comes through their words: the sense that the *inner* eye has been opened to the One Presence. Once we understand that **the nature of the hero's journey is a quest for perspective *and integration,*** we can see that his role is to bridge worlds that have been sundered: to bridge male and female; familiar community and cosmic mystery; knowing and feeling; past and present; perspective and Being. But his ultimate task is to bridge the human world with the all-aware unity of the divine whole.

> Myth remains, necessarily, within the cycle, but represents this cycle as surrounded and permeated by the silence. Myth is the revelation of a plenum of silence within and around every atom of existence.... Even in the most comical and apparently frivolous of

its moments, mythology is directing the mind to this unmanifest which is just beyond the eye.[183]

The supreme achievement of the hero, then, is *to resensitize us to the silent Source.* In that regard we might say of myth, as T. S. Eliot said of poetry, that the chief use of the 'meaning' of a myth may be to satisfy one habit of the reader, to keep his mind diverted and quiet, while the myth does its work upon him[184]—enabling him to feel the 'unmanifest'. By the same token, we can understand that the great mistake of the tyrant is that he *"has occluded the source of grace with the shadow of his limited personality,"*[185] as Joseph Campbell put it, and so he believes that his strength is his own. Mistaking the shadow for the substance, his efforts are doomed to failure. But of course the tyrant's delusion is precisely what our culture in its core believes and exults in—the conviction that its strength is its own. And as long as we persist in that delusion, we will be charging towards the tyrant's demise. We see no need for mediation between worlds because we recognize only the corrupted world of multiplicity, every part of which is ultimately knowable; in such a world there is no unmanifest, and all is amenable to our control.

The journey of the hero is shaped by two grand mythological adventures of integration: with the Divine Female and with the Divine Male. The Divine Female element, or the goddess, is the love that brings forth forms from the unseen dark via the yielding midwifery of 'what is'; she also sustains those forms and draws them back into the dark when harmony requires it. In that regard she is the Source that can be seen in every falling leaf and mountain range, heard in every birdsong. The Divine Male, or the god, is the Source that cannot be Seen: the Imperishable Perspective, the Law that no man can read, the Plenum of Silence around every atom, the Ordering that has no order, the Governance that needs neither hand nor force. The unseen wholeness of the world is a revelation of their marriage—the union of the sacred female mystery with the sacred male mystery—and that marriage begets a universe suspended in stillness and churning with fecund transformations. What we have spoken of as the One Presence, the Logos, the Tao, the Great Spirit or Christ consciousness, then, is neither male nor female, but is rather the deep, deep harmony that arises when those two sacred aspects dance as one.

The supreme hero, too, stands beyond male, beyond female, beyond name: he cannot otherwise integrate what has been rent asunder, nor rise above the limitations of personal hopes and fears and the blind spot of the self. In opening his eye to the One Presence, as Campbell explains, he

> no longer resists the self-annihilation that is prerequisite to rebirth in the realization of truth, and so becomes ripe, at last, for the great at-one-ment. His personal ambitions being totally dissolved, he no longer tries to live but willingly relaxes to whatever may come to pass in him; he becomes, that is to say, an anonymity. The Law lives in him with his unreserved consent.[186]

Whether the hero's adventure carries him to a meeting with the goddess or a reconciliation with the god, it transpires in both cases that "the hero himself is that which he had come to find."[187] The One Presence is the truth of his own life, as much as it is the truth of the world; in the end, **the One Presence is the ultimate perspective to be incarnated and lived.** It is in the One Presence that the world's spiritual center of gravity is discovered. In order that his newly-won perspective can be carried back to the community and integrated,

> a transmutation of the whole social order is necessary, so that through every detail and act of secular life the vitalizing image of the universal god-man who is actually immanent and effective in all of us may be somehow made known to consciousness.[188]

When the astronauts came back with a simple photograph showing a god's-eye perspective of our planet, the image traveled across the world and into some of its remotest corners; but we struggle to integrate its message of fragility and organic seamlessness. When Christ returned to his community, his message spoke so forcibly against the trappings of power and so passionately about the love that binds us all, and he so consistently showed by example the need to honor and cherish the female element in each of us, that the powers that relied on the "organized inadequacy" of his community retaliated. Not only was Christ slain by those he wished to save, the message he brought back has been repeatedly subverted and manipulated to serve the vested interests of tyranny—all, of course, in the name of Christ's love.

The Heart's Gate

In general, the values of our culture *require* that perspectives remain unintegrated—for once it is integrated, a perspective gives us sensitivity rather than leverage; kinship rather than ownership; responsibility rather than power; and an attentiveness to the present rather than to schemata. Our patrifocal culture warns that such sensitivities are hindrances to our willpower—and we learn our lessons early, so that our resistance to the integration we so desperately need is often too subtle to notice.

And just as the vested powers of a community may resist the integration of the hero's insight—even ferociously—the same is true of the vested powers of the male element within us. If our journey brings us to the brink of a new perspective that contradicts what has been frozen as the 'known self', we either relinquish what is frozen and allow it to melt, or we resist and become stuck. Sometimes it is only in the aftermath of a personal crisis, when the scaffolding of the 'known self' collapses and the painted scenery of the 'known world' falls away, that what is frozen in us can finally thaw; and then the gift of a possibility awaits us, if only we can recognize it as such: that left facing the unknown we might feel ourselves reflected there. Once we do, the gentle, patient work of integration can finally begin.

As we saw in the story of Orpheus and Eurydice, myths warn us that even when male and female have united, there is an ever-present danger that the male element will want to 'check up' on the progress of the female by looking back, thereby losing her and plunging the self into the divisions of self-consciousness. If the male element is not looking back, of course, it is facing forward. But how do we translate that from myth to experience? In the moment when Orpheus turns back, he has just made the transition from the inner world to the outer—but Eurydice, following, has not. We earlier identified that gateway between the worlds as the heart: it is the heart's energy, its love, that opens inner world to outer. Facing forward, then, is the heart's surrender to the world as it is. As Lao-tzu wrote, "The Master gives himself up to whatever the moment brings."[189]

If the gateway of the heart is closed, we are looking back—a state of self-consciousness that isolates the intelligence of the felt self from the present, causing it to languish and vanish, as Eurydice did when Orpheus looked back. When the corridor within is cut off from the present, we feel alienated and confined and anxious. What opens that corridor to the light and *grants us the spaciousness of the world* is the gateway of the heart. The heart, ultimately, is a gateway to our own sensitivity—and at any moment the access it provides is clear, because paying the least attention to your heart will tell you whether it is heavy or light. A heavy heart is a heavy gate—slow and reluctant to open to the world, and so unable to nourish the sensitivities of the felt self. A light heart is a light gate, opening to the world without resistance. Facing forward, then, is no mere idea or attitude: it is an instantly recognizable physical sensation of ease in the heart that welcomes the world in gladness and so brings us into relationship with it. And what sustains the heart's lightness is love: a love of Being, a love of life itself, which places us in the specificity of being here, now, whatever it might bring.

Light-heartedness is essential to the hero's act of self-achieved submission. To wit: if we submit with a heavy heart, with reluctance, or with a sense of foreboding, then our submission is not truly self-achieved, but foisted upon us by circumstances. In short, we are offering compliance. Only if we submit with the light-heartedness that might characterize a child at play can our submission truly be called "self-achieved"—for a "self-achieved submission" is one that is utterly at peace. It may be a little bizarre for us to think of a carefree or cheerful or peaceful submission, but that is exactly what the spirit of the hero asks for: a sense of "Here we go, come what may," trusting deeply in the self and in the revelations of the felt present. As the adage says, "Life, when lived fully, dances lightly from test to test." To live fully is to live with a cheerful acceptance of the wounding and wondrous and ordinary world that is constantly calling out to you and supporting you in all you do.

When we talk about the felt self, then, as a unity of consciousness by which we "rest in the pelvis and act from the heart," we have to guard against any misconception that when we act through the heart, we do so willfully. When our impulses are driven by willfulness, the male element is in charge: supervising and looking back and determined to achieve certain results—all of which clenches the heart. The felt unity of our consciousness is something altogether different: at rest in the pelvic bowl, our awareness of the self as a whole joins the stillness of the present, which receives all, and from which all impulses arise to greet the world. When the heart's gateway to the world is lightness itself, such impulses rise through us and, empowered by the heart's love, pass into the world to discover the fullness of our being in action.

It helps to recognize that when we look back, we are looking for **anything that will substitute *perspective* on the unknown for an *experience* of it.** Our reflex to 'look back' and grasp for the certainty of a perspective is so profound that *it takes us over even when we are doing nothing.* Whenever a gap is encountered in our regimen of doing, for instance, we tend to fill it with waiting. Waiting is a peculiar state in which doing doesn't cease; it is just restrained, like an impatient horse. We wait in lines, we wait at bus stops, we wait at red lights, we wait for elevators, we wait *in* elevators—we wait for the show to begin. **Such waiting puts us in a kind of limbo in which we can't stop doing even though there is nothing to do:** closed off from the energy of Being, our hearts grow tense as we strain towards a better future when we will finally be able to start doing again, as if by so straining we could hurry time along. We are addicts, and doing is our fix. As a society we have so thoroughly divorced ourselves from the female element, and have so thoroughly forgotten how to just *be,* that some people spend most of their lives waiting—waiting for the big break, the next step, for *their* show to begin—as if life itself were up ahead, waiting on the horizon. In fact, the habit of waiting is so deeply entrenched in our culture that many of us feel uncomfortable if we are *not* waiting for something. We feel vaguely lost. The present will always be insufficient if we are insufficiently present.

I have often found that if I really want to get at a deeply established personal pattern such as waiting, or the incessant need to 'look back' and grasp at perspectives, I need the equivalent of a disclosing dye—those little red tablets that, when dissolved in the mouth, bizarrely show up all the areas on your teeth that have not been properly brushed. And so I have a handful of questions I return to, simple, potent questions that reliably disclose my own abstractions—questions like, "What happens if I let my heart open now?" or "What happens if I stop doing and just pause?" I find that second question especially useful when it is especially inappropriate. And it often triggers a knee-jerk reaction ("I can't pause now!") signaling that the stakes are high, that something important will be threatened, that calamity will befall if I should be so foolish as to actually allow the pause to happen. It is a calamity, of course, only to the 'known self'. The essence of such a pause is to release us from the confined, driven agenda of doing, allowing us to float through the heart's gate into the nourishment of the world. When God rested on the seventh day, it wasn't because He was tired; He was creating The Pause, directing us to rest in the nourishment of Being in order that our work might never lose sight of it. "And God blessed the seventh day, and sanctified it."

Our culture suggests that nourishment derives from doing rather than Being. In any enterprise we obsess over what we do, how we do it, and often how quickly we do it. To be sure of success, we undertake those whats, hows and how-quicklys willfully; the train of thought that drives them hurtles through the scenery of our lives, and we customarily watch that scenery pass by the window of our compartment, noting it without being nourished by it. Spectators, as Thomas Merton observed. The idea of stepping out of the compartment of the 'known self' and getting off the train seems plain pointless. We believe that if we are in the compartment in the train, we are really getting somewhere in the world. But in reality we can't be, because we are not in the world in the first place; being there is such a different experience—to actually step onto the earth, and breathe the scents on the air, and hear the awakened present all around you.

Consider though, that to risk the pause, sabotaging the locomotive that drives the 'known self', is to risk an opening of the heart that reunites Orpheus and Eurydice with the world; it is to give yourself over to a little adventure into the felt unknown. Into reality. Such a pause constitutes a form of prayer—a union with the oneness of Being. When you allow that pause to happen, you may have a sense that the world around you is brought into sudden focus. In fact, what is coming into focus is your felt self, newly discovered.

Energy, Ideas, Trees and Trust

In that moment when you pause and unite with Being, you hold on to nothing, you brace against nothing, you neglect nothing. You simply come to rest in the receptivity of the pelvic bowl. Much as a surfer continuously falls through the wave that continuously rises up beneath him, you ground in the still point, falling continuously through the present, even as the present moves continuously through you. And to address what it takes to remain in that place, rather than speak of a *willingness* to give yourself up to the wave of the present, we might speak of *love*: a love for the stirrings of the present that awaken your whole Being; a love for the dance of the present that transforms everything and never pauses to own any of it; a love for the stillness of the present which, like the depths of the sea, silently receives the message of every ripple on its face, and of every living being that moves within it; and a love for the abandon that enables you to give yourself up to the wild peace of the world as it endlessly runs its course. What is being loved in all those cases is essentially Being itself—the great creative flux of all that is, making everything new. Just as the sky needs the earth, that love of Being is rooted in our deep, personal need for completion, and in the wordless joy of finding it. That love is as passionate as was the love of Orpheus for Eurydice, and it lies at the very core of the heroic element within each of us.

And here we can articulate one of the major themes of this book: the choice the male element faces between uniting with female Being or separating from it is a choice we make between Energy and Idea. Visceral thinking, which is empty of idea, is a sensitive confluence and harmonizing of the energies of the present; the cranial brain, which is insensate, is nonetheless filled to the brim with ideas—and the function of its ideas is to capture energy and hold it still so they can marshal it and organize it. If our awareness is dominated by our ideas, the male aspect of our consciousness has dissociated from the female and is binding up energy. If our awareness turns towards the energy of the present—the energy of its vibrations, of its stillness, of its coursing dance—the male aspect is surrendering its wealth to the female, rather than hoarding it. Such a surrender expresses a love of life that celebrates the energy of 'what is' and the gifts and losses that come in its wake. The choice we consistently make in our own lives, then—the choice to which the timeless myths sensitize us—is between the love of Being, which releases the male element heroically into the energy of the unknowable present, and the tyrant's fear, which encloses the male element from that energy within the consolidations of idea. We might also say that **in assenting to the heroic element we express our allegiance to Energy; in assenting to the element of tyranny, we express our allegiance to Idea.**

Of course, Idea is indispensable to an evolution of consciousness. The hero metaphorically leaves the "organized inadequacy" of his community for just that reason: to gain perspective that, once integrated upon his return, will liberate and revitalize his community. In other words, when the Energy of his community has settled into a stasis that cannot evolve, the hero ventures into the unknown to gain a critical perspective that, carried home, will topple the 'known' and liberate the Energy of life, which is and always will be a mystery, breathing through and sustaining the vibrant present. The heroic act plays itself out on the scale of communities and societies, but it also plays itself out within each of us. If you open your eyes to the world and feel its particulars to be largely 'known' phenomena within your catalogs of Idea, you are gazing out of a window in the stronghold. The alternative is simple enough: to drop into the pelvic intelligence, look upon the world around you and grow utterly passive to it, so that you feel stirring within the whole the Energy of its life in this moment; if you can do that, you have begun the ordinary, heroic surrender to Being. In that context we can understand that **when perspective is integrated, it sensitizes us to the Energy of the world; by contrast,** *everything within your consciousness that is not experienced as Energy is Idea that has not been integrated yet.*

If we are to greet the Energy of the present as one would a lover, we would be wise to acknowledge the archaic meaning of *greet*, which was "to weep." The cost of moving on is always loss—but it is precisely the transience of 'what is' that makes it so precious. Only Idea seeks asylum from that transience. But how far you will entrust yourself to the Energy of the transient now is established by *how much of yourself you are willing to discover in the world around you.* "If you receive the world, the Tao will never leave you." We turn away from the world to seek refuge from its uncertainties, and from our own. But the refuge we seek lies in a duplicate of the world. To face backward is to lose the self in its own fiction.

We think of 'fiction' as being at the opposite end of the scale from 'truth', but in our moment-by-moment choice between Idea and Energy we could more poignantly consider a scale that ran from 'fiction' to 'trust'. When Orpheus is told to trust that Eurydice is with him, he is being told symbolically to resist the fiction that a perspective will render Being knowable. **No truth in the world can survive the vanities of perseity; conversely, only a deep trust will enable a deep integration.** It's not surprising, then, that *trust* and *truth* are connected, both springing from the Indo-European base *dru-*, which also gave us *tree* and meant "firm as a tree." Historically, *tree*, *truth* and *trust* have a long-standing association. Buddha's moment of truth came while sitting under the Bo Tree—The Tree of Enlightenment. Christ's came while on the Tree of Redemption—The Holy Rood.[190] Odin found truth by hanging himself on a tree:

> I ween that I hung on the windy tree,
> Hung there for nights full nine;
> With the spear I was wounded, and offered I was
> To Odin, myself to myself,
> On the tree that none may ever know
> What root beneath it runs.[191]

As Odin points out, we may see the tree, but not its nourishing roots. That is perhaps what makes the tree so apt a symbol for "true expression," as Grotowski commented; for when we *do* know the roots of our own expression—when we look back to ascertain them—then our expression lacks both trust and truth.

Integrative Genius

The tree is an expression of trust, giving itself to and sustained by its world. Great artists and athletes alike understand that kind of trust, and occasionally they talk about the experience. Athletes refer to it as being "in the zone," and they instinctively know—or quickly find out—that the zone, like Eurydice, disappears the moment they doubt or question it. When Catfish Hunter pitched a perfect game against the Minnesota Twins, he said it was like being in a dream: "I wasn't worried about a perfect game.... I was going on like I was in a daze. I never thought about it the whole time. If I'd thought about it I wouldn't have thrown a perfect game—I know I wouldn't."[192] To be "in the zone" is to have passed beyond Idea and the chattering in the head that serves it, beyond all the doubts that make you ask, "Am I in possession of Buddha consciousness?" and beyond all need to 'look back'. Goalie Ken Dryden talked to a friend of mine about the way his glove hand would reach out and catch a puck that he couldn't even see through the throng in front of his crease. The hand was guided by an instinct he had learned to pay attention to, and integrate, and trust. Michael Murphy's book *In the Zone*** is replete with similar examples. You trust the Energy of Being, or you disconnect from it, reflexively. All sports are different ways of learning to trust the present: learning how to just *be* in the midst of the extremities of doing.

The quality of being "in the zone" is not unique to athletes—it is something with which gifted artists, mathematicians, chess players, stand-up comics, public speakers and many others are acquainted. On August 2, 1999, *The New Yorker* published an article by Malcolm Gladwell called "The Physical Genius," in which he looked at a range of accomplished individuals who regularly performed "in the zone." They included neurosurgeon Charlie Wilson, baseball player Tony Gwynn, cellist Yo-Yo Ma and hockey great Wayne Gretzky. What distinguished them was what Gladwell called "a special feel" in their field of expertise, one that gave what they did "a distinctive fluidity and grace." He dubbed them "physical geniuses." In describing Charlie Wilson, Gladwell writes,

> Wilson has a plainspoken, unpretentious quality. When he talks about his extraordinary success as a surgeon, he gives the impression that he is talking about some abstract trait that he is neither responsible for nor completely able to understand. "It's a sort of invisible hand," he went on. "It begins almost to seem mystical. Sometimes a resident asks, 'Why did you do that?' and I say"—here Wilson gave a little shrug—"'Well, it just seemed like the right thing.'"[193]

Gladwell emphasizes the role imagination plays in physical genius, but I am wary of the confusion that the word *imagination* might create in this context: the word literally means "forming images"—something at which the fantasies of our enclosed head-consciousness excel. Physical geniuses do not attend to an image of reality—a duplicate— but to its living pulse; and in that their genius is *physical,* it attends to that pulse *sensationally.* In fact, their genius is to feel what the rest of us cannot: specifically, "the thing as a whole." Wyndham Lewis once

---

* Michael Murphy and Rhea A. White, *In the Zone: Transcendent Experience in Sports* (New York: Penguin, 1995).

wrote, "The artist is always engaged in writing a detailed history of the future *because he is the only person aware of the nature of the present.*"[194] I could agree with that rather rash claim if we can appreciate any physical genius as an artist: like Orpheus, acutely present, and uncannily sensitized to the converging and shifting vectors of energy that reveal their world. As a colleague of Charlie Wilson explained,

> If I look at a particular field—tumor or aneurysm—I will see the gestalt after I've worked on it for a little while. He would just glance at it and see it. It's a conceptual thing, a spatial thing.... He could do it (the operation) because he had the picture of the whole anatomy in his head when he picked up the instrument.[195]

One characteristic that physical geniuses seem to share is that they put in hours and hours and hours of practice. As a kid, Wayne Gretzky had to be hauled off the ice long after everyone else had gone home—even when temperatures hovered at minus thirty degrees centigrade. Practice alone, of course, does not make perfection. In fact, repeating the same activity over and over can have the opposite effect—it can deaden you to it, make it mechanical. So we have to understand that physical geniuses were doing something else than mere repetition—something they hungered for and couldn't keep away from, something that uniquely fed them. And here we begin to get a sense both of what it means and what it takes to integrate new perspectives.

Gladwell noted that Charlie Wilson didn't have a lot of perspective on why he did certain things, didn't completely understand them—they just felt right. In reality, Wilson couldn't *afford* to have perspective— he couldn't afford to 'look back', to stand outside 'what is' and deaden himself to it; he couldn't afford to give allegiance to Idea, which knows a phenomenon in part, according to a range of perspectives gathered from lectures or case histories or studies. It's not that he was without such perspectives—it's that they had been so fully integrated that their effect was beyond any fixity of abstract knowledge; they were able to inform his movements from a place of wholeness, guiding them as though by "an invisible hand." Perspective, when integrated, heightens the mind's sensitivity—and so helps our consciousness to evolve.

Wayne Gretzky was also guided by an invisible hand. His most famous advice to other players was: Don't skate to where the puck is—skate to where it's going to be. Knowing where it's going to be isn't something you calculate; it is something you feel. When the best hockey players go out on the ice, they are not guided by any stand-alone *perspective* on how to play the game: as Catfish Hunter intuitively understood, *the 'zone' lies beyond perspective and beyond all its forms of self-tyranny*—"I never thought about it the whole time." They enter a zone of still sensitivity in which they feel the thing as a whole, attuning to the other players, the quality of the ice, the flex of their stick, the weight of the puck, the energy of the crowd, to all the sensations of the present that can be felt, seen, heard and smelled. They even observe telltale details that escape the rest of us. Gretzky's sensitivity to the whole of the rink and to the weaknesses of the moment is what made him so dangerously effective. His powers of observation seemed to include the sixth sense. Coach Darryl Sutter once observed that Gretzky wasn't that big, and he wasn't the most talented player—but he was the most insightful player there was.

Even those of us who are not the Gretzkys or Wilsons of the world know full well what it is to lose all perspective by integrating it. Can you imagine trying to catch a ball using reason—calculating velocity, trajectory, wind speed, drag, spin, and tallying where to put your hand when and how fast to close it as the ball flies towards you? We don't run our bodies according to such unintegrated perspectives, because they would interfere with our natural physical responsiveness. Suppose we had an instruction manual on how to ride a bicycle, elucidating *every perspective* it involves, from the biomechanics of the ankle to the curvature of the space-time continuum that we experience as gravity, to the workings of the inner ear that convey a sense of balance. However exhaustive any such manual might be, and however diligently studied, the perspectives it provided could never enable a beginner to hop on a bike and ride away.

You learn to ride a bike by gaining perspectives and integrating them. At first you tend to overcompensate when you lose your balance, unable to feel what the bike as a whole is doing. Later you can steer with one finger, or even with no hands, as you learn to feel the unity of bike, road and world in ways so subtle you might, like Charlie Wilson, not even be able to articulate them in words. Once that happens, your front wheel is continuously adjusting right and left to maintain your balance—but there is no authoritative little voice in your head saying, "Now right. Now left." There are no cybernetics. You make your adjustments according to a "special feel" that devotes its attention to Energy and requires neither perspective nor supervision. That is the nature of physical genius, and that is what integrated perspectives feel like.

The potential for physical genius lies in all of us. And so a seasoned carpenter can hold a two-by-four and feel the weight it will bear; an engineer practiced in aerodynamics can stand in a landscape and 'see' the turbulence of the wind coursing across it; a master builder from medieval Europe, without recourse to span tables or compression strength charts, can 'feel as a whole' the design for a towering cathedral, and oversee its construction, and know it will last for centuries. When your physical genius has patiently integrated the perspectives that bear on a phenomenon, sensitizing to the whole of it, you will be informed by the whole. To cling to an unintegrated perspective is to turn away from the very whole that guides you.

As the above examples indicate, our integrated perspectives promote our ability to heed the guidance of the world—whether we are riding a bike, reading an invisible breeze or designing a cathedral. That is true even of those perspectives that might initially make us self-conscious. If I were to comment to you that tension in your abdomen and sacrum and pelvic floor is restricting your breath and keeping it from contact with the soft depths of the body, you might consider that perspective, and compare it to 'what is', and find it to be true. If you react to that perspective by pushing the breath into that region willfully, it will gain you nothing but mechanics that will quickly fatigue. To integrate that new perspective means something else: it asks us to bring consciousness to those soft depths—releasing the tension that strangles awareness—so that the pelvic floor can yield to the breath as it drops in. Eventually breathing with such awareness will simply feel so much better than carrying around tension all day long that it will be integrated into what you recognize as a feeling of well-being. The soft responsiveness of the pelvic bowl, now beyond the supervision of any perspective, simply becomes a part of your sensitivity, a part of the spacious corridor within that enables you to feel whole and join the whole.

We might note that the intelligence of the body as a whole *specializes* in integrating information—even when we have no conscious awareness that it is doing so. In fact, as Nick Herbert explains in *Elemental Mind,* the amount of information we process without being aware of it is at least a trillion times greater than the information we process consciously.[196] The countless processes of the body's oceanic flux of molecular exchanges is just one part of that; we also smell pheromones, and are attracted to someone without really knowing why; we subliminally hear the breathing of the person we talk to, and are informed about their rhythms of being; we can see people do things and sense what they are experiencing without being aware that our mirror neurons are mapping their actions through our own bodies. Other information processed unconsciously is less obvious: a close friend of mine, as a schoolchild, stood up from his desk in the middle of a lesson and ran out of his classroom, out of his school and all the way home to find his mother lying on the kitchen floor in a pool of blood, hemorrhaging. As he came through the door she said, "Thank God, Jack, I prayed you would come." By doing so, he saved her life. We might also appreciate that the subtle vibrations that inform animals about thunderstorms or earthquakes or imminent danger pass through our bodies as well; and they might register more clearly in them if our bodies were more available to the coursing Energies of Being.

Anything that relaxes the body into its sensations heightens its consciousness and its ability to integrate perspectives. We can literally increase that ability with a massage or a walk in the woods or a soak in a warm bath. In England they have a saying that the greatest scientific discoveries have occurred in the three Bs: the bath, the bus and the bed. Each is well suited to the deep work of integration that the body carries out, in that each provides a situation in which our willfulness is more or less put on hold: you can't lie in bed and will yourself to sleep; a bus ride can induce a pleasing kind of passivity as you are carried towards your destination; and a bath is often a ritual as much for melting away cares as for washing. As the will is lulled into quietude it releases the perspectives onto which it has fastened and you can simply 'be': the muscles of the body, taken off alert, are allowed to soften, and the intelligence of the body is released to do its work—which can include newly integrated, startling scientific insights into the nature of reality.

When a perspective is integrated, it is accommodated by the intelligence of the body as a whole. The axis of that intelligence rests on the pelvic floor, informed by the world in ways that are utterly beyond the cause-and-effect logic of which our culture is so fond. In its function, the embodied center of being within us has many of the qualities of what physics has dubbed the quantum vacuum. As systems scientist Ervin Laszlo describes the quantum vacuum, it is

> the locus of a vast energy field that is neither classically electromagnetic nor gravitational, nor yet nuclear in nature. Instead, it is the originating source of the known electromagnetic, gravitational and nuclear forces and fields. It is the originating source of matter itself.[197]

The integrating genius of the pelvic intelligence is the quantum vacuum of the self: touched by the present, it receives into it all the perspectives of our living, and then rebirths them as the living sensitivities of the felt self, awakening it to the mutual awareness of reality.

The integration made possible by the female genius of Being excludes nothing—not mathematics, not rocket science, not art, not molecular investigation: Friedrich Kekulé famously ushered in the science of organic chemistry as he dozed by the fire and dreamed of a snake biting its own tail—the secret to the benzene molecule. *Any such integration of perspectives constitutes an evolution of consciousness, the merging of male and female; and it is the only means by which such an evolution can be achieved.* Einstein has been popularly quoted as having said,

> The intellect has little to do on the road to discovery. There comes a leap in consciousness, call it intuition or what you will, the solution comes to you and you don't know how or why.

It is left to us to trust the intelligence we cannot command and submit to it attentively, allowing the self to integrate with it, even as it integrates the self. Without that trust we will always be Looking Back to the parts and missing the whole that calls to us.

Exercise Six: The Elevator Shaft

When a perspective is integrated, it ceases to be a duplicate and becomes a sensitivity. The integration of a perspective happens once it is brought into relationship with the pelvic intelligence. If the corridor of the embodied axis is wide open and we are at rest in the pelvic bowl, the integration of our perspectives is a continuous dance that accepts the world as its partner.

As we have seen, we are tacitly advised from childhood to retreat from the corridor and seclude ourselves in the head. Our cultural evolution over the past eight thousand years has been shaped by the migration of our center of consciousness from pelvic bowl to cranium; the corridor we have abandoned has been partitioned into a many-chambered catacomb. This exercise simply reverses that trend. It carries the center of our consciousness down the corridor, toppling walls on the way as it conveys the male element back to Eurydice. In practice, it is evocative of the two-headed Celestial Serpent of Mayan myth, accepting the rising sun into its Eastern mouth (the cranial skull), passing it through the body, and discharging it from its Western mouth (the pelvic skull) at sunset.

The Elevator Shaft can be done standing, sitting, lying down, running or walking; but I have found it easiest to learn while standing. Start with feet comfortably apart, knees soft, hips floating and the breath dropping in and releasing out through the whole body. Bring your awareness to the center of your visceral intelligence, which you might imagine as a mindfulness that sits deep within the pelvic bowl. Then feel within the body a spacious shaft that includes the spine but sits just in front of it and runs from above the scalp, down through the torso and out through the pelvic floor. Allow yourself to feel the dissociated male aspect of your consciousness residing in your head—your conscious center, your thinking self. Feel that center as specifically as you can, so that you can actually shift the *center of your awareness* around inside the cranium like a little ball of energy, moving it up, down, or side to side. Try letting

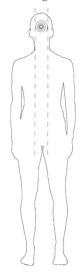

that center rise through the cranium and through the scalp itself to hover just above the head; and then allow it to drop through the shaft like an elevator until it passes down past the pelvic floor. With practice you'll be able to feel its descent quite tangibly, as if a sphere of energy were descending through the flesh of your body. Once it is slightly below the pelvic floor, allow it to rise just enough that it comes to rest in the mindful center of the inverted pelvic skull.

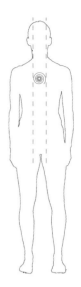

Be patient with yourself while finding your way into this exercise: you are reversing eight thousand years of cultural conditioning; you are retracing the journey of Orpheus to the underworld; you are discovering *you,* here and now, as you open your sensitivities to include the genius of your integrative intelligence. The exercise is not something to 'get right', but to play around with. Feel the descent as specifically as you can along the corridor, opening the conduit within you. Whenever that descent is stalled, pay attention to the partition standing in its way, welcome it with love, and then ease your way down through it. The energy contained by that partition, released from its confines, will naturally follow that descent and merge with the welcoming genius of the pelvic intelligence. You can also play around with the depth to which you can drop through the elevator shaft. Can you drop your center to sit at knee level? To your feet? To below your feet? Playing with your center like that eventually makes it easier to let it come to rest in the pelvic bowl; once it is there, resting, notice how that changes the center, and changes how you feel, and changes how the world around you feels.

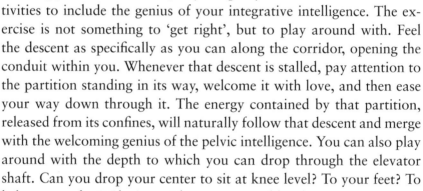

A variation on the Elevator Shaft will give you a direct experience of *what it means to integrate a perception and birth a sensitivity.* Take any simple perspective and render it as a phrase, such as, "I am here" or "The tree is tall" or "The rose is red." Feel that idea in your head, and then allow it to drop down the elevator shaft until it comes to rest in the pelvic bowl. If you are patient enough to carry the idea into the

pelvic intelligence, you will find that the borders of
the idea fall away as it dissolves in sensation. The first
time I invited others to try this, one person took "Fire
is hot" as an idea, carried it down the elevator shaft,
and felt it as sensations of heat in the pelvic bowl.
Another who took "Roses are red" felt the roses
come to life there. Perceptions, when integrated, become sensitivities—and so enrich our presence in the
world. We live by words every day, but until the word
is made flesh, Idea will rule; the more we are ruled
by Idea, the more we stifle the Energy of Being. As
we have seen, our 'headism' specifically prevents the
word from becoming flesh, so that our thinking can
operate independent of our Being, chattering away to
itself. **If we are literally to *incorporate* our thinking—**
**which constitutes the integration of idea or perspective—we have to
surrender it to the flesh.** This is the metaphoric journey of Orpheus to
reunite with Eurydice, reenacted within the body's depths. Eventually,
you can carry the present itself down the Elevator Shaft, to rest in the
pelvic bowl; and when that happens, the present becomes a sensitivity
rather than an idea, and its sensitivity is recognized to be the thinking
self. At that point you are truly "feeling the thing as a whole."

The Elevator Shaft exercise does several things. First of all, it gives
us an experiential understanding of how the perceptions, ideas and
thinking of the male pole of our consciousness can submit to our being
and merge with it to become sensation: the prototypical homecoming of the hero. It also shows you right away where the spaciousness
within the body is too compromised to allow your male perspectives
to travel down through it; it improves your ability to ground yourself
within the pelvic bowl; and it tangibly carries you from a unipolar to
an axial consciousness. The Elevator Shaft can be repeated as often as
necessary, and you can practice it virtually anywhere, anytime: in line
at the grocery store, while traveling to work, while sitting at a desk,
working. With a bit of practice you will find that in the course of a
day, if you notice you are caught in your head, it only takes a few seconds to drop through the elevator shaft to come to rest in the pelvis:
the mythic homecoming.

7 | The Corational Corridor

A Fence against the River

We who live in our heads are pretty familiar with the way the male aspect of our consciousness thinks when it becomes unipolar: identified with the mythological tyrant, it holds its logic independent of the Logos and, by consolidating the body, refuses to integrate experience. That consolidation—that construct of clenched muscle tissues and fixed idea that we have called the 'known self'—also changes how we think and what we can think about. For simplicity's sake, we might dub that dissociated thinking of our male consciousness **the hetabrain mode.** *Heta,* which sounds a little like 'head', is the name of the Greek letter from which we got our letter 'H', and the Greeks originally borrowed it from a Semitic letter that means "fence, barrier" in honor of its shape: **H.** In that meaning we find precisely the state of the consciousness that requires the 'known self': **that mind-set seeks to fence the self in, so that its thinking can work from behind a barrier**—a barrier that specifically rejects the female pole of its axis. For our purposes, then, we might be well enough served to say that when the male element of doing takes over, our experiences of self, body and world phase into the hetabrain mode.

We have already looked at how our experience of the body changes as it enters the hetabrain mode. We also have a sense that, *as water is locked into crystals when it freezes, hetabrain thinking freezes the world into symbols or duplicates, which constitute its basic language of thought.* We might consider furthermore that water represents a more energetic state than ice. Quite simply, you have to add energy to ice to melt it, or strip energy away from water to make it freeze.

Something comparable occurs when we phase into hetabrain thinking. We have to strip energy away from a tree, for example—obviate its particular life, its individual expression, forget about its here-and-now process in which we share—to treat it with the foregone assumptions we would accord a symbol. When our knowledge about it is neat and tidy, what need is there to open to the energy of its particular reality? Similarly, we open the fridge to find the ketchup and don't usually notice the ordinary qualities that make the bottle unique—we notice it generically. We notice people, insects, apples and birdsong in the same way. But when we strip energy away from the world, we also strip away its ability to energize us.

Each of us is at every moment standing in the river of the world's energy. Either we choose to brace against it or we submit to it. The hetabrain braces against it in myriad ways, which we so take for granted that our reflex to resist is seen as normal, necessary and prudent. I learned a big lesson about such resistance from a little river in Ontario called the Coldwater River; and there is no question as to how it got its name. I was building a barn late one summer on a property through which the river ran, and I was determined to find a way of swimming in it that did not send my body into panic. Every evening over weeks I would walk down to the river, step into it, take the plunge, and face the panic. I was warm, the water was cold, and the panic was my way of trying to keep them apart. As I did that night after night, I came to realize that I wasn't really *feeling* the water; I was too busy fortifying myself against it. Bit by bit it became easier and easier to enter the water until—as I have come to understand it now—I learned to release all the tensions in my body that were trying to secure the 'known self' against the cold, and instead let my body come to rest, whole and in the moment and resonant to it. When I was able to feel the body as a whole, I could walk into the rushing cold and *submit* to it, without resistance or prejudice or effort. The plunge was a kind of bliss, leading to a few moments of utter serenity beneath the swirling surface. And, quite contrary to what common sense would predict, once I was willing to *feel* the cold, I didn't *become* cold. My body, unlocked and free to respond to the frigid currents, could adapt to them. Since then I've just as easily waded through shore ice to dive into a wintry lake; or through rush-hour crowds to enter a subway station. To release yourself from the divisions and effort of the hetabrain mode is to give yourself the chance of merging with the aliveness of the felt present around you; *to allow yourself to transform—even while submersed in ice-cold water—is to allow yourself to remain whole.* Resting, you change.

Furthermore, only by submitting to the energy of the world can you connect with the roots of your own Being, for those roots do not lie protected and static within you, but are living conduits that bring you into relationship and exchange with the world. *By giving yourself over to the energy of the world, you are, in effect, unlocking your capacity for relationship.* By fencing yourself off from that energy, you are cutting away your own roots.

The Tao Te Ching observed, "what is rooted is easy to nourish."[198] That metaphor comes alive for me when I think of running. There was a time when I would go out for a run and supervise my body to help it achieve its optimum pace. Eventually, slowly, I recognized the shimmering flux of energy all around me, and I found that if I just opened myself to its companionship, without design or specific aims—if I allowed all that energy to course into and through me—it would carry me the way a leaf is carried along by a river. As the isolated 'doer' melted into the space around me, I felt I was 'being run' rather than running. At its finest, such running opens me to a state of grace. But that possibility of grace is always available, whether running or standing still: to be present in the river of the world's companionship is to be supported by its coursing energy. **And although we can and do brace ourselves against it, there is in fact nowhere to stand *but* in that river—it is all we have.** To open to it is to open to the grace of Being, which is the gift of life.

Man, we are told, has been given choice; and I think the choice that most fundamentally distinguishes humanity is the one that enables us to lock ourselves out of the world's fluidity behind the walls of stubborn, insensate fantasy. No other animal seems able to do that so well. The ability is made possible by the simple fact that **you cannot integrate unconscious flesh.** Ultimately, then, the fence behind which the hetabrain retreats is constituted of just that: our own desensitized flesh. All the spheres of the 'known self' have that in common. In all of them, the mind's sensitivity hides itself and calls that feat self-mastery. That is the choice that turns us away from the female, fragments our view of self and world, and relieves us of the inconvenience of feeling the present. It also enables us to forge such deep attachments to a set of ideas that we *feel* the truth of those ideas passionately and mistake 'feeling an idea' for 'feeling the whole'. The advice to "live by your convictions" is certainly laudable up to a point, but it can all too easily become a slippery slope into obdurate insensitivity. Living in relationship to the world as a whole is a moment-by-moment revelation, an entirely different experience from living in relation to ideas about it. As a culture, though, we persist in trying to solve our problems by finding the right perspective on them, as though that is where redemption lies, as though we needn't really bother with the messy business of integration. That tendency is not just wayward, but destructive. In fact, **I think the most dangerous individuals are those who feel their convictions more intensely than they feel the newness of 'what is'**— whether their convictions concern corporate entitlement, religious ideology, social engineering or the solutions afforded by technology. Such rigid convictions exhort us to actions that are heedless of the whispering currents of the living present.

The Analog Axis and the Great Wave Phenomenon

The way the felt self thinks is exactly what Parmenides so persuasively urged us to turn our backs on 2,500 years ago; so that even though we have all experienced its thinking in one way or another, it remains shrouded in shadows. In fact, that thinking remains precisely as obscure to us as our neglected pelvic intelligence, on which it largely depends. The thinking of the felt self finds its complement in the ever-moving, paradoxical process of the present: in its wild peace, its earth and sky, and in the abiding stillness that underlies its continuous transformations. Unlike the unipolar thinking of the 'known self'—housed in the head—the axial thinking of the felt self occurs when the embodied corridor opens to a balanced interplay of exchange and renewal between its two poles; and then takes the next step of opening to the guidance of the world. When it does that, we begin to feel a second axis of consciousness, one through which the felt whole of the self comes into accord with the felt whole of the world. And just as *perspectives are converted into sensation* as they move along the embodied axis, our clear sense of 'I' is converted into a clear sense of 'We' as our consciousness opens along this second axis. But another, more curious thing also happens: *sensations are converted into insights*. How that happens, and what the nature of the second axis is, we can begin to understand by drawing a comparison from the recording industry: the differences between analog and digital recording technologies.

To begin with, the differences between those two technologies illustrate what the old lady was trying to explain to the novice Noh actor: digital technology is like "knowing the thing in part"; analog technology is like "feeling the thing as a whole." How so? Collecting digital information is a lot like "copying facts point by point." The information on a digital recording of music is compiled of samples that are collected 44,100 times per second. Each sample is like a snapshot: it measures one instant of the music and converts that measurement into a binary number. The process creates 44,100 discontinuities in each second of music we hear—the spaces between the snapshots—but who could ever hear such fleeting interstices? When all those snapshots are run sequentially—ten seconds of high-quality sound require almost half a million samples and more than seven million bits of information—we can create a duplicate that sounds convincingly like the real thing.

In an analog recording, nothing is measured or quantified—there are neither facts nor snapshots. To understand how an analog recording works, it helps to understand that sound is the energy of mechanical vibrations, which alternately compress and expand the air around them. Those vibrations travel as waves through the air, move the eardrum, and are heard as sound. The sensitivity of the ear is astounding: it can detect density changes of sound of less than one ten-millionth of one percent. Analog recordings store sound in impressions that are made by the original sound wave. On a vinyl LP, for instance, the original waveform of the music is physically shaped along the groove of the record, in the form of ripples along its walls. In making those grooves, the original sound wave moves the microphone, which sends an electric impulse to a cutter, moving it in the same way; the cutter creates a groove as it moves through a soft material and leaves behind the impression of the waveform. When you play an LP on a turntable, a stylus rides through the groove, and the ripples move the stylus, which recreates the waveform in another electric impulse, which is amplified and goes on to move the speaker in your living room.

It is easy enough to see how these different recording technologies correspond to the differences in thinking between the hetabrain and the felt self. Digital information is similar to unintegrated perspectives: as the hetabrain quantifies and consolidates perspectives into a static concept, so too a digital recorder quantifies perspectives on a waveform and consolidates them into a static sequence of numbers. Digital information is broken information—made of discrete, discontinuous facts. And in the same way that the young actor's copied facts do not themselves resemble an old lady, the sequence of numbers does not resemble the music: both are abstract duplicates purified of life *and cannot fulfill their function until they are interpreted*. The word *digital* comes from an Indo-European base *deik-*, which means "to show," and is related to our words *judge, judicative, verdict* and *dictator*. It came to us through a group of Latin words that conveyed the sense of "to point at," the way you might *indicate* something with a finger. And that is reminiscent of Meister Eckhart's observation that because an idea "always points to something else," it cannot bless us. Metaphorically, then, we might speak of the intelligence of the hetabrain, which stands apart from the Energy of the world and indicates it with a system of duplicates, as 'digital knowing'.

All of our senses are informed by analog impression rather than measurement: the world's energy presses upon them, as the pressure of a door handle upon the palm of our hand. And much as a stylus is informed by the waveforms in a record groove, our senses are informed about the energy of the world by vibrations: the eye sees waves of light, the ear hears vibrations, and we feel heat and cold, wind and texture, all as vibrations. Similarly, the consciousness that joins self and world is analog, and *the energetic potential for exchange between them* might be named **the analog axis**. In the way that analog audio technology leans on the vibrating source—the music—and enables its waveform to shape the groove in the LP, *the analog axis allows our sensitivities to lean on the One Source—the present—and receive the impression of all the subtle waveforms of Being*. Taken together, those waveforms, those currents of exchange, are the one reality. On the subatomic level, even so-called 'particles' can be understood in those terms. Physicist Heinz Pagels explains,

> The electron is not a particle ... it is a matter wave as an ocean wave is a water wave. According to this interpretation ... all quantum objects, not just electrons, are little waves—and all of nature is a great wave phenomenon.[199]

We might also say that **Being is a great wave phenomenon**—and that its every ripple conveys information. It is through vibrations that a baby in the womb learns about its world, which is first and foremost its mother. And as a baby belongs to and is immersed in the vibrations of its mother, we belong to and are immersed in the vibrations of the great maternal energy around us. When we clear the body of its rigid presumptions and consolidations and open our hearts to the world, then what passes through us is the humming reality of Being. The grace of the maternal harmony, the vibrations of the One Presence, traverse the analog axis and permeate our core. The vibrations of Being become our vibrations—the energy of the world felt within the body's stillness. In its essence, **the body is a vibratory medium**—but only our receptivity to the great wave phenomenon we call 'the present' makes us aware of that, just as it is only through that receptivity that our analog axis is ushered into consciousness. It is of some interest to us, then, that our word *vibrate* is linked through the Indo-European base *weib-* to the English word *woman*, and also to a German word *Wipfel*, which literally means "the swaying part of a tree."

Our analog axis enables us to feel the energy of the world; our digital knowing enables us to represent aspects of that energy with static ideas. As the touch of a finger will silence a tuning fork, the tyrannies that drive consciousness out of the body will silence our analog axis: quite simply, it becomes incapable of moving to the world's subtle currents. When such tyranny advances sufficiently far, *it reaches a threshold at which the unity of the present cannot be detected.* When you can no longer detect the all-informing present, you no longer have reason to believe it can offer you guidance. The present then becomes a mere idea—one you can track by the number on your digital watch. Detached from the Logos, you devote your faculties of intelligence almost entirely to unintegrated perspectives; and then the meaningful currents of your own life slip between the discontinuities of your broken analysis of things as water will run through your cupped digits.

The word *analog* originally comes from roots that mean "according to the Logos." To know any part of reality according to the Logos is to experience the living currents of that part directly, which themselves accord with the Logos: every wave of being contains inexhaustible information about the great wave phenomenon from which it arises. The impressions that pass through the analog axis are of the utmost sensitivity and speak to your heart; they speak as directly as a mother to her child; and they speak to a core that has fully surrendered to the present—either through a self-achieved submission that razes the fence of the hetabrain, or through an event in your life that does the same and leaves you naked to 'what is'. The analog axis cannot come into existence until the self is felt as a whole: once we have swept away the shadows of our neglect—its lethargies, its dullness, its anxieties—we can replace them with the sensitivity of stillness. It is into that stillness, then, that the waveforms of the present are received—as the stillness of a pond will receive the merest breeze floating over its face. When the body is grounded in stillness, the analog axis can open us to an exchange with we know not what intelligence it is that breathes through all things. And that intelligence can guide us as surely as a mother's loving touch will guide her child.

Once the impression of that loving touch passes into the body, more subtly than any idea, you will discover that **all of nature is your primer**. Give the attention of your entire being to a tree, or a river, or the night sky, open your love to the present, allow it to touch your core, and its guidance will be felt vividly. Your analog axis joins you to the present by welcoming its energy. The subtlety of nature's lessons can be equal only to the stillness to which you abandon yourself, but they begin simply enough.

> The trees teach us how to stand.
> The sea teaches us how to breathe.
> The flower teaches us how to open our hearts.
> The waterfall teaches us how to ground ourselves.
> The mountain teaches us how to rest.
> The river teaches us to move on.
> The moon teaches us calm reflection.
> The spider's thread teaches us sensitivity.
> The starry night teaches us companionship.
> The blue sky teaches us patience.

Our culture assures us that anything we do has to be overseen by our enclosed intelligence and chaperoned by our willfulness. But the medium of the world in which we live is thought, as a fish lives in water. To open the second axis of our consciousness is to open to that medium, in all its vibratory stillness. Because the harmony of the felt present occurs within the spaciousness of a field that knows no boundaries, opening to that field requires a commensurate spaciousness: a sensitivity on which you yourself have placed no boundaries. And so it is that as the mind's sensitivity opens through the widening spheres of its awareness, the chatter of the nagging, bullying inner judge falls silent, replaced by an immersion in the experience of the present: the caress of its waveforms speaks to the heart with intimate eloquence. That experience will make it clear to you as no other: **the alternative to judgment, the antidote, is sensitivity.** Judgment contracts the world; sensitivity dilates it into the truth and immediacy of the fluid present.

Fluidity Is Information

Our understanding that "all of nature is a great wave phenomenon" tells us that all of reality is essentially fluid. In the shift from 'known self' to felt self, we leave a frozen realm of division and fixity and enter the essential fluidity of 'what is'. Mysticism and science give us different ways of understanding that fluidity; a remarkable book by Theodor Schwenk, *Sensitive Chaos,* blends those views to present a compelling vision of it. In the book he shows how our organs and bones and the bark of trees and river deltas and a multitude of other forms all testify to the flow that gave them shape and continues to shape them. Fluidity embodies information and facilitates exchanges, whether in the world around us or within. Physician and author Larry Dossey refers to the endless give and take of atoms that sustains all life as the "biodance," which he describes as follows:

> *Biodance*—the endless exchange of the elements of living things with the earth itself—proceeds silently, giving us no hint that it is happening. It is a dervish dance, animated and purposeful and disciplined; and it is a dance in which every living organism participates. These observations simply defy any definition of a static and fixed body. Even our genes, our claim to biologic individuality, constantly dissolve and are renewed. We are in a persistent equilibrium with the earth.[200]

As for the self, Alan Watts provided us with a metaphor that radically underscores the fluidity of our continuous exchanges with the world: "Man as an organism is to the world outside like a whirlpool is to a river: man and world are a single natural process."[201] He explained,

When I watch a whirlpool in a stream, here's the stream plowing along, and there's always a whirlpool like the one at Niagara. But that whirlpool never, never really holds any water. The water is all the time rushing through it.... And so, in just precisely that way, every one of us is a whirlpool in the tide of existence, where every cell in our body, every molecule, every atom is in constant flux, and nothing can be pinned down.[202]

The intelligence of the felt self resides in our fluidity and is processed through the exchanges along our embodied axis; but ultimately, too, the intelligence of the felt self resides within the fluidity of the great wave phenomenon of the present, and is processed through the exchanges along our analog axis. In fact, we could liken its intelligence to a womb in that it receives the world and integrates it and thereby births the self anew in each moment. We might even call that *its first and foremost function: to receive the world's coursing harmony that it might discover the reality of its own. That ability is its genius.* And it is, to be sure, a physical genius, one that is guided by the subtle thinking of the world. We might think of that bodily intelligence, in fact, as the womb in which the Tao or the Logos is received and conceived. Oneness cannot be found, Logos cannot be heard, the Tao cannot be felt, unless the two axes of consciousness that constitute the genius of the felt self are sensationally processing 'what is' as a whole. In recognition of its genius for "feeling the thing as a whole," we might name the united functioning of those two axes of our consciousness the *logosmind*—**the mind that receives and conceives "the thought that steers all things through all things," the mind that vibrates to the harmony of the whole, the intelligence that becomes whole through the whole.**

The logosmind, then, is the thinking of the felt self. It enters the experience of the felt present just as you might ease into a hot bath, releasing every cell to the warmth of the water and yielding to the luxury of its sensations. It is a self-achieved abandonment in which you offer yourself completely and with gladness to the world around you, sensationally merging with it. The thinking of the logosmind thrives in the inner corridor and is liberated when it unites with the pole of the swirling present. Analytical thinking can play along the corridor and inform being and be informed by it—but the thinking of the logosmind does not rely on duplicates and is not predominantly analytical. But if it is not analytical, what is it?

Analysis is the separation of a whole into its component parts, and comes from a Greek word that means "loosening"—similar to the root of *solution*, which, as we saw, comes from a Latin word that means "to loosen." And indeed, when you want a solution, analysis is likely to facilitate it. Like Alexander's sword, it cuts the world into parts that retain no vestige of the perplexity that belongs to the whole; the divisions of analysis allow you to ponder the qualities and relationships of those parts. We commonly think of *synthesis* as the counterpart to analysis—and for good reason, because it means, as its Greek roots indicate, "a putting together." But that is not how the intelligence that feels the world works: *the world is together; it doesn't **need** to be put together.* Its togetherness is, in fact, immutable, indissoluble and inescapable, evincing a depth of interrelationships that we cannot begin to compass. If we tried to put the world together, we would undoubtedly end up with a synthetic duplicate. Patently, another word is needed, one that suggests the unity by which the logosmind feels the world in itself and its self in the world.

The word *assimilate* suggests both of those aspects. The OED lists two related meanings for the word: "to make or be like" and "to absorb and incorporate." The word is related to other English words such as *similar, same, ensemble, simple* and *single,* and all of them trace back to an Indo-European base, *sem-,* which means "one, together." The word *assimilate* aptly describes the thinking of physical genius: Gretzky stepped onto the ice and *assimilated* what was happening there in its entirety; Charlie Wilson looked at an aneurysm and *assimilated* it; and that's precisely what the old woman was urging the young Noh actor to do: not synthesize his facts into a performance, but *assimilate* the role—feel it from the inside and embody it, as the stylus of a turntable yields to and reveals the waveform of the orchestra. Of course, the ultimate affinity towards which the logosmind is drawn is an assimilation of the One Presence. To honor that natural affinity is to find yourself in the presence of the One Mind even as you find it within you. Assimilate this, let this assimilate you: that is the heroic surrender.

Understanding that the logosmind thinks predominantly by assimilation suggests the fluidity and openness of a mind in which all things are allowed to come into relationship with all things. It also provides us with a means of calling ourselves to account. When you stand and converse with someone, do you assimilate the present, or switch out of it into the kind of role-playing expected of you by your relationship with that person? What might happen if, while conversing, you *allowed* yourself to assimilate the present—just as the hero journeys into unknown Being? When you walk down the street, can you assimilate the present? Or while in the grocery store? Or while eating a meal? As soon as you can answer "yes" to such questions, you have activated the thinking of the logosmind, which will illuminate the whole of your life with a newness and truth that reveal the realm of the felt self.

We can further call ourselves to account once we understand that the rigidities of the hetabrain are organized to secure results and the fluidity of the logosmind is an attunement to process. The differences between process and results are familiar enough to most of us; but those words take on a new significance when we scratch them to look at their roots: *process* comes to us from the Latin *procedere,* "to go forward, advance," and *result* from the Latin *resultare,* "to leap back, spring back, rebound." Process, which is always about assimilation, carries us forward into the felt perplexity of the present; a concern with results, or doing, pulls us back into the familiar duplicates of the 'known self'.

Consider this: we seek, expect and even demand convenience in our lives. We feel entitled to it. Convenience, of course, is nothing other than the ease of getting results. But it would follow then that **the more convenience we enjoy, the more we disconnect from process—** and, by extension, the more we disconnect from Being. We tend to take for granted those things on which the convenience of our daily living depends, and feel no obligation to honor the complex and sophisticated processes that sustain them. As Jean Houston observed,

> Most of our ancestors knew process all the time. They planted the seed, they chased away the birds, they nourished the plant, they baked the bread. We just stand in the supermarket line. Maybe much of our social pathology is a lack of process—we have no sense of the moral flow of things.[203]

A similar observation was made by science activist David Suzuki: "We live in a shattered world.... It used to be that everything you did carried certain responsibilities."[204] When we accede to convenience, we undermine relationships and our own ability to assimilate reality. Are you on a first-name basis with your bank manager? I don't even have one—I use a virtual bank with ATMs. As a kid I knew the milkman, the fruit and vegetable man, and the butcher—who once told me that to get the sawdust for their floor they had George in the basement with a handsaw, cutting up boards all day. In the summers we occasionally bought produce directly from a farmer, who lived in a different rhythm and always had time to chitchat. These days the chicken for sale in our brightly lit supermarkets comes from birds that have suffered an inhumane existence, shelved in a factory like a mere commodity and as rigidly hidden from the light of day as the hetabrain's ideas are from the Logos. Fruits and vegetables have been irrigated with aquifer-depleting waters, doused with chemicals and flown or trucked thousands of miles. I find there are certain 'normalized' conveniences I can no longer assent to—the personal cost of dissociation is too great.

As our addiction to results and convenience diminishes our relationships with the world, it bolsters the amnesia of our abstractions on every scale, so that we forget to feel; but our patterns of thought and behavior don't need feeling: they drive themselves, fixated on results. Deafened to the ways in which the world calls out to us, we obsess over our personal agendas. And those often concern the problems of money, because *money represents an entitlement to sidestep process and demand convenience.* The dreams of the hetabrain, built on its scaffolding of duplicates, occupy us relentlessly, even as the womblike ability of the logosmind to receive 'what is' and process it is numbed with neglect.

I have a confession to make. I was out for a long run on a bright spring day, trying to feel my way with every available faculty towards a metaphor by which the intelligence of the felt self could be understood, when the image of the womb came to mind. I was under a large willow tree on the edge of a trout pond and I stopped in my tracks, letting the metaphor settle into and through me. And a part of me flinched. A part that, despite my understanding about male doing and female Being and self-tyranny and heroic submission and all of that, still flinched at the prospect of identifying so closely with the female element. On the one hand, standing stock-still under the shifting sky it was so clear to me—I am a womb; more specifically, the intelligence I experience through my body, unlike the enclosed knowing of the hetabrain, can only be fully honored and fully realized when, like a womb, it is allowed to receive the world into its emptiness; when its genius is free to work in ways I cannot understand or control, but *can* feel; and when I wholly attend to the guidance of the whole as it is born within me. On the other hand, a product of my culture, I flinched. It passed, easily enough. But I will never forget that it happened.

Unipolar versus Axial Thinking

We have suggested the whirlpool as a metaphor for the logosmind, wherein the fluidity of the self attunes to and reveals the currents of the world. As for the barricaded hetabrain, I can't think of a better symbol than Professor Pippy P. Poopypants. The Professor is a character from the brazen comic book series by Dav Pilkey, *The Adventures of Captain Underpants*—a scientific genius who, having been stung by mockery and humiliation, decides to take over the world. Obsessed with renaming everyone on the planet, he creates a man-shaped robot ten stories high with a glass-domed control room for a head. Standing in that head he can watch the world outside, assess it from that perspective, and impose his will upon it by operating the robot.

Amidst its playfulness and comic-book zest, Professor Poopypants, housed within his robot, is the archetype of the hetabrain in action. He is a tyrant of self-achieved independence who ensconces himself in the head of a mechanical creation of his own making and pursues an agenda of such acquisitiveness it would mean the destruction of the world. Being a male Professor, he not only represents the element of doing, he is cast as an authoritative patriarch. Confident in his own superior intelligence, he excels at manipulating abstract concepts, which he does from the headquarters of his robot body, busy with the cybernetics of controlling it, obsessed with his agenda of names/labels/symbols and what he must do to carry it out, all the while buffered from the sensational processes of the world, which he monitors through the robot's domed window.

As the image of Professor Poopypants illustrates so clearly, the hetabrain inhabits a headquarters of its own making, one that renders the body as a mechanism and the world as exploitable. By contrast, the logosmind lives with the world as its complement: its willing passivity to 'what is' enables it to enter a mutual awareness with a felt whole. Whereas the hetabrain contracts into the consciousness of tyranny, the logosmind rests in the consciousness of being. Other differences between the hetabrain and the logosmind might be compared as follows:

The Hetabrain	The Logosmind
identifies with the dissociated male element and thinks with a unipolar consciousness	identifies with the whole and thinks with an axial consciousness that marries male and female, self and world
is centered in the head	is centered in the body
isolates its perspectives from being	converts its perspectives into sensation
is dedicated to doing	is devoted to Being
understands the world in four dimensions	experiences the world in five dimensions
functions on a coarse scale within a world that can be 'known'	lives within the unthinkable subtlety of a world that is fluid
sees the world as a sum of parts	feels the world as an indivisible whole
attends primarily to Idea	attends primarily to Energy
experiences the physical, emotional, mental and spiritual energies of the self as related but separate	experiences the physical, emotional, mental and spiritual energies of the self as a single, integrated consciousness
knows by analysis	understands through assimilation
looks at the world as though through a windowpane and interprets it	opens into the world as though through a door and joins it
has a digital intelligence that stands apart from the world and freezes its perspectives into bits of knowledge	has an analog intelligence that stands in the river of the world, knowing the whole by the movement of the whole

differentiates its intelligence from the body and is forgetful of the whole	understands its intelligence through the body and is continuous with the whole
experiences the body as a consolidated thing	experiences the body as a vibratory field of intelligence
sees a world of discrete objects	sees a world of indiscrete fluidity
prioritizes results and inhabits an interpreted world of duplicates	prioritizes sensitivity and dwells within the fluid processes of renewal
recognizes no guidance in the world, but seeks and complies with the authority of its duplicates	recognizes no authority, but listens for the calling of the world and submits to its guidance
clenches against the world and seeks mastery over it	yields to the world's flux and attends to the mystery of it
thinks in a monologue directed at itself	thinks in a dialogue with the world
through its doing implements its own solutions	through its Being realizes the world's grace
is a victim of the past	is a companion of the present
accumulates abstract knowledge and rules	assimilates waveforms and principles
uses symbols as its language of thought	recognizes sensation as its language of thought
characteristically holds and pushes	characteristically changes and rests
feeds on anxiety	rests in serenity
drives towards the future willfully, governed by the past	is carried forward gracefully, guided by the present

Corationality

The Universal Law of Interrelationship is the strength on which the logosmind builds; the illusion of perseity is the foundational premise

230 I TWO AXES, ONE PURPOSE

of the hetabrain. It is also the premise of our culture. Of course, our adherence to four dimensions will never turn perseity into a real phenomenon. We can consolidate the known and avert our gaze from fluid mystery; we can obsess over our duplicates and neglect the living guidance of the moment; we can seek refuge in the smaller self and disconnect from the larger Self; in short, we can refuse in any number of ways to open ourselves to the full dimensionality of the world; but we cannot create perseity. Not in physics, genetics, art, meaning, self, careers, families, human behavior, nations or nature. As physicist Lee Smolin reminds us, the world is

> a vast, interconnected system of relations, in which even the properties of a single elementary particle or the identity of a point in space requires and reflects the whole rest of the universe.[205]

His observation raises a question that is particularly pertinent to an understanding of ourselves: **if there is no perseity, what is the nature of our thinking?** Does a single thought "require and reflect the whole rest of the universe"? Or are all our personal thoughts created within the seclusion of our craniums, independent of the universal flux? Is our thinking somehow an exception to the Universal Law of Interrelationship? Should we draft up an exemption for ourselves? The hetabrain views thought according to the computer model: an enclosed rationality that looks at the world as though from behind the screen of its monitor. The ideal of *pure rationality* epitomizes the characteristics of perseity, being associated with self-enclosure, autonomy, authority and the right to rule. Fictions all, but they communicate such a seductive story that Darwin himself was prompted to write, "Of all the faculties of the human mind, it will, I presume, be admitted that Reason stands at the summit."[206] That summit, of course, is the prospect that provides us with objective perspective. But detached reason—divided from the world by the very altitude it seeks, determined to elevate itself above the messiness of feeling—cannot *assimilate*. Its digital duplicates cannot '*yield to what is*'—the basis of physical genius. Its judicative perspectives, however thickly piled one on top of the other, cannot *create a whole*. In this context, Rachel Carson's suggestion, "It is not half so important to *know* as to *feel*,"[207] acquires a particular poignancy, and provides a stark contrast to Darwin's.

We sometimes mistakenly imagine that *thinking* is synonymous with *reasoning*. As we have observed, though, thinking is necessary to catch a ball or ride a bike, and such thinking is not reason; it is sensational thinking, the thinking by which physical genius is able to process the whole and respond out of wholeness directly, without a need for mediation. Sensational thinking guides the aerialist aloft on his tightrope, and the mother's love for her child, and the limitless understanding that that love bestows. It guides our understanding of Bach or Rembrandt. **Sensational thinking is what alerts the 'self' aspect of consciousness to the 'world' aspect of consciousness and brings those two complementary poles into mutual awareness.** It is through their interplay that our consciousness derives new harmonies and new insights. Yet the hetabrain has the nerve to declare reason to be the supreme faculty—and then it adds insult to injury when it dismisses the thinking of the logosmind as *irrational*. When we remember that the root of *rational* is found in a word meaning "to join," the description seems downright ironic. The hetabrain, working in the splendid isolation of its own abstract concepts, is the truly 'disjointed' faculty.

But it is easy enough to understand how the hetabrain came to think of the logosmind as irrational: the analog axis of the logosmind functions in fluid partnership with the world; *it can no more think by itself than one leg can walk without the other.* Now imagine that you overheard someone alone in the next room talking on the phone, and that you didn't know such things as telephones existed. Hearing only his side of the conversation, you would think him mad, or irrational. That is precisely the case with the hetabrain: when the logosmind is thinking hand in hand with the Living Logos, the walled-in hetabrain overhears half of the conversation and, alarmed, proclaims the logosmind to be irrational. As a popular saying frames it, "And those who were seen dancing were thought to be insane by those who could not hear the music."

In much the same way, we may be inclined to think that the shamans and oracles of the world are off their rockers. Actor David Niven wrote of an incident in which he and his wife were staying with friends in the country. A hunt had been organized, but when it was time to leave for it, David found his wife reading a book. She calmly explained to him that she wasn't coming. He asked why, and she replied that if she did come, she would be shot. He was disappointed by her decision, *reasoned with her that it was quite irrational,* and implored her to change her mind. She finally relented, saying, "All right, but I'm going to be shot."[208] And so she was, in a freak accident that nearly left her disfigured.

All of us have probably had, or know someone who has had, such direct, 'irrational' insights. My friend Jack saved his mother's life by heeding what he 'irrationally' knew, leaving his classroom to run home. When my wife was a teenager she was driving down a winding mountain road into the setting sun when the car ahead of her, which had no brake lights, suddenly stopped. She hit the brakes hard, and her car skidded to a stop, narrowly avoiding a collision. When she got home, her mom asked her anxiously, "Are you all right?" About twenty minutes earlier, at the time of the near collision, she had had a terrible feeling of impending danger for her daughter.

The description of the logosmind as *irrational* has been foisted upon us by the hetabrain and helps to keep us in its thrall. It's time to free ourselves from that deceit. After all, who would ever trust themselves to a faculty that they truly believed was irrational? It would be … well, irrational. **But the thinking of the felt self isn't *ir*rational, it is corational**—literally "joined together"; and the mystery, the begetter of the interweaving perplexities around which we gather ourselves, the hidden harmony of things, the Logos, is its unseen partner in thinking—specifically, in sensational thinking. The logosmind is bestirred in a give-and-take with the currents of the great wave phenomenon around us, and from that wordless, sensational interplay the felt self is gifted with insights that emerge from Being itself. And so it is that *the analog axis of our consciousness converts sensations into insights:* insights that tell you, for example, that you will be shot if you go hunting today; that as you sit in class, your mother is dying; that your daughter is in danger; or even, if you attend patiently and sensitively and devotedly enough, that $E = mc^2$. Einstein wrote of the act of discovery, remember, that

> The intellect has little to do on the road to discovery. There comes a leap in consciousness, call it intuition or what you will, the solution comes to you and you don't know how or why.[209]

As Heidegger suggested, "essential thinking is an event of Being."[210] When the self aspect of consciousness unites with the world aspect of consciousness, the thinking self recognizes its identity as the felt whole, and its insights arise from Being itself. *Sensational genius, then, is not something you possess—it is a property of the dance of opposites in which you stand; and the more sensitively you awaken to that dance and yield to it and participate in it, the more fully you enable that genius.* You also begin to realize that certain anecdotes that we normally make palatable with a grain of salt, or consider to be quaint or metaphorical, are actually saying exactly and literally what is intended. Einstein was not being allegorical, but merely accurate, when he wrote that the harmony of natural law "reveals an intelligence of such superiority that, in comparison with it, all the systematic thinking of human beings is an utterly insignificant reflection."[211] Morehei Uyeshiba, the founder of aikido, was also being factual rather than poetic when he commented that

> the secret of Aikido is to harmonize ourselves with the movement of the universe and bring ourselves into accord with the universe itself.... When an enemy tries to fight with me, the universe itself, he has to break the harmony of the universe. Hence, at the moment he has the mind to fight with me, he is already defeated.[212]

When Heraclitus wrote, "Listening not to me but to the Logos, it is wise to acknowledge that all things are one,"[213] he didn't feign listening—*the Logos was his real, unseen partner in corational thinking,* just as the harmony of the universe was for Uyeshiba. To feel "the harmony of the universe" is to feel the coherence of the transforming whole advising us, ushering perspective into sensation and sensation into insight. The immediacy of such an experience is beyond all 'rational' understanding, beyond reason, but also beyond doubt: baffling and frustrating to the hetabrain, it is recognized as direct, primary, relational truth by the logosmind. On his return trip from the moon with the Apollo 14 mission, Edgar Mitchell looked out the window at Earth floating in the vastness of space and received a life-shaking insight about the hidden harmony of things and the palpable presence of divinity. As he later explained, "The knowledge came to me directly."[214]

It should be clear by now that the thinking of the felt self does not disdain the analytic aspect of our male consciousness; rather, it brings that faculty into relationship with the pelvic intelligence, where perceptions interact with a host of sensitivities that locate them in the present. That interaction is transformative: once an insight comes out of isolation and joins the present, it is experienced sensationally, and will be sensationally informed by the present. That conversion of a discrete perspective into sensation is analogous to the way nuclear fission converts bound matter into energy. The energy that is released as sensation is ungovernable, and where it might carry you is unknown; for that reason, it is feared by the hetabrain.

In the symbolic language of myth, we might note that when a male perception forsakes all urges towards tyranny, it can venture in submission down the corridor to the chthonic realm of female being, to be made whole by joining the whole. That journey changes the perception, as we have said; what is more difficult for us to understand is that it also alters the present—which unfailingly shifts as the fusion of the perspective into being converts it into energy. The Global Consciousness Project lets us see that effect on a grand scale: for instance, as the ceremony of Princess Diana's funeral converted the public consciousness of her death from a fact to an integrated, sensational understanding located in the present, random-event generators around the world registered the event: the shifting of the present.

The second form of conversion carried out by the thinking of the felt self—from sensation into insight—arises from a deeper partnership with the present. As our sensational union with the world shifts our spiritual center of gravity into the dark beyond, it often draws our attention to a potential source of grace; if we attend to that shapeless, sensed phenomenon before us, we become increasingly sensitized to it. Suspended in the dark emptiness between the poles of self and world, it acquires more and more presence, until finally it is released into the light of consciousness as a full-fledged insight. The liberation of such insights is also liberating: they are so deeply integrated, and so sensationally informed, that they accord with and reveal the whole from which they arise. They can take the form of a deep truth that speaks to your own life, or a line of poetry, or the revelation of a scientific principle: $E = mc^2$, for instance. Once such a gift of insight arrives, it triggers the energies of the felt self in a profound, sometimes soul-shaking wash of sensations; and those sensations in turn, once integrated, provoke further insights, so that the dance between the male and female aspects of our consciousness carries us deeper and deeper into the subtle sensitivities of the mindful present. That, then, is the true nature of our corational thinking—and I have come to trust it deeply, for there is no other means by which I could have written this book.

It turns out, then, that the analog axis of our consciousness is actually more than a means of receiving the waveforms of the world, in the way that a stylus receives the waveforms of an LP. Like the embodied axis, it enables an interplay between its poles in both directions. Through the analog axis, we not only receive the world: we behold it and are beheld. It is the axis by which the self aspect of consciousness and the world aspect of consciousness join in mutual awareness. It is along the analog axis that the sphere of our sensitivity opens to the corational nature of consciousness. An apt metaphor for the analog axis was expressed by Hiroyuki Aoki, the founder of Shintaido—a martial art founded on and shaped by its expressly spiritual concerns. In speaking of our duty as humans, Aoki said,

> The unconscious soul of the universe with which we are unified is completely reflected in the heart of great Nature.... And because we are such a small part of the natural world, it is good to imagine that there is a large pipeline connecting everything—earth, self and solar system—and that it is our task to clean and enlarge it.[215]

The trinity of "earth, self and solar system" evokes the mythical axis mundi that unites earth, man and sky—and it reflects the inner trinity of pelvic bowl, heart and cranial brain. And just as the embodied axis of that inner trinity is supported by a corridor that grows more spacious within us as we grow more sensitive, the analog axis of our consciousness is supported by "a large pipeline connecting everything"— a pipeline that we might refer to as the **corational corridor**. Our task is to "clean and enlarge it," as Aoki says, so that as its spaciousness grows, our sensitivity grows, until finally all the world around us is seen to be a vast, corational corridor, revealing "the unconscious soul of the universe with which we are unified."

Our corational partnership with the "unconscious soul of the universe" forms the basis of what I consider to be among the most transformative of prayers: "Thy will be done." To the casual observer, the prayer might seem ridiculous or even arrogant: that an individual should think that she can request of God that He enact His own will, or somehow give her permission for Him to do so—as if she had any say in the matter. In fact, the prayer is a profound expression of self-achieved submission, an abnegation of will and an awakening to the hidden coherence of all that is. It is transformative of self and world—inextricably linked as they are—precisely because it brings you into accord with that limitless harmony; it is empowering because it relinquishes force and the fiction that drives it, and celebrates the great dance of renewal and the sensitivity that enables us to feel it. Only by submitting to what is can you feel what is. And so we might come to understand that those whom Gladwell called physical geniuses might also be called geniuses of corational thinking—geniuses for being able to devote their attention to a challenge to which they have been called, and to "feel what is" in its living reality. **We help the world not with willpower, but with sensitivity.**

A key to the thinking of the felt self is found in an early Buddhist text that observed, "When the mind is disturbed, the multiplicity of things is produced; but when the mind is quieted, the multiplicity of things disappears."[216] The multiplicity of things arises from a mind attached to the fiction of four dimensions, which presents a world made up of innumerable independent objects. The imagined autonomy of those objects provides the central conceit of control on which the hetabrain depends, for mastery is possible only over the bits and pieces of a world that is artificially broken up—like the Gordian knot sliced apart by Alexander's sword. Similarly, mastery is possible only over the bits and pieces of a *self* that is artificially broken up. When the harmony of Being is broken, Authority takes over, chattering away in its incessant, distracted monologue, obsessed with systemizing the world's multiplicity.

The thinking of the felt self, then, is grounded in stillness, which reveals the world as a unity. If we cling to the idea that our intelligence is our own personal computer, plugged into our brain stem, shielded from interference by the blood-brain barrier and ready to calculate solutions to our problems, we forget stillness and trust in the application of force. If we understand that our true genius is found in our capacity to clean and enlarge the pipeline, heeding the all-informing companionship of the present, we will trust in the felt mystery and the calm sensitivity in us that accords with its guidance. That is the state of a corational genius who, like an accomplished surfer, rides the unfolding wave of the present without fear or consolidation; the rest of us are too busy looking for ways to exert control over the board and the self to really feel the wave—the Logos—that carries us.

We might finally note that when love roots the felt self in the stillness of the present, its vibratory calm reveals, above all, that you are not alone: you breathe with all things as they breathe with you, sensitized to the grace of mutual awareness. To look upon the world, immersed in its wild peace, is to know that you are known. The union between love and corationality is made memorably clear in a story that was told to Matthew Fox by a car mechanic. As Fox tells it, the mechanic

> was depressed at work but stuck with his job because of family responsibilities. Then he encountered a Sufi teacher who said to him, "Each time you turn the ratchet as you repair a vehicle, speak the word Allah." The mechanic did so, and his whole life changed, the whole relation with his work changed. "Now," he said, "I love my work. I love cars. They are alive. It is a mistake to think of animate versus inanimate. A car will tell you, if you listen deeply enough, whether it wants to be repaired or whether it wants simply to be left alone to die."[217]

By the same token, I have found it immensely helpful to recognize that *any time you feel alone in doing something,* it is a sure sign that you have detached from the present, abandoned your own wholeness, and entrusted yourself to the unipolar realm of doing and willpower. What pulls you into that realm is easily identified: by detaching from the present, you render the world four-dimensional, whereupon the corational corridor blinks out of existence, like Eurydice; and then you have nowhere else to stand but in that realm. In fact, it becomes clear that just as **a collapse of the inner corridor creates a unipolar** *consciousness,* **a collapse of the corational corridor creates a unipo-** lar *existence:* in the absence of the corational corridor, you become trapped in the self—watching the world as though through a window, fundamentally desensitized to it. Of course, we are all directed into a unipolar existence by our culture's story. What other fulfillment could our belief in perseity provide us? It denies the call, refutes the relationships that constitute Being, sanctions self-absorption, and dismisses any notion that our spiritual center of gravity might lie in the felt unknown beyond the self. We feel that by accepting our culture's staunch axioms we are keeping to reality—but as we have seen, reality is a union of opposites that dance the world into being. Only when we open to that dance—to the diversity, energy, newness, calm and harmony that thrive between its vibrant poles—can we feel the dance and join in. And there is literally a world of difference between *standing* in a unipolar realm and *dancing* through the energized expanse that is held between complementary opposites. It is only in the spacious companionship of that dance that we can "feel the thing as a whole," and find our peace in it.

Finding peace while holding a mechanic's wrench or in the midst of our commonplace chores and activities is not always easy—and there are no shortcuts to it. Peace is not a matter of stress management; it is more than the absence of anxiety. Peace is a full acceptance of the whole of your life and an engagement with the whole of your truth; it is what opens you to the transforming present. Any parts of you that are chronically not at peace—any parts that carry judgment or plans or resentments—cannot be made to conform to peace, or go quiet: they live in the body and have to be processed by its fluid intelligence. You cannot join the present until you offer your entire body to the present—so that the felt self can come to rest in the pelvic bowl, quickened to the subtle stirrings all around it.

The Subtle Dialogue

When the poet A. E. Housman was asked to define poetry, he famously replied that he "could no more define poetry than a terrier can define a rat";[218] but he added that he thought both he and the terrier recognized their quarry by the physical symptoms it provoked in them. Like the terrier hunting a rat, an artist pursues the resonant life of his artwork with gestures or syllables or daubs of paint or notes of music; and like the terrier, the artist is guided in his pursuit by the physical aliveness of his response, which tells him it's the real thing. When the artist eventually stands back and declares the artwork to be complete, it is not because he has achieved something fixed, solid and eternal, but just the opposite: **the artist knows his work is complete when it has acquired such sensitivity that each part is fluidly responsive to every other, so** that as he looks at the whole of it, it won't hold still, but moves with the subtle slipperiness of a living perplexity.

The same truth obtains for us with regards to the body: just as an artwork is fully realized only when it achieves consummate fluidity, it helps to recognize that **you are fully present to the world only when your body is completely unlocked to the currents of the present.** Only movement can know movement, as the whirlpool knows the river. That is the aim of the best bodywork: to awaken the body into a state of awareness and flow, freely responsive to the perplexity of 'what is', so that the wave of each breath ripples through the body as a whole and the whole is experienced as a borderless field of energy attuned to the felt singularity of the present. Whenever the body yields to that kind of fluid harmony, the merest reverberation in the core of your being will ripple through the whole of it. As the world aspect of consciousness and the self aspect of consciousness come into relationship as complementary poles—each the beholder, each the beheld—the subtle, yielding, sensational, insight-birthing currents that run along the analog axis between them are literally a dialogue; and it is in that dialogue that you truly "feel the thing as a whole," even as the whole is feeling you.

Just as our word *analog* traces back to the Greek concept of Logos, so does *dialogue:* it comes from *dia* and *logos,* which combine to mean literally "through the Logos"—*and through the Logos is precisely how the felt self thinks:* when the pole of the self recognizes its complement in the living present, and opens to it so that what is passing through the Logos passes through the corridor of your being, then your core will answer as a compass needle does to the far poles of the earth. And so the dialogue begins. All information is shared information.

"Feeling the thing as a whole," then, is not a striking and grand accomplishment that is achieved by standing back and taking it all in from some überperspective; it occurs as you enter a living conversation with the whole—and that can only happen on a very subtle scale: a scale revealed by stillness. *A surrender to Being is a surrender to its intimate dialogue.* Be still, and know that life is subtle.

The subtlety of your relationship with the living present is revealed only to the degree that the subtlety of the body is brought into awareness. That awareness is not some rarefied abstract ideal; it is what you begin to feel when you grow fully passive to the mindful body and honor its merest sensation as being fully worthy of your attention. It is only on the scale of such subtlety that the body can be experienced as a vibratory medium, and the logosmind revealed. We have been advised to regard the subtle stirrings of the body's energy as the unintended offspring of various biochemical processes of physiology, often nuisances at best and barely worth our attention: but they are much, much more than that. **They are the stirrings of our unnamable and acutely sensitive attempts to assimilate the present and accord with it as a whole.** The consciousness of the named 'I'—your 'known self'—resides in the hetabrain; but the consciousness of the ineffable felt self resides within the subtle stirrings of the body. *If those subtle energies are in conflict, the 'I' is in conflict; if those energies are coherent, the 'I' exists as a whole and can come into relationship with the present as a whole.*

Subtle energy does not lie. It is what it is. It is beyond the reach of any of fantasy's coarse fabrications. As the sphere of our sensitivity dilates to take in more and more of the world, it is specifically opening more and more to the world's subtlety. Once you start to lift the curtain on that humming universe, you will find that the subtle energy of Being suffuses everything: it illuminates the teacup, and answers your heart's gaze; it sifts between the pine needles, and seeps through them, even as it sifts and seeps through you. The subtle currents of the world strengthen the mechanic's wrench as he speaks "Allah" and guides it with grace and companionship.

There is a poem by Bashō that was written while he was traveling *The Narrow Road to the Deep North:* his house sold, his heart "filled with a strong desire to wander," he was well into his journey, being led along a path on horseback, when he addressed the farmer leading him:

> Turn the head of your horse
> Sideways across the field,
> To let me hear
> The cry of a cuckoo.[219]

The horse, like the part of us that persists in doing, is brought to a stillness; and off to the side, across the field, comes the quiet, bright song of the present: the Self calling to the self.

The One Purpose

The thinking of the felt self, as we have seen, begins along the embodied axis: once that axis unites cranial brain and pelvic intelligence, the self can be felt as a unity; and then the analog axis can bring the self aspect of consciousness and the world aspect of consciousness into mutual awareness. The union of those two axes is what we might call the crux of our consciousness. That much is clear, but that clarity raises a larger issue: if we have a purpose in our lives, individually as well as collectively, surely the capacities with which we were born and from whose interplay our very natures are forged would give us the most direct indication possible as to what our purpose might be.

It is clear that our first task as humans is to unite the poles of consciousness within us; and, indeed, the task of joining male and female in full, embodied consciousness gives most of us fodder enough for a lifetime's work. But let us suppose that we learn to still the fears of the tyrant and to open our hearts to the fragile beauty of the world around us. Let us say that we finally come to see that the only way to bring male and female into balance is to say, "First, being"; and that the driven, anxious, dissociated male grows passive enough to all the subtle currents and energies of Being to feel them and fall in love with them and fall into them. And suppose that in that spirit of adoration our male perspective surrenders its strength to the all-integrating genius of Being, and the two are united—and that their unified sensitivities then open to find their complement in the singularity of the felt present. What then? What does that newborn mutual awareness enable? What does it prepare us for? Through what work could it fulfill itself?

The sensitivity of the felt self enables us to venture into the mountains and valleys of the human enterprise all around us, into the mysteries of great nature, and gain perspectives of utter clarity on our world, and *integrate* those perspectives so that they deeply enrich our ability to see and understand the world—and, living in that renewed seeing and understanding, to feel more clearly our relationships with 'the thing as a whole', attending to it so closely that sensation converts into perspective, illuminating the felt mystery of the Logos. The effect of such a venture is to sensitize us to all the relationships that constitute our being; and that, in turn, sensitizes us to the One. As we find ourselves more and more deeply reflected in the world around us, **not only will our responses to the world bring our core into full relationship with it—they will bring our core into its full and irrevocable responsibility to the world.** It is in that awakening to responsibility that our strengths find their purpose and that we are carried into the grace and poignancy and power of our own lives. It is in the illuminated, ordinary relationships of that responsibility that we find our presence, our true freedom, and our limitless creativity. It is through the actions into which that responsibility carries us, and with which it challenges us, that we will undertake a personal journey of discovery that will not just bring us into harmony with the world—it will enable us to actively deepen that harmony.

And so it is that the heart, dynamically awakened by the energy of the embodied axis within us, opens to discover its self in the world around it, and to recognize that self as the One—and to be carried by its intimate love of the One, its love of life itself, into the revelatory, activated gifts of sacred responsibility. That is the single purpose to which our true nature is born. It is the journey the world asks you to take, and it is on that journey that the world will most profoundly bless the days of your life. The world is inviting you on that journey right now—if only you could hear its invitation all around you.

Exercise Seven: The Flower and the Cello String

The crux of your consciousness lies in the meeting place of self and world. It is there that the embodied axis engages in interplay with its complementary pole in the embodied world, activating the corational axis. Naming and even feeling that crux is one thing; finding a way to center yourself in its coursing intelligence is another. We have looked at the whirlpool as a metaphor to help us feel and understand the logosmind. This exercise helps us feel and understand the felt self.

The dynamic of the felt self, as we have said, is one in which you rest in the pelvis and act from the heart. It finds its complement in the dynamic of a simple flower: its roots are sunk deep in the stillness of the dark earth, and its many-petaled blossom, like the heart, opens to the world. That dynamic heightens our affinity for flowers, since it also stirs deep within us. To connect with it, begin by standing upright, knees soft and hips floating, and allow the breath to drop into the pelvic bowl and release out. In this relaxed state, allow the elevator to drop down the shaft (see Exercise Six) and come to rest on the pelvic floor. Once your sensitivity has gathered in the pelvic bowl, feel the roots of the flower securely and deeply grounded there, and feel its stem carrying the vibrational energy of your being from those roots up to your heart, which blossoms within your breast and shares that energy with all the world.

As you feel the roots, stem and blossom acquire presence and specificity within you, you might note how your sensitivity attunes to the world differently. You might also be aware of a tendency to focus on the blossom—just as we forget the roots when we cut flowers and arrange them in a vase. It is from the roots, though, that the flower draws its life-sustaining nourishment. If you put your attention on the roots, allowing them to ground themselves in your pelvic intelligence, you may also feel them rooting themselves in the present; and then you can understand that it is not any energy you *possess*, but the energy *of the present itself*, that streams up from the roots and opens the heart to the world—an opening that is connected to and expressive of the pelvic bowl of being, in which male and female unite.

We have spoken of the energy of Being as a vibrational energy— the great wave phenomenon. Like the Tao, that energy cannot be lost, but it can be found. When the vibrational present touches your core and lives there, the stem that carries its rooted energy through the heart and into the world might be experienced almost as a cello string—vibrating along its length within you, between pelvic bowl and heart, singing to the world and with the world. Without that living

correspondence between the pelvic center of your being and its love-supported portal to the world, your soul's energy will be at a loss to greet the world and join it. Similarly, if the portal of your heart is open to the world, but not rooted in the depths of your being, it will disconnect from your place of rest.

The vibrational flower of the felt self is a guiding image I return to frequently, and it is a practice that all the other exercises in the book are designed to support. Once you have activated that image within you, though, allow it to disappear. Like any other exercise or metaphor or system of understanding presented in this book, if the flower is taken to be a solution, it will stand between you and the world as surely as any duplicate. The image is useful only to the extent that it opens a door and newly sensitizes you to 'what is'. So let go of the image, and step through the door it reveals. If roots, stem and blossom were all clearly felt as a unity within you, then where the flower was you will likely find, lingering within you, the awakened, dynamic crux of your consciousness, sensitized to the corational corridor all around you. A direct experience of the great wave phenomenon of being, and of you as an indivisible part of it, will itself begin to heal the deepest schisms we live with: the rupture between our thinking and our being; the disconnect between our pelvic intelligence and our hearts; and the artificial divide of self from world.

Those schisms, incidentally, show up for all to see in what our culture accepts as normal adult posture. If you look around at people as they stand or sit or walk, you will notice that the angle between the neck and the upper back is an obtuse angle—that is, it falls somewhere between 180 and 90 degrees. The angle tends to get smaller with age; in some people it can even approach a right angle. If our torsos were erect, that angle between neck and torso would leave us all looking at the sky (Figure A); but our chests have so collapsed upon our hearts that we are actually looking forward (Figure B). In our culture, the chest tends to progressively collapse as we age, so that we have to lift the head more and more to continue seeing in front of us.

Fig. A

Our culture's 'normalized' collapse of the chest cannot be wholly explained by aging, or the effects of gravity, or osteoporosis; it is a direct result of our unipolar existence, which dissociates from the present, and our unipolar consciousness, which dissociates from the body. As a result, the energy of the heart is unsupported by the energy of our being. When the energy of the heart flags, the chest sags, and the tilt of the head adjusts to compensate.

Fig. B

Fig. C

There are many exercises and techniques for improving our posture and our biomechanics. I suggest that the ones that really work are those that help us, inadvertently or not, to open our hearts and ground them in the energy of our being. The flower of the felt self takes the direct approach: it connects the heart's energy with the vibratory energy of our pelvic intelligence, which opens the heart to the living energy of the present and supports us in all we do. When the crux of our consciousness is awakened like that (Figure C), the body's energy follows: the angle at the back of the neck becomes a gentle, elongated convex curve, and we stand up straight—not because it is the 'correct' posture, and we 'should' stand that way; not because we need to house an inflated ego; but because, by surrendering to the energy of the present, we open to it and celebrate it.

There is a remarkable time-lapse video of a lily blossom opening that perfectly coveys the affinity between the opening of a flower and the opening of the heart. I could watch it once a day. It can be viewed at http://www.seantamblyn.com/island/Last%20Day%20Lily_100.swf

Part III

The Exchanges of Being

Those who set out to serve both God and Mammon
soon discover that there is no God.
—Logan Pearsall Smith

How could the soul not take flight
When from the glorious Presence
A soft call flows sweet as honey, comes right up to her
And whispers, "Rise up now, come away."
—Rumi

... And I have felt
A presence that disturbs me with the joy
Of elevated thoughts; a sense sublime
Of something far more deeply interfused
Whose dwelling is the light of setting suns,
And the round ocean, and the living air,
And the blue sky, and in the mind of man,
A motion and a spirit, that impels
All thinking things, all objects of all thought
And rolls through all things.
—William Wordsworth

8 | The Heart's Compass

Refusing the Call

With the parlor trick that collapses the axes of our consciousness—retracting it into the head and evicting livingness from the world—we find ourselves surrounded by things that, for the most part, have no personal relevance to us except as obstacles or resources. Our perspective on them tells us what, if anything, we might want from them; but the very idea that the world might want something *from us,* and might be calling to what is most personal in us to communicate that, is frankly nonsensical. Our culture's story assures us that the world is ultimately no more than atoms moving through the indifferent vacuum of space-time; dead matter is insensate: it cannot want; it cannot call. That fiction leads to irksome conclusions, though: if the above were true, then we ourselves are ultimately no more than atoms within the indifferent vacuum of space-time—and yet we want, and we call. Might it be, then, that only *some* atoms—the ones we possess—can participate in consciousness? More to the point, might that last suggestion be more nonsensical than the conclusion from which it tries to save us?

In *The Book of Tea,* Kakuzo Okakura wrote, "We boast that we have conquered Matter, and forget that it is Matter that has enslaved us."[220] To my mind, those words offer a succinct summation of the place to which our evolving self-tyranny has brought us. We conquered Matter not only with the parlor trick that expelled the One Presence from it; we also subjected it to our every whim and use, baffled at the few lonely voices speaking of the need for respect—a claim that may seem wholesome in a New Age sort of way, but which can be no more than a sentimental overlay onto matter that is fundamentally dead and expendable. Ultimately, though, in conquering Matter, we became enslaved to it. That is, we conquered matter by eliminating its living dimension, which meant we then had to define ourselves as lifeless matter biochemically animated, and our existence as unipolar; and once we are so defined any concepts such as inherent sacredness, mystery and spirit appear to be no more than sentimental overlays on who *we* actually are. And so Matter triumphed over Mind, and holds us hostage: trapped in an idea of ourselves that is cut off from the un-manifest, abiding, all-creating stillness that enfolds self and world, we are slaves to the belief that our entire experience is a by-product of the ineluctable laws of biochemical materialism. Until we can escape that idea of ourselves, we will remain prisoners within the four dimensions of dead Matter, and will continue to devote our lives to its material bidding, its material pursuits and its material limitations.

The great Karlfried Dürckheim wrote an astute diagnosis of the trap into which our parlor trick has carried us. What we have called the construct of the 'known self', he calls the I-prisoner.

> In the conduct of practical daily life the I-prisoner shows an anxious striving for demonstrable security, and as he does not possess that fundamental trust in life which comes from an openness towards Being, he has no choice but to rely upon himself alone. **His self-confidence rests solely upon what he knows, has and can do.** So he is always concerned with improving and preserving his position, always in fear for his material security, in society very sensitive about his dignity, and when he feels himself attacked he stiffens or turns sour—becomes "knotted up inside." ... **Because of the rigidity of his preconceived ideas he is not even in contact with himself.** He cuts himself off from all that fullness and unifying strength in life which, deep within his being, wants to unfold and be at one with others. Thus, by admitting only what does not upset his tenaciously held position he not only cuts himself off from the powers flowing towards him from the outside, but to the point of sterility, he is cut off from his own creative powers.... And lastly no amount of

success in the world can serve to satisfy his inner need. **For every success which he attributes to his own efforts only strengthens and heightens the wall separating him from his own being.**[221]

Of course, we ourselves are the jail keeper watching over the 'I-prisoner'. But how did that that fundamental separation of self from being come about? Myth gives us a clue, in what Joseph Campbell calls the "Refusal of the Call."

> Often in actual life, and not infrequently in the myths and popular tales, we encounter the dull case of the call unanswered: for it is always possible to turn the ear to other interests. Refusal of the summons converts the adventure into its negative. Walled in boredom, hard work, or 'culture', the subject loses the power of significant affirmative action and becomes a victim to be saved. His flowering world becomes a wasteland of dry stones and his life feels meaningless—even though, like King Minos, he may through titanic effort succeed in building an empire of renown. Whatever house he builds, it will be a house of death: a labyrinth of cyclopean walls to hide from him his Minotaur. All he can do is create new problems for himself and await the gradual approach of his disintegration.[222]

To refuse the Call is to refuse the mutually animating, corational exchange between self and world. By denying the analog axis, it impoverishes the embodied axis. The consequences of that refusal constitute the primary crises we face individually and collectively. It is the basis of our mistaken identity, which isolates us in our own skins and places us in a world of mere dead matter and physical laws. It disconnects us from the living world—so that our actions can only be insensitive and willful. As James Hillman observed, "The coming ecological disaster we worry about has already occurred, and goes on occurring. It takes place in the accounts of ourselves that separate ourselves from the world."[223] And finally, it leads to our unipolar, inner patriarchy: deafened to the world's ability to guide all that we do, we then have to guide *ourselves* in all we do: we have to invest one part of us as the supervising authority, to issue orders to the other part. In other words, **to refuse the Call is to insist on the solutions of tyranny.**

As we have seen, the solutions of tyranny are willful, detached from the present, and deeply patterned. In fact, those solutions pattern us. Our word *pattern* derives from the Latin *pater*, which means "father." The hetabrain is the inner patriarch, in charge of the self and enforcing its *agendas*—literally "things to be done." It stands at the helm of the self, issuing commands, guiding the cybernetics of the divided self with nonstop directives. We might even refer to that relentless chatter in the head as the **Pater-patter**: the authoritative monologue in the stronghold of the skull that is forever issuing advice on what to do and how to do it, and overwhelming the call of the world with busy warnings and congratulations and calculations and blandishments and judgments. Of course, there is no true authority in the world; there is only companionship. Authority is an abstraction we create in order to govern what has lost touch with the guidance of Being. That is as true of our social patriarchies as it is of the unipolar patriarch within.

I have no desire to confuse fatherhood with the mythological tyrant, any more than I would wish to confuse the disembodied male element with men in general, or motherhood with the female element of pure Being: no one in the world has more to *do* than a mother. And as for fatherhood—it is one of the greatest gifts to have blessed my life, and I cherish it every day. I also know, though, that my ability to cherish it, and my own abilities as a father in general, have been guided by the vivid and sad memories of the extent to which my own father bought into the prevailing culture that said he was the head of the household—"master of a house" is the literal meaning of *husband*. As conceived of by that culture, his job was to rule and control. His natural vitality was hardened by those rigid assumptions: he was as remote from my childhood as is the hetabrain from the body.

When the body is patterned and controlled by inner patriarchy, it is so incapable of natural response that, as Moshe Feldenkrais observed, the "conscious wish to perform a reflex action is sometimes sufficient to stop it or interrupt it even when there is stimulation that is normally infallible." He cites a range of examples, including this story by Charles Darwin:

> Many years ago I laid a small wager with a dozen young men that they would not sneeze if they took

snuff, although they all declared that they invariably did so; accordingly they all took a pinch, but from wishing much to succeed, not one sneezed, though their eyes watered, and all without exception had to pay me the wager.[224]

A natural response is uncontrolled, something that insults the very premise of the patriarchal hetabrain. The sole resource of the hetabrain lies in its bank of consolidated knowledge: it stores patterns, recalls them, revises them and adds to them; but without the crux of consciousness that unifies the self and locates it in the world, the hetabrain can never step outside of that fortified bank and open to the newness of 'what is'. Newness comes upon us sensationally, as Archimedes leaped from his bath with "Eureka" echoing in the air; the hetabrain is sheltered from newness within the insensate *skull*—a word that comes from the Indo-European base "to cut, cleave, split," the meaning of which closely resembles that of the Latin *scindere*, "to cut, split, cleave," from which we get our word *science*. The Call is newness itself: it is freshly here, now, summoning through the present, fully awake to you. To be cut off from newness is to be immune to the Call and insensate to the felt mystery from which it issues.

The Laius Complex

Myths abound in which tyrants refuse the Call and set themselves up as the Authority. As I have said, my greatest interest in such myths is *in their representations of our most significant struggle: the struggle to overthrow inner patriarchy and integrate our thinking with our Being.* When Freud famously considered the Oedipus myth, he approached it in a different way, to shed light on an ageless dynamic among mother, son and father—and that insight has certainly proven its relevance. The narrowness with which that relevance can be applied—to certain males struggling with the problems of adolescence—is commensurate with the narrowness with which Freud looks at the myth. He neglects most of its inconvenient details, such as the fact that Oedipus only attacked his father after his father had twice tried to kill him. In fact, the tyrant Laius didn't ever encounter Oedipus *without* trying to kill him. These and other events in the myth take on a new significance if we understand the story not as a struggle of son against father but as something more personal: the struggle we all face against the fearful tyranny of the self by the male element.

It was foretold to King Laius that his son would one day kill him, so Laius mutilated his baby's feet at birth—as the Messenger tells Oedipus in the play by Sophocles, "the tendons of your feet were pierced and fettered"—and sent him to die of exposure on a mountainside. To illuminate the symbolic meaning of that act, we might understand that the father's heart was moved by an absolute refusal to let his son stand on his own. For *father* and *son*, of course, we can substitute *hetabrain* and *self*.

The wounds gave the baby his name: *Oedipus* means "swollen feet." When father and son next meet, the son has grown to young manhood and knows nothing of his real father. He is traveling along a road, as the play makes clear, on his own two feet. His father, a "*head* of state," happens along the same road riding in a vehicle: a carriage pulled by horses. He is attended by five servants whom he commands from his seat of power. When they encounter Oedipus standing on his own, Pater Laius orders his men to thrust Oedipus off the road, as if to say, "The way belongs to me," which pretty much sums up the attitude of the inner patriarch. Oedipus, angered, strikes the coachman who pushes him. Pater Laius sees that and waits until Oedipus passes by the carriage, whereupon he again tries to kill him, striking Oedipus "full on the head with his two-pointed goad."[225] Oedipus, enraged, unseats Laius from his carriage and kills him, as well as four of his attendant minions.

If this myth is taken as a message encoded by the self to be later discovered by the self, the message would read "**kill the pattern, or the pattern will kill you.**" Kill the Buddha, kill the patriarch of the law, as the Zen motto put it. Joseph Campbell pointed to precisely that as the hero's task: "the mythological hero is the champion not of things become, but of things becoming; the dragon to be slain by him is precisely the monster of the status quo."[226] Marion Woodman and Elinor Dickson address the same issue when they write,

> To cut off the head of patriarchy within us is to cut
> off the power drives—the injunctions, the rules, false
> reasonings, false values that separate us from our
> reality and take our voice away.[227]

The reason it is so vital to slay the internalized Pater is simple: the Pater refuses the Call, barricades the inner corridor, neutralizes the corational corridor of Being, and so imprisons us in its self-tyranny. Equally, then, we can see that the Zen motto is saying, "Kill who you know yourself to be, or it will kill you." But we should also appreciate that our facility for perspective is what gives us the choice to get past "the monster of the status quo" and transform with the "things becoming": **perspective reveals pattern**; perspective that is rooted in Being becomes insight that enables the hero to look the tyrant in the eye and vanquish him; in other words, *perspective helps us liberate ourselves from the segregations of perspective.*

As the story of Laius demonstrates, the Authority would rather kill what is new in us than risk being eclipsed by it. Trusting only in its hoard of fixed knowledge, the inner patriarch willfully shapes self and world in its image; its motivation is anxiety, its obsession is control, and its claim is entitlement—which considers the true self to be aloof from or more special than the ordinary world that calls us into Being. The bundle of tendencies that constitute the Authority make up **the consciousness of inner patriarchy, or the *Laius complex*.** Quite simply, the Laius complex is what inevitably becomes of us when we refuse the Call and step back from our primary relationship with Being. It is to the Laius Complex that Charles Davis addressed himself when he wrote,

> The core of disorder lies in the self. The self has to be healed; **its attempt to control the universe is a sickness to be cured, not a source of remedy.**[228]

Similarly, Lao-tzu warns us that:

> Not-knowing is true knowledge.
> Presuming to know is a disease.
> First realize that you are sick;
> then you can move towards health.[229]

"Presuming to know" is the disease of Laius within us: it grows like a scab between us and the Energy of the present, effectively arresting our personal evolution. *Forever guided by the Authoritative Pater, our lives remain infantile:* unfulfilled, egocentric, grasping, reactionary, and irresponsible in its most literal sense: "not able to respond." It is impossible to demonstrate response-ability to what cannot be felt. Of course, to step out from under the aegis of the Pater's rule—to move from four-dimensional doing to five-dimensional Being—is to step into the unpredictable sensations of genuine experience; and that exposes us to genuine vulnerabilities. As Campbell points out,

> Original experience has not been interpreted for you, and so you've got to work out your life for yourself ... You don't have to go far off the interpreted path to find yourself in very difficult situations. The courage to face the trials and to bring a whole new body of possibilities into the field of interpreted experience for other people to experience—that is the hero's deed.[230]

On the uninterpreted path of Being, the streets are naked—the Pater's rules and signs and sidewalks are stripped away—and there you are, naked to the energy of the present. In your passivity to the subtle intelligence coursing through the body you begin to assimilate the unknown currents in which you stand: the axes intersect, the corridors accord. That harmonic brings you into relationship with the present, and into the mutual awareness of Being—a tangible dialogue in which all the particulars of the world talk to you, and through them, behind them, the aliveness of the world is felt. Once you feel that aliveness as acutely as you feel your own, then you will recognize the fathomless sensitivity that embraces you in understanding; and the small step that takes you from that recognition to saying, "Guide me," or "Comfort my friend," or even just "Thank you," is the step that will carry you into prayer.

The Mother and Her Summoned Child

The reality of our mind-suffused world, by calling to us, calls also to itself. But how do we actually attend to that reality—and how can we recognize the Call? For a first clue we could turn to a poem by Rumi:

> All day and night, music,
> a quiet, bright

reedsong. If it fades,
we fade.[231]

Of course, the Call does not exist objectively: its reedsong exists for us only when we confront the present as life confronts life; when we meet the present as a child's gaze meets its mother's. In the loving intelligence of that mutual recognition, the present will talk to us. *When our attention retreats from the reality of the present, though, the Call fades and we too fade.* When the Call fades, the felt self fades, and the patterns of Laius take over—pulling us from kinship into isolation, from the energy of being into idea. The analog axis sustains the felt self in its limitless capacity for relationship, even as the felt self sustains the Call; and both sustain the bright spaciousness of Being.

The reedsong of the Call is neither esoteric nor obscure. Children live for it and dance to it. If you watch young ones you will see them suddenly stirred to engage with the world, and you will notice that they respond to its Call unfettered by self-consciousness or anxiety: they simply answer it, in tune with what their whole resonant Being communicates to them. And the world calls to them without generalization: it calls specifically and personally, suddenly illuminating a corner of their world with a special significance. As Mozart was called by the keyboard, another child might be called by a snowboard or a chessboard or a diving board or a ballet slipper. In *The Soul's Code* psychologist James Hillman cites example after example of children seized by the desire to engage with the world through a certain activity. Elsewhere I remember reading that Baryshnikov as a child couldn't stop dancing. My elder daughter was three when she appeared in a performance at her nursery school's spring concert. Once the children had lined up across the stage, she stepped out of the line to come downstage center, where she remained for the whole program. She didn't calculate that; it was just right for her. Some months before she turned seven, my younger daughter held a violin for the first time; it struck such a chord in her that she announced that she didn't care if she got nothing else for her birthday but please, *please,* could she have a violin. I've never wanted a violin in my life—it makes me a little nervous just holding one. The world calls me in other directions.

Of course the world does not call primarily to children; but it calls most reliably to those who have retained—or, more likely, regained—the innocence that makes children receptive to the Call. In childhood we are surrounded by giants, and the world is enormous and mysterious; by the time our childhood becomes a distant memory, the world has typically so shrunk in our adult awareness that it has largely become a 'known' entity—and our own presence within it, by comparison, can seem quite significant in its scale. Such bloat fantasies are born of layers of neglect, and are incompatible with the innocence that enables children to walk through the ordinary world knowing it as an extension of the Mother's lap. A child feels its mother's love expressed in its essential relationship to Being; an adult who can open his eyes to the present mystery of Being, and trust in it as a child trusts in its mother—who can feel the maternal caring and love expressing itself through all that is—will hear the world call him by name to undertake with heart and soul and dedication the work that will renew the world, even as it renews the self. Hearing that call, he will respond as a child summoned by its mother.

No one simply remakes oneself as a 'summoned child'—it happens as the outcome of an unswerving honesty about one's own life and a dedication to one's own personal journey towards wholeness. **Once you understand the fundamental nature of your relationship to the world as that of a child summoned by its mother, you will never lose your sense of the world's wholeness**—and you will heed its Call and dedicate yourself to it, and express your unity with it in all that you do.

A friend of mine, musician Marty Reno, once told me that his favorite saying was, "God will give you your heart's desire." He expressed dismay at those who construed it to mean, "God will give you *what* you desire"; for Marty it means just what it says: *God's gift is the desire itself—specifically your heart's desire.* It is a gift that pulls your entire life into focus; it lights up the world for you and illuminates you within it. And it is worth stressing the point: your *heart's* desire never conforms to the tyrant's desire to acquire, or to the prideful desire of the 'known self' to manipulate its fiction. It is something else—something that threatens to upset your world, to challenge you and transform you. You awaken to a mere possibility shimmering in the darkness beyond, and your whole life is tugged towards that new horizon on its way to an adventure. And that adventure could be of any sort whatsoever: intellectual, physical, romantic, spiritual, or all of them at once.

The inner, physical resonance of the calling can come as a momentary touch of guidance, or as a huge thing that seizes you and sustains years of dedication—which is what happens when you find your 'calling in life', or your true *vocation*, a word that comes from the Latin *vocatus*, "called." Whatever the nature of the resonance, **it always calls you into the unknown, and it always calls you towards wholeness, and it always calls you to come and play and risk.** It calls you to follow your soul's valence, to leave the safety of your own organized inadequacy, to find something out and to grow. By responding to the Call, you knowingly or unknowingly undertake *a deepening of your responsibility*.

It seems paradoxical that in leaving behind the segregated realm of your 'known self'—every part of which seeks your individuation—you more fully discover and grow into your own individuality. But once you have cast off the smothering constraints of 'who you know yourself to be', you will be open to the world's perplexity, which calls you to be changed and challenged who knows how. By heeding that call, you are following what in mythological terms is the hero's call to submission: the quest begins, the search is underway, driven by the need to find something out. It is through the quest that you shed your own consolidated 'norms' and discover yourself anew. It bundles certainty and uncertainty together at the same time: the certainty of your heart's desire moving you forward, grounded in the world and awake to it; and the uncertainty of what lies ahead. *But the certainty you feel does not rest, as our culture's story would advise, on your having* '**found the answer**'. *The certainty with which the hero moves into the unknown rests on his having* **found his quest**—*which, as the word suggests, is empowered by a* **quest**ion *that has you in its grip and calls you to life.* Indeed, both words *quest* and *question* take us back to the Latin word *quaerere*, "to seek." A quest is the basic human activity—our search for wholeness—brought into focus and writ large.

In his novel *The Seeing Stone*, Kevin Crossley-Holland presents an astute observation: "Each of us needs a quest ... and the person without one is lost to himself."[232] **Your quest is your compass: it orients you to the world and unites you with your heart's desire.** When Joseph Campbell famously encouraged his readers to "follow your bliss," he was urging them to heed that compass. And just as the needle of a compass doesn't 'decide' on its orientation, but is aligned by the far poles of the earth, we don't decide on our heart's desire. It is awakened in us by the felt unknown, perhaps by the unblinking, steadfast stars returning our gaze. Our word *desire* contains that exact image: as the remarkable linguist Ernest Klein explains, the word comes from the Latin *de*, "from," and *sideris*, "star," and originally meant "to expect from the stars." And how many times has someone sat in solitude under the night sky and, glancing up into the stars, found herself connecting then and there in a wholly personal and ineffable way with her own compass? Once the unknown world calls to us like that, we recognize it in our core. And in the same way that a mother's milk is let down when her baby cries, so too sensation is let down into the body when the world calls. The body enters a kind of fluid harmony such that the merest reverberation of the compass needle will ripple through the whole of it. You become you, you *feel* your self—fully present and alive and activated, world-conscious rather than self-conscious. And at that point you face a decision: whether to heed the Call or pull back from it.

A decision to heed it will be life-altering. As the radical Christian theologian Dietrich Bonhoeffer once wrote, "When Christ calls a man, he bids him come and die."[233] To follow the Call into the Energy of the unknown world is to leave behind the world stitched together by Idea. On the other hand, if you refuse the Call, you refuse your compass, your means of orienting to the world. In that case, your only recourse is to willfulness, and its abilities to lobby on behalf of the fictions of the 'known self'. However splendid a house you build for yourself, it will be a many-chambered house of death. Warnings to that effect are embedded in myths, as Laius demonstrates—but they are also found in the substructure of our language. The word *vanity*, for instance, is cousin to a Sanskrit word that means "insufficient, wanting." The state of spiritual torpor, the state of someone who, as Crossley-Holland puts it, is "lost to himself," is described by the Middle English word *accidie*, which is from the Greek and means "not caring." "I don't care" is the anthem of youth who are lost to themselves; but equally, there are CEOs who are out of touch with their heart's desire and are lost to themselves; or successful movie stars who are lost to themselves. The story is a familiar one.

When we speak of someone "being lost to himself" we are spelling out the idea that a person can stray from what might be called his true self, which can therefore exist independent of his person. In effect, we are invoking the ancient recognition that a double, or spirit self, is always there, ready to guide you in your truth. Our expression of that ancient notion, though, is disguised and rather pale; in fact, the idea of a double could *only* have survived for us in an etiolated state, because our fiction of four dimensions would balk at a more robust expression. If we sidestep the literality of the double for a moment and look at the different cultures that speak of it, and at the various ways in which they understand the concept, we find that one essential feature is constant: the double is understood to be a part of us that is informed by or in touch with the unseen, unbroken whole. **If the consciousness of the felt self consists of a 'world' aspect and a 'self' aspect, then the 'double' would be the 'world aspect'—the vivid, mysterious part of the self that is aware of the unbroken whole, indivisible from it, and limitlessly informed by it.** Understood in that light, the idea of a double may look less like naïveté and more like a wake-up call, for it embodies the idea that *there is a part of you that directly knows the larger harmony, can possibly help guide the events of your life to manifest it, and can even—where your surrender is sufficient—offer the bottomless possibility of attuning your inner Being to it.* If that possibility should be realized, then your moment-by-moment living would manifest that harmony. That is the mystical view, and it is nonsensical to anyone who has bought into our culture's unintegrated perspectives of self and world.

Our culture's attitude towards the possibility of a double can be seen in various reactions to the Third Man Factor. In a book of that name, John Geiger looks at dozens of cases in which a seen or unseen presence appears to someone in trouble—often in the most extreme circumstances imaginable—and plays a significant role in his or her survival. The presence affords calm companionship, and often guidance or advice—leading one man from the eightieth floor of the south tower of the World Trade Center moments before its collapse; helping a scuba diver find her way out of a cave system just before her air ran out; guiding an explorer to safety through the tropical mists, heat haze and rainstorms of the New Guinea jungle. Other firsthand stories came out during a radio show about the book. One listener described how, driving along a mountain road, she heard her deceased father's voice come from the backseat, clearly saying, "Take it easy." She slowed down and drove on cautiously, only to turn a bend to see dust rising from a rockslide that would have hit her car. Another listener told of flying a plane through thick fog when she heard a voice telling her to climb. She did, only to see a mountain suddenly come into view that she would otherwise have crashed into.

Of course there is a stampede of specialists falling over one another in their haste to demonstrate how all of these phenomena must be biochemical hallucinations of the stand-alone brain. Just as, no doubt, my friend's dash home in the middle of a school lesson just happened to coincide with his mother's imminent death, and was actually caused by a random biochemical brain burp. The need to reduce all such phenomena to four-dimensional mechanics bespeaks a profound fear of the transformative sensitivity of female Being; and any such fear will render the Call—in any of its manifestations—as undetectable as Eurydice became to Orpheus.

Entelechy, the Exchange of Gifts

Many cultures understand that an individual's journey in the world is assisted by a nurturing spirit, a double, who summons and guides us. Plato called this soul-companion our *daimon;* the Romans called it our *genius;* in many native North American traditions, it is an animal spirit or an ancestor; Australian aborigines refer to their "bush soul"; in the Philippine languages it is called *kadua, kakambal, kaluha* and many other names; even in our contemporary culture, people refer to their 'guardian angel'.

In early Egypt one's double, called one's *ka,* was seen as an identical twin born at the same time as an individual, to accompany him through life—guiding, sustaining and supporting, much like the Third Man Factor. *Ka* is, suitably, a perplexing, many-layered concept—but a concise summation of it is found in the appendix of Julius Lester's novel *The Pharaoh's Daughter.* There we read that *ka* was understood in three overlapping ways as,

> (1) the spiritual essence of a person that was the guiding force of life; (2) an astral being that existed alongside a person and had its own individuality; (3) an aspect of the divine essence on which all existence rested.[234]

Among those three meanings of *ka* we can find links to innumerable cultures around the world. Working backwards through them we find that the third meaning—the divine, vital spirit of life—is akin to the Sanskrit notion of *prana,* the Chinese term *chi,* the Japanese *ki* and the Hebrew *ruach*, among others. The astral being of the second meaning is like one's guardian angel, or animal spirit, or ancestor, and is found in philosophies in India, in most Philippine ethnic groups and among North American aboriginal tribes. The first sense is a lot like Aristotle's notion of *entelechy*: the immaterial drive that carries living beings towards their ultimate form. It is the entelechy of an acorn, for example, to become an oak tree. The term *entelechy* has fallen in and out of fashion over the centuries, but it was mostly out of fashion during the twentieth century, and it remains so, as scientists have sought to liberate biology from the taint of anything not purely of four dimensions; if there is a driving, organizing force, they argue, it must have an explanation that is purely mechanical. As we have seen, though, all attempts to contain life within the perseity of interacting *things*—whether genes or electrons—have so far failed; and if the Universal Law of Interrelationship is anything to go by, they will continue to fail.

In the meantime, the term lives on in a different context. Psychologist and philosopher Jean Houston has given it a contemporary relevance. A leader in the Human Potential Movement, Houston identifies entelechy as an innate sense of our essential reason for being. Entelechy is the inner quest that, once awakened, will unlock our energy and engage us with the world: "Contact entelechy, and all circuits are 'go'. Tune into it and another order of perspective is at hand."[235]

I sometimes feel my own entelechy—quite tangibly—as what the spirit seeded within me wants to become, or as what a loving attention to the world calls me towards. Of course, **entelechy is not located either within, like a seed, or without: it is located in the clarity of a relationship between the two—seed and world, each pole recognizing its need for the other.** Contact entelechy, and you become Orpheus drawn by your own Eurydice, willing to risk as much, and able to trust as deeply. *When the world calls to your heart-seeded entelechy, it births a quest in you, a hunger*—a longing, a need to engage, to make, to act, to move towards a spiritual center that summons you from an unknown landscape. The hunger birthed in you by entelechy is something to which your every faculty awakens. It is something entirely different from the tyrant's insatiable appetite for acquisition, or for self-aggrandizement: it is a recognition of the work you were born to undertake, and to which you must give yourself. That recognition is liberated in you by a heart's gate that is wide open to Being—and the hunger it births summons your every faculty into growth and discovery. That hunger—the passion of it—is also what makes us who we are. Without it we collapse into self-absorption, lost to ourselves. Without that hunger, in a real sense, we are nothing.

The concept of entelechy does not suggest that there is such a thing as who any of us is 'meant' to be, or that our individual destinies are somehow predetermined or foreordained. The calling is the invitation, not the destination; entelechy initiates and guides and transforms rather than limits. The very idea of Fate belongs to the fable of perseity: it tells us that the future is sealed up and enclosed; beyond change; preordained and inevitable; fixed, solid and eternal. That may be a comforting fiction to some people, in the same way that the fiction of the 'known self' is comforting; but comfort is not a measure of reality, and the fiction of Fate is as vulnerable to scrutiny as is the fiction of the 'known self'. As we are developing, so is the world. When the needle of my compass quivers and points me towards the unknown, my stepping into the unknown will change not only me, but the world as well. There is no fixed storyline, no predetermined end for either of us. There is just the ongoing game in which world and self are cocreators, each in its way caring for the other, exchanging gifts. As James Hillman wrote of the daimon, "Not only does it bless us with its calling, we bless it with our style of following."[236]

In the original sense in which Aristotle coined the word, *entelechy* was made up of two words that combined to mean "to have completion." We all yearn to be complete, to find wholeness in our lives; in amplifying that original sense of *entelechy* we can understand something very basic, yet rich with implications: **every living thing is born to complete itself by receiving the energies of the world, processing them, and releasing them back into the world.** That is the universal drive in the acorn, the amoeba, the grasshopper—and in us. It is in the midst of that exchange and transformation of energies that we thrive. It is through that exchange that we live our purpose and our own becoming. Similarly, it is through that exchange that the hero's journey is shaped: venturing into the unknown, he *receives* the energy of his newfound perspective; in receiving it, he *processes* it, even as it processes him; and he returns home to *release* that energy back into his society—to which, if it is integrated, that energy will bring new life.

If we can understand it in those terms, we can see that **entelechy**

forms the basis of all relationship and as such forms the basis of all reality. To come into relationship with anything is to exchange energy with it. Where there is no exchange of energy, there is no relationship; where there is no relationship, there is no reality. We saw that in the case of tachyons, the hypothetical particles that can only travel faster than the speed of light. If they don't interact with our universe on this side of the speed of light, they cannot exchange energy with our world, and so they simply don't exist in it.

The exchange of Energy—and specifically its limits and forms of optimization—shapes all life on earth. It is entelechy that shapes a tree, and it is into that exchange of energies that a tree grows. A poplar tree is optimized for a different exchange than the ones that shape either the oak or the fir tree. Conversely, the *similarities* in morphology that can be seen among beetles, cats, horses, and elephants have been shaped by the limits and optimizations for similar exchanges. The eye of the beetle and the eye of the elephant are similar insofar as they are both shaped by an exchange in which the energy of light is received, processed, and released into the nerve ways. We might further note a fundamental entelechy in which all life participates: the exchange of energies between the earth and the sky. We eat and breathe earth-transformed sun energy, even as we further transform it to return it to the earth. I feel it is not insignificant that, like the trees, we spend most of our lives upright, our embodied axis aligned along that exchange between earth and sky: between the integration of the ground at one pole and the perspective of the sky at the other; between the consciousness of Mother Earth and the consciousness of what used to be called the welkin, where angels dwell.

How we evolve as individuals, we might further note, is largely made possible by the exchanges that run through the axes of our consciousness. Each axis, remember, is the energetic potential for exchange between two poles: in the case of the embodied axis, between the male and female aspects of our consciousness; for the analog axis, between the self and world aspects of consciousness. When you can feel the potential for the coursing of an exchange through the corridor within you, each pole of your consciousness yearning to know itself through the other; or when you can stand in the corational corridor that is the mindful present, and feel between self and world a recognition, a stirring of dialogue, a mutual awareness that bespeaks a necessity; when you can feel those axes illuminated by the pulsing call of complementary opposites for each other, seeking completion, then you are feeling your own entelechy.

As such, we can understand our axes of consciousness to be the means that reveal our entelechy; and we can understand entelechy to be the dynamic that engages us with the world and most fully brings us into relationship with it. Like the poplar, each one of us is optimized for a particular exchange of energies: everyone has particular gifts to offer, particular blessings to receive. Not just our lives but our very bodies and souls are shaped by the ways in which we choose to— or choose not to—give ourselves to that exchange. And it is through that exchange that we acquire poignancy in our lives. As Buddha said, "Your work is to discover your work and then, with all your heart, to give yourself to it."[237] *Creativity* itself is precisely about receiving the energies of the world, processing them, and releasing them. But the same could be said of *presence*: to be present is to be here, now, fully sensitized and awake to the world—assimilating it and giving over to what it calls from you without resistance or hesitation. The same can also be said of the third leg of our metaphoric stool: *freedom*. The caged tiger cannot live in an open exchange of energies with the world; the tiger treading the bamboo grove is fully participant in it. In fact, the currents of energy that make up your exchange with the world *are what you feel as your life*. **You are most fully in reality, then, and most freely in reality, when your exchange of Energy with the world is most free: when the inner corridor is uncluttered and the corational corridor wide open.** And just as entelechy is the basis of all reality, we might also recognize that unintegrated Idea is the basis of all *un*reality: cutting across the axes that join us to self and world, it imparts to both the aura of a fantasy we watch as though through a windowpane, shielding us from the threat of any real exchange. The effect on your own sensitivity is to numb you to the harmony and deafen you to the Call, which will give you more than enough reason to deny that either exists. And then you will neither feel blessed nor sense your ability to bring blessings upon the world. In such a scenario as that—a very familiar one, unfortunately—you could only equate the notion of freedom with the need and ability to acquire.

It should not come as a surprise, then, that the world's great spiritual leaders tell us that we most fully realize our own humanity when we receive the energies of the world *as a gift* and, in processing them, release them back into the world *as a gift*. That view represents entelechy as an exchange of gifts; indeed, each breath we take in brings a gift of oxygen from the plant life of the world, and each exhalation carries in return a gift of carbon dioxide. All forms of thanksgiving—whether prayer, song or ritual—celebrate the exchange of gifts, and acknowledge it in all the phenomena of the world.

The Egyptian glyph for ka depicts the calling of the world as a gift being extended: ka was represented by a picture of two arms outstretched in a gesture of calling, offering and support. That image could also serve as a depiction of the self as it opens along the analog axis, welcoming 'what is' and supporting the world in an openhearted exchange. It is when you actively attend to the present that you *reverberate* to its call and discover the self as a *verb* rather than an object. To recognize that Call in the present is to recognize yourself in the present. Look to it and there you are, calling yourself. The genesis of your wholeness commences there—with the summons, the Logos—and with the quivering needle in your core that answers. And when we think of that compass needle quickening in response, it helps to bear in mind that the root of *compass* is an Indo-European base that means "to spread out," and is also the root of our word *petal*. By issuing through the present, the Call roots you in it; by summoning you from the felt unknown, the Call summons the energy of your being through the heart, which blossoms at the touch of its currents. The Call and the cello-stringed flower of the felt self are complements—each a realization of being. As Dürckheim said, whatever exists

> does not realize its inner truth unless it allows Being to manifest itself in its particular form. We can say that man is truly in his center when he has become conscious of his own path as an innate truth and as a personal call, and that he is capable of consciously realizing it through the simplest activity in daily life.[238]

Ordinary activities are often the most challenging in which to consciously realize your own path and your personal call. It helps to recognize that **the ordinary world always calls us to live more fully in the present; the 'known self' always warns us to live on a leash of anticipation.** The inspiring theater teacher and director Robert Barash once commented, "The greatest gift you can give anyone is just to be present with them." To be present with others in simple appreciation of who they are, without expectation or anticipation, is also to make a gift of 'being' to yourself.

The Voodoo of Authority

The heart's compass is drawn to its true bearing by the world. Our culture distracts our attention from the reedsong of the present with messages inciting self-absorption and compliance. They tell us that the truth of our relationship to the world lies inside us, and we should take hold of the compass needle that orients our truth, seize it in our hands, point it at what we want—and pursue it. In all of the grasping and pushing that follows, the Call of the world is forgotten—as Rumi observed, it fades and we fade.

Turning to an appointed Authority can equally deafen us to the Call—and in our culture, doing so is as deeply ingrained a habit as heeding our inner patriarch. That habit is nowhere more evident than in a phenomenon that I call Lab Coat Voodoo. It is practiced by experts and is endorsed by the population at large; it effectively casts a spell over our personal relationship to the guidance of the world and endarkens it. To illustrate, a personal anecdote: while I was out for a run one day my left foot landed on a stick, which rolled sideways and wrenched my ankle. Over the next week I was slowed down but I carried on with my life, which included wiring in a 200-amp electrical panel and climbing onto the roof to hook it up to the power lines. I wasn't ignoring the pain—on the contrary, I was deliberately and gently attending to the ankle; but after a week it wasn't much better, so I cycled to the local hospital, where a doctor sent me for X-rays. When he returned with them in hand, he told me my ankle was broken. I thought he was joking, but he said, no, it actually was broken. As his words sank in, *I lost my ability to walk*. Never mind that I had been up and down ladders and lugging things to work and cycling around town in the past week: I suddenly couldn't take a step. Lab Coat Voodoo.

The doctor intended me no malice, to be sure, but the power of his word "broken" and the authority of his expertise were sufficient to override both the sensations of my body and my ability to be gently guided by them; he had issued a verdict that was fixed, solid and intractable. All too keenly aware of the absurdity of my reaction, I recovered from the effect of his words within a few minutes; but the ability of those words to disable me, to extirpate my thinking from my Being with a single utterance, was profoundly disturbing.

Recent research by Gregory Berns has demonstrated that expert advice suppresses areas of the brain that involve our judgment. As Berns noted, "The study indicates that the brain relinquishes responsibility when a trusted authority provides expertise,"[239] a finding we might also interpret literally as "the brain relinquishes its responsiveness to Being." Once we are alerted to that phenomenon, we find it in every sphere of our lives, presenting us with empowered words that magically displace us from the guidance of the world—and from the peace of mind that it fosters. Experts are called upon to tell us when to eat, what to eat, how much to eat, as well as what not to eat, when not to eat, and how not to eat. They tell us how and when to exercise. What to wear and how to look. How to make love. What to say when. What to think. How to judge others. Never mind that their edicts vary from year to year—the seductive persuasion of Lab Coat Voodoo oozes expertise. And so its practitioners persuade us not by pushing pins into little dolls, but by jabbing us with statistics and studies; by piercing us with images of people depressed or anxious and who simply need the right solution to perk them up. Or they prick us with images of actors and models who have been paid to present happiness such as can only be found on TV, and we are led to believe, knowing that it is not true, that their happiness comes from the right consumer product that has filled an emptiness in their lives.

Our culture promotes an underlying message that happiness is fatalistically determined by certain mechanics. Certain solutions. Certain answers. Forget the quest that unites us with the felt unknown. Forget the soul-shaking submission that awakens the crux of our intelligence to the corationality of Being. We just need to breathe the right ions or use the right vitamins, wear the right colors, practice the right secret, drink the right tea, hang our mirror in the right place or say the right mantra. As we have seen, **such fatalism is a form of endarkenment that can keep you from your own experience; it can distract you from turning your attention to the most pertinent question of all:** *What keeps you from being present?*

If we turn our attention to that question, we find that *what keeps us from being present is always a resistance to the Energy of the present.*

And that resistance always shows up in *a deliberate impairment of our consciousness:* dividing up the corridor within and constricting the pipeline that carries us into corationality. To open our consciousness to the world's calling is to discover that the present challenges us to develop even as it supports that development: entelechy is a process, and the present is your midwife. Learning to live in the Energy of the present is a journey of trust, honesty and evolving sensitivity. That journey brings not happiness, but felicity; not acquisitions, but grace; not importance, but ease; not fixity, but aliveness; not knowledge, but understanding; not personal conquests, but gratitude; not meaning, but experience; in short, not solutions, but wholeness.

The reason we so readily acquiesce to the dictums of an external authority is because we practice acquiescence every day of our lives, whenever we bow to the tyranny of our own internalized patriarch. We bow to his instructions instinctively; we follow them as a way of life. So when it comes to Lab Coat Voodoo we are sitting ducks. We naturally want to be told what to do and what is best. How else will we know? And who better to tell us than experts? If you meet a Buddha, kill him. If you meet an expert, kill him.

Not all experts in our culture practice Lab Coat Voodoo, of course: some raise questions rather than presenting answers; some encourage experience rather than prescribing behavior; some gently shake the house in order to help you strengthen it from within, rather than handing you more things to tack onto its facade; some nurture playfulness rather than dictating the road you should follow; some even point you to the unknown that calls you by name, and do so with compassion and encouragement. Voodoo experts uproot us from the source of presence, creativity and freedom in our own lives; real teachers return us to it. They also help us pay attention. Once the male element grows sufficiently passive to enable us to hear the world calling, body and world merge in mutual awareness—and then our doing acquires the grace of Being itself. If it is that simple and rewarding, though, why in the world don't we do it more often?

Wounding, Truth and Gratitude

The grace of Being is quintessentially corational: as your analog intelligence yields to the present, feeling the whole in all its fluid harmony, that harmony lives in you and guides you, at one with the ordinary reality of where you are. To submit to the grace of Being is not just to pay attention to the ordinary world the way you might pay attention to the scenery outside your window; it is to be no other than ordinary yourself, so that the ordinariness of where you are runs through your core as the smell of your mother did when you were a small child. When that happens, it will induce resonances and feelings that are beyond your control.

And that is the issue. Losing control. Once you hear the Call and begin your journey, you expose yourself to reality as it is—the unknown terrain that lies beyond interpretation. In myth, the hero's vulnerability in answering the Call is graphically presented to us in countless storied metaphors. *Vulnerable* literally means "able to be wounded." **Answering the Call, then, expresses and is made possible by a willingness to risk being wounded.**

You cannot live and escape wounding. But I think many of us make the choice to wound ourselves, thereby at least asserting some control over how we are wounded, rather than risk being wounded by the unknown. Mythically this is represented by Laius, the patriarch within, skewering the feet of his newborn son Oedipus, the child within. The scars of our self-wounding are the consolidations that dull us to the world, blocking and constricting the rush of sensations through the body. We are largely blind to our own consolidations, forgetting entirely that they are not just the givens of what is normal, *but were at some point created by a choice not to integrate the present.* We overlook the significance borne to us by the fact that every consolidation in ourselves is itself actually a wound. That lack of self-insight is surprising in that we can plainly see the same kind of wounding in everyone else around us. It is visible because the scar tissue of those self-inflicted wounds actually shapes people's bodies: the way we move, hold ourselves, look, listen, gesture, breathe and speak reveals those consolidations for all to see. They show up because they constrain us and pull at us—like toughened calluses that resist movement and feeling, or like a face partially disabled by Botox.

The purpose behind such self-inflicted wounding is to dull ourselves to pain; in fact, those patches of scar tissue diminish not just pain, but all sensation. The practice is in keeping with a tacit deal our culture has brokered, based on the belief that an individual has a right to be free of pain. That belief would be hard to argue against if it did not by implication give everyone the nonsensical right to be free of living. Pain accompanies everything of value: love, self-knowledge, the hero's journey, the lessons of failure—which lessons themselves can turn any failure into a gift of learning. Essentially, *pain is communication*; the most accelerated learning in my life has been guided by suffering of one sort or another. On the other hand, when we try to avoid pain by self-wounding, we fall into a vicious cycle: our anxiety about pain prompts self-wounding; the scarring diminishes sensation; the diminished sensation abstracts the world around us; and that abstraction itself creates more anxiety, et cetera. Self-inflicted wounding directs us into a cul-de-sac.

When I work as an actor I know that I cannot 'inhabit' a character until I have found his particular body in my own—his stance, his rhythms, his carriage; I also know that those qualities are primarily shaped by the wounds of his unique anxieties. Those wounds literally represent *who* the character knows himself to be, which in the course of the play usually comes into conflict with *where* he finds himself—a conflict expressed by: "What is happening to me is not who I am." That in a nutshell is the germ of both tragedy and comedy. I have also found that the more innocent the character, the less scar tissue he carries. *Innocent* literally means "doing no harm," and I take its true meaning not to be doing no harm to others—you would have to check before each footfall as you walked so as not to crush any insect, and what would you eat, and how could you speak truth without the risk of hurting someone?—but to be more fundamentally grounded in inflicting no wounds on oneself. An innocent heart is one that has not hardened itself with scar tissue. An innocent heart is what enables you to see the world anew. The patriarch within, the Laius part of us, wounds our innocence with his two-pointed goad, because our innocence is what enables us to hear the Call and discover that our true relationship to the world is that of a child, summoned. By bringing us into that relationship, our innocence enables the wound of our 'spectatorship' to heal. Even as I watch my young daughters lose innocence, I continue to learn from them about how to regain my own.

We employ *self*-inflicted wounding to forge an enclosure within which our self-tyranny can reign—an enclosure that keeps the world out even as it traps us within. When the *world* wounds us, something very different happens. Sogyal Rinpoche has written about the world's wounding with a lucid and uncompromising simplicity:

> So each time the losses and deceptions of life teach us about impermanence, they bring us closer to the truth.[240]

In its unflinching clarity that statement reminds me of an insight into art that is as beautiful and true as any I've read, and which appears in the form of a question in *The Medusa Frequency*, a novel by Russell Hoban. Halfway through the book, a character asks: "**Is not all art a celebration of loss?**"[241] The character asking that question is, felicitously, Orpheus—or more accurately, his severed head. Wounding is always a loss of one sort or another. To celebrate loss is to celebrate the perplexing truth it brings in its wake. Sogyal Rinpoche paraphrases the poet Rilke, observing that "our deepest fears are like dragons guarding our deepest treasure."[242] Yet another take on wounding seems to me equally insightful. The late Isaac Vogelfanger was more intimately acquainted with wounding than most of us could imagine: he was a survivor of Stalin's death camps. He later came to Canada, where he taught medicine, and was able to write of his ordeal:

> Wounds heal and you become whole again, a little stronger and more human than before.[243]

How is it, though, that being wounded can make us "more human"? It isn't easy to say what makes us human in the first place, but a wound will do several things that help awaken us to our humanity. First, as Sogyal Rinpoche pointed out, a wound will teach us about impermanence: by doing so, it will challenge every assumption of the 'known self', which clings to the idea of permanence and control and assiduously avoids looking directly at the implications of its own impermanence—which happens to be the ground of truth and the source of all that is precious in life.

A wound will also nourish compassion: how much easier to put yourself in someone else's shoes and open your heart to him from the perplexed understanding that your own wounds have nurtured. And the more human we become, the more that compassion extends to all living things, and recognizes all things as living.

Wounding also makes us more human to the extent that it makes us more grateful. There is nothing like a broken leg, for example, to release a newfound gratitude once you are able to walk again; or the loss of a family member to bring the rest of the family closer, newly appreciative of what they share. As Joni Mitchell astutely observed, "You don't know what you've got till it's gone."

The gratitude that wounding teaches us, at its most extreme, is a gratitude for life itself, and for the opportunity to be here, now in its rich and poignant mystery. I remember lying in a hospital bed after a construction accident in which my thumb had been crushed and deboned. Once I was left alone in the room I began weeping: they were tears of gratitude for the wonder of the life in which I was so blessed to participate—a blessing made vividly clear, paradoxically, by the naked bone and sagging flesh of my thumb.

More than any single perspective on the present, I think that to be *grateful* for what is here will *place* you here; gratitude opens us to Being and lets it penetrate our core. By doing so, it summons the crux of our consciousness to flower forth into all that is. It is perhaps for that reason that religions and shamanic traditions the world over and without exception give thanks in prayer or song or poetry or ritual. Thanksgiving is rooted in the ground of truth: that reality consists of the exchange of energies. Thanksgiving is itself a gift, given in exchange for gifts received. It connects you with your own entelechy and opens you to the transient present. And so it was common not that long ago to give thanks before every single meal we ate; to give thanks in our prayers before going to sleep; and to go to church at least once a week and sing songs of thanks. If someone didn't learn to be thankful, it wasn't for lack of practice: all the social rituals were in place to support it.

Nothing has come along to replace those ancient rituals, which leaves the discovery of gratitude up to the individual. I have nothing against the personal learning curve, but in our culture this one is a particular challenge. Our belief in perseity and our cult of self-achieved doing make it hard enough; beyond that, though, the benighted persuasions of entitlement wage an assault against gratitude on every level. 'Entitlement' is as close as we are likely to come to naming gratitude's dark counterpart, and it seems to be woven into the very cloth of our culture. Consider the extent to which our thinking—especially on political issues—is clouded by the agenda of individual rights: I have a right to that, but she has a right to this, which violates my right to those, and so on. If I have a *right* to something, I cannot receive it as a gift and there is no reason to feel gratitude for it. Such entitlement also makes deep compassion, such as that which prompted the desegregation movement in the United States, functionally redundant. Entitlement doesn't require compassion; it requires policing. We'll just sort out who has a right to what and enforce it. The miasma of entitlement taints even our most personal reckonings: if I should be wounded, forget about becoming more human—I'm entitled to happiness and my rights have been violated. Someone should pay. As writer Curtis White succinctly put it,

> In its most extreme and universal form, our constitutional rights are reducible to the right not to have to love our neighbor. The irony is that the more energetically we pursue our individual, socially isolated right to "life, liberty and the pursuit of happiness," the deader the social and natural worlds become.[244]

Rights are a representation of what 'should be', and adherence to them dulls our responsiveness to 'what is'. We don't need to be really touched by a given situation if we can sort out who is entitled to what. And when our *ability to respond* is off the hook, so, of course, is our *responsibility*. It used to be understood as a maxim that it was a community's responsibility to care for the common good. **A responsibility is a *relationship* within a larger whole; by contrast, an individual right is a *possession*, something you have and defend.** When we accept responsibility, we transcend perseity; when we focus on the rights of individuals, we fortify it. The fight for racial equality in the United States was not a fight for personal rights, but for social justice. The fight for human rights in totalitarian states remains critical, because policing can remain unaccountable in such states, and legislated rights are the most effective way of curtailing it. In Western cultures, though, the entitled pursuit of individual rights often erodes the most valued asset of a society: the sense of community. A mind-boggling practice was long ago legalized in the United States: a corporation, which is created from and sustained by the larger community, is granted the rights of an individual citizen by law—and is also reified as a stand-alone entity. So much for the common good. Optics replace compassion; gratitude is useful only if it increases stock value. Which of course it can't.

If the focus on rights undermines a personal sense of gratitude, an even more invidious influence is wielded by the fictions of advertising,

which generally appeal directly to self-centeredness. You can't move
very far in a big city without being confronted by billboards dominating the skyline, or ads on the subway, or videos in the elevator, all
proclaiming the same message: "You deserve more. You deserve better.
You could be happier. You are *entitled* to be happier." Those blandishments are like candy to the hetabrain—but our stampede towards
acquisition funnels ineluctably into a closed loop. Once gratitude at-
rophies, we can never quite be satisfied; to ease our dissatisfaction, we
acquire what promises us "better, more, happier"; we may be thrilled
by the act of acquisition, but learn nothing about gratitude from it,
and so have nothing to return to but our ever-present dissatisfaction.
As we persist around this closed loop, our actions are fueled by restlessness, and we eventually come to mistake any diminution of that
restlessness for being truly at rest; or a diminution of white noise for
the reverberant signal of being; or the tugging need to acquire for the
calling of the world.

To experience deep gratitude is to experience a profound opening
to the spacious present: the Indo-European root that gave us *gratitude*
literally means "to praise, to welcome." But establishing any grounds
for gratitude is almost impossible if you buy into perseity, for it only
prompts questions: gratitude to whom? And for what? I would suggest, though, that the first step towards gratitude may be found in
just being present—beyond all ideas or calculations or agendas. If you
find that difficult, you might remember that **if you don't love being
here now, you will resist it**—and such resistance is always successful.
Standing before the king of the underworld and his queen Persephone,
Orpheus explains how it was that he, alone of all mortals, was able to
make his way into the heart of their realm: "Love had greater strength
than I."[245] The strength of his love enabled a calm acceptance of whatever woundings his journey might bring—enabled him to 'be' in his
life exactly as it was, without resistance. Just how subtle such resistance can be is pointed out in a story by Shinichi Suzuki, the founder
of the Suzuki method for teaching the violin:

> When I was at junior high school, there was a time
> when four of the neighborhood children and I used to
> visit our local shrine every evening. We talked about all
> sorts of things on our way to and fro. That is all there
> was to it, but it was a pleasant daily task. Then one

day my father asked me, "What do you say when you visit the shrine?" I replied that I asked for protection for all of my family. But my father remonstrated, "Stop being so selfish. When you go to the shrine each day, all you should say is, 'Thank you very much!'" ... I realized that what my father was trying to teach me was that although man is prone to always be waiting for something, that is wrong.[246]

As Suzuki's father understood, if we are waiting, we lack true gratitude; and without gratitude we are always waiting, ready to be somewhere else, never truly here. Never fully present. To detach from gratitude is to slide into self-absorption. No wonder Meister Eckhart advised that "If the only prayer you say in your whole life is 'thank you', that would suffice."[247]

If self-inflicted wounding reinforces the 'known self', and the woundings of the world bring us the gifts of humanity and strength as we return to wholeness, then we can appreciate why it is that so many journeys to enlightenment, to the ordinary mind, have been precipitated by crisis and loss. The transition through wounding from the dark and isolated fantasies of the 'known self' into a sensitivity that is wide open to ordinary, luminous Being is stunningly captured by William Golding in his novel *Free Fall*.

The protagonist, Sammy, having been interrogated in a Nazi prisoner-of-war camp, is then shut up in a pitch-dark concrete cell, where he is terrorized as much by his own imaginings as by anything else—just as the tyrant of the enclosed consciousness is "self-terrorized, fear-haunted." Sammy's crisis plummets him into an abyss of fear, whereupon he is unexpectedly released from his dark enclosure into the spacious light of day; there he finds the ordinary world transformed. He saw things shining

with the innocent light of their own created nature.... I lifted my arms, saw them too, and was overwhelmed by their unendurable richness as possessions, either arm ten thousand fortunes poured out for me. Huge tears were dropping from my face into dust; and this dust was a universe of brilliant and fantastic crystals, that miracles instantly supported in their being. I looked up beyond the huts and the wire, I raised my dead eyes, desiring nothing, accepting all things and giving all created things away. The paper wrappings of use and language dropped from me. Those crowded shapes extending up into the air and down into the rich earth, those deeds of far space and deep earth were aflame at the surface and daunting by right of their own natures though a day before I should have disguised them as trees. Beyond them the mountains were not only clear all through like purple glass, but living. They sang and were conjubilant. They were not all that sang. Everything is related to everything else and all relationship is either discord or harmony. The power of gravity, dimension and space, the movement of the earth and sun and unseen stars, these made what might be called music and I heard it.[248]

Sammy is introduced to the uninterpreted world by a dissolution of the 'known self'. As he later says, "I was surrounded by a universe like a burst casket of jewels and I was dead anyway myself."[249] Who he knew himself to be had perished, and the five-dimensional present was resplendent around him and through him, expressing its Call through every molecule. He was nothing and everything; ordinary and extraordinary; submissive and uncompliant; wounded and whole; a witness to the full revelation of Being and suffused with wonder and gratitude at it. And when Being is heard as song, as music, we are reminded again of Orpheus, the archetypal artist and the archetypal shaman, singing the world into harmony.

Exercise Eight: **Just Receive**

Entelechy is the basic drive towards a fulfillment of what the spirit seeded within you wants to become, of what the world calls you towards. That fulfillment proceeds through the exchange of energies with the world—which we spoke of as an exchange of gifts. That exchange, which sustains and constitutes reality, involves the receiving, processing and release of energy. Receiving is the beginning of our journey beyond the enclosure of self-tyranny. As Lao-tzu put it, "If you receive the world, the Tao will never leave you."

Any faculty will atrophy without use; but in our doing-obsessed culture we rarely give ourselves the permission or space to just receive. That's what this exercise is about. Receiving, without labels or judgment or naming. Receiving what the sensational language of the logos-mind brings to you, in all its subtlety.

To begin, lie on your back with your eyes closed, and allow your attention to take in the sensations of your breathing. Receive the touch of the cool air on your mouth or nose, and notice the cascade of sensation in your body as the breath wave washes into your body and then releases out in a stream of warm air. Without interfering with your breath any more than a baby does, just receive all the sensations throughout the body that accompany it. You may do this for as long as you wish, which might be two minutes or twenty.

When you are ready to move on, let your attention welcome and receive all the sensations of your body making contact with the ground as your weight presses into it.

Receive the sensations of your clothing on your skin, and the touch of air on your exposed skin.

Receive the sounds nearest to you, without naming them or judging them. Just receive them gently, as they are. Then receive whatever sounds reach you from the middle distance and then from far away.

When you wish to, open your eyes and just receive the colors and textures and shapes of whatever comes to them. If you are moved to do so, look around at the world that surrounds you and just receive its particular energies, without any need to name them.

When you feel ready, sit up slowly, receiving all the sensations of your own movement as you do so. And pause there for a bit, receiving where you are.

Then slowly stand, again receiving all the sensations that accompany your moving. Receive where you are standing, which is so different from where you were sitting.

Finally, try walking about, receiving the sensations of your own body resting on the ground as it moves through space, and all the sensations of the world around you that each moment brings.

Of course, this exercise really comes into its own when carried into the world: to walk down the street, and receive all its energies; to converse with someone, and truly receive his presence; to sit on a park bench and just receive 'what is'. In a state of receptivity, the nourishment of Being is bottomless.

9 | Becoming Conscious
of Consciousness

Mind over Matter

As we have seen, the transition from the sensitivities of the 'known self' to those of the felt self represents a quantum jump in consciousness, one that enables the felt whole of the self to come into relationship with the felt whole of the present. The 'known self' is primarily preoccupied with the task of managing the various warring factions within the self and between self and world—a task that involves analysis, duplicates, judgment, willfulness, plans and agendas. The forces that bind the awareness of the 'known self' to that task are the anxieties that embed division and neglect within the body, confounding its consciousness and deadening it to the consciousness of the world.

The transition to the felt self begins with a dissolution of the inner barriers and baffles that separate the male pole of consciousness from the female; and the transition is fulfilled once the self opens to its full axial consciousness and finds its complement in the world. When that happens, the felt self becomes primarily conscious of consciousness itself—the defining trait of mutual awareness: the mind discovers all the world to be a corational corridor; it finds it can enter all things, and join them and learn from them, as it increasingly recognizes the One Mind that brings them all into relationship. Whereas the 'known self' experiences matter objectively from a mind materially confined to the head, the felt self experiences mind subjectively *through the consciousness-infused matter of the world.*

Okakura, remember, observed, "We boast that we have conquered matter, and forget that it is matter that has enslaved us." The felt self represents the triumph of a sensitivity attuned to mind over one that is

281

bound by the constraints of mere obdurate matter: mind over matter, we might say. The emergence of the felt self undoes our boast and our enslavement. It is a phase shift of such liberating power that its effect on self and world is multidimensional, and shows up in a wide range of perspectives. Among other effects that can be seen, the transition carries us

- *from self-consciousness to mutual awareness.* We could well consider this to be the primary shift in consciousness, the one from which all the others issue, and which helps to explain them.

- *from doing to being.* When doing comes first, being vanishes. When being comes first, it empowers our doing.

- *from self-achieved independence to self-achieved submission.* Myth personifies these two latent tendencies of the male element as tyrant and hero— roles determined by their relationship to Being. The tyrant, withdrawing into himself, rejects being and becomes unipolar; the hero, by submitting, opens the inner corridor first to his own being, and ultimately to the mutual awareness that sustains the felt unknown all around him.

- *from enclosure to receptivity.* This perspective epitomizes the shift from 'fenced-in' hetabrain to the resonant crux of our consciousness, through which self and world transform together.

- *from knowing to feeling.* The enclosure we have built is made of unintegrated bits of knowledge that stand against sensation—and so against the present itself. When that knowledge is surrendered to the pelvic intelligence of being, we begin to feel perspectives as sensation, and "the thing" as a whole.

- *from self-conflict to grace.* The effects of the phase shift can be seen in our actions; before the shift, our actions reveal the conflicts of Jerzy Grotowski's divided performer; after it, they reveal being in a grace of expression that is limitlessly informed.

• *from Idea to Energy.* The purpose of stand-alone ideas is to split up the energy of the world and freeze it in discrete, fixed shards that diminish the reality of relationship and abstract the exchange of gifts.

• *from bits to waves.* When our thinking is shielded from Being, our 'spectatorship' reveals a world of isolated particulars, just as an observation of a wave of light reveals it to be a particle. When we see the world in bits, we naturally want to order it and rule it. When the self shifts out of spectatorship into the wide axes of its embodied, corational consciousness, we experience a vibratory intelligence that belongs to "a great wave phenomenon"—every ripple of which carries complete evidence of the whole from which it arises.

• *from cybernetics to responsiveness.* As the mindful sensitivities of the body awaken, we begin to experience it not as stubborn matter, but as a field of intelligence that has no need of a helmsman. Instead, the body enters a partnership with the corational present.

• *from coarseness to subtlety.* As self and world come into fluid, mindful relationship, the coarseness of our ideated thinking melts into the sensational subtlety of the present.

• *from four dimensions to five.* The rigid demarcations of time and space lose their verdict of absolute separation, as all things are found to reflect all things, and consciousness is found to be not a stand-alone phenomenon that defies the Universal Law, but a dimension of our reality in which all things interfuse.

> • *from generalization to specificity.* As the hetabrain's patterned divisions of class and category dissipate, the dull generality of the world around us falls away to reveal a ravishing specificity in which every tree, every stalk of grass, every cup of tea is its own unique and voluble manifestation of Being.

Of course, the above is only a partial list. In particular, there are five other dramatic changes by which our sensitivities become conscious of consciousness: they show up in our relationships to the ordinary, to spaciousness, to play, to gentleness, and to the harmonizing of the world. The rest of this chapter is devoted to a consideration of them, one at a time.

The Wonder of the Ordinary

We are so in thrall to the male element that we see its power as the agent of success even when it isn't. It wasn't Wayne Gretzky's power as a hockey player that made his career so outstanding—it was his sensitivity. It wasn't Einstein's powers of deductive reasoning that cracked open the riddle of relativity—it was his sensitivity to the interplay among mass, length, time, the speed of light and, by his own account, "the mind of God." It wasn't Barack Obama's power as an orator that carried him into the White House—it was his sensitivity to his own truth, to the issues facing America, and to the hearts of the people. Of course, Gretzky was a powerful player, as Einstein was a powerful thinker and Obama a powerful speaker; *but their power was in service to their sensitivity, not the other way around.*

Misinterpreting the success of others, we tend to resort to willfulness in overcoming our own problems, which obliterates the sensitivity that could guide us through them and find guidance in them. And just as power is the quality that is formalized in any hierarchy—so that the transcendent king or CEO at the top wields more power than those lower down—power is seen by the male element as a means of transcending what is inconvenient or ordinary or simply standing in the way. **We take transcendence as our polestar and are guided by the urge towards it in everything we do.** This notion assigns supremacy to the male element—and that proves ruinous to the female element of Being every time and on every order of human organization: from individual to familial to communal to national to global. But why shouldn't we transcend? Who wants to be ordinary? Our phrase "ordinary as dirt" reveals our associations with that word; and it's telling that the name we use for our planet—the ultimate embodiment of female being—is *Earth,* which is synonymous with *dirt* and *soil,* words that also mean "filth."

Our need to transcend Being is taken as natural, just as our fear of the female is taken as a prudent entitlement; and so it is that we seek for ourselves the tyrant's acquisitions and his splendid bubble of privilege. Our pursuit of them has been radically successful: we take up residence in the head, and look down upon the body as a sort of fashion accessory to be whipped into shape by a personal trainer. Most of us in the West live as powerful tyrants of old could only have dreamed of doing: we can have whatever food we want, whenever we want it, in season or out; we can listen to whatever music we crave, wherever we are, with thousands of choices at our fingertips; we can travel half the globe in a matter of hours; and when we come home, we enter a private space and lock the door behind us. Inside, our hands are kept as far as possible from demeaning contact with the ordinary: they push buttons on the dishwasher, and on a proliferation of remote controls, and push 'send' and 'command' and 'talk' buttons on an array of devices that enable us to communicate with almost anyone at any distance. In our urban centers we surround ourselves with forms of architecture that not only proclaim our superiority to nature: they actually announce its irrelevance—except as accent or decoration—to what really matters in our vision of human progress.

Our tyranny over every facet of the natural world is relentless, and everywhere that tyranny exerts itself, it reinforces our culture's fantasy of what it is to be human: to rise above the *mundane*—literally, "what is of the earth." And so we transcend earth and meadow with the help of concrete and asphalt and homogenized lawns; we transcend time with facelifts and jet travel and instant meals; we transcend ordinary death by buying our meat prepackaged at the grocery store, and making up our corpses to look like they are sleeping, and watching death every day on the news as if it belonged to another, somehow smaller and more remote reality. We transcend everyday weather with air conditioners and heated cars, and with malls and underground concourses where you can buy anything and never see the light of day. And when we buy, we are not attracted to the ordinary, but to the best: the best pen, the best stereo, the best watch; not because, for example, the $8,000 watch tells time better than the $80 watch, but because it distinguishes us, sets us apart, shows that *we* are not ordinary. The farther we remove ourselves from what is ordinary, of course, the more we disconnect from Being. In fact, we show such callous disregard towards the life over which we have been "given dominion" that one might be forgiven for thinking that our gaze is fixed on the fantasy of some promised afterlife—the tyrant's ultimate dream of transcendence: everlasting abundance liberated from all responsibility.

Alden Nowlan, in his searching humanity, wrote a poem that stands against that trend and sides resolutely with the ordinary. It recalls an event he shared with his wife and son and is called "Great Things Have Happened":

> We were talking about the great things
> that have happened in our lifetimes;
> and I said, "Oh, I suppose the moon landing
> was the greatest thing that has happened
> in my time." But, of course, we were all lying.
> The truth is the moon landing didn't mean
> one-tenth as much to me as one night in 1963
> when we lived in a three-room flat in what once had
>   been
> the mansion of some Victorian merchant prince
> (our kitchen had been a clothes closet, I'm sure),
> on a street where by now nobody lived
> who could afford to live anywhere else.
> That night, the three of us, Claudine, Johnnie and me,
> woke up at half-past four in the morning
> and ate cinnamon toast together.
>
> "Is that all?" I hear somebody ask.
>
> Oh, but we were silly with sleepiness
> and, under our windows, the street-cleaners
> were working their machines and conversing in
>   Italian, and
> everything was strange without being threatening,

even the tea-kettle whistled differently
than in the daytime: it was like the feeling
you get sometimes in a country you've never visited
before, when the bread doesn't taste quite the same,
the butter is a small adventure, and they put
paprika on the table instead of pepper,
except that there was nobody in this country
except the three of us, half-tipsy with the wonder
of being alive, and wholly enveloped in love.[250]

Because the polestar of male doing is transcendence, it chafes to sever ties with the earth altogether, to rise above its verdant, ordinary filth and achieve something that really stands out, like landing on the moon; something that might proclaim the extraordinariness of the 'doer' for all to witness. By contrast, the Zen archer who makes a perfect, nigh-impossible shot bows deeply to honor the unknown "It," for the shot is understood to manifest not the archer's self-achieved excellence, but his self-achieved submission to the whole that informs and guides him. He remains an ordinary part of that whole, and knows that his art depends on it.

If you look through Alden Nowlan's poems, you will find most of them warmed and heightened by the ordinary details of our world, which often carry a poem's significance out like a ripple to meet the horizon. Those details are rooted in a specificity of moment and occasion and sensibility. Similarly, the Japanese poet Bashō surrendered his remarkable talents to the commonplace particulars of his world—and through those particulars Bashō allows the world to speak. The sense of particular and unbounded presence in such poems is conveyed by what is most ordinary in them. But how?

The roots of *ordinary* lead back to a Latin word meaning "to begin a web, lay the warp," and back farther to a Greek cousin with the same meaning. Ernest Klein suggests that its earliest traceable origins lead to the same base that lies at the root of *art* and *harmony*: the Indo-European base *ar-*, "to join." **What is ordinary belongs to and reveals the web that is joined to all else—it embodies and reveals relationship.** When you hold an ordinary object in your hand you are touched by its particular history, which is woven from the fabric of the whole universe. The material that constitutes a simple twig, for instance, was born in stars, eventually to be drawn through the soil and the air and stitched together by sunlight, which also sustains us. Its shape tells us about the winters and rains and bright days that have marked its growth; and before that its story weaves continuously back through the succession of its ancestors that breathed oxygen into the world and helped sustain your ancestors. Similarly, Arthur Miller noted that

> the shadow of a cornstalk on the ground is lovely, but it is no denial of its loveliness to see as one looks on it that it is telling the time of day, the position of the earth and the sun, the size of our planet and its shape, and perhaps even the length of its life and ours among the stars.[251]

An old teapot acquires a patina from all the hands that have held it and used it with care. It was fashioned from clay that lay in the earth for thousands of years until someone's spade uncovered it and dug it out. Its shape was felt only in someone's imagination before her slippery hands drew it forth from the clay; the touch and imprint of those hands can still be seen, having been fired into fastness. An old teapot may have served tea to people who were children once and now are old. Held in the hands, it connects us to all that and more.

An ordinary object, like an ordinary person, doesn't stand out but *fits seamlessly into the world around it*—the very fate we fear will befall us, which is why we imagine perseity and create artificial seams, wounding both self and world. But whatever is essentially ordinary— a child's wooden toy, a roadside flower, the sound of rain on a tin roof—shares the same qualities as the teapot. In fact, **wherever we find ordinariness, we find kinship;** and finding kinship in the world cracks the door open to our partnership with it. That kinship is metaphoric in that an ordinary object has a history and a life we can identify with; but it is also literal. As Father Thomas Berry has pointed out, the trees and grasses are our kin, our relations, our genetic cousins; the rocks of the earth are born of the same star matter that made us. How apt, then, that Thich Nhat Hahn should write of washing a teapot "with the kind of attention I would have were I giving the baby Buddha or Jesus a bath."[252] Even an old teapot is a window on the harmony of the world; and that makes it a window on the dialogue of Being. The ordinary is our access into the living web of mutual awareness: "if you love it enough, anything will talk to you."

The ordinary and the extraordinary are commonly thought of as two distinct and contrasting classes of things. And yet Bashō's poems are extraordinary, as are Nowlan's—though both are steeped in the ordinary. And classical Japanese Noh theater, which is resolutely ordinary, is also breathtakingly extraordinary. When I reflect on the extraordinary moments in my own life, I think, for example, of the first present my elder daughter gave me, when she was barely two: it was a little grey pebble she found on the ground as we walked home together. I still remember her tiny fingers placing it in my hand—a moment that illuminated my whole life and brought it into sudden focus.

It seems to me that the ordinary and the extraordinary are different sides of the same coin. People tend to turn their backs on the ordinary in order to seek an experience of the extraordinary; but in fact it is through our connection with the ordinary that the truly extraordinary unfolds before us: the ordinary, resplendent with the weave of the world, awakens us to it. The word *extraordinary* literally means "outside of the ordinary"—**and what lies outside of any ordinary event is the extraordinary web of time and process that births that event from the universe.** Only the ordinary can manifestly reveal that web, as the teapot reveals and connects us to Being. Similarly, it is when an ordinary artwork resonates with the world around it that we can experience the extraordinary through it. The ineffable harmonies of the Taj Mahal are unforgettable for just that reason, in spite of the number of tea towels and trinkets that bear its image. Or the Venus de Milo. And if you consider the Venus de Milo, you will find that it is not just the sculpted contours that captivate us—it is also the marble, in itself both ordinary and extraordinary, forged in the earth's mantle, hauled into the light, and chiseled and shaped by hand. Imagine exactly the same contours cast in plastic or stainless steel, and the potency of the kinship afforded by the earth-forged marble becomes apparent.

The connection to Being provided by ordinariness is also behind the advice given in *Hagakure,* a samurai book written in the 1700s: "Matters of great concern should be treated lightly. Matters of small concern should be treated seriously."[253] When we treat light matters seriously, even so light a matter as the gift of a grey pebble, it grounds us in the present, which contains all the mystery of the world; when we treat serious matters lightly, it helps us locate them in the ordinary and keeps them from becoming abstract. The martial arts technique *heijoshin*—the ability to retain ordinary or everyday mind in the face of danger—addresses the same issue. As long as the world remains ordinary, you are brought into relationship with it, seeing and hearing it clearly; when you abstract the world—something that fear always does—you mask its specificity and occlude the source of your natural responsiveness.

If we want to understand the ordinary better by naming its opposite, we could do worse than look to abstraction. Whereas the root of *ordinary* tells us about "beginning a web," the root of *abstract,* you may remember, literally means "to pull away from." The forgetfulness of abstraction is usually the tool of choice when we are looking for a *solution*—which, as we saw, comes from a root meaning "to cut off." When the 'known self' cuts away from the ordinary world, it asserts its own *rarity,* which is the opposite of fitting seamlessly into the world even down to its etymology: *rare* comes from the Indo-European base *eri-,* "to loose; to split, separate, be rare."

The meanings associated with *abstract*—pulling away from, cutting off, separating—suggest a severing of relationship; and indeed, the more we abstract our world, the less grounded we are in Being and the more we isolate ourselves from it; and isolation, remember, is hallucinogenic. The billionaire Howard Hughes, once a daring aviation inventor, pilot and movie producer, is not the only rare celebrity to have so cut himself off from the ordinary that he descended into paranoid madness. We can take only so much abstraction in our lives before all reality leaks out of them.

Actors learn that lesson, and for the purposes of their craft they adjust what they do depending on the relative ordinariness or abstraction of the medium in which they are working—whether theater, cinema or television. Those related media occupy so many of our waking hours—television especially—that it is worth taking stock of their different degrees of abstraction. Of the three, the process of making theater is the most ordinary. An audience assembles to witness ordinary people moving around and speaking in their own, usually unamplified, voices on an ordinary stage. Everything about theater at its best is patently ordinary. And an actor learns that as long as *he* remains grounded in the ordinary—resisting all urges towards self-achieved, rare accomplishment—then he can submit to whatever energies run through the world of the play so that they run through him too, heightening his physical responsiveness and awareness; and should *he* be ravished by a sensitivity to the felt unknown that is present here and now, the *audience* will be touched by it too. I love films, I love working on them and watching them; but no film has carried me into a direct experience of the blossoming mysteries and wonders and *reality* of life in the way that theater has. In my lifetime a small handful of performances have shaken me to the core, leaving me so opened that a breeze could meander through me. I believe it is the very ordinariness of the theatrical experience that enables it to fulfill its most exalted function—which is to render the invisible visible.

The processes that make cinema are less ordinary. The audience watches not people, but images of them projected onto a screen. The earliest screen actors quickly found that a heightened responsiveness to the world looked ridiculous on the screen—in fact, the screen will only fall in love with an everyday approach to acting. It was originally speculated that this was due to the large scale of the cinema screen, that acting just had to be smaller to compensate; but even on a tiny screen so-called 'theatrical acting' looks melodramatic and weak. It seems rather that the medium, lacking ordinariness, has to adhere to it in other ways. So even though the circumstances of a movie may be extraordinary—Bruce Willis battered and bruised and standing alone against world terrorists, for example—the actor's responses need the kinship of the ordinary ("Oh well, here we go again") for the audience to relate to them. We accept that the issue is one of realistic depiction, but of course it's not. The underscored ordinariness is an artifice that actors, screenwriters and directors have had to master, a way of compensating for the abstraction of the medium. The earliest heroes of cinema may not have understood that conceptually, but they certainly knew how to appear endearingly ordinary: Charlie Chaplin, for example, or Clark Gable, who described himself as "a lucky slob from Ohio."

The processes that bring television into our living rooms make it the most abstract of the three media. A signal is sent over a wire or through the air (but how that happens remains vague for most of us) from somewhere (most of us have never passed by the television stations and probably don't know where they are) and enters a box that translates it (how does *that* happen?) into images in a screen (not even on the screen, *in* it—and what *is* inside a television screen anyway? All we really know is that a tube screen will explode if it's broken. Would a plasma screen leak plasma?). Then there is its content: an ordinary story is continually sliced and diced by random messages that urge us to go shopping for life-enhancing products. One is tempted to speculate that the medium is so divorced from the ordinary that it can only compensate by becoming banal. And it is banal, even down to the etymology of the word. *Banal* originally meant "compulsory," and is related to the Old High German word *bannan*, "to command or forbid under threat of punishment": a demand for compliance if ever there was one. And sure enough, television is beamed into our living rooms with laugh tracks that cue us to be amused, and to what extent; scripts that tell us what to think; music that instructs us in what to feel when; and acting that directs the audience in their every response. The medium is so abstract that the viewer usually has to be taken by the hand and walked through what a show means every step of the way. Ambiguity banished, perplexity nowhere to be seen, the world flattened into what can be signified. In exchange for its familiar tyranny, television entertains us—that is its one task and it does it well. Of course, the word *entertain* literally means "to hold between," and that, usually, is the effect of television: to temporarily suspend us between realities, so that we are in neither the revelations of the present nor the remembrance of an artwork. The abstraction induced by television is a form of forgetfulness—similar to that induced by nepenthe, the mythological drug of forgetfulness. *The effect of that forgetfulness not only renders the visible ordinariness of things invisible—it induces in us a neglect of the body, and of our capacity to be present with 'what is'.*

Considering the abstractions of the medium, it is instructive to look at the ways in which television mirrors and complements the privately screened world of the 'known self'. We might recognize, first of all, that we often turn on the television not because watching it feels good, but because by watching it *we feel less*—we withdraw from sensation. Television is a peculiar form of companionship that offers little but the antephialtic of distraction, and asks even less of the viewer in return. It is called escapism for a reason; but its appeal dims a little when you realize that what you are escaping is the intelligence of your own Being. Television holds us in its sway in part because, totemically, it actually represents our head-centered mode of existence. Encased in its skull-like enclosure, it stares out at us through its bright windowpane, chattering away endlessly in scatterbrain fashion, offering a continual drip feed of commercials and flashy inducements not to channel-hop. It can never rest because it can never escape its own abstractions; and so it anxiously frets its way through a rapid-fire succession of images, each one infused with predigested meaning—while the disconnected body on the couch moves into a deep sleep of lethargy in which the tyrant's values are reinforced at every turn. And even when television displays images of our larger, shared body losing its life—images of widespread extinctions, dying lakes and rivers, air turning brown with filth—we note them, as we might note our leg has fallen asleep on the couch, but we don't really feel them. Just as we know, but don't really feel, that they represent the very processes that give us life.

The Spaciousness of Being

The phase shift from the 'known self' into the sensitivities of the felt self, then, carries us from the nagging need to transcend, and grounds us in the ordinary; but it also carries us from enclosure into spaciousness. The assimilating intelligence of the logosmind depends on a sense of spaciousness: only when there is spaciousness enough in our sensitivities to accommodate the whole can we feel the whole.

Spaciousness is so fundamentally a part of the natural condition of things anyway, one wonders how we could ever *lose* our sense of it. All the matter of the universe was just a mere speck in the moment before the Big Bang; that mere speck is now dispersed across the unfathomable stretches of the universe—all the rest is empty space. Sir James Jeans pointed out that if you "put three grains of sand inside a vast cathedral, the cathedral will be more closely packed with sand than space is with stars."[254] A physicist looking into your body on a subatomic scale would see something pretty similar: a vast emptiness, occasionally punctuated by pinpoints of energy.

And yet we live in bodies that feel dense and tense, in a world that feels squeezed for time, and in a mental environment that is often strained with congestion. It is not in the nature of the world or the body to so constrain us, but in the nature of the 'known self'. Sogyal Rinpoche helped us understand that when he wrote, **"All effort and struggle come from not being spacious."**[255] When I first read that statement, I was pulled up short. A daily torrent of half-digested verbiage has lulled us into glossing over words, forgetful of their ability to point with care and felicity to the world's relationships. I knew of the precision that informed the writing of Sogyal Rinpoche—but could he really mean that *all* effort and struggle come from a lack of spaciousness? I lived with the statement for weeks before I was ready to accept that not only did he mean exactly that, but I couldn't find an exception to it.

Sogyal Rinpoche's statement pertains directly to the choice we face between *inhabiting the tension* and *inhabiting the world*. To inhabit the *tension* is specifically to inhabit the patterns of willfulness (or "effort") and self-conflict (or "struggle") that resist the world's energies. To inhabit the *world* is something quite different. You cannot inhabit the world without inhabiting its spaciousness; to turn away from its spaciousness is to *fortify* yourself against the world, a word that shares the same root as *effort*. We create spaciousness inside us as we dismantle the baffles that confound the corridor within. It is into the spaciousness of the corational corridor we call 'the world' that the heart's gate opens us, dilating the spheres of our sensitivity. Your very existence is so intimately bound to and supported by that spaciousness that we might say that **only by inhabiting the spaciousness of the world can you inhabit the unpatterned source of your true self.** That unpatterned source, of course, is antithetical to the status quo—and inhabiting it is the mythic task to which the hero is called.

Given how central spaciousness is to reality itself, it is odd to note that although we have the word *proprioception* to describe "our sense of the body in space," we have no word to describe "our sense of the space in the body." That oversight is natural enough in our male-inflected culture: our sense of 'the body in space' enables us to act on the world and 'do' things even as it underscores our apartness from the world; by contrast, our sense of 'the space in the body' enables us to 'be' in the world, even as it draws us into relationship with it. But natural though it is to us, that oversight is also dangerous: language is what delivers our awareness into consciousness. As the young Helen Keller was delivered into a world of clarity once she learned to 'sign', we need to discern and bring our awareness to the spaciousness within the body and the patterns that compromise it if we are to be delivered into our own wholeness: for *the body's spaciousness activates the corridor, and the heart's spaciousness opens us to the Call, delivering us into mutual awareness.* Once the crux of our consciousness finds its complement in the spacious, mindful Energy of the present, it becomes the unpatterned source of our truest responses and our fullest life.

We might name the sensitivity that reveals how much spaciousness we are allowing ourselves in the body our *spatioceptive sense*. Once you become aware of your spatioceptive sense, you can subtly scan your body at any time and discover which parts of it feel spacious and which feel dense or congested; you can feel where the flow of energy through the corridor is baffled and impeded. What compromises our spaciousness is always our own divisions: they are the source of the effort and struggle that bind our subtle energies in neglect and self-conflict. They represent our choice *not to integrate our experience*. As you detect those consolidations and consciously ease them into relationship with the core of your being, you reclaim the spaciousness within, so that every part of the body becomes responsive to every other part, and it moves as a mind-suffused unity: every breath is then a whole-body breath; every tilt of the head ripples up through the spine; every lift of an arm is supported by the floating, responsive hips.

There is a direct relationship between our spatioceptive sense and our mind's sensitivity. An activated spatioceptive sense is our surest defense against the fixities of the 'known self': willful doing relies on the baffles within. When we surrender our inner corridor to spaciousness, we liberate the body's cellular intelligence to do its work. When the mind's sensitivity offers the spaciousness within to the spaciousness of the world, so that each lives within the other, then it dilates into the fullness of its partnership with the present.

Play and the Felt Unknown

The transition of our consciousness into the felt self also carries us from the compliance and tyranny of the 'known self' into a spirit of welcoming playfulness. The nature of Being is elusive: contained within a perplexity, it is hidden, and it is hidden, and it is hidden, as Rumi said. *Elusive* contains a vestige of the Latin word *ludere* from which it comes, and which means "to play." If the elusiveness of Being is inherently playful, we might also note that the playfulness of Being is the quality in which we can most readily and seamlessly join it. For instance, as an artist tracks a shimmering perplexity, which he recognizes by pure feeling, it plays among all the ins and outs of the world it inhabits, slipping and sliding, showing and hiding; and as he chases it through its world with brushstroke or phrasing, the work of art remains behind as the evidence or the record of that play. The prototypical artist, Orpheus, brought the world around him into harmony by *playing* his music. Any activity, it seems to me, acquires more life and immediacy and effectiveness when buoyed by the spirit of play. Muhammad Ali brought that spirit into the boxing ring; Shakespeare brought it to the theater; Socrates brought it to philosophy. The remarkable neurosurgeon Charlie Wilson brought it to the operating table: as a colleague commented, "He was like a cat playing with a mouse."[256] I remember interviews with teammates of Wayne Gretzky when they were preparing for a big hockey game. Most of them spoke in terms of "psyching up to take on the other team," and "gearing up for the challenge," or their determination to "get out there and win." Gretzky's attitude was of an altogether different character: "I don't go out there for the challenge, as a challenge—I go out there to have fun. I go out there saying, 'I want that puck—and you can get your own.'" He wasn't just playing hockey—he was *playing*. As coach for the Canadian team at the 2006 Winter Olympics, he told them—after they had just been shut out two games in a row—that if they couldn't go out there and have fun, they were missing the whole point of being there.

The central importance of playing in human health and development was perhaps the foremost message of psychologist Donald Winnicott. He believed that in playing, and only in playing, are you able to use your whole personality; that playing is the basic expression of the creative impulse, which is active in all healthy individuals; and that playing is the basis of all spontaneous living. It is the basis of vital conversation, of good cooking, of a pleasant walk in the woods. The spirit of playfulness is best embodied by children: unless they are fearful, they play at everything; they are agents of chaos. The world calls aloud to them to come and play, to just try things out and see what happens.

Playing is fun, creative and enriching; it can also be dangerous. The eminent scholar Ernest Klein traces our word *play* to the old English word *pleon*, "to expose to danger, risk." That applies precisely. Playing is not about reverting to fixed solutions; it is about chasing the resonance of a perplexity into the unknown. When we undertake those chases, we are most alive, most free, most open to experience—and most open to risk: the word *experience,* remember, is a cousin to *peril.* When Winnicott points out that "playing is inherently exciting and precarious,"[257] he also notes that "this is the precariousness of magic itself."[258] Magic, of course, is about transformation; the unknown is always an agent of transformation. That's why we are so uncomfortable with the unknown, because to the enclosed self it smells of death, not rebirth. In fact, it is redolent of both. The unknown into which Orpheus stepped literally *was* death: Hades itself. To step into the unknown is to expose yourself to transformation, and transformation demands that what *is* must pass away, or die, to be replaced by something newborn. When we play, we step into the unknown and risk encountering ourselves in a perplexing light—one that might ask us, like the snake, to shed an old skin. That risk also carries a reward, for it opens the door to self-revelation; and to discover the self anew is to discover the world anew.

We have already noted that the tyrant is identified with the spirit of *acquisitiveness,* and at this point we can see why: **when someone cuts away from the perplexing whole to which he belongs, he turns instead to the things that belong to him.** By contrast, insofar as the hero heads into the perplexing unknown, he is identified with the spirit of *inquisitiveness,* the desire to find something out, to achieve a new and transforming perspective. Inquisitiveness is a form of play that leaves what is known and pursues a perplexity as a moth tracks light—without needing to stop at answers, solutions or meaning. We are warned that "curiosity killed the cat," and without doubt it has claimed a few of them over the years; but a *lack* of curiosity will kill a kitten ten times out of ten: what there is of the kitten dies off, leaving behind a cat, prematurely old. If curiosity is a feature of youthfulness at any age, it might also be recognized that perplexity nourishes the soul—calls to it directly and challenges it to grow. *Inquisitiveness* leads to an evolution of consciousness that brings us more deeply into relationship with the world; by contrast, the possessions of *acquisitiveness* stand as a bulwark against any such evolution.

Donald Winnicott wrote extensively about playing, but he also wrote about what he considered to be the dark counterpart to playing: compliance. Compliance, we might note, is the sine qua non of self-tyranny; but compliance also sounds the death knell of play. In comparing them, Winnicott contended that **"living creatively is a healthy state ... compliance is a sick basis for life."**[259] *Any* act of compliance tacitly empowers the authority it obeys, whether the authority justifies its demand on the basis of its claim to knowledge or by its ability to inflict reprisals. When the self is divided into a part that orders and a part that obeys, it complies with and thereby sanctions rule by Idea; the more authority we give to an idea, the greater its power of endarkenment, and the deeper the compliance that binds us.

Of course, the very idea of authority is a fantasy we construct; the Energy of Being, the one reality, answers not to authority, but to harmony. The differences between a compliance to authority and the companionship of play are telling: compliance 'looks back', play faces forward; compliance conforms to expectation, play defies expectation; compliance subjugates curiosity, play is fueled by it; compliance abstracts the present, play is awake to it; compliance is guided by the 'known self', play is guided by the mystery of 'what is'; compliance stultifies the exchange of energies with the world, play exults in it; and finally, compliance is characterized by a sense of seriousness or heaviness (each delicate foot of my younger daughter used to weigh at least ten pounds the moment she was asked to do something she didn't want to do), and play is characterized by a sense of welcome or lightness. If the spirit of isolation thwarts play—and so too any real possibility of transformation—the spirit of play, by contrast, is rooted in companionship; and real companionship, it turns out, expresses a willingness to be changed.

The Deepening Harmony

Another aspect of the shift that moves us from 'known self' to felt self is that it carries us from a siege mentality to one that finds repose in harmony. The hetabrain feels under siege and encloses itself in response. In the Indo-European family of languages there is a host of words related to *enclosure*, and together they tell a story: their meanings include *hook, club, knotty stick, peg, nail, bolt, lock, to bar, to be caught on,* and *to shut up.* Images of aggression, defensiveness and fixity. It is an appropriate set of responses to a hostile world—and **that raises an essential question, a question to which the spiritual path provides one answer, and classical science another:** *is the world alive to you, and a source of guidance and nourishment, or is it a place of hostility and indifference?* Is it a place in which to be at home, or is it an environment in which you won't survive unless you build and fortify your own private bunker? Is it a random outcome of strictly material, four-dimensional interactions, or is it an all-aware miracle in five dimensions? The stance this book takes is clear enough, but it is a question that each of us can only answer in our own hearts. In what follows I offer my own thoughts on it, with the hope that they might provide you with a source of reflection.

As we have noted, science has chosen to describe a four-dimensional world in which consciousness is but an insignificant by-product—a world described originally by the rules of mechanics and, more recently, by those of statistical probability. At best, such a world is indifferent to man—an opinion our culture generally considers to be realistic. Darwin left us a somewhat darker legacy: "survival of the fittest," an idea inspired by his work, paints a picture of scarcity in which the individual has to *compete* against the world to earn the right to continue living. This is a culturally biased outlook that both suits and feeds the consciousness of tyranny with which the West has identified. It is also so circuitous an idea as to be almost worthless. When we say "survival of the fittest" we might ask—"the fittest for what"? The answer would have to be "the fittest for survival"—which establishes a standard that is self-defining only after the fact, conveniently adapting the idea of fitness to accord with whatever happens to have survived.

Nevertheless, we embrace this message of popular Darwinism as if it were lucid gospel, and retreat to our fortified enclosures, sensing hostility all around. *Competition* in its ancient Latin roots used to mean "to strive together"—and indeed, when you race with someone, each of you is helping the other to do his or her best. Nowadays we compete *against*—often for financial gain, which is our culture's most trusted determinant of status: if I own more than you, I am ipso facto more fit for survival, and therefore a superior specimen. Money breeds entitlement. The almighty *quantity* we accumulate in our lives becomes our substitute for *quality* in our lives, which always beckons to us from somewhere in the future, just over the horizon, something we have to work towards—and that's ironic, of course, because real quality can only be found where you are right now.

'Survival of the fittest' is the tyrant's ultimate self-justification. According to its flimsy logic, to control or dominate someone is to demonstrate that you are *fit* to control or dominate her. You are entitled to. That can happen at any scale: in the hetabrain's tyranny of the self; in a boss bullying an employee; in a corporate tyranny within the competitive marketplace; or in a society's tyranny over other cultures. The arrogance it breeds is not merely obscene: it is capable of blinding us. The idea, for instance, that we in the developed world—who foul our own nests with such toxicity that we threaten the very life of the earth that mothers us—are more 'fit for survival' than, say, traditional Australian aborigines is downright preposterous. And yet, it persists as a self-evident truth for many. In the dog-eat-dog scheme that 'survival of the fittest' extols, we have amply demonstrated our superiority, after all.

But is it really a dog-eat-dog world? Paleobiologist Blaire Van Valkenburgh has found that fossil records of prehistoric dogs in North America tell an interesting story. About thirty million years ago twenty-five canine species roamed the west and south of what is now the United States. Typically those species show an evolutionary trend towards getting bigger and stronger—in fact, some were the size of grizzly bears. So 'survival of the fittest', as our culture understands it, seems to be a rule of thumb. At a certain size, though—somewhere between 20 and 25 kilograms of weight—'bigger and stronger' becomes a liability. It takes too much effort to survive on smaller prey, so the diets of such carnivores become more specialized: they are forced to kill prey as large as or larger than they are. Higher energy needs lead to lower population densities, and that makes the species vulnerable to food shortages. Fossils reveal a clear pattern: extinction comes fastest to the canine species that are 'fittest'—that is, biggest and strongest, as we typically think of fitness. Some would counter, though, that if one canine species survives while a larger one dies off, it is self-evident that the surviving species was more fit. Whatever fitness means.

Perhaps the dizziness induced by such arguments is what keeps us from reflecting soberly on our notion of the dog-eat-dog world and stating the obvious: **for any species in the natural world, its survival is a product of how well it can harmonize with that world.** There is more to this issue than semantics—the principles of 'fitness' and 'harmony' are radically different. Fitness appeals to the hetabrain because, although it won't lend itself to a meaningful principle, we can isolate the quality of 'fitness' from the world and satisfy ourselves by measuring what we believe to be its various aspects: speed, strength, reproductive rate, size, weight, et cetera. We could even compile those measurements in a weighted formula and come up with a number that represented the specimen's Fitness Quotient—much as we currently measure someone's faculties of abstract reasoning and call that number his Intelligence Quotient. Harmony, on the other hand, cannot be measured, because it cannot be isolated. Furthermore, unlike fitness, it *does* lend itself to a meaningful principle—a principle of dynamic balance in its give and take with the world. To survive, a species needs to be in harmony with its food supply and its predators, and also with the fluctuating seasons of its world, and ultimately with the entire intricate web of the ecosystem to which it belongs and which it helps to sustain. Without such a sensitive balance, the species will perish through overpopulation, dwindling food supply or an inability to adapt within an increasingly imbalanced environment. What natural selection actually favors is the ability to harmonize with the world.

Habit might lead us to imagine that 'survival of the most harmonious' is the same as 'survival of the most adaptable'; but mere adaptation is a reactionary and passive idea, a throwback to the isolationism of perseity. Harmonizing with the environment is an exchange of gifts, a reciprocal relationship. Examples of such relationships abound wherever a species is studied within its environment, but I know of none that more clearly illustrates the point than a story about the prairie dog cited in the *New York Times*.[260] In the 1950s, government officials were concerned about the damage done to sparse desert grasses on the Navajo reservation near Chilchinbito, Arizona, and recommended an extermination of the extensive prairie dog population. Navajo elders objected, saying, "If you kill off the prairie dogs, there will be no one to cry for rain." Amused by this superstition, and knowing full well that prairie dogs had nothing to do with rainfall, scientists went ahead with their plan. Today, that area is a virtual wasteland. It turns out that the millions of burrows acted much as the alveoli of our lungs do. As the moon moved the water in aquifers up and down, it pumped moisture-laden, ion-charged air out of the earth and into the atmosphere, which helped create the moisture on which the grasses depended, which the prairie dogs then ate. Their burrowing also kept the soil loose, allowing the rainfall to penetrate and nourish the grass roots. The prairie dogs had not just adapted to their environment— they were an inseparable component of its living harmony.

Our potential for harmonizing with the natural world is obscured by our instinct to dominate it. In fact, the five-dimensional reality of that potential is so far beyond anything our female-fearing culture prepares us to contemplate that we can gain some inkling into it only by looking at examples from hunter-gatherer cultures, which have been shaped by it. Elizabeth Marshall Thomas, daughter of two anthropologists, grew up on Africa's Kalahari Desert among the Ju/wa Bushmen.

In her book *The Tribe of Tiger,* Thomas writes of the relationship between the Ju/wasi and the lions: though they hunted the same prey, the tribes and the prides had established a sort of understanding. Her brother once joined a group of four Ju/wasi as they trailed a wildebeest they'd wounded with a poisoned arrow. When they came upon the animal after several days, it was very ill and was surrounded by a large pride of lions, perhaps thirty in all. The Ju/wasi spoke "firmly but respectfully" to the lions, threw some clumps of earth at them, entered their circle, killed and butchered the wildebeest, and left with it. The whole time the lions rumbled and paced among the surrounding bushes, but kept their distance. As Thomas observed, "the people-lion relationship wouldn't have worked unless both sides had participated."[261] By the time Thomas returned to the Kalahari thirty years later the Ju/wasi had disappeared—driven off by white ranchers—and the harmony of the truce was long forgotten.

Another example: in *Searching for the Lost Arrow,* Richard Nelson describes his stay at an Inupiaq whaling camp off the Alaskan coast. Winds had closed the open channels in the ice that whales use for migration, except for one large lead, at which the Inupiaq placed their camp. No whales had been seen for a couple of days, so everyone was staying warm inside the tent. Their conversation was suddenly interrupted by Igruk, an elder in his seventies who had been lying on a soft bed of caribou skins with his eyes closed: "I think a whale is coming, and perhaps it will surface very close." Igruk was respected as a great whaler, and at his words, everyone hurried outside. Sure enough, seconds after Richard had stepped outside to join them, "a broad, shining back cleaved up through still water near the opposite side of the opening, accompanied by the burst of a whale's blow."[262]

To begin to grasp how examples of such harmony are possible we need to appreciate that they are enfolded in the dimension of consciousness, which suffuses and sustains all reality. As Hugh Brody has noted,

> Hunter-gatherers believe in the spiritual link between the creatures they hunt, the places they travel and themselves.... And shamanic knowledge to some extent depends on the possibility of communication between humans and animals. It accepts without difficulty analogous communication between animal species.

> Shamans embrace mystery not as a temporary failure
> of explanation, but as an integral way of apprehending
> the world around them.[263]

Shamanism is a vital element in the culture of such societies. Our attempts to dismiss it as ignorant superstition betray the evidence: shamanism has survived because such societies rely for their survival on the ability to read the truth of the world around them; and shamanism—along with detailed observation, a living attunement to place, and a culture of respect—provides that. At its best, shamanism is a way of listening to the subtle energy of the world in order to harmonize with it; and to the best of our knowledge no hunter-gatherer society has survived without it.

To the hetabrain, of course, 'survival of the most harmonious' doesn't sound anywhere near as convincing as 'survival of the fittest'. For starters, *the hetabrain is incapable of recognizing harmony,* as we have seen. When it looks to the world, it seeks and detects *order,* which promises to facilitate control. What a difference it would make to your soul's journey and to your kinship with the world if you sought to harmonize with it—*if you took **that** to be the cardinal necessity.* It would change how you step out of your front door and onto the street. It would change how you wake up in the morning—opening your eyes to mutual awareness and seeking to listen to and harmonize with the world's five-dimensional aliveness, rather than waking up already trapped within the machinery of your agendas as they grind away at you and the world to get things done.

I think 'survival of the fittest' was obliquely introduced to us in the sixth century B.C. by Zoroaster, who saw the world as the battleground in which the good God was perpetually in conflict with the evil God. All of nature, including human nature, was implicated in that struggle for domination. Joseph Campbell's observation on the effect of that worldview shows how deeply it still runs within us: One is not to put oneself in accord with such a world, but to correct it. And in your efforts to correct it, *nothing can impart a sense of entitlement more thoroughly than the knowledge that your actions are sanctified by the good God, and are made on his behalf, and that what you oppose is impure and not deserving to survive.* Zoroastrianism, though still practiced, is dying out, condemned by its own standards of purity: membership is restricted to those whose parents both belong to the faith. Its hostile interpretation of the world thrives, however, in many of the world's great religions, as well as in the dualistic 'isms' that haunt our thinking: every 'ism' that represents an adherence to doctrine—racism, sexism, despotism, communism, fundamentalism, capitalism, authoritarianism, whatever—is in its essence a division of the world into an entitled elite and an undeserving other.

And that reminds us that *to see the world as a testing ground for fitness is to empower the inner tyrant,* who is ever ready, as Campbell observed, "to battle back the anticipated aggressions of his environment." The gravest effect of that outlook is anticipated by our theme "as it is with the world, so also with the body." To be at home in the body is to be at home in the world; **but to experience the world as a place of hostility—as an environment from which to maintain your distance and over which to seek control—is to experience the body in the same way.** One is not to put oneself in accord with such a body, but to correct it. *The tyrant, afraid of the female, is afraid of being in the body.* And so we alienate ourselves from the body by withdrawing into the head, and we assert control over the body, and stifle its breathing, and drug it into submission when we need to, and make it get fit enough to assuage our vanity, and accept as natural and inevitable the schisms and conflicts and scarcities that rage through it. Or we so dissociate from it that when we feel the body nagging at us for attention—needing to experience its own consciousness—what we give it instead is food, and more food.

So much for the outlook that is promoted by pure science. The spiritual path is the path of the ordinary hero, and it sees the world very differently. The entire spiritual journey is one in which the individual learns by degrees to see and read the world as an all-nurturing miracle of guidance in which we have a role as cocreators. It is a path that teaches us—deeply, deeply teaches us—that **the state of no effort is our greatest strength, for it is also the seamlessly integrated state of Being that enables us to harmonize with the strength of the world.** Eventually that teaching leads us to the understanding that the world itself is enlightened; to join the world is to die to the endarkened ego and give yourself to the supreme light of intelligence all around you. Enlightenment is not something any individual can possess, any more than someone could possess the Logos or Buddha consciousness. Spiritual enlightenment in an individual is nurtured by a profound dissolution of the anxiety that separates us from the world, so that we can at last join it, seeing and understanding "the real as the play and work of love," as Andrew Harvey put it.[264] To join the enlightened world is to awaken to a place of ceaseless renewal and revelation; a place of companionship in which you are fully known in everything you do, even as you sensationally discover and serve the world in everything you do; a place in which alienation and existential isolation are seen to be creaky illusions, because in fact you know yourself to be an indivisible part of all Being, intimately and companionably sustained by it; a place in which endless gifts arise from the deep mystery that suffuses everything ordinary.

When you come to that place, you become like the tree or the prairie dog, which move to and express the harmonies of the world—but which, more than that, also deepen and support those harmonies. That too is the story Orpheus shows us: the harmony of the world calls forth music from the artist—but equally, the artist can call forth harmony from the world. I have been fortunate to have experienced this in performances: John Gielgud and Ralph Richardson performing in *Home* in London; Monica Mason dancing *The Song of the Earth* at Covent Garden; Claudia Bruce performing *Cross Way Cross* in New York; Iben Nagel Rasmussen performing *Itsi Bitsi* in Holstebro, Denmark; Hosho Hideo performing the Noh play *Sotoba Komachi* in Tokyo. It has been said that "Noh has been a purification of the Japanese soul for 400 years"; Noh has also been called 'healing without medicine'. It is hard to explain exactly how or why that happens, but the same is true of all of the above performances: each one of them called forth from the world a new harmony that could not be resisted, and which unleashed life-giving energies. All great art does that—it sensitizes us and makes it possible for us to relate to the world anew: newly harmonized, and harmonizing in turn.

It is tempting for us, of course, to explain away such phenomena as matters of psychological affect. That temptation is supported by a feature of our culture that is not without irony: we devote ourselves to controlling and fighting 'what is' without ever really *attending* to 'what is'—and then we proclaim ourselves the most reliable *arbiters* of 'what is'. Evidence abounds, though, that there is the potential for an exchange of gifts within the corational corridor around us in ways that our idea of 'what is' just doesn't prepare us for. I'll cite two small examples. Jay Gluck, who wrote *Zen Combat* in 1962, arranged to bring five United States military police and a high-speed camera to meet with

Morehei Uyeshiba, the founder of aikido, who at the time was eighty-five. In a demonstration, Uyeshiba took on the military police, who were supported by a further six Japanese martial artists armed with oak swords. As Gluck explains, the film shows this tiny old man—he stood four foot ten—moving amongst his charging assailants with a contented smile on his face. No one even touched him until he let several of them grasp him in any way they wanted, whereupon he floored them all simultaneously. Gluck wrote that the film "showed nothing but a smiling old man moving unconcernedly amidst intense, charging GIs [who were] seemingly unaware that he existed."[265] The modern mind wants to explain this phenomenon in terms that are entirely inconsistent with Uyeshiba's writings and training and teachings; but only so much can be explained away as trickery or coincidence before those explanations begin to sound overly defensive.

The second small example (and there are literally thousands we could look at) took place in South America in the spring of 1998. The story was followed closely by the media there, and was also picked up in Europe and North America. The account that appeared in the London *Daily Telegraph* on April 4 is so enjoyable that I present it to you in its entirety.

Tribesmen Call in Divine Power to Halt Forest Fire
John Clemens, *London Daily Telegraph*

RIO DE JANEIRO - Kukrit and Mati-i are the new heroes of the rain forest. It took the illiterate Kaiapo tribesmen from the Mato Grosso half an hour of mysterious ritual on a river bank this week to break a five-month drought in the northern Amazon region of Roraima, which had been turned into an inferno.

Their ancestral powers ended what was rapidly turning into one of the world's largest ecological disasters.

Within hours, torrential tropical downpours had put out over 90 per cent of the huge jungle fires that had run out of control and destroyed thousands of acres of savannah and rain forest in an area the size of Wales over the past two weeks.

Kukrit and Mati-i—they are unsure about their age as tribal forest Indians count only up to two, all the rest is "very much"—were flown from their tribal village 2,400 kilometres away by the government's Indian Foundation. It was a desperate act which defied all the latest technology and white man's science. The official forecasts were gloomy. Data sent by channel 2 of the NOAA-14 weather satellite and interpreted by the high-tech computers at the Brazilian space center in Jose dos Campos, thousands of kilometres away in the far south of the country, indicated rain in the region was still "at least two to three weeks away."

Hundreds of firefighters were engaged in a hopeless battle against the advancing flames, United Nations emergency aid was offered and considered, army helicopters were dropping "waterbombs"—all to no avail. Enormous tracts of virgin rain forest were being devoured and no one could stop it.

Kukrit and Mati-i were unperturbed by their first flight. After they had crossed hundreds of kilometres of jungle they settled in a three-star hotel in Boa Vista, capital of Roraima state in the extreme north of Brazil, took a shower and had a leisurely dinner. Then they went out to the banks of the nearby Curupira River, carrying cipo leaves and taquara branches from their homeland. They were worried that their tribal brothers of the local Yanomami nation would be "eaten" by the flames. "We will make water fall," they promised as they asked to be left alone to perform their ceremony in the dark.

Satisfied, they returned to their hotel 30 minutes later and went to bed, a novelty to them as they are used to hammocks. "It will rain," was all they said before sleeping.

Less than two hours later, the first reports came through on the radio at the army fire task emergency center in Boa Vista. "It started raining here," an almost incredulous voice said from the jungle town of Cacarai.

An hour later, similar reports came in from Apiau, in the region between the Surunu and Majari rivers in the north. When dawn broke, Boa Vista was hit by one of the heaviest downpours in living memory. People danced in the rain in the streets before breakfast and the airport, closed several times in the past few weeks because of smoke from the forest fires, was shut again—this time because of poor visibility caused by the impenetrable rain curtain.

By the end of the day, 25 millimetres had fallen. The fires petered out and humidity rose back to its "normal" 97-per-cent level.

Satisfied, Kukrit and Mati-i returned to the Mato Grosso. They did not give an explanation. All they said was that they had talked to Becororoti, a famous ancestor gifted with divine power, who, when he died, went to heaven and was turned into rain.

Orpheus flies out of the jungle and, in an exchange of gifts by the Curupira River, calls the world into harmony. Unfortunately, the harmony that is so natural to Kukrit and Mati-i is not only unsupported by the dominant cultural paradigms of the West—it is directly undermined by them. Our culture is devoted to the myth of individuality; it sees unipolar thinking as the rightful ruler of the individual; it reveres dissociated perspectives as 'pure' truth; it believes the world is strictly four-dimensional; it considers an individual's accumulated wealth or status to be emblematic of his success; and it considers the ideal lifestyle, accessible only to those with a deluding amount of wealth, to consist largely of being shielded from any contact with the ordinary, and from any responsibility but to one's own security.

Just as damaging, our culture believes that our thoughts don't matter to the world, and sees the problems around us as strictly mechanical problems that require mechanical solutions—whether they are problems of socioeconomic malaise, personal illness or the health of our planet. But consider this: Kukrit and Mati-i brought harmony to rampant natural destruction with prayers, leaves, branches and a sensibility attuned to the universe. Is it not possible, then, that the discord and conflict in human consciousness worldwide might be contributing to the discord and conflict we see around us in the natural world? As

Roger Nelson commented, "We may be connected together far more intimately than we realize."

For myself, I believe that the main challenge of our age is to usher our corationality into consciousness—so that we live within the subtle dialogue of reality rather than inside our self-absorbed monologue. When you consider all the problems our society faces—in the environment, in the economy, in our shattered sense of community—it's clear that they are problems of systemic imbalance. It is not by mere accident that those problems exactly mirror the imbalances we perpetuate within the thinking of the self by dissociating the male element from the female. Until we evolve beyond the fetters of our own mistaken identity—until we can evolve from a consciousness of tyranny to a consciousness of consciousness—the idea of restoring balance to the world will remain no more than a half-baked fantasy.

The Way of Gentleness

The Apocrypha is a selection of books that were included as an appendix to the King James Version of the Old Testament. The word *apocrypha* comes from the Greek for "hidden things," and in one of its books, Ecclesiasticus, is written,

> Many are in high place, and of renown; but mysteries
> are revealed unto the meek.[266]

It is a familiar sentiment, expressed in a wide diversity of spiritual writings and practices. But according to one of the central themes of this book—*the world we create around us replicates the one we experience within*—we would expect to find the prototype for that truth at work in the individual. The hetabrain, of course, is seated on high, and houses a self that is of *renown*, a word that literally means "named"; the 'named self' is the 'known self'. The passage contrasts those "in high place and of renown" with the meek, to whom "mysteries are revealed." The word *meek* as it is used in the Bible has none of the modern connotations of "weak," "shy" or "spineless." In fact, those connotations are provided by the hetabrain, just as it misunderstands *co*rationality to be *ir*rationality, or self-enclosure to be mastery, or harmony to mean order. The tyrant views *meekness* as a timid, retreating demeanor that betrays a lack of strength, or a tentative sense of presence. Such forms of meekness exist, and are ways of minimizing certain relationships with the world; in fact, they result from their own kind of self-conscious enclosure and tyranny.

The Biblical meekness is something altogether different: a form of grounded presence that enables you to stand in the world's stillness in innocence. Such meekness doesn't cringe defensively in the world but stands tall in it, precisely because meekness is not weighed down with the burdens of self-absorption. In fact, because such meekness fully surrenders to the present, the heart's gate will fully open to the present: standing tall in humility before the spacious present, you leave room for it to come to rest within the pelvic bowl. Meekness in the Biblical sense is a vulnerability born of strength, a state of mind that is free from anxiety—a striking contrast with arrogance, which cloaks anxiety beneath the smug assurance of knowledge. **Meekness surrenders the blinkers of 'knowledge' before the limitless presence of 'what is', and accompanies it into the felt unknown; meekness is literally made possible by heroic courage.** Christ, who preached meekness, exemplified such courage: he did not submit to any man, nor to any law of man, because he found the strength to submit meekly to the truth of his own life and to the Logos—the mind of God—that all the world expresses.

The word *meek* comes to us from the Old Norse *mjuk-r,* "soft, pliant, gentle". One meaning that the OED lists for *meek* is **"patient and unresentful under injury and reproach"**; and that is the real test, in a way. It is one thing to cultivate a sense of spaciousness—a full acceptance of the world as it is, untainted by resistance or anxiety—while sitting by the seaside or walking through a meadow. It is another thing to remain in the world, *gently* in the world, when under duress.

When Jesus says, "Blessed are the meek, for they shall inherit the earth,"[267] he is merely stating a fact: only the meek *can* inherit the earth; others can't, for the simple reason that they are enclosed from it; with the world kept at a distance, they can inherit only the specters of their personal, self-achieved fantasies. *A grounded gentleness of heart—or meekness, as the Bible says—ushers us into a relationship with the present that is fully sensitized to it.* To inherit the world is to live in it as it lives in you, "feeling the thing as a whole."

Gentleness of heart—or meekness—attunes you to the blessed *subtlety* of 'what is' and begins weaning you away from the habit of *abstracting* 'what is'. In its quiet attentiveness, gentleness receives the mysteries—the pulse of the present and the touch of its invisible guidance. When an athlete finds himself "in the zone," he has found in the utmost extremity of his sport an inner gentleness that lets him hear, as in the calm eye of a storm, the subsonic whisperings of the world around him: the delicate currency of Being that informs his every move. And who among us can guess with what subtlety Kukrit and Mati-i tuned in to the web of life, or how gently they turned its course with their cipo leaves and taquara branches?

Standing in the river, in the world, knowing it and being known, is the only true blessing we have—and the only one that is always right here. As Christ's words and those of Ecclesiasticus point out, only a gentle surrender can attune to those subtle currents. **Your capacity for relationship—the true measure of your ability to 'be' in the river—cannot outgrow your sensitivity; and it is in the medium of grounded gentleness that your sensitivity is truly nurtured.** And to be quite clear, what we are talking about here has nothing to do with the appearance of gentleness; it is not something to be achieved by cultivating certain mannerisms of speech or demeanor or deportment. The focus is not on gentleness per se, but on what its subtle yielding opens you to and the vivid companionship it illuminates. It is a means, a doorway—not a destination: the submission of the hero is specifically a self-achieved gentleness that allows what is here, now, to speak to your core. In the midst of your exchange with the world you might even appear ferocious or wild or uncouth or aggressive. During one martial arts sparring match, Aoki was monitored by an electroencephalograph. Of the results of the EEG, which were published at the time, he said in an interview,

> When they analyzed the wave patterns, they found that I entered into deep meditation even while in the midst of violent movement, using a technique, in the manner of the Zen adage, "motion in calmness, calmness in motion."[268]

The more completely you are at peace with the present, the more sensationally you will be informed by its subtle currents—and the more sensitively you will respond to what it calls from you. Furthermore, **the more extreme the circumstances in which you find yourself—the**

more fully you are called upon to *do*—the more gently you will need to abide in the wild calmness of Being itself. Aoki has spoken of entering a state of such calm clarity that any opponent who even thought of attacking him would fall down. When he was asked by the interviewer whether he really did nothing at such a time, he responded, "No! If I do anything, it's no good. It's a state in which I myself do nothing."[269] In such a state there are no cybernetics, there is no white noise, there is no willful doing; the pure signal of Being resonates through the pipeline in a seamless, unfettered exchange of information and creativity with the world. By contrast, we typically have difficulty walking down Fifth Avenue—or holding a banana peel—in a state of peace.

The whole idea of gentleness runs contrary to the impulses of a culture that believes doing requires effort and misapprehends the world as a place of hostility—so it is worth a closer look. The word *gentle* comes from the Latin *gentilis*, which means "belonging to the same family." That brings to mind Thomas Berry's observation that the trees and grasses are our genetic cousins, our kin; and that the earth itself is born of the same star matter from which we are made. When we pick up a teapot gently, we embrace the kinship of the ordinary world. To see that subtle kinship around you, to see family, is to open your heart to your life; to be gentle with the world is to feel the kinship of it. In gentleness, the ordinary heart meets the ordinary world and they are found to beat as one.

Gentleness has limited value as a mere idea—gentleness is a yielding love for 'what is' that involves your whole being: emotional, spiritual, intellectual and physical. To engage with the world that way, gently and wholly, is to return to the sort of unenclosed sensitivity that Henri and H. A. Frankfort described in our ancient forebears, who experienced the world "as life confronting life, involving every faculty of man in a reciprocal relationship"[270]—a precise description of the dialogue of Being. But that gentle wakefulness to the world, insofar as it involves reciprocity, also reminds us of the essential nature of gentleness: gentleness is not static by nature, nor is it found in any action per se; the quality of gentleness is only revealed in interaction—it is fundamentally a quality of relating, or relationship, in the same way that grace is. Because gentleness is grounded in the stillness of the present, it is a quality of relating that arises from wholeness and answers to wholeness. **In its essence, gentleness is not a state—it is a subtle, two-way conversation, and does not exist independent of that**

conversation. If you gently move a baby's arm, that gentleness shows up in the sensitivity and care and patience and mindfulness of your interaction with the baby. A gentle gesture is a highly informed gesture: it begins in attentive unknowing and is guided by Being; like Being, it is in flux, adapting to and revealing the world's subtle currents. Whatever is gentle bespeaks a capacity for relationship. As such, it carries us out of the isolating wound of our self-consciousness and reunites our thinking with our Being.

Because gentleness brings you into relationship with the world, it maximizes the world's reality for you. And the more reality the world has for you, the more it will activate you and engage you. Gentleness is not weakheartedness. It is about entering the full reality of mutual awareness. To move into gentleness is to step into a serene wakefulness that moves on and out, like ripples in a pond. Its patience is like a shot of oxygen to the loving logosmind, and it quickens your whole Being to the specificity of the present. Its fluid, welcoming spirit carries you forward, hand-in-hand with the world, fully activated. And that, more than anything, is what places gentleness on the side of life: because gentleness yields, it allows us to move forward in partnership with 'what is'. Whenever we lose gentleness, we put on the brakes and arrest our own life. Reality is sensational. Fantasy is sensationalistic.

Zeami, in his advice to actors, expressed something that carries profound implications for our culture: it is a mistake to understand a lack of tenderness as strength.[271] True strength is something you discover as you open to the subtle currents of Being; and you can truly connect with Being, with 'what is', only through gentleness. Anything else is a form of resistance. The moment we lose gentleness we topple into fantasy and preoccupy ourselves with embellishments on its dark logic. Gentleness of heart will deliver you from the shadowed cell of the ego, and carry you into the bosom of Being, in which the mystery that slides through each moment sings its love. True gentleness enables you to rest in the pelvic bowl, and it lightens the heart's gate that it may open with ease to the world's currents. It rescues you from the driven highway of doing and allows you to sail the river of being.

Understanding grounded gentleness as the medium in which the mind's sensitivity flourishes, we might further recognize it as the medium of love that enables anything to talk to us. There are many ways in which gentleness can quicken our analog intelligence to the dialogue of Being, and all of them are important. First, and perhaps most challenging, is to forego willfulness and be gentle with yourself: with your breath, your seeing and hearing, your moving, your self-doubts and self-accusations and missteps. Similarly, you can be *gentle with your emotions*: with your own excitement, your own disappointment, even with your own grief and joy and rage. Gentleness is not a means of subduing the emotions or homogenizing them. It is just the opposite. Emotions are energy on the move, and they have the potential to bring the vividness of the world into focus. It is more often the case, though, that our emotions preoccupy us and *separate* us from the world. They bury us in ourselves. Sometimes the emotions that ambush us and hang on are an expression of the shadow self: a part of us that we are unwilling to acknowledge and bring into relation with the whole—often a part of us that has been hurt or fearful from a young age, and remains defensively reactionary. John Sarno, a medical doctor and pioneer in the practice of mindbody disorders, has done remarkable work in demonstrating how such emotions, rage in particular, will manifest in the body as painful symptoms. A calm, gentle acknowledgment of such dark passions is sometimes all that is needed to bring them into relationship with the whole and eliminate the pain. As well, the liberated energy of those emotions will bring the present newly into focus, and leave the intimacy of the world in its wake.

By contrast, when you apply the brakes to an emotion, you wrench yourself out of the world and terminate the two-way conversation. The emotional energy then has only the barricaded fantasy of your 'known self' to move through, and around and around it goes until it settles into the body and hardens. In general **we always lose gentleness when there is something we would rather not feel, often simply because we perceive that feeling it is not going to help us achieve our goals.** And so we decide that we don't really require the participation of our pelvic intelligence. With that decision we align with the tyrant's unipolar choice to "know the thing in part."

The gentler you are with yourself, the more fully you will be present. When you can be gentle with your whole life, your whole life will be present. Of course, gentleness is soft, but its effects are not. It opens the door on the flux of the world, the only reality, which moves with the power of a whirlpool. Not everyone chooses to give over to its pull. If you do make that choice, your grounded gentleness will carry you into an ocean of truth.

In being gentle with yourself you prepare the way to be gentle with all the particulars of the living space around you—and that loving attention will reveal the 'mutual awareness' on which your true consciousness depends. When you behold the world beholding you, it welcomes you into the reality of 'what is'. As that mutual awareness gently grows, you respond with increasing ease and genuineness to what is around you. In so responding you discover responsibility—for the link between gentleness and responsibility is immutable. Your 'ability to respond' depends on the yielding spirit of gentleness, and whenever gentleness is offered, your 'responsibility' will be activated.

The link between gentleness and responsibility takes on a larger significance when applied to the discovery of your personal path. Nothing will throw you from that path more quickly than the spirit of resentment or blame or victimhood by which we hold others responsible for how we feel or what we do. Gentleness, on the other hand, which has no brakes, returns you to the source of your life and accommodates whatever integration is necessary to carry you forward: **to bring the spirit of gentleness to your own living is ultimately to take responsibility for your own life.** Sometimes, as our gentleness carries us into a profound realization of kinship with the world, the responsibility we feel will have such reality, such Quality, that it will appear to be sacred. The remarkable theologian Dietrich Bonhoeffer, who argued on behalf of a "religionless Christianity,"[272] rejected the rigid moral standards of the Bible, and argued that right and wrong are determined purely by the "loving obligations of the moment."[273] It is reported that when he was hanged by the Nazis, there were tears in the eyes of his guards.

There are other ways of being gentle as well. Sogyal Rinpoche tells us, "The most essential thing in life is to establish an unafraid, heartfelt communication with others."[274] What most consistently interferes with such communication is the part of us that can't resist being judgmental. *In that regard, offering gentleness to someone is the opposite of offering her your judgment.* When you gently open to another's Being, the shimmering reality of your exchange with her overwhelms any mere fantasy you might wish to construct.

To be gentle with the present moment is to open yourself to its wild eternity: **to be gentle with the present is to *be* present.** And you may find that it is possible to be in the moment so gently that you merge with it. When that happens, you enter a state of bottomless grace: the bliss that occurs when your thinking merges with your Being and finds peace and nourishment within the harmony of 'what is'.

In this chapter we have looked at some of the changes that occur as the two axes of our consciousness—the inner and the analog—bring us more and more fully into relationship with the reality in which we live. But if we are to truly overthrow the entrenched habits and tenacious hallucinations of our self-tyranny, it would help to know how it all began. How did we come to live in our heads? How did the male element dissociate from the female within us? And why? How did we turn away from the guidance of the world to such an extent that we can no longer detect it? How did we move so deeply into self-absorption that, ironically, we lost our ability to feel the self? Whatever forces guided the evolution of our consciousness into the enclosure of dissociated doing, they are the forces with which we must now contend. The next section of the book, then, takes a look at the historical journey that carried the center of our consciousness into the cranium and bottled it up there.

Exercise Nine: **The Milk Jug**

Our self-tyranny, under whose influence we all live, seeks to make of the body a house of death: it becomes an organized inadequacy, a stranger to its own energy. How, then, to call that tendency to account? The breath is our most tangible and immediate experience of the body's energy. The question then becomes how to *submit* to the breath and receive its sensational information, rather than anticipate and control its journey. Most people have heard of the importance of breathing deeply, but I have found that when I encourage students to breathe deeply, they often try to accomplish that by pushing the breath down into their bodies, as if filling the lungs from the top down. Such breathing is the work of willful manipulation rather than receptivity. As such, it tends to reinforce the baffles that divide up the corridor, rather than opening it to your being. You will never see a baby pushing its breath down into its body.

To foster a different experience I use the image of milk being poured into a jug: it drops freely into the jug until it hits the bottom, and as the pouring continues the milk fills the pitcher from the bottom up. Similarly, try that with the breath: stand in a relaxed position and let the breath drop straight down through the spacious corridor of the body until it hits the pelvic floor, and then fills the body from the bottom up, and finally releases out again. If you find that difficult, try to be aware of where you may be holding tension and allow it to relax, submitting to where the experience may take you. As you bring ease to the jaw, tongue, chest, and especially the muscles deep in the abdomen you will become aware of the pelvic bowl receiving the breath, bringing all the sensations of the body into relationship with your core. Once that begins to happen, the inflow and outflow of the breath will begin to liberate the entire energy of the body as a whole. Just let the breath drop in and release out and carry you into newness.

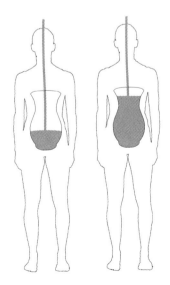

Part IV

The Body as History

I have learned many English words and could recite part of the Ten Commandments. I knew how to sleep on a bed, pray to Jesus, comb my hair, eat with a knife and fork, and use a toilet.... I also learned that a person thinks with his head instead of his heart.
—Sun Chief, of the Oraibi Hopi

Inuktitut has no words for "vermin" or "weed." There is no demarcation between the life of an animal and that of a human—no word for "it." There is no hierarchy of classes of people or ... of rights to land use.
—Hugh Brody, *The Other Side of Eden*

Some primitive people were once visited by an American scientist, and when they were told that Western people think with their heads, the primitive people thought that the Americans were all crazy. They said, "We think with the abdomen."
—D. T. Suzuki, *Lectures on Zen Buddhism*

10 | Leaving the Hub

The Migration towards Perspective

In trying to trace the historical arc that took our culture from an embodied consciousness to a unipolar consciousness, we are looking specifically for the forces that separated our thinking from our being. Etymology is one of the few means available to us for hacking into our ancestral memory banks: the shifting evolution of a word over time often traces out fundamental shifts in our ideas and relationships. As we have mentioned, for example, ancient Greeks had a word, *phren*, that can only be translated into English with two very different words: "diaphragm" and "mind." That double meaning is still found in our word *phrenograph,* which the OED defines as,

> (a) an instrument for recording the movements of the diaphragm in respiration; (b) a phrenological description or 'chart' of a person's mental characteristics.

For the Greeks, though, there was no double meaning: the mind was the diaphragm. The issue here is not that some early Greek anatomist simply misunderstood the functioning of body parts; the usage traces back to a time when the ancient Greeks experienced their thinking in the upper torso, just as we experience our thinking in the head. In Homer's writings in the eighth century B.C., which drew on an ancient oral tradition, phren was most often used in the plural—*phrenes*—and it denoted a multifaceted faculty that was located in the chest area. In her study of the subject,[275] Shirley Sullivan explains that the distinctions we make between physical and psychological, between

321

immaterial and material, are blurred in Homer's world—and so it is with *phrenes*: a center of consciousness, it had physical, intellectual, emotional, volitional and moral aspects. That sense is preserved in Richmond Lattimore's translations. In Book Twenty of the Odyssey, for instance, Theoklymenos says, "I have eyes and I have ears, and I have both my feet, *and a mind inside my breast which is not without understanding.*"[276] What the term *phren* suggests, then, is that in the time of the Greek oral tradition, which culminated in Homer, the center of thought and self was experienced roughly midway between the cranial brain and the pelvic brain.

We can hack our way back another three thousand years or so if we trace the ancestry of our word *navel*. It has its earliest detectable roots in an Indo-European base that is hard to reconstruct—it could have been *ombh* or *nobh* or *mbh*—but we know it meant "navel." Through all its transformations over time, it has retained that original meaning. We have to be careful, though, not to imagine that because its ancient meaning was "navel," it meant no more than what navel means to us today. Indo-European words are characterized by a dynamic energy that reveals not fixed, independent meaning but active, metaphoric relationship. Ernest Fenollosa and Ezra Pound, writing about ancient Sanskrit roots, observed that almost all of them

> are primitive verbs, which express characteristic actions of visible nature. The verb must be the primary fact of nature, since motion and change are all that we can recognize in her.[277]

When we search through the linguistic relationships that might suggest what the activated meaning of the navel was, we turn up some interesting clues. Sanskrit, which was introduced to India around 1500 B.C., provides some of the oldest writings of any Indo-European language. The Indo-European base for *navel* became the Sanskrit word *nabhih*, "navel," but it revealed itself in two other meanings as well. One of its alternate meanings, intriguingly, was **"relationship."** The other was **"the hub of a wheel"**—the round hole in the middle of a wheel through which the axle is passed. The association of the navel with the hub must have been fundamental, because it also shows up in English via a completely separate route. The English word *nave*, no longer a common word, also means "the hub of a wheel" and also traces back to the same Indo-European base. In fact, many of the Germanic languages, to which English belongs, have similar words for "hub" rooted in the same base. By yet a third route, that base also became *nabis*—again, "the hub of a wheel"—in Old Prussian, an extinct Baltic language.

Terminology for wheeled vehicles is widespread in early Indo-European languages. Archaeology tells us that wheeled vehicles were invented in the fourth millennium B.C.; by around 2500 B.C. they acquired spokes. In trying to understand the tenacity of the metaphor identifying the wheel's hub with the body's navel, it helps to bear in mind that prehistoric metaphors are not displays of cleverness or whimsy. They achieved currency because they captured experiential relationships—they 'hit the nail on the head'; and like that modern metaphor, their aptness springs first and foremost from what the body understands. It is their fidelity to that cellular memory that gives those metaphors their vitality and durability. Consider, then, what it means to watch a wheel turning about its hub, and to relate that hub to the experience of the body, and to find that it accords with the navel: as *the center of the wheel* is found at the hub, *the center of the self* was found at the navel. As the wheel revolves around the hub, the sensations of our thinking being revolved about the navel. As the center of a hub rests in stillness, so too the center of the self. The hub of the self stood as the place from which one related to the world, and as the place at which one's *relationships*—like the spokes of a wheel—converge. As a metaphor, the hub is close to the Japanese concept of *hara* and is strikingly similar to the whirlpool metaphor suggested by Alan Watts: both the wheel and the whirlpool turn about, and even into, a still center of emptiness.

Most of us would face difficulty in trying to consciously experience the navel as the center of the self, for our consciousness has too radically dissociated from our visceral brain, the center that allows us to consciously 'be'. In fact, your normal 'hub of activity' is probably centered in the cranial brain. In an ironic contrast, we associate the idea of 'navel gazing' with the enclosure of self-contemplation—an association at odds with the hub of being, which connects us to the world. Like Neolithic cultures, we also have a wheel metaphor that situates the hub of the self; but when you look at someone who is deep in thought and tell him, "I can see your wheels turning," where you 'see' those wheels is in the head—not, for instance, in the belly. And so it is that if you try to grasp the Neolithic navel metaphor by means of your 'wheels turning' in the hub of your conscious thinking, you will never get more than an *idea* of it—like an appealing bauble that can be set within a ready structure of concepts. Or perhaps the idea will just seem like a bit of spurious speculation to be dismissed out of hand. To awaken to that metaphor within your body, though—the shifting sensations of your being centered on the navel, the still hub that integrates all thought and feeling—is to begin to heal the ancient cultural schism that has split your thinking from your being.

The prehistoric metaphor of the navel as the center of Being shows up on a grand scale at the oracle of Delphi. The temple there was originally devoted to the goddess Gaia; it literally represented the earth's center, which was marked by a conical navel-stone, or omphalos. The goddess Gaia was later overthrown and replaced by the god Apollo, as goddesses were overthrown across Europe. But the navel stone remained there, and Delphi became the most celebrated of the Greek oracles—suggesting perhaps a lingering recognition that the greatest truths issue from the chthonic mystery of Being that lives beneath the navel.

We also inherited from the Greeks the story of Omphale and Heracles. As penance for a murder, Heracles—symbol of male doing if ever there was one—became a slave to the Queen of Lydia, Omphale, whose name means navel. When he submitted himself to this queen of Being, she made him dress like a woman and do woman's work, such as spinning wool, which he didn't take to very well. This myth tells us about a transitional phase, when the hetabrain was struggling for supremacy and resentful of the tempering influence of the female element of Being. The birthright of the hetabrain was not servitude—it would much rather be out in the world, doing heraclean tasks.

The Greeks were among the last major cultures in Europe with a remembrance of the navel as the center of Being. The oracle at Delphi was shut down in A.D. 390 by the Christianized Roman Empire, which was fully committed to a different center of Being. The new hierarchy is pretty much summed up by the two convergent meanings of the Latin word *capitalis:* "pertaining to the head," and "capital, chief, first." That convergence tells its own story: the male prerogative of conscious thinking, held aloof from being by its own abstractions, is the supreme faculty and rightful ruler. The supremacy of head over hub—which was characterized by the cultural phase shift from logosmind to hetabrain, from integration to perspective, from five dimensions to four, from embodied consciousness to unipolar consciousness—was by then well established. The intervening centuries have merely fortified and secured its right to rule.

Creating a Paradigm Shift

So we see sketched out in the history of words a transition from the Neolithic hub of being to modern hetabrain, from Being to doing—but how or why did the new kind of human arise from the old? To account for it, we need to be clear about the forces that precipitate cultural change. Very often, I think, we identify cause where we are actually observing effect. Many people, for instance, lay blame for our mind/body split at the feet of Descartes, noting that he was the first to ascribe to the body the machine-like characteristics of the pocket watch by which he kept time, or of the larger clockwork that wheeled the stars and planets through the heavens. By doing so, the story goes, he gave birth to the Cartesian duality that bears his name. The implication is that his act of putting that view into words is responsible for creating the split. Well, that accusation just doesn't hold up. If Descartes had made the same pitch to a group of Tibetan monks or aboriginal Australians, or to the First People's Nations of North America, his idea simply wouldn't have made any sense to them. End of story.

No, what distinguishes Descartes is that **he was the first to express something that people were already experiencing**: as they heard it described they recognized its truth, because it fit with their experience. A new paradigm does not *create* a new experience; experience outgrows the inherited patterns of understanding, generating a tension that builds up until eventually another paradigm comes along that expresses what is being experienced. The emergent paradigm acts as a midwife, pulling the experience from the darkness into the light. And there is no question that the new paradigm affects our experience—it helps it develop and "fixes" it, in the same way that the developing process helps to reveal and fix an image on photographic paper. The potency of any new paradigm is determined by how faithfully it reveals what is *already* being experienced.

What can we say, then, of the forces that are able to reshape the experience of the self so far beyond an old paradigm that it loses its relevance? There are many forces that push on people from the outside—economic, military and otherwise. But even the systematic power of the early Roman Empire could not thwart a Christian experience of the world. One's experience of the world sustains one's belief system—but one's belief system also sustains one's view of the world. Force is not a sure way to change either.

If the Romans had handed out cell phones, on the other hand, the empire might have inflicted considerably more damage on Christianity. Nothing changes our experience of the world more radically than the development of a powerful new tool. That effect has long been recognized, but it seems to me to remain underappreciated. The earliest ages of man—Stone Age, Bronze Age and Iron Age—were identified in 1816 by a Danish archaeologist based on the materials used for toolmaking, each of which ushered in a new era. Winston Churchill observed, "We shape our buildings; thereafter they shape us."[278] William Mitchell of MIT took the idea further: "we make our tools and our tools make us: by taking up particular tools we accede to desires and we manifest intentions."[279] But it was Marshall McLuhan who most vividly called our attention to the effect of tools, and his insights have proven prophetic.

I once attended a lecture by McLuhan at the University of Toronto, during which he stressed the fact that while talking on the telephone, we become disembodied. I wrote a somewhat smug little piece for an arts magazine, saying in effect that I hadn't noticed that my body was particularly absent from the scene while I was talking on the phone. Thirty years later, of course, cell phones are everywhere, and studies have found that the ability to drive a car while talking on one is on a par with someone well over the legal limit for blood alcohol. Marshall—if you are listening, I repent.

Some new tools, such as phones, create a new medium for communication; but McLuhan observed time and again that the most significant message of any new medium was not what it communicated by, say, the words on the page or the images on the screen; **the most significant message any new medium conveyed was, in effect, the new experience it provided of what it means to be human.** Of course, it is from our culture's array of such experiences that its story derives. In my view, then, McLuhan's greatest accomplishment was that *he turned our attention away from how tools or technologies affected what we could do and directed it onto how they affected our being.* In a culture obsessed with doing, that suggestion was radical.

McLuhan observed, for example, that to assess the impact of the printing press by evaluating the new things it enabled us to do was to miss the real revolution; its impact could be understood only by appreciating how it altered our experience of *who we are:* like any tool, print works as an extension of man, shaping and transforming "his entire environment, psychic and social."[280] McLuhan carried his critique well beyond a study of media and applied it to both concrete and conceptual tools; he showed that the new use of a language or hammer or clock would alter our experience of both self and world, and so forever alter us.

Consider, then, the technological advances of the Neolithic Revolution, which was underway in the core of Europe by 6000 B.C.: it saw the development of agriculture, the creation of permanent settlements that sometimes amounted to towns (Catal Huyuk grew to 8,000 people and 2,000 homes) and the domestication of animals, among other accomplishments. Because our culture sees and understands according to the values of 'doing', it is natural for us to focus on how those developments changed man's efficiency and migration patterns and enhanced his opportunities for survival. But if we assess the Neolithic Revolution in those terms alone, we miss its real message. McLuhan would urge us rather to consider how those developments altered man's psychic and social environment—his Being. To begin to do so, we need a sense of what man's psychic and social environment was prior to the Neolithic Revolution.

Old Europe

Henri and H. A. Frankfort were a husband-and-wife team who specialized in the ancient Near East and helped us understand that the world of ancient man was not the four-dimensional decor our eyes see around us today. Most notably, whatever ancient man looked upon was alive—there was no such thing as dead matter. Nor was any line drawn to divide the realm of nature from the realm of man. **The world of phenomena was a living presence that surrounded him and beheld him and communicated with him.** Every part of it expressed a presence that was never fully knowable, but to which a personal relationship was as natural as breathing. The world was a revelation of Being, and as such had the unprecedented, unparalleled and unpredictable character of an individual, a presence known only in so far as it reveals itself.... [The world] is not contemplated with intellectual detachment; it is experienced as life confronting life, involving every faculty of man in a reciprocal relationship. Thoughts, no less than acts and feelings, are subordinated to this experience.[281]

In that it is reciprocal, the relationship constitutes an exchange of gifts. In that his world had the "character of an individual," we can see that ancient man was "feeling the thing as a whole"—feeling the world as a Thou:

The whole man confronts a living "Thou" in nature; and the whole man—emotional and imaginative as well as intellectual—gives expression to the experience.[282]

One might surmise that in ancient man the male pole of conscious thinking was not as sensitized to the possibilities of perspective as we have become—but his capacity for reason, as the Frankforts explained, was by no means negligible. For instance, people

explained phenomena in terms of time and space and number. The form of their reasoning is far less alien to ours than is often believed. They could reason logically; but they did not often care to do it. **For the detachment which a purely intellectual attitude implies is hardly compatible with their most significant experience of reality.**[283]

That last sentence raises a simple question with bewildering implications—*is the detachment of an intellectual attitude compatible with* **anyone's** *most significant experience of reality?* In fact, just how significant an experience of reality could an attitude of intellectual detachment provide even at the best of times? And yet, that is the attitude to which the abstract-loving hetabrain devotes itself and fetters us in turn.

Understanding that the world of ancient man was five-dimensional—suffused with Mind—we can better understand the findings of Marija

Gimbutas, an archaeologist whose work reconfigured our view of Stone Age Europe. The Stone Age began with the Paleolithic period, which lasted over two million years and was characterized by hunting and gathering and the use of simple stone tools. The Neolithic or 'New Stone Age' was marked by the emergence of agriculture, the domestication of animals and permanent settlements. A popular view considered Neolithic Europe to be the precursor to real civilization, but Gimbutas countered that civilization ought to be gauged by "its degree of artistic creation, aesthetic achievements, nonmaterial values and freedom which makes life enjoyable for all its citizens, as well as a balance of power between the sexes."[284] By those standards, civilization thrived in Neolithic Europe—especially in the period prior to the arrival of what has been called the Kurgan influence, which we shall look at later; Gimbutas referred to the period of pre-Kurgan, Neolithic civilization as Old Europe.

What we know about Old Europe has been methodically pieced together on the basis of archaeological discoveries ranging from the Atlantic coastline to Russia. Gimbutas points out, for example, that many settlements in Old Europe were unpalisaded villages that were typically located on sites endowed with natural beauty: people usually chose the most enjoyable places to live without consideration for how vulnerable they might be to attack—even though there is some evidence of warfare and, as the eminent specialist J. P. Mallory has noted, "even mass slaughter on a few occasions."[285]

Their arts and culture, too, suggest that life in Old Europe was generally characterized not by fear and enclosure, but by a wakefulness to the great sustaining forces of nature and a sense of belonging to them. As Gimbutas observes, "celebration of life is the leading motif in Old European ideology and art. There is no stagnation; life energy is constantly moving as a serpent, spiral or whirl."[286] Those images, which recur throughout Neolithic art, represent Being as a sensational gathering and dispersing: at the center of the world's transforming energies is its self-aware stillness.

On the basis of its art and culture, Gimbutas concluded that Old Europe worshipped a Great Goddess. Modern scholarship disputes her thesis of a single Goddess worshipped by Old Europe—and, in fact, the very notion there was worship of objectified goddesses. And from the point of view of this book, the idea of an individuated goddess runs contrary to what one would expect from a culture attuned to

Being, for Being suffuses all the world's particulars and speaks through them as the One Unbroken Whole; objectification results from perspective, the male strength. If there was no sense of an objectified goddess, though, there is ample evidence to suggest that Old Europe was matrifocal. If, then, we take the literality with which Gimbutas describes Old Europe's relationship to *the Goddess* to be instead a metaphoric description of their relationship with *the Divine 'Thou' of Female Being*, then what Gimbutas has to say acquires a renewed significance and poignancy. For instance, she tells us,

> In fact, there are no images that have been found of a Father God throughout the prehistoric record. Paleolithic and Neolithic symbols and images cluster around a self-generating Goddess and her basic functions as Giver-of-Life, Wielder-of-Death, and as Regeneratrix.[287]

In a culture that is attuned first to Being, it is natural that representations of female being should preponderate. And as for the lack of a hierarchical "father figure," we might consider that in the Mosuo community in China, one of the few matrifocal societies that still exist, there is not even a word for "father." Other aspects of the matrifocal realm also seem strange to us: time was not linear but cyclic—there was no death that was not followed by regeneration. Bones were compared to seeds, and burials represented a return to the fertile womb of the earth. Divine Female Being lived through nature and was physically manifest in all its phenomena: she was the source and power of all life.

We get a sense of the central concerns and sensibilities of the matrifocal culture if we look to its art. In an overview of the findings at Catal Huyuk, the largest Neolithic settlement to have been studied, Ian Hodder noted that women were usually depicted in three dimensions—think of the famous 'Venus' figurines—and are naked; they are not 'doing' anything: they just are.[288] Men were usually depicted in the more abstract medium of two-dimensional wall paintings; in general they were clothed and engaged with the living mystery of life and death through activities such as hunting. Man's daily agriculture or domestic tasks were not the subject of this art: its focus was the power and fluid mystery of wild nature.[289] This strikes a contrast with the contemporary art of our own patrifocal culture, which tends to gather around and celebrate new ideas.

If we go farther back in time to the Paleolithic, we find that the male prerogatives of doing and abstract planning played an even smaller role in how man related to his world than it did in the transitional Neolithic. People of that era were concerned first and foremost with noticing what is. When shelter was needed, they would gather the branches of Divine Being that were waiting for them and build a hut, or find a cave and crawl into her womb. When food was needed they would walk into her abundant meadows and forests and notice and gather what she provided; or they would take up a spear and ask her to bless its throw. The tangible companionship of Divine Being was the dominant feature of their world.

Tooling a New Human

Paleolithic Being gave way to Neolithic doing. In light of their developing technologies, we would expect "the entire environment, psychic and social" of emerging Neolithic societies to undergo an unprecedented upheaval; and in that our descriptions of the world derive from how we experience the self, we would also expect a change in their descriptions of nature. Let's look first at the *message* that was conveyed by the medium of Neolithic developments, and at how it *transformed the user.*

The domestication of plants, for starters, reorganized every realm of human activity so profoundly as to leave no activity untouched by it. In order to plant in the spring, you need to have gathered and stored seeds the previous fall. You need to prepare the earth for the seed by cutting and hacking at what you know to be her living bosom. By virtue of your work, you stake out and assume *ownership* of the planted land and its crop, which had always belonged to the seamless domain of Divine Being. Certain of her animals are now seen to be vermin, robbing you of crops, as certain plants are now seen to be weeds. And when you do finally harvest, you are harvesting the fruits of *your own labors.* That isn't to say that Divine Being is not a part of it all—the harvest still depends on her blessings of sun and rain—but her role has been scaled back. Sustenance is no longer just what appears on the trees and bushes of her magical groves and rivers, or on the hillsides and meadows that manifest her Being; it now appears mainly by dint of a whole new perspective that is fortified by knowledge and craft and planning and labor. Man appropriates land and transforms it willfully; and the *manpower* of 'doing' that is needed to create a successful crop on that land is quite distinct from the *goddess* power of 'Being'. **Attention has started to shift from noticing and respecting to imagining, planning, dividing, subduing and reshaping.**

The cycles of planting, cultivation and harvest required people to settle in one place. In the Paleolithic era, people largely sheltered in caves or huts they built for themselves, and moved according to seasons and food supply. In Old Europe, by contrast, Gimbutas tells us that there were

> towns with a considerable concentration of population, temples several stories high ...[and] spacious houses of four or five rooms.[290]

And so the idea of transient or found shelter gave way to the concept of the year-round man-made house. That provided a potent new perspective on what it is to be human—and so *changed* what it is to be human. Consider this: the permanent space a house defines is not borrowed from Divine Being, but appropriated, and so establishes for the first time in man's experience a substantial division between his realm and the realm of nature; and that independence from nature is self-achieved, to revisit Joseph Campbell's term, like the tyrant's. **The purpose of a house is to effectively and securely shut out the world of nature**—its sun and rain and cold and wind and animals and plants; when you close the door of your house, you are deliberately closing the door against the world of Divine Being. You are shutting *her* out of *your space.* And to be fair, that space isn't exactly a house of death—but it is, by design, less amenable to life.

The construction of a settlement alters the look of the very landscape, which eventually proclaims the accomplishments of "Man" rather than the transformations of Divine Being. Construction also encourages man to look at her forms—her trees and rocks and mud and grasses—as raw materials voided of any sacred presence, to be reshaped and used willfully. And those raw materials are shaped first not by hands, but by the imagination. The most wondrous part of building a house is to watch as what has lived only in the imagination acquires dimension and form and eventually stands before you for all to see. Just as God conceived of a world and created it, so it was with man and his house. **By his own efforts he created a space for himself that was governed by will and secured against Nature's fecundity. By his own efforts man was becoming godlike.** Suddenly, when the storm raged, it and the Divine Being it expressed were 'other'; they were *out there,* battering at the border of one's protected space *in here.* So crucial was the house in defining our relationship to the world that we call nature the "outdoors." In time, the enclosure of the house became a metaphor for the self, and the whole of what lay outside of the protective barrier of the ego became 'other': **by his own efforts, then, man created in the body a space for the self that is governed by will and committed to doing, and which secures the door against the fecundity of Divine Being.**

The house so radically redefines what it is to be human that some aboriginal tribes identify white men just by reference to their houses. When the Indians of North America portrayed the white men on their sacred wampum belts, they depicted rows of houses. To the Warumungu of Australia, white men were *Papulanyi,* "enclosure dwellers." Those tribes couldn't have found a more appropriate symbol for our peculiar idea of the walled-in self. Freud and Jung also recognized it— both spoke of "the house of the self" as a fundamental metaphor for who we are and how we see ourselves—but I don't think either of them examined the extent to which that metaphor is a cultural construct.

Neolithic man also domesticated animals. To get a sense of what that step meant is to start to untangle some of our most basic assumptions. Paleolithic man lived in a world teeming with creatures, each a revelation of Divine Being. He hunted a few of them—and if the flight of his spear was blessed, the hunter would give thanks to Divine Being and also to the prey. Contrast that to the Neolithic development of taking a fellow creature captive and keeping it for breeding and slaughtering. That act turns the animal into your property—it becomes subject to your will; it is alive to serve your needs. The effect on your psychic and social environment is incalculable. When you assume ownership of an animal, you also assume the role of the deity, and some of her power. You, rather than Divine Being, determine the moment of the animal's death, and, having made the decision, you rather than Divine Being are the bringer of death. You decide when the beast will feed and what it will eat; often you dictate where it goes when. Often you also decide if the animal will breed, and you may select its partner; and if it has offspring, you always consider those fellow creatures to be your property as well.

The very lives of domesticated animals were to become man's first great symbol of personal wealth. When we say someone is *impecunious,* we are invoking an Indo-European root thousands of years old that tells us he is "without cattle." Robert Graves also suggests that the name Laius comes from the Greek *leios,* which means "having cattle." The kind of entitlement that the ownership of animals encourages is at the heart of the Laius Complex; and just as the pastoralist herds and manages cattle, the Laius Complex herds and manages the sensations of the body. The domestication of animals seems to grant superiority to the male element both in the self and in a society: Margaret Ehrenberg has pointed out that in all societies in which animal husbandry plays a large role, women are the subservient gender.[291]

These three main developments in the Neolithic era—the beginning of agriculture, the building of houses and the domestication of animals—each radically reconfigured man's relationship to nature. Each made the mysteries of Divine Being more banal or less immanent; each increasingly defined the realm of man as something set apart from the realm of nature; and that newfound apartness promoted the emerging fiction of four dimensions. Man was climbing into the role of a 'doer' on structures of control provided by new perspectives—perspectives that enabled him to systemize the cycles of agriculture, and imagine new tools to make it easier; to organize the design of a large house and the materials and steps required to erect it; and to manage the herding and penning and feeding and breeding of animals.

Because we can recognize ourselves in the descriptions we give to nature, we would expect the changes wrought in man by acquiring agriculture also to give rise to some changes in the way Divine Being was described. Sure enough, Gimbutas tells us that the Neolithic Earth Goddess acquired a male partner

> who appeared in the spring, matured in the summer, and died in the autumn with the vegetation. This God cannot be traced in the Paleolithic and is associated only with the cultivation of agriculture.[292]

That new male partner, in other words, came to life when the male element of doing was needed in the spring, and died when the harvest was complete. He represented the emerging reality—which dawned with agriculture—that Divine Being was self-sufficient only in the dead of winter. That change in the perception of Divine Being was also shown by other new companions: figurines of animals noted for their strength, such as the dog, bull and he-goat. There is something slightly out-of-sync in those animals attending the metaphoric goddess, for they facilitate doing and are impotent to assist Divine Being, which just is. But the male element of doing had to express itself somehow: like a newly discovered muscle, it was flexing its fresh powers and seeing the world with new eyes. And those new powers, notably, were all used in service to abstract concepts. A new hierarchy was being established. Quite simply, **the successful implementation of any abstract concept establishes its supremacy over the material world**: an idea is born, and the material world is then refashioned according to its dictates. The implications of that supremacy are made more profound when we remember that our word *material* comes from an Indo-European base that means "mother." By dominating the material world, we are demonstrating our superiority to female Being.

To even imagine achieving control over the material world is already to stand apart from it, so that the seamless, subtle consciousness—the felt dimension that binds all things to the processes of the unknown world—vanishes from sight, like Eurydice; and then the pieces of your world suddenly appear to be stand-alone objects rather than manifestations of the Great Swirl of Divine Being: doing over being leads to matter over mind. In their life-deprived abstraction, stand-alone objects appear to be knowable, things you can explain, anticipate, regulate, divert and transform; but being products of neglect, they also breed neglect.

The more *power* you have, the more *control* you can assert—so the acquisition of power and of the emblems of power become ends in themselves. Also, the more power you acquire, the greater is the level of systemization you need to sustain and implement it. The hetabrain comes into its own, and once it develops a taste for manipulating Being and beings to its own purposes, it doesn't take long before it turns its attention to *its own* being—because the systemization of the world ultimately requires the isolation, ownership, patterning and control of the self. And then the die is cast: doing gains supremacy over Being, *because control is chosen over sensitivity.* Control even attempts to masquerade as freedom. But, of course, they are not the same: control rules the self, the way the helmsman steers the ship or the rider the horse.

Exercise Ten: **Figure Eights**

If we are to unlock our unipolar consciousness and awaken it to the hub of our being, we have to reacquaint ourselves with the energy of the pelvic bowl. This exercise, more than any other I know of, slowly but surely stirs its sensitivity to wakefulness. I learned the exercise from the great Butoh performer and teacher Yumiko Yoshioka. Butoh is a modern theater/dance form that originated in Japan.

To start, stand in a relaxed but alert position and imagine a steel ball at the midpoint between the navel and the coccyx (tailbone). Keeping the steel ball centered in the pelvic bowl, slowly move the hips from side to side on a plane parallel to the floor so that the steel ball traces out a figure eight. Let the path of the figure eight gradually diminish in size, and the movement of the ball become gradually faster, until to an outside observer you would not be seen to be moving at all, so tiny is the figure eight that is being traced out by the speeding ball.

Then do the same thing with a figure eight also on a plane parallel to the floor, but which moves from front to back. And next with a figure eight that moves up and down perpendicular to the floor and aligned with the plane of your body, also getting gradually smaller and faster.

The final step is to connect the three figure eights, so that the ball traces a large figure eight side to side which leads into a front-to-back figure eight, which leads into an up-and-down figure eight, which leads again into a side-to-side figure eight. Again, the figure eights gradually diminish in size and the speed of the ball gradually accelerates, until eventually the casual observer would think you had stopped moving. I find that at the end of the exercise, if I just stand in a fairly neutral position, the energy in the pelvic bowl remains vividly present, the steel ball a calmly pulsing, bright-burning point of awareness.

11 | Horse and Rider

The Original Power Trip

The first horse and rider appeared in the Neolithic era and marked a development that contributed in such a singular fashion to who we are that it came to provide the primary metaphor by which we live. When man domesticated the horse and started riding it, he created a symbol that characterized the hetabrain atop the dumb beast of the body, and he gave expression to a new kind of human that is with us still.

There is abiding controversy as to when horses were actually domesticated. David Anthony and his associates have done some truly remarkable research with a scanning electron microscope on the teeth of a stallion that was buried sometime around 4000 B.C.; that research establishes beyond reasonable doubt that the stallion had been fitted with a bit, and had been mounted and ridden.[293] Although this tells us that horses were domesticated by 4000 B.C., it cannot set a date for how much earlier than that they might have been ridden with bits, or indicate how long they might have been ridden before bits were invented. Gimbutas argued that the horse was domesticated by 5000 B.C. and that it was used in warfare from around 4300 B.C. I think it unlikely that the first horse ever to be ridden would happen to be the one preserved for six thousand years and found, and I find the arguments made by Gimbutas for an earlier date of domestication compelling.

Whenever it happened, though, man's domination of the horse gave an immediacy to his experience of dominating nature that was unparalleled by any other development. We are all acquainted with the effect that slipping behind the wheel of a high-powered sports car can have on someone—but that could not begin to compare with the effects on the first rider who roped a horse, even the relatively small horses that were first domesticated, and mounted it, and subjected it to his will: stopping, galloping and turning on command. Furthermore, **to sit astride one of the largest creatures in your world and subjugate it to your wishes is to challenge the sacred immanence of Divine Being: if she is truly immanent in the horse, then you have harnessed the power of Being with your doing.** On the other hand, maybe the real god is more like you—a male god, sitting on high, issuing commands.

By climbing up onto the horse's back, that first rider achieved a new kind of independence from the ordinary world. Perched on his powerful beast, he could move through the landscape without even touching it; he found himself elevated above all around him and closer to the immaterial sky—literally the "nonmaternal" sky. Kings, emperors, knights, generals and landowners would later insist on this position for the privilege it affords. And even today, if someone puts on superior airs, we may suggest that he should "get down off his high horse." The implication is clear: getting off his horse would bring him back to earth and dispossess him of his arrogant sense of superiority.

The Neolithic horse rider wields a power that was entirely without precedent. When he sits on his horse, dogs can't bite him, streams can't soak his boots, people can't easily grab him and if they try he can trample them or outrun them. The horse is big and powerful, and he is its master. And with that mastery, distance shrinks for the first time in history, speed is attained for the first time in history, and the power of a man increases fivefold. With the speed of the horse, the rider can run down prey, and with the strength of the horse, he can drag the carcass home. With a few companions on horses, he can herd hundreds of animals and slaughter them at will. And once the rider is used to dominating and slaughtering animals from horseback, it's not such a stretch to think about overrunning people in the same way.

Horses were not indigenous to the Mid-East, and were abundant in Europe only in the area of the Russian steppes and eastward. They were first domesticated there by pastoralists. In his book *A History of Warfare*, John Keegan notes that, historically, pastoralists "have been more warlike than their hunting ancestors or agricultural neighbors." He cites a number of factors that contribute to that pattern. To the pastoralist, flocks of sheep and goats represent "no more than food on the hoof"; also, "Dealing a lethal blow, once, quickly and neatly, was a principal pastoral skill, heightened no doubt by anatomical knowledge gained in regular butchery." But then he adds,

> It was flock management, as much as slaughter and butchery, which made the pastoralists so cold-bloodedly adept at confronting the sedentary agriculturalists of the civilized lands in battle.... [The pastoralists] knew how to break a flock up into manageable sections, how to cut off a line of retreat by circling to a flank, how to compress scattered beasts into a compact mass, how to isolate flock leaders, how to dominate superior numbers by threat and menace, how to kill the chosen few while leaving the mass inert and subject to control. All pastoralists' methods of battle as described at later dates in history disclose just such a pattern.[294]

Once horses were domesticated and used for attacks, they spread unstoppably across Eurasia and eventually the Americas to become the prime war machine worldwide. As Keegan notes,

> The horse and human ruthlessness together thus transformed war, making it for the first time 'a thing in itself'. We can henceforth speak of 'militarism', an aspect of societies in which the mere ability to make war, readily and profitably, becomes a reason in itself for doing so.[295]

Because our culture is entirely familiar with horse and rider images, it's a stretch for us to appreciate how someone who has never seen a horse before would react at being suddenly attacked by warriors on horseback. Our mythological centaur probably comes from such early encounters, in which horse and rider were seen not as two creatures, but as one. Even in our own culture, a cowboy would more reasonably be called a horseboy—except that the horse is subsumed in the man's identity as an implicit extension of his will: a metaphoric centaur. In fact, horses are culturally so much an extension of the self that—as with cats and dogs—most societies balk at the thought of eating them.

Myths depicted the centaurs as powerful and, with one notable exception, uncouth and aggressive; they were also exclusively male. In spirit, centaurs live on today—not as cowboys, but as members of biker gangs. The horse image, fittingly for our times, has been replaced by a machine, for the real issue of power no longer lies in the sensation-filled experience of dominating nature directly, but in controlling the machines that dominate nature, like the archetypal robot body of Professor Pippy P. Poopypants. And that begs the question: did the man make the motorcycle, or did the motorcycle make the man? It is a chicken-and-egg question—a question that was actually solved long ago. The egg came first because, in the progress of evolution, each egg represents a new step in chickenhood. Similarly, man built the motorcycle, and became a new man by riding it—McLuhan showed us that much. Just by sitting atop the engine, which roars at his command, the rider is suffused with a new perspective on his own potential, and a primordial sense of power and entitlement to go with it. And, of course, with the new man came a new culture—in this case, the black leather, the jargon, and the tribal identities and values.

The arguments of this book would lead us to expect that **if domesticating the horse so profoundly altered who man was, then the descriptions given to nature by the first horse riders should represent a radical departure from the matrifocal culture of Being.** Archaeologists have traced the domestication of the horse back to a group of seminomadic tribes that lived in the Russian steppes north of the Black Sea. Much of their culture has been reconstructed, and it has proven to be an anomaly in its time. According to Gimbutas, these pastoralists evolved what seems to be *the earliest patriarchal society in Europe of which we have any evidence.* In fact, it was not just patriarchal, but also hierarchical: a classed society with a warrior chief at its head and in which women could achieve status only by association with their male relations.

In keeping with the new, elevated status of the male element in their culture, these horse riders also evolved male gods who, by the second half of the fourth millennium B.C., were depicted in carved images with axes, daggers, maces and bows. Later the gods rode horses and drove chariots. These gods were growing independent of nature and superior to it: they no longer appear to be immanent in it, like the Goddess, but sit apart from it—just like the male strength of commanding perspective. They were associated with the bright, immaterial sky and its phenomena: the sun, thunder and lightning. Life was no longer created by female deities, but by these male gods, who also brought death. These newly conceived gods, of course, represent a newly conceived description of nature. Just as man built the motorcycle and became a new man by riding it—catalyzing what was latent in him—a similar thing seems to have happened on a different scale with these early horse riders. Marija Gimbutas noted that the domestication of the horse "must have contributed to the transition from matrism to armored patrism."[296] Her contention that the horse was "used in warfare from at least the middle of the 5th millennium B.C."[297] is based on archaeological findings that concur with existing linguistic and mythological evidence. **As the riding of horses exercised and emboldened the male element, a new culture was born to express its new perspective.** Seven hundred years later, that new culture was full-fledged—its classed society, its patrifocal values, its male gods, its weapons and its raiding parties were all in place. Gimbutas noted that the agricultural societies of Old Europe were hit by three waves of incursions from these horse riders. She writes of the first of those incursions,

> Around 4300 B.C., horse-riding pastoralists from south Russia created the first shock wave and population shifts in the Danube basin. The flowering of Old Europe was truncated.[298]

As the influence of the horse riders spread, so did palisades around villages; in tandem with that, as the influence of male doing grew, so did the palisades of the hetabrain.

Black Life, White Death

Marija Gimbutas studied this new culture of horse riders extensively and named its people *Kurgans,* the Russian name for the round burial mounds they built. She reports that later burial mounds were filled with weapons; eventually kings and chieftains were joined in their tombs by their wives, servants, children and animals. After a funeral, food continued to be brought to the tomb to sustain the dead in the afterlife. Those practices tell us that the Kurgans understood time to be essentially linear—a perspective endowed by the shift to doing. The cycles of nature were straightened into an arrow that sailed into the newly imagined future, its path delineated by a succession of accomplishments and accomplishers. Bones were 'housed' rather than being seeded back into the earth as part of an ever-renewing cycle—*because the individualistic, action-based idea of self lives in relationship to the future, not to cycles.* In the Kurgan culture, the dead traveled to an underground world—cold, swampy and overseen by a male god. There one's self-achieved independence continued after death, sustained by the emblems of power that accompanied the burial.

Among all the polarity shifts that the horse-riding Kurgan culture underwent—from Being to doing, from matrifocal to patrifocal, from earth goddess to sky gods, from cyclic time to linear time—one of the most telling is the shift from black to white; it almost affronts our sensibilities to try to imagine black as the color of life and white as the color of death, but that is how they were seen in Old Europe. It was under the Kurgan influence that they switched.

To understand the Old European association of black with life we might understand that Being itself—which Heraclitus reminds us is a secret process—can never be brought into the light and known. But it can be sensed as though "through a glass, darkly"—and in sensing it we discover ourselves. Of particular relevance, it is also in the dark unknown that we discover someone else. What you actually see of someone is largely objectified: you can look at a person's face; you can look at his hands, at his lips, at his belly; you can examine the whites of his eyeballs; you can look at every square inch of him and notice many, many particulars; but those particulars do not add up to the whole. When you look into the darkness of someone's pupils, though, you encounter her non-objective self—her Being. And let's be clear about this: the pupils are black holes—they are empty and the retina beyond is black; to look at a pupil is not to look at an object any more than looking into the darkness through the mouth of a cave is looking at an object. There is nothing in the dark emptiness of the pupil to actually see or describe or objectify or know, and *yet:* by looking into it you connect with someone's *life;* you encounter her *Being.* And in that encounter you precipitate an exchange of energies in which you are both participant.

When the Old Europeans opened their eyes on the world, they were looking towards its life; they were looking to encounter its Being. They did not learn *about* nature; they learned *from* it. They looked past the bright surface of the world and into its hidden darkness; they sought out and encountered the *pupil* of the world gazing back at them—a word that comes from the Latin *pupilla* and literally means "the little girl" of the world, the female element of Being in all its newness. And just as people and animals alike feel a mutual exchange of energies when they look into the pupils of each other's eyes, so too the Old Europeans felt an exchange of energies when they encountered the newness of Being—the "little girl," the Thou, the Logos—hidden beneath the world's brightness. As Heraclitus observed, "The hidden harmony is stronger than the apparent."[299] Similarly, the Bible notes, "You have hidden the truth in darkness; through this mystery you teach me wisdom."[300] What is felt in the empty darkness among the effects of the world is Being itself, the source of all life.

White, on the other hand, is revealed directly to the eye; it represents the known, which is what enables the hetabrain to think and act, in contrast to unknowable black, which can only be felt. **For the Kurgans, in other words, white, the known—which we have recognized as endarkenment—became The Good; and black, the unknowable—which we have recognized as Being itself, and the source of guidance—became The Feared.** And so began the trend of seeking mastery over the world from within a sterile realm of bright ideas that can never quite fuse into a whole.

But what of the terrors of the dark that are so real to us? What of our seemingly instinctive dread of that which waits in the blackness beyond, and our need for the assurance of light to dispel it? The tale of Gilgamesh—man's earliest surviving epic, composed at least 1,500 years before Homer lived—contains a passage in which Gilgamesh and his soul mate Enkidu enter the dark Cedar Forest to defeat its guardian, the monster Humbaba. Humbaba's powers are fearful: he breathes fire, his garments are the seven terrors, and his face changes into a thousand nightmare forms. To flush him out, Gilgamesh and Enkidu begin to cut down his sacred cedars. Humbaba charges out of his den and confronts them with dire threats, whereupon fear seizes Gilgamesh's soul, and he is unable to go on. Enkidu rallies him and they attack Humbaba together; but their battle does not go well until the god Shamash sides with them and pins the monster down with the four winds. Gilgamesh then leaps upon Humbaba and holds a knife to his throat, and the tempests abate. Now face to face with him, Gilgamesh finds Humbaba mild-mannered; Humbaba even offers to help

Gilgamesh as a friend. Enkidu grows jealous, and persuades Gilgamesh to cut off Humbaba's head.

The confusion Gilgamesh and Enkidu experienced in the dark forest is described in hallucinogenic terms—the demon's face changing into nightmarish forms, their feeling of being haunted; and that reminds us that the 'known self', being isolated, trusts only the light and feels no kinship with the dark. Even when they eventually meet Humbaba and discover meekness behind the bravura, their fears are not abated. The episode brings to mind a night I spent while cycling through France. I had no tent, preferring to sleep on the forest floor. Just after I had fallen asleep that evening, I was brought to by a rustling of leaves among the dark trees about five feet away from me. An animal was moving slowly and erratically along the ground, and my heart beat and my mind raced—and although I knew from the sound that it couldn't be very big, I could not put my anxiety to rest until I dug out my bike light, switched it on, and discovered the threat: a brown toad. I was face-to-face with Humbaba. The hallucinations subsided, and thereafter I slept outside in the dark through Europe, the Middle East, India and Japan—still aware of the night noises, but unperturbed by them.

One of the most magical evenings I have enjoyed in my own community occurred during the massive blackout in North America in the summer of 2003. The city was hushed as night fell—traffic lights, street lights, house lights all out—and the darkness was felt as both a novelty and a comfort. It imparted a gentleness to the world. People came out of doors to walk around, and they greeted each other, and looked into the fathomless black of the clear sky, and stood together beneath the spreading galaxies and stars, and expressed the wish that such a thing could happen more often.

Being resides in the seen without being seen; it sings through the heard without being heard; it calls through the silence without disturbing the silence. Shakespeare, whose sense of metaphor was almost preternatural, had the war hero Coriolanus address his wife as "My gracious silence."[301] Although the phrase may rankle modern sensibilities, it takes on a different significance when considered as a greeting of adoration by the male element of doing to the female element of Being. Being—silent, unseen and unknowable—supports your every perception, your every breath, your every deed. And in noting that Shakespeare dubbed the silent female element of Being "gracious," we might further appreciate that it is from that dark, silent, unseen element, and only from there, that thought, word or deed can acquire the quality of grace.

The Domino Effect

In 1783 Sir William Jones was sent to India to serve as a judge. Once there, he found that some Indian laws were written in Sanskrit—an ancient language that had been preserved largely by priests who had passed its sacred hymns, the Vedas, down through the generations orally. To familiarize himself with the Indian laws, Jones passed his evenings teaching himself Sanskrit. As he learned it, he began to notice uncanny similarities among Sanskrit, Greek and Latin—words for numbers, animals, plants, relationships and natural phenomena were often strikingly congruent. "Three," for example, is *trayas* in Sanskrit, *trias* in Greek and *tres* in Latin. So numerous were such coincidences that Jones presented a paper in 1786 to the Asiatik Society of Calcutta in which he stated that Sanskrit bears to Greek and Latin

> a stronger affinity, both in the roots of verbs and in the forms of grammar, than could have been produced by accident; so strong, indeed, that no philologer could examine all three, without believing them to have sprung from **some common source** which, perhaps, no longer exists.[302]

His daring and unprecedented statement has been amply confirmed in the two centuries since he made it, and it marks the starting point for the modern study of historical linguistics. That common source is now widely recognized to have been the language spoken by the Kurgans, our horse riders from the Russian steppes. It is referred to as Indo-European, because its influence is found in a family of related languages ranging from India to Europe. If the symbolism and gods and patrifocal values and burial practices and language of the Kurgans sound familiar to us, there is good reason. Somehow that small collection of tribes from the Russian steppes sparked a cultural revolution that swept Europe, the Middle East and India with a power that not only transformed languages—it also transformed belief systems, social relationships and the worldview of Western civilization, literally turning black into white. In the wake of that revolution the Indo-Europeans—the Kurgans—emerged as the cultural and linguistic ancestors of almost half the population of the present world.

How their influence spread remains one of the greatest mysteries of Neolithic prehistory. Like a brush fire, it incinerated the local languages, customs, and belief systems of the great matrifocal culture of the prehistoric West. As J. P. Mallory wrote in his definitive work, *In Search of the Indo-Europeans,*

> A society identified as essentially matrifocal, that is, centred on females, and which is emphasized by virtually thousands of female clay figurines, abruptly disappears under the Kurgan warriors whose religious attention was more attracted to warlike sky-gods and sun worship.[303]

So radical was the scope of that transformation that it has been likened to the effect that the European invasion had on the cultures of the American continent. Today, not only does almost half of the world's population speak an Indo-European language as their native tongue; even more have bought into the Indo-European description of the world. That is significant, because we describe the world in terms that reflect how we experience the self. As our center made its journey from the navel to the noggin, as the abstract monologue of the Pater-patter acquired more presence in the individual than the pulsing, subtle intelligence of his or her own Being, patriarchy took hold in us all.

There is controversy when it comes to accounting for a force potent enough to have transformed the cultures of Europe, Asia Minor, Persia and India. Gimbutas contends that the peaceful, undefended settlements of Old Europe were easily conquered by the weaponed, aggressive, horse-riding Kurgans. True enough, but the Kurgans' direct influence was relatively contained: some argue that they extended no farther west than Hungary. But if the Kurgans didn't travel to Ireland or India, how did their language and culture move on to conquer the homegrown varieties? Some have tried to find a mechanism to account for it. David Anthony suggests that the Kurgan's horseback riding "provides a possible mechanism for their dispersal."[304] Others, most notably Colin Renfrew, argue for another mechanism: that the

Indo-European transformation followed the spread of agriculture; but Gimbutas asserts that "there is no possibility" that the new culture could have *evolved* out of the belief system of Old Europe. Black didn't evolve into white. It was an ideological conquest.

But what if we have been looking for the wrong kind of explanation? What if the Kurgan influence wasn't spread by a mechanism? What if, as McLuhan would encourage us to consider, the new tools of the Neolithic Revolution—which was underway in much of Eurasia—so redefined man's Being and the world that *they created a pressing need for a new vision of nature?* Specifically, for a new story in which independent, empowered doing—as exemplified by a warrior on horseback—played a major role. The shimmering presence of *Divine Being* could not evolve into that role; her magic was eroding as her world was being systemized and dominated; she was being evicted from the 'resources' over which man was asserting control. Even in cultures that hadn't domesticated the horse, the Neolithic Revolution was recreating man as an empowered 'doer' who could control the lives of animals and the materials of nature to suit his purposes. Man's major accomplishments, whether kurgans, pyramids, highways or skyscrapers, disdain the bounds of nature, disdain the cycling seasons, and tell a story of time, space and self in which man stands at the helm of his own power.

When the Kurgans arrived on their powerful horses, **they represented a revolutionary new brand of humanness, one that trumpeted man as a matchless doer and the world as a resource over which he could assert dominion.** Their potent new description included their two primary deities, both male, described by J. P. Mallory as: "**dyeus paeter,* the god of the clear sky, charged with the maintenance of religious order, and **perkuno*—the god of storm, thunder and patron of war."[305] The new male gods acted in linear time, behaved like action figures and, rather than inhabiting the world around us, lived above it, ordering it and acting on it. Eventually the presence of Divine Being, which had suffused and lived through all things, was replaced by a single God who stands apart from the world ("Our Father, who art in Heaven") just as we do, is possessed of an omniscient perspective, and governs by rules and reprisals, just as we do. The materials of nature, deprived of their sacred immanence, became 'raw' and were now up for grabs.

The Kurgan story of the self and the world was irresistible. It wasn't a *mechanism* that propelled the dispersal of their influence, although we naturally seek such an explanation; nor was it a conquest fueled by superior technology. Aggressive though the mounted Kurgans were, the ideological and linguistic conquest was achieved by *the persuasiveness of their new vision of what it is to be human*. People had been primed for that new paradigm of self and world by the Neolithic Revolution, and they capitulated to it like dominoes. Their *being* had been so profoundly altered by their new tools that they could no longer recognize themselves in the images and symbols of a matrifocal culture. They needed a new story. **What set the stage for the Indo-European 'conquest', then, was the tension between the old paradigm and the newly acquired experiences of abstract perspective and domination: cultures needed a paradigm that represented human beings as empowered doers, unencumbered by old cultural ties of devotion to female Being; it was a paradigm uniquely provided by the Kurgan culture.** The scope and power of the Indo-European 'conquest' evidences how deep and widespread the need was for that new paradigm. And it acted precisely as a catalyst, hastening to ripeness a change that was already underway.

With the ripening of that change, the elements of patriarchy were upon us—and they did result from male domination, but not from the domination of women by men: that was an effect, not the cause. **The root cause of patriarchy lies in the domination of the *self* by the male element**—in the subjugation of our being and in the newfound entitlement of the abstract hetabrain. Our historic subjugation and mistrust of women precisely parallels the subjugation and mistrust of Being itself: *our patrifocal culture expresses to the world the hierarchy to which we as individuals subjugate ourselves.*

There is an ancient Mesopotamian hymn to the goddess Nidaba, preserved in cuneiform, that praises her as the goddess of grasses and grains, and it is clear that she was the grasses and grains. Where there were no grasses or grains, there was no Nidaba. Her power was in her immanence, and it neither acted nor willed beyond those plants. Nidaba would have been right at home in Old Europe. A much later hymn to the Mesopotamian god Enlil provides a striking contrast. He helps man not by being, but by what he does, which is directed towards control:

> Enlil, by your skillful planning in intricate designs—
> their inner workings a blur of threads
> not to be unraveled,
> thread entwined in thread, not to be traced by the eye
> –
> you excel in your task of divine providence.
>
> You are your own counselor, adviser and manager,
> who (else) could comprehend what you do?
>
> Your tasks are tasks that are not apparent,
> your guise (that of) a god, invisible to the eye.[306]

It is a hymn to Enlil, but in the particulars of each phrase it could just as well serve as a hymn to the newly fledged hetabrain. What Enlil represented—the power to plan, design, advise, manage and execute *independent of any counsel*—was characteristic of both the emergent patriarchal gods and the hetabrain, which refuses the Call and secretly busies itself with planning and implementing its agenda. By the time the Greek gods arrived, even creation was the preserve of the male: the goddess Athena famously sprang from the forehead of Zeus, a physical process that virtually defies imagination, but which makes perfect metaphoric sense—the hetabrain was supreme, even in the act of creation. After all, it was re-creating man's world all around him.

Riding the horse is a big thing, and it leads to big things. It imbued man with a sense of destiny and embedded his accomplishments in linear time. The fact that on a horse one is faster, stronger, more eminent among men and more powerful is supremely seductive. Even today, the underlying promise of car ads is that of self-transformation and entitlement, and often that promise is explicit: with "more muscle" you can "own the road," and "your friends won't recognize you." The greater the horsepower you are controlling, the greater the transformation you can expect. The lessons that riding a horse taught Neolithic man about power and entitlement and control are with us still. Cultures soaked up those lessons, which descended from the Kurgans, and then "taught a lesson" to other cultures. In McLuhan's terms, the horse is the medium, we are the content, and the message is a redefinition of what it is to be human, one that has altered the world. It is that new definition that was carried on horseback to the Indus valley and beyond, and which transformed the agricultural world from Ireland to India into one of raiding and trading. **The horse didn't just enable people to dominate; it taught them to want to.** The four horsemen have been with us ever since. The Apocalypse arrived long ago.

The Possessed Self

Riding the horse may have been the catalyst that crystallized a new definition of man—but the profoundest lesson it taught us is one that to this day dominates our experience of the self. The lesson presents itself naturally enough: as the hetabrain learns to assert its control over the world, it begins to turn its attentions to the self—the ultimate conquest. The hetabrain finds the natural model for that conquest in horse riding. Consider the way in which you "override" the intelligence of a horse from your position in the saddle; by doing so you can exert your will not just upon the horse, but through the horse upon the world. That is just how we have come to relate to our bodies. **In our head-centered culture we have become, in effect, the willful, thinking rider sitting on top of his big, dumb body,** *overriding its intelligence and telling it what to do.* Were that not our perception, cryonics companies would have no customers. And so we typically go through our days never fully entering the sensational, analog intelligence that places us where we are. In effect, we have made hostages of ourselves, and as hostages we typically feel anger and frustration and resentment, chafing at the bit—without realizing that we ourselves hold the reins.

It is noteworthy that the most frequent group of symbols that appeared from the Kurgan's new ideology centered around solar imagery; and among the engravings on stelae—which represent the richest source for the study of those early symbols—are often to be found, as Gimbutas put it, "solar signs (circles, radiating suns, and a circle with groups of long rays) engraved in the area of the head."[307] Once the self withdraws to its *head*quarters, we live according to the 'known self', which we possess and defend. We speak not only of "having a body," but of "having a life," or even of "getting a life," as if they were all possessions. But then, almost everything in the world around us is seen to be a thing that someone or other possesses—is there even a tree left on earth that is not 'owned'?—so that our role has become one of *managing what is ours.* And just as managers typically don't "get their hands dirty," **our managerial role keeps us at a distance from the fecund nourishment of our own living.** We try to do a good job as we manage our health, our eating habits, our problems, our spiritual growth, our pain, our vitamins, our relationships, our emotions, our weight, our household, our property, our expectations, our finances, our careers—we even seek to manage our happiness, something many popular 'self-help' books promise to make simple. Analysis is the manager's modus operandi, and to facilitate it we seek perspective on everything. The language of managing is familiar enough to us—we like to be 'in charge' of our lives, and managing puts us in 'the driver's seat'; but the most crucial issue of personal freedom each of us faces is the challenge of how to assimilate the present and *enter* our life instead of managing it as though it were a duplicate: therein lies the mythic choice between the hero's path and the tyrant's. That issue connects to a much larger story when we scratch the word *manage*: it comes from an Italian word, *managgiare*, which means "to control a horse."

The Invention of Authority

The passing centuries have witnessed a number of developments that have helped to confirm the hetabrain's right to rule. The ascendancy of television in the last century is staggering in its impact, as is that of its smaller, more versatile brother, the computer. But there was another development, already underway in the Neolithic era, that I think was even more staggering in its impact: written language.

Writing started as pictures of things; over time it became pictures of words; but not until 1400 B.C. was the North Semitic alphabet invented, the first to represent a sound with a sign. Although that alphabet represented only consonants—so that *but, abut, bat, batty, bit, bitty, bet, abet, Betty, bite, bought, beat, boat, boot, booty, bout, about, bait, abate, beta* and *abbot* would all have been written "bt"—the ability to freeze sound on parchment provided a huge sense of empowerment. In 800 B.C. the Greeks appropriated the Semitic consonants, didn't need them all, and turned the leftovers into vowels. With that innovation, as Ivan Illich has noted, a reader no longer needed to breathe life into the bare bones of consonants: "The Greek picks the sound from the page and searches for the invisible ideas in the sounds *the letters command him to make.*"[308] We might further note that those stand-alone letters represent the atoms of speech—the smallest units of sound from which it is constructed.

The etymology of our word *read* sounds exactly like a description of the Pater-patter of the hetabrain. The Old English word from which it comes, *raedon,* means "to advise, counsel, discuss, deliberate, rule, guess, interpret"—all the things the authoritative little voice in our head does. Anthropologist Wade Davis has commented from his considerable depth of experience on the ways in which our literate tradition "made for a different human being,"[309] and we can begin to see why. Phonetic writing is the first digital language—a language made by the fingers, divorced from the body's breath. Its development opened the doorway to a world of abstract concepts beyond anything man had dealt with before. Ultimately, *the power of the written word even superseded the Logos of ancient Greece: Logos* was translated into Latin to mean "word"; to write "In the beginning was the Word, and the Word was with God, and the Word was God"[310] is to raise above all else the word of God as a law or rule, which is a far cry from the unreadable, living mind of the world that steers all things through all things—the meaning, as we have seen, that Logos had for ancient Greeks.

Written language helped us grow into a mode of being in which the sensations of the body can be an irrelevance, an inconvenience, and even a nuisance if they express discomfort. Learning to read requires an enormous effort of abstraction, an effort we tend to forget ever happened once the skill is mastered. I was reminded of it watching my daughters. Consider the steps that someone who is learning to read needs to go through to decipher a word like *but*. First she recognizes the "b," and makes sure it is not a "d." Then she remembers the sound that "b" makes, and she says it out loud. Then she recognizes the letter "u," which makes two sounds. She picks one and says it out loud. The same with "t." Then she has to remember the succession of sounds "b," "u," "t" and string them together out loud; and then she has to recognize in those sounds the word she has been made to say. It is a check/go/stop/check/go/stop process that happens predominantly in an abstract realm—that is, it necessitates a certain forgetfulness.

I used to watch each of my daughters go stock still in silence ("Hold your horses"), barely breathing, hovering above a page with intense focus, learning to decode sound from 'atomic' symbol, and word from sound. More significantly, though, in *learning to withdraw from their sensational bodies they were learning how to grant supremacy to the hetabrain.* Once we learn to read fluently, of course, we no longer need to translate from symbol to sound to word, but by then we have thoroughly mastered the primary lesson of reading: the forgetfulness of the body and the potency of the unipolar hetabrain. It makes me wonder whether phonetic writing in the West may have contributed to the different sense of self than that developed in the East, in which written languages are based on pictures.

The changes in our experience of the self that were brought on by the Neolithic Revolution, and given added impetus by such developments as writing, are widely evident by the eighth century B.C.. We know from the word *phren* that by the eighth century in Greece the thinking of the self was being experienced at the chest. In India at the same time, as the earliest Upanishads show, the heart was considered to be the seat of waking consciousness. At the same time in Egypt a slab of basalt, known as the Shabaka Stone, was inscribed with a sacred text we call the Memphite Theology, and it similarly tells us that the mind is found in the heart—a sentiment that had actually been held by Egyptians for a long time. When ancient Egyptians prepared bodies for mummification, the heart—the center of intelligence—was the one internal organ left in the body; the abdominal organs were carefully preserved in jars; and the brain was thrown on the trash heap—the exact opposite of our practice of cryonics. By 700 B.C. in Egypt, India and Greece, then, the experiential center of our thinking had moved from the pelvic intelligence—the hub of Being—more than halfway to the cranial brain. The effect on our "whole psychic and social complex," as McLuhan put it, was cataclysmic: *what had been one—thinking and Being—was being split into two.*

Eventually the embodied axis was disabled and our thinking—divorced from being—was centered in our heads. Unipolar thinking is by nature schizologic—"split from the Logos." We could sit at a distance from our own being or from the world and think *about* them, like Orpheus looking back; we could also scrutinize them for the fulcrum points by which they could be levered and manipulated to our advantage. But the privilege of insisting on unintegrated perspectives came at a cost: an emotional, physical and spiritual exile from the natural world and the fullness of our own being—a fullness that belongs to the unity of the felt self. Over the centuries our culture has lost the ability—and to a large extent even the wish—to experience that unity.

Those who do seek that experience face a personal struggle against the very cultural edicts that have shaped who they know themselves to be.

The separation of thinking from Being created a crisis in man's relationship to the world—a crisis that came to the fore in the eighth century B.C. across Eurasia and lasted for six hundred years. During those centuries various attempts were made to solve that crisis, giving rise to classical philosophy in Greece, including Socrates, Plato and Aristotle; to the principal Hebrew prophets in Israel, including Elijah, Isaiah and Jeremiah; to Confucianism and Taoism in China; to the Upanishads and Buddhism in India; and to Zoroastrianism in Persia. In 1949 philosopher Karl Jaspers, appreciating the significance of that era, named it "the Axial Age." As Jaspers wrote, "in this age were born the fundamental categories within which we still think today, and the beginning of the world religions by which human beings still live."[311]

There has been considerable debate among historians about what causes might be adduced to explain the rise of the Axial Age, but the context of this book suggests it is a direct and natural outcome of the path on which we embarked with the Neolithic Revolution: namely, the shift in our allegiance from the female element of Being to the male element of doing, by which perspective was gained and unity was sacrificed. That loss of unity gave rise to the unipolar state of self-consciousness that frames such questions as, "Who am I?" "What is the meaning of life?" and "Am I in possession of Buddha consciousness?" Those questions, which we live with still, characterize and were formative of the Axial Age. They are potent questions that can impart a search with urgency; but unless the passion they spark can break through to a new set of questions, **they can lead only to insights that are self-referential, because the questions all tacitly imply perseity.** For instance, "Who am I?" is asking "What essential individuality do I possess?"; "What is the meaning of life?" is really asking "What meaning does my life possess?"—similar in its assumptions to "Am I in possession of Buddha consciousness?" *Possession, a fiction of perseity, is the anchor by which the 'known self' seeks to locate itself in the sea of Being.* Our reliance on that anchor makes it all the more difficult for us to understand how other cultures, such as that of the Inuit, could have no verb by which to say, "I own" or "You own" or "He owns."

As the Axial Age progressed, our growing addiction to the glories and triumphs of the newly liberated male element pulled us farther and farther from the pelvic intelligence, rupturing our connection to being and so dividing us from the world as well. Across Eurasia, remarkable individuals stepped forth to understand and remedy the division between self and world. Some of those individuals sought to restore our relationship with the world by bringing to light the *principles* on which it depended. Others sought to replace the loss of that relationship with the world by bringing us into relationship instead with written *rules*. Their efforts formalized the authority of laws or texts that paradoxically promise to hold the world together by cleaving it into unambiguous judgments of good and bad.

The year 500 B.C. stands at the epicenter of the Axial Age. In that year Buddha in India, Heraclitus in Greece, Confucius in China—and, some scholars say, Lao-tzu—all walked upon the earth. Buddha, Lao-tzu and Heraclitus were each, in different ways, struggling past self-consciousness to find union with the world's living consciousness—to wake up, as each would say. Also alive in 500 B.C., Parmenides applied a philosophical guillotine to our relationship with the world—cutting the head off from the body's sensations and urging us towards pure reason. In his wake came the Greek philosopher Melissus, who fore-shadowed the classical model of the atom and the self when he argued that the One Sphere of Parmenides, which makes up all existence, could consist of many little, independent spheres, each eternal like the One—a view of the world that has endured doggedly ever since. Also alive in 500 B.C., and ruling over a Persian Empire that stretched from the Asiatic Greeks to the Indus valley, Darius I was the first ruler to put his head—his face, his ego, his known and singular self—on a coin, rather than selecting an image from nature or myth. He attempted to solve man's relationship with the world by using the force of his empire to institute a system of laws that his subjects were to obey without question. His laws were tied to Zoroastrianism, which was the first religion to divide the world into categories of good and evil, thereby overturning the mythic message that all the world's particulars issue from a single, unique source of Being beyond all polarities. As Joseph Campbell points out, the message of Zoroastrianism was that

> the world in which we live is mixed of good and evil.
> Man is therefore not to put himself in accord with
> nature—as in the ancient and oriental worlds—but to
> make a decision for the good, put himself in accord

with the good, fight for justice and the light, and correct nature.[312]

The emphasis is Campbell's. Zoroaster's vision aligned law and order and control with the good, thereby formalizing a mind-set that began to emerge when hunting and gathering gave way to farming. As anthropologist Hugh Brody explains,

> The farmer has the task of controlling and shaping the world, making it yield the produce upon which agricultural life depends. If this is done well, the crops will grow. Discovery by discovery, change by change, field by field, control is increased and produce is more secure. The dichotomies of good and evil, right and wrong express this farming project: control comes … [by] working with determination and consistency against all that might undermine this endeavor.[313]

Ideas of right and wrong beget rules, which distract us from the energy of Being. As Stephen Mitchell observed, "When the Tao is forgotten, people act according to rules, not from the heart."[314] If the West had taken more heed of Heraclitus, we might have attended more closely to the Logos, as the East attended to the Tao. But before Heraclitus had died, Parmenides gave expression to a paradigm that fit people's experience of themselves and their world so well that virtually everyone assented to it; that paradigm stood as the cornerstone of Western philosophy until the twentieth century. As we have seen, the core of his premise was, *"Don't believe the experience of your body— the senses are unreliable. Only reason can lead you to the truth."* Whereupon he reasoned that nothing can move. Literally. Fifty years later Democritus was finally able to demonstrate that, logically, things could move, and everyone breathed a sigh of relief; but he didn't lay a finger on Parmenides' underlying premise—*which specifically instructs us not to think about the whole in a manner that is whole.* The world, it asserts, is knowable only through insensate reason and analysis, and only the purity of abstract knowledge represents true knowledge. Of course, to claim in effect that you can be liberated to the truth only by rendering the body unconscious is to burn the very bridge that connects you to the full dimensionality of your truth.

Around this time, tellingly, the very concept of what 'reason' is underwent a profound change. The word *reason* comes from the same Indo-European base as *art, harmony, ratio* and *rational*: the base *ar-*, which means "to join." That indeed is the sense in which Heraclitus used the word—as something joined to the world, a part of its mutual awareness; but as John Mansley Robinson explains, all that changed:

> For Heraclitus reason is embedded in the very nature of things; it is only reflected in man because man is himself a part of nature. But Democritus does not view reason as embedded in nature; it is peculiar to man—a possession which at the same time sets him apart from nature and enables him to control it for his own ends.[315]

Thereafter, corationality was relegated to the shadows of our culture, to be discovered and fully appreciated by relatively few—some of whom were persecuted for that sensitivity. Reason became a strength we think of as our own, like the prideful tyrant. A little while after Democritus, sometime not much before 350 B.C., Plato wrote one of his last books, *Timaeus,* in which he gives an explanation of how the gods made us:

> They copied the shape of the universe and fastened the two divine orbits of the soul into a spherical body, which we now call *the head, the divinest part of us which controls all the rest;* they then put together the body as a whole to serve the head, knowing that it would be endowed with all the varieties of motion there were to be. *And to prevent the head from rolling about on the earth, unable to get over or out of its many heights and hollows, they provided that the body should act as a convenient vehicle.* It was therefore given height and grew limbs which could bend and stretch, and with which it could take hold of things and support itself, and so by god's contrivance move in all directions *carrying on top of it the seat of our divinest and holiest part.*[316]

Socrates commented that the speaker offering this explanation "made a wonderfully favorable impression on the minds of his audience." Of course he did, because the guillotine had dropped and they could feel their "divinest and holiest part" in their heads; they had so demeaned the pelvic intelligence as to have disconnected from it; and they experienced the body as "a convenient vehicle." They would have been keen to hear about cryonics.

That's pretty much it, then: by 350 B.C. our journey to stand-alone brain is more or less a done deal. In about 40 B.C. Sallust captured in a few succinct phrases that new image of what it is to be human—an image that has guided us ever since:

> All our power lies in both mind and body; we employ the mind to rule, the body rather to serve; the one we have in common with the Gods, the other with the brutes.[317]

The self has set up shop in its stronghold in the head, its private isolation chamber; our consciousness is unipolar; and the body is like the horse—a brute power for serving the commands of its divine ruler. The hetabrain has triumphed. Doing rules. Entitled taking feels more natural than any exchange of gifts with the world. Cybernetic anxiety feels more secure than attending to the Call. Four dimensions feel more secure than five. And the existential angst of isolation—stepsister of perseity, the inevitable hostess of our unipolar existence—has become our constant shadow. As Jean-Paul Sartre expressed it,

> Man is alone, abandoned on earth in the midst of his infinite responsibilities, without help, with no other aim than the one he sets himself, with no other destiny than the one he forges for himself on this earth.[318]

In 1971 molecular biologist Jacques Monod expressed it in even starker terms:

> Man must at last wake out of his millenary dream and discover his total solitude, his fundamental isolation. He must realize that, like a gypsy, he lives on the boundary of an alien world; a world that is deaf to

his music, and as indifferent to his hopes as it is to his sufferings and his crimes.[319]

In announcing that the world is deaf to man's music, Monod was declaring, in effect, "Orpheus is dead." His sentiments seemed to sum up the findings of four-dimensional science perfectly, but his call to 'wake' to our total solitude never quite caught on as a paradigm: it was countervailed by the hope-inspired cultural upheavals of the sixties. What remains interesting about Monod's view is the seductiveness of its pull, which derives from the purity of its hetabrain assessment of reality. When you read Monod's text closely—"total solitude," "fundamental isolation," "on the boundary of an alien world"—you realize that he is describing the hetabrain in terms that are consistent with the clinical view of autism.

Autism is generally characterized by a withdrawal from the world, a withdrawal from sensation; autistic behavior is typified by a preoccupation with the repetition or manipulation of patterns. In the context of this book that sounds familiarly like the hetabrain at work. Industrialized countries are experiencing an exponential increase in cases of autism, which currently affects four boys for every one girl. A Cambridge psychologist, Simon Baron-Cohen, has done extensive research on autism and considers it to be an extreme form of what he calls the male brain. He is very clear about the terms by which he distinguishes between "the male brain" and "the female brain," and he is careful to note that "some women have the male brain type, and some men have the female brain type, or aspects of it." Baron-Cohen characterizes the strength of the female brain as 'empathizing' and the strength of the male brain as 'systemizing':

> "Empathising" is the drive to identify another person's emotions and thoughts, and to respond to these with an appropriate emotion. Empathising allows you to predict a person's behavior, and to care about how others feel.... "Systemising" is the drive to analyze the variables in a system, to derive underlying rules that govern the behavior of a system. Systemising also refers to the drive to construct systems. Systemising allows you to predict the behavior of a *system*, and to control it.[320]

Within Baron-Cohen's terms we can again see an expression of the familiar female and male elements of Being and doing. Empathy acts by attending to the unknown, the hidden darkness of another's Being, and feeling it as a whole: our analog intelligence at work. Systemizing belongs to the realm of male doing, which seeks perspectives by which it might discern patterns and analyze them: our digital intelligence at work, seeking to predict and control the system. An extreme male brain lacks the ability to empathize: Baron-Cohen has described autism as a state in which one is *"mind-blind,"* incapable of insight into another's mind. If one were to characterize the evolution of the self within our culture as a whole, I think one could say *we have all been shifting towards the extreme male brain:* dissociating from Being, drawn by the Siren song of tyranny. The "fundamental isolation" of which Jacques Monod writes is our credo, and the vision of reality he articulates has dominated the way we see and live our individual lives: the attention we lavish on the self overwhelms our ability to attend to the world; the presumptions of entitlement obscure our occasions for gratitude; we invent ways of parceling the world up wholly for ourselves instead of discovering how to give ourselves wholly to the world; the priority we give to the creation of systems overrules our respect for the sacred weave of creation; and the fictions of the 'known self' and the 'known world' are sustained by elaborate abstractions that distract us from the miracle of the ordinary. **As a culture we have become "Mind-blind," so incapable of insight into the One Mind of the world that we are effectively blind to it.** So it is, for example, that we naturally assume Einstein was speaking figuratively when he said, "I want to know the mind of God. Everything else is detail." But what if he actually meant what he said?

In his book *The Other Side of Eden: Hunters, Farmers and the Shaping of the World,* anthropologist Hugh Brody offers a detailed meditation on what was lost when our Paleolithic ancestors made the transition from hunting and gathering to agriculture. As Brody observes, the survival of hunter-gatherers depends on a sensitivity that has expanded its sphere of awareness to attune to the very spirit of the land that supports them.

> A fluidity of boundaries, a porousness of divisions, can be seen as useful and normal. This ever-present possibility of transformation is both the opposite of,

and an equivalent to, control. Rather than seeking to change the world, hunter-gathers know it. They also care for it, showing respect and paying attention to its well-being.[321]

We, who drive ourselves through the agendas of our lives like autonomous cars, have exiled ourselves from any such transformative sensitivity. Transformation is anathema to the 'known self', and a direct threat to the hetabrain; we have baffled and confounded our inner corridor, and with it the porosity that makes corationality possible. Without that porosity, we lose our sense of place; without our sense of place, we lose our ability to be present. We do not situate ourselves in the Energy of the living world around us; we rather determine where we are according to measurements of our success and by the ticking of the clock. As long as we remain numb to the world's intelligence, all its unthinkable diversity will be impotent to guide us, even as we persist in dismembering it. The effects of our willfulness may end our tyranny before we do.

The way ahead for us is clear, without being clear at all. That is, if we are to move forward as individuals and as a culture, our aim cannot be to solve our problems by acquiring the right perspectives on them and enforcing the solutions they suggest. We want to believe that technology and social engineering can save us; but technology in the hands of tyranny cannot bring redemption: it cannot sensitize us to the five-dimensional world; nor can it deliver us from greed, self-absorption, cybernetics or our senseless disregard of harmony. **What we need is to deliver ourselves from the self-achieved impoverishment of our own sensitivity; what has been divided inside us must now be made whole**—and that cannot happen willfully: it cannot even *begin* if the male element is in charge. That healing requires the ordinary hero's journey of submission, which alone enables us to pay attention with the kind of passivity that welcomes whatever the moment brings. And welcomes what every moment brings. In other words, the male element needs to give up its agenda of control—needs to come down to earth, still itself, and surrender its perspectives to the "massively connected" pelvic intelligence, which awakens us to the world of the manifest mind. The world calls to each of us individually to grow into our gifts of sensitivity; and as we learn to give ourselves to the present, it has gifts ready to exchange, moment by ordinary moment.

Exercise Eleven: **The Horse**

We are used to sitting on top of the body, like a rider on his horse, and telling it what to do. This exercise turns that relationship upside down. It was developed by Steven Rumbelow, a pioneer of physical theater in Britain, who was looking for a way to help actors step out of a head-centered approach to acting and into relationship with the vibrant, earthy, holistic intelligence of the body. One day he was having a picnic with his theater company in the countryside. Beside him were some horses in a field. As he watched them, one of the horses suddenly bolted, ran a little ways off, and then settled to graze again. Like Grotowski's tree, what the horse expressed was beautiful and ineffable and true. But the horse didn't move because it wanted to express, nor did it *decide* to move. It was at one with its own energy, and with the energy of the moment, and was carried by it—and so expressed it. From that simple event the Horse exercise was born, and it remains an invaluable tool for anyone wanting to connect with the primal, analog sensitivity of the logosmind.

The exercise can be done for as little as a few minutes. In Rumbelow's theater company it was occasionally done for a couple of consecutive days. It begins simply enough. Your body was meant to move and integrate its experience, but typically has been kept from what it

needs by the will, in ways too numerous to detail. Still, within the body is the desire to shrug off its unseen tethers, and be free, and be in a free exchange with the world. The exercise leaves no room for decision or calculation or judgment—there is merely submission.

The intelligence of the body is a responsive intelligence, and the exercise begins by simply paying attention to its promptings. If you stand still and relaxed for long enough, your body will want to move. Let it. That is the exercise. The body leads, and you follow, honoring its innate connection to Being and trusting in its revelations. There is no proper way of doing the Horse—no kind or speed or quality of movement that is right, no certain way the exercise should look. In fact it can really begin only when you let go of those considerations and simply cut your body loose to horse around. When you truly enter the exercise, there is no longer a rider: there is no division; there is no expression; there is no little voice directing this, judging that, anticipating or controlling. There is only the urging of the body as it moves and processes and explores. There is only the unified, vital, connected energy of the horse.

At times that energy will guide you into movements that seem completely irrational; but you may begin to discover that they are, in fact, completely corational. The Present is unimaginably rich, and this exercise liberates the body to respond to and dance with the Present in its full, unmediated richness. Sometimes it feels like a spring gale blowing; sometimes it feels like the coursing of a deep, slow-moving river. And occasionally it may feel like a dance of the sort that a tiger might do after being released from a cage where it had been enclosed for a long, long time.

Part V

Recovering Our Senses

Walls not only keep others out, but keep us in. Yet, we can afford to tear down those walls only if we are willing to surrender to a sense of connectedness deep within ourselves.

—Marion Woodman and Elinor Dickson

We are like flies crawling across the Sistine Chapel. We cannot see what angels and gods lie underneath the threshold of our perceptions. We do not live in reality; we live in our paradigms, our habituated perceptions, our illusions, the illusions we share through the culture we call reality, but the true ... reality of our condition is invisible to us.

—Jean Houston

I paused, wondering what to ask next. We drove along for a while in silence. Then I said to him: "What is power?"

Without a blink of hesitation, he answered: "Transformation. Transformation is power."

—Hugh Brody in conversation with
Harold Wright, a Nisga'a elder

12 | Our Elemental Sensitivity

Air: Unleashing the Dragon

As we have seen, our view of reason has altered dramatically since the time of Heraclitus. As he saw it, whatever man discovers in himself merely reflects what belongs first to nature—just as man himself does. Our fundamental belief in perseity tells us otherwise—that reason is a quality unique to man; but common sense suggests that Heraclitus was right—and the Universal Law insists that he is. There is no element of which we are constituted that is peculiar to us or is even possessed by us. That is true not only of reason, but of the mind's sensitivity as well.

The ancient Greek philosopher Empedocles held that everything is made from four elements: earth, air, fire and water. And because his culture did not consider anything to be divorced from spirit, Empedocles also identified the four elements as the four spiritual essences, "the four roots of all things."[322] Carl Jung spoke of the four elements symbolically as the four types of consciousness: sensation, thinking, intuition and emotions. We are intimately linked to those elements on every level: earth, air, fire and water are not just basic to our lives as humans, they also symbolize the diverse energies from which we and all else are made—including our mind's sensitivity. As we have seen, what impairs that sensitivity are all the unintegrated parts of ourselves, both perspectives and emotions, that we cannot reconcile with the whole. The result, whether we intend it or not, is that those parts stand like battlements between us and the whispering world to which we belong. Once we recognize the elements of earth, air, fire and water within us, we recognize the world's sensitivity within us; and then we

367

can experience the battlements coming down and discover within us a clarity of being that imparts felicity to our every response and action.

Air, for instance, is the very stuff we breathe. Our relationship with it is often uneasy. Whenever people struggle to keep their feelings under control, they stifle their breathing to prevent it from moving too far into the depths of the body. When they become willful, they hold it or force it. Breath is dangerous because it liberates feeling, and thereby also liberates the sensational thinking of the logosmind. But it also represents life itself: we find that the roots of our words *animal*, *psyche* and *spirit* all trace back to different words meaning "breath."

Breath is an all-in-one agent of transformation and renewal and integration. This is as true of the physical process of *respiration* as it is for the spiritual process of *inspiration*. Physically, the in-breath carries dissolved world stuff into the body to become part of its intelligence; the out-breath carries dissolved parts of the body away to unite with the world's intelligence. Spiritually, a whole-body breath unites thinking and being; as such, a whole-body breath reveals and activates the embodied axis. We were all born as whole-body breathers, but as the isometrics of neglect take up residence in our bodies, we incrementally lose that ability, and may eventually even forget what a whole-body breath is. The sense of what we mean by 'a whole-body breath' is potently conveyed in a single phrase by Chuang Tzu:

> True men breathe from their heels.
> Others breathe with their gullets,
> Half-strangled.[323]

I consider myself fortunate to be an actor for many reasons—but foremost among them is having had to pay scrupulous attention to the united energy of body and mind, and to where I was dividing it or willful with it, and then learning over time how to release the 'frozen' parts of myself. You can't release the breath as a whole without releasing the whole of the body; and you can't release the whole of the body without releasing any ideas or feelings that are frozen within— feelings that are suppressed or edited or judged or manipulated. When you do release all that on the breath, it enables you to "feel the thing as a whole." Allowing yourself a 'whole body breath', it turns out, is essential not just for the actor's truth, but for anyone's. And frankly, it took me months of study with a remarkable voice teacher, David

Smukler, before I learned what it meant to release the whole body on the out-breath and to allow the whole body to answer to the in-breath. David helped me understand that the pulse of the whole-body breath originates in the responsiveness of the pelvic bowl, and that the sacrum—that triangular bone at the base of the spine—is crucial to that responsiveness. The sacrum actually releases down and back to welcome the breath into the body, and settles down to the center to release the breath into the world; in doing so, it also sends a wave of release up the entire length of the spine—and when the spine is released into fluidity, it eases the rest of the body into fluidity. When David first introduced me to that notion, I was so out of touch with the pole of my conscious being—the Neolithic hub of relationship—that I could barely feel what he was talking about. Now it is second nature.

In the eyes of the Laius Complex, the breath presents the most powerful interference with which it has to contend, a natural force of unpredictable consequences. A deep, relaxed, abandoned breath will unleash sensations of life that buoy you into the unknown. The internalized Authority senses that journey as an insurrection, and will want to restore order by imposing patterns on the breathing—often in ways so familiar we fail to notice. Those patterns are the instruments of self-tyranny, constraining the spirit of breath with the cybernetics of will; and a body deprived of its own sensitivity cannot notice the world's.

Constricting the breath flow turns mindful flesh into obdurate matter. But if you start to pay attention to your breath flow, you will be rewarded with insights into habits of consolidation that are otherwise invisible. If you release the breath on a sigh, can you passively attend to your body's intelligence and simply experience the sensations precipitating through it? Do you put your breath on hold as you get into a car or get up from a chair? As you concentrate on a fine-motor task, or push a heavy weight? When you stand to deliver a speech? When you reach for something? When you meet someone? Or when you catch something that is thrown to you? If so, you are reverting to the cybernetics of the hetabrain mode. And then the most interesting question to ask is: what would you risk by releasing the breath flow? And the most interesting answer is to go ahead and try it.

As a liberator of the energies of your Being, breath is aptly symbolized by the dragon. It's telling that the traditional views of the dragon in East and West are so radically at odds. The differences between them are summarized by Kakuzo Okakura:

> The Eastern Dragon is not the gruesome monster of mediaeval imagination, but the genius of strength and goodness. He is the spirit of change, therefore of life itself.[324]

Substitute "breath" for "dragon" in the last half of that quote ("breath is the genius of strength..."), and you have a pretty good description of its latent power. Symbolically the dragon serves to remind us that the whole-body breath unites the various elements of the world. He swims in the *sea,* lives deep in the *earth,* flies through the *air,* and breathes *fire.* The mnemonic is useful. It has often been said that we carry *the sea* around with us, as evidenced by the percentage of saltwater in our blood; but more tangibly, the swell of the sea lives on in the huge internal wave that each breath initiates and to which the whole body responds. As we breathe from our heels, the whole body is sensitized to *the earth* we stand on. *Air,* of course, is the element we breathe in, taking into our core the intangible energy of the space around us. And *fire* lives not just in the life-giving oxidization that rips apart molecules in our bodies, but also in the spiritual fires sparked by breathing, which turn to ash the structures of the hetabrain. It's no wonder the hetabrain wants to keep this dragon on a short leash—by doing so it keeps change on a leash; but it also tethers "the genius of strength and goodness."

In the West our relationship to the dragon is epitomized by the legend of St. George, which was recounted in the popular medieval book *The Golden Legend.* We don't need to look far into it to see what this story was communicating. St. George was a knight, and like most knights he was buffered from the world's sensations by his armor and is found riding his high horse—an evocative image within the context of this book. The famous fight took place at the dragon's lair, where the king's daughter was being held captive. Dragon and knight clashed with each other, and the dragon was badly wounded. St. George did not finish him off though; he

> said to the maid: Deliver to me your girdle, and bind it about the neck of the dragon and be not afeard. When she had done so the dragon followed her as it had been a meek beast and debonair. Then she led him into the city.[325]

Whatever you do, don't head downtown without your breath on a leash.

In the particulars of this tale the male element of doing protects the female element of Being from the dragon, whose single most dangerous aspect was his breath: with it he "venomed the people." The male element tamed the breather by bleeding the vitality from it, so that the female element could keep it on a leash. In more symbolic terms, what St. George saved this virgin maid from was her own energy and sensuousness as awakened by a whole-body breath, which was venomous to the kingdom of the hetabrain. Her girdle—used, as girdles are, to constrict breath and feeling—is placed around the neck of the Dragon, the narrow divide between head and body that, like a drawbridge, protects the thinker in the head from interference by unbidden feelings. The symbolic value of that girdle lives on in the necessary badge of the modern businessman: the necktie—the wearing of which signifies a tacit pledge not to breathe or feel too deeply. Fewer sights are more indecorous to our sensibilities than a display of unchecked emotion by the wearer of a necktie. By symbolizing control, the tie represents a tacit promise that the male element will remain in charge.

The encoded lesson of St. George and the Dragon has been well learned over the centuries. To this day the male element of doing protects our female element of Being from the sensational energies of the breath: we breathe and speak according to will and muscle, rather than from the sensuous, mindful present. "Everything breathes together," [326] as Plotinus once observed; but only as we move beyond willful breathing do we, too, begin to breathe with all else. In fact, you might quite simply note that **if you are not breathing with the world, you are breathing alone; if you are breathing alone, you have achieved discontinuity from the present.** There is a further lesson that the astute reader could draw from this tale: be careful what you demonize.

Water: The Emptiness of Fluidity

Water is the element that enables the exchanges of life itself; and the exchanges made possible by fluidity, which water represents, constitute the sensitivities of the logosmind, of entelechy and of reality. On a small enough physical scale (sub-atomic, for example) or within a sufficiently large time frame (think of a time-lapse film of a galaxy forming) the essential fluidity of all matter becomes manifestly apparent. We don't notice that a hunk of marble or steel is in a state of flow, but it is. In the dimension of consciousness, too, nothing is fixed: self, world, thought—everything is in process.

As we have identified the 'known self' with ice, we have identified the felt self with water. The fluidity of water is a quality that brings everything into relationship: a dolphin off Nova Scotia sends ripples across the Atlantic. The very fact that everything in the universe exists only in relationship tells us that it exists in a state of yielding flow. That is exactly what makes fluidity so essential to our elemental sensitivity: when we relax the body into its natural fluidity, the heart comes into relationship with our core—the cello string a wave medium—as do our emotions and perceptions, and around us, the present itself.

To feel the subtle *fluidity* of your body, your world and your life is to enter their essential *reality;* it is also to reclaim an ancient identification. We do not normally speak of a "*body* of earth" or "air" or "fire"—but when we stand by a lake and call it a "*body* of water" it is because, on a deeply intuitive level, we identify it with our bodily self. We intuitively understand our *soul* in a similar way: the word comes from a Teutonic base for a body of water, *saiwa-z,* which means "lake" or "sea." Our thought, too, is associated with images of water: we speak of the 'stream of consciousness', and might politely excuse ourselves for interrupting 'the flow' of someone's thinking. And as for our emotions, our language is full of metaphors in which they gush, or come in waves, or flow through us. Such associations remind us that the fluid subtlety of the logosmind is one in which body, soul, thought, feelings and world all participate without division. The love-based intelligence of the logosmind liquefies the world; and when we release ourselves into its fluidity, we release ourselves into the subtle currents of Being.

In my experience, the most reliable barometer of consolidation in the body is the spine. It is sensitive to any tyranny we might exercise: at the slightest impulse towards willfulness, the spine tends to pull back from Being and contract into itself. By contrast, allowing the spine to lengthen into fluidity is a small adventure of ordinary heroism. In fact, all healthy movements of the body tend to open fluidly to the unknowable present, rather than retracting into the consolidations of the 'known self': the body is a field of intelligence, and the spine a river running through it. As we release the energy of that field into the felt present, the body as a whole is released into its essential fluidity—and as should be clear by now, **that essential fluidity of the whole *is* the felt self.**

Water's elemental fluidity defies the fixity of any *pattern,* and so it eludes all tyranny. Instead, water gives itself to innumerable, never repeated *forms:* rivers, waves, waterfalls, rainfalls, clouds, trees, animals and whirlpools. Alan Watts's image of the whirlpool is a particularly apt metaphor for the loving logosmind in that it has no clearly defined border, but is fed by and is continuous with the watery world in which it stands—whirlpool and river belonging to the same strength. In fact, if we consider any of the living forms of water—whirlpools, waterfalls, clouds or human bodies—we can see that each is a process through which the energy of the world constantly courses. That energy is not incidental to those forms, but actually creates and sustains them; and any of them is devoid of so much as a molecule to serve as a permanent fixture within it.

As we have seen, the heroic surrender to ordinary being reveals the body to be a fluid expression of mind—a form always in transition, and never the same twice. Everything within us that is patterned aims at resisting transition; what is fluid within us is form in flux, revealing in its ease our intention and the guidance of the present. When the energies of the present and our own intention course through us like that—transforming matter and carrying it into the newness of each moment—we are experiencing the nature of reality as described in a Buddhist scripture known as the Heart Sutra. Its most famous passage reads: "Form is emptiness; emptiness is form. Emptiness is not other than form; form is not other than emptiness."[327] Alan Watts explains this apparent paradox with great simplicity, by reminding us of the two meanings of our word *clarity.*

> We think of clarity at once as translucent and unobstructed space, and (also) as form articulate in every detail—as what photographers, using finely polished lenses, call 'high resolution'—and this takes us back to what Lao-tzu said of the usefulness of doors and windows. Through perfect nothing we see perfect something.[328]

When we are empty of the hetabrain's desire to supervise and pattern what self and world become, then we surrender to a clarity of being that is informed by the world around it. We can then feel the self and the present to which it belongs "as a whole," with a lucidity that is at the same time a dialogue. We feel form in emptiness. Just as we feel emptiness in form. In fact, we might understand that the Heart Sutra is also telling us *informed presence is no other than emptiness; emptiness is no other than informed presence.* All of the illusions that Buddhism seeks to help us move beyond are rooted in a refusal to be informed by the world—a refusal that clings to the vanities of perseity. The Dalai Lama, writing of the Heart Sutra, says:

> In sum, the production and disintegration, increase and decrease, and so forth of forms are possible because forms are empty of self-powered existence. Phenomena such as forms are said to dawn from within the sphere of the nature of emptiness.[329]

The Dalai Lama's idea of "self-powered existence" echoes the tyrant's age-old urge to "self-achieved independence"; both ideas underpin the assumption on which every action of the hetabrain is founded: that the self is enclosed in the body. That much is clear, I think. But what can it mean to say that all the forms of the world dawn from within the nature of emptiness? In fact, we can understand it as a natural corollary of the Universal Law of Interrelationship. The Buddhist philosopher Nagarjuna helps us to see the connection. Sometime shortly before A.D. 200 he bucked the prevailing idea that something could be called real only by virtue of its inherent, independent nature—which is essentially the view of perseity. Nagarjuna claimed that **nothing is in possession of its own independent nature.** As he wrote, "things derive their being and nature by mutual dependence and are nothing in themselves."[330] This idea of the essential emptiness of things was not nihilistic. As Alan Watts explains it,

> first of all, emptiness means, essentially, "transience," that's the first thing it means. Nothing to grasp, nothing permanent, nothing to hold on to. But it means this with special reference to ideas of reality, ideas of god, ideas of the self, the brahman, anything you like. What

it means is that reality escapes all concepts. If you say that there is a god, that is a concept; if you say there is no god, that's a concept. And Nagarjuna is saying that always your concepts will prove to be attempts to catch water in a sieve, or wrap it up in a parcel.[331]

That explanation helps us to understand that the terms *emptiness*, *fluidity* and *spaciousness* provide different ways of talking about the fundamental nature of reality—a nature we fundamentally resist with our need to conceptualize. Our word *concept* traces back to *qap-*, "to seize, hold, contain," the same Indo-European root that gave us *haven*. We employ our concepts as havens to contain the world's parts and keep them static; but when you try to hold the world *captive* (from the same root as *concept*), you actually hold *yourself* captive, like an animal in a net. To fight against the net is endlessly tiring. But if you surrender to emptiness, no net can hold you—you simply slip out of its knotted patterns, shedding concepts as a snake sheds its skin. **Reality is essentially fluid, and fluidity is no other than emptiness:** there is nothing permanent in reality to grasp, nothing to hold on to—but in its ceaseless, all-aware currents, there is everything to feel.

To say the reality of the *world* abides in emptiness is one thing; to say the reality of the *self* abides in emptiness is something else. But the emptiness in which the self abides is what remains once we shed the patterns and structures and fixities of the 'known self'; once its baffles have dissolved within the embodied corridor, and the grounded heart has opened to mutual awareness; once we sensitize ourselves to the fluid present and surrender to its living guidance. Only in the afterglow of such emptiness can we truly receive 'what is' and exchange with it. It is an emptiness that surrenders to the world, like heroic intention; it is the emptiness of a flower vase ready for a bouquet, or of a flute ready to be played. It is an emptiness made possible by an awakened confession of ignorance before the mystery that is our most intimate counselor. When you confess your ignorance and let go of what is 'known', you tangibly empty yourself to the world: by emptying of concepts, you empty of will; by emptying of will, you empty of muscular tension; by emptying of muscular tension, you empty of discontinuities; by emptying of discontinuities, you join the fluidity of the world; by joining the fluidity of the world, you join the present. *Every time the body's sensitivity returns to emptiness, it returns to experience,* like an animal cut loose from a net. In that regard, to return to emptiness constitutes a form of patricide: **our surrender to fluid spaciousness annihilates not the self, but the fearful, patterned, isolated, willful Pater in the head.** It makes us like the tree—open to the world, *in possession of nothing.* Not even, we might note, in possession of the self.

Now, to lack willfulness is considered a catastrophe within our culture. As we commonly see it, to lose your will is to lose your identity, your purpose, your power, your ability to engage with the world. As with 'irrationality', that is strictly a hetabrain view of things. The fact is that the *more* willful you are, the *less* you are able to engage with the world—in the same way that the more absorbed you are by the monologue in your head, the less able you are to attend to the present. All willful effort displaces Being; by teaching us to solve our daily challenges with effort, our culture teaches us daily to separate thinking from being and bury the female. We cannot learn how to be whole until we understand what it is to eat with no effort, to listen with no effort, to speak our truth with no effort; until we understand what it is to give ourselves to the present as we might calmly enter the currents of an ice-cold river.

There is a psychological term, 'abulia', which literally means a loss of will, and refers to a pathological inability to make or act on decisions. But although abulia seems to result from a lack of will, I think it *more specifically results from a breakdown of the cybernetics on which the will relies;* in other words, **abulia is symptomatic of an enclosed system that can no longer self-regulate and yet willfully refuses to relinquish its insularity.** The resulting stalemate is a form of stasis. That syndrome seems to be implicated in most disease as well, once we understand the cellular tensions observed by Candace Pert and the repressed emotions observed by John Sarno to be forms of insularity. In fact, *that syndrome represents the blind canyon of self-absorbed independence into which our tyranny leads, and is the source of much of our frustration and despair and alienation.*

It would be a mistake, then, to look at the accomplishments of physical genius as accomplishments of the will. Physical genius is rather a heightened sensitivity that is open to the world's guidance, and so is characterized by "a distinctive fluidity and grace," as Malcolm Gladwell observed. Its fluidity is its empty analog intelligence, attending to the whole; and its grace arises from its dance with the whole.

Grace cannot be self-achieved: it is quintessentially corational; nor can it be scooped from the river and possessed: it is a quality of reciprocity, of relationship; and it is made possible not by knowledge, but by the responsive sensitivities of empty intention.

As the sage Lieh Tzu wrote, "he who for knowledge substitutes blankness of mind really does know."[332] A blank mind, of course, is one that has allowed its perspectives to join the fluidity of the whole that they might be informed by the whole. Meister Eckhart wrote passionately and perceptively about the fluid state of blessedness in which you are empty of will, empty of knowledge and empty even of God. In fact, Eckhart tells us that "God is neither a being nor intelligent, nor does he understand this or that. Thus God is empty of all things, and thus he *is* all things."[333] In general, though, the West has tied itself in knots over the concept of emptiness or nothingness, because emptiness cannot be quantified or measured or patterned or systemized or *known*. How can it even be real? We long ago transferred our allegiance from the black of Being to the white of manifest knowing and doing. Parmenides found the very idea that *nothingness* could *exist* so preposterous he preferred to conclude that any movement was impossible because "all is full of what is." Descartes filled the heavens with a liquid that pushed planets and stars around rather than give his assent to heavenly emptiness. That liquid was conceptualized by Newton and others as ether, a concept that stood until Michelson and Morley failed to detect motion relative to it, and Einstein demonstrated that space and time were not relative to any medium, but rather to the speed of light.

Just as the West has remained uncomfortable with emptiness, and sought to fill the heavens, we seem to feel most assured when the body is so filled with the isometrics of neglect that no room is left for newness. The corridor within is stopped up; the corridor that is the corational world around us is filled with dead matter, mute as a corpse. The task we have taken on, though—in effect, to fill and partition the empty river of Being—is one that gives us no rest. We even work to fill extensions of the self: we fill our bank accounts and our houses, we fill our lawns with uniformly clipped grass, we fill our daybooks, we fill our closets, and we fill the quiet of our environment with nonstop distractions. Nothing new, not even a breath, can be poured into what is already full.

As we have seen, the consolidations of the self create a refuge from life—a shelter, a house—the very architecture of which is determined by the cellular tensions that make up the 'known self'. Tellingly, *house* comes from the Indo-European base "to cover, to hide": you cannot live in the world until you come out of hiding; you can only arrive home once you leave the 'house'. *Home,* as we have seen, comes from an Indo-European base meaning "to lie, settle down"—and indeed, to be at home in the world is to be settled within it: at rest in its fluidity, ultimately, which is also to be at rest in its emptiness. And here we are treading into paradox again: only by returning to emptiness can we be truly full; only by dissolving the self in spaciousness can we come home to the self; only through absence can we come into full presence; the dialogue of Being can only be manifest within the nonbeing of will-lessness. Emptiness, it turns out, despite being a negative, has a positive value. As Lao-tzu observed:

> we shape clay into a pot,
> but it is the emptiness inside
> that holds whatever we want.[334]

It is helpful to note that the yardstick of time tends to banish both emptiness and fluidity. Calibrated time is a tyranny: immune to the Energy of the present, it cannot be hastened or slowed, but can only be identified by the strict numbering of clocks and calendars. In reality, though, the regimented numbers on clocks and calendars are Ideas that can tell us nothing about the present. They can *identify* 'now' according to the nonexistent realms of 'then'—but they do nothing to *illuminate* 'now'. Time is never here—only timelessness is here. Time is a fugitive, fleeing the present; if you join time, you become a fugitive as well. As Ludwig Wittgenstein wrote,

> If we take eternity to mean not infinite temporal
> duration but timelessness, then eternal life belongs to
> those who live in the present.[335]

To join the present is to enter its eternity. To understand that the present is timeless—literally 'without time'—is to see that life itself is timeless, for life exists nowhere else but in the present. We cannot experience life until we let go of all anxiety about experiencing it and drop our awareness into the body's center of fluid wakefulness: the pelvic bowl, which is empty of time. If sensation is our bridge to the present, anxiety is our rampart against it. Mythology frames the pull of anxiety quite specifically: **any time you feel anxiety, you are actually feeling the tyrant within straining towards self-achieved independence.** Straining to make two of one; straining to revoke your natural porosity, to shelter your thinking from the body's sensations. But when we exile sensation from our field of awareness, we stop being where we are: our subtle sense of place falters and is superseded by the urgent proddings of the tyrant time.

If the pelvic bowl and the present are empty of time, it is noteworthy that light, which is widely associated with consciousness and divinity, is also empty of time. Einstein showed us as much: at the speed of light, time literally ceases. From the perspective of the starlight that enters your eye from a galaxy a hundred thousand light-years away, it has spent not so much as a millisecond in transition. All corners of the universe, as far as light is concerned, are right here, right now, and exist timelessly.

The anxieties of calibrated time absorb your attention with issues of what might happen and what you might do about it—*issues that treat the present as a place for solving the problems of the future.* That view of the present is the overriding perspective of our culture. And the farther your anxiety carries you from the timelessness of the pelvic bowl towards the head, the closer doomsday comes and the less time is available—just as the higher you climb a mountain, the less air is available until, in the upper atmosphere, the air becomes so thin you can't catch your breath. The upper reaches of anxiety confine us in the Authority of the head, where we suffocate between the rarefied pressures of past and future. Caught in that citadel of abstractions we grow breathless in the atmosphere of insufficient time. Leaning on the calculations of the hetabrain, we anxiously strive for more control, when what we really need is more breath.

The timelessness of the pelvic bowl is very much like the eye of a wheel or a whirlpool or a hurricane. Its *stillness*—from an Indo-European root meaning "to place"—is what locates us in the specificity of place and the easy, fluid presence of the body: be still, and know that you are here. For the ancients the stillness of the pelvic bowl revealed the place from which we relate to the world; and in that the self exists only through relationships, we can see why that motionless hub is also the center of Being: it is the nexus through which we massively connect with the world around us. The still eye of the whirlpool is also the 'I' of the soul, a dimension of the dialogue that, like Logos, births within us the truth of the present. In that regard, **the still emptiness at our center is the stillness of the present as it lives within us.** It is the quantum vacuum, birthing all forms. If the elemental sensitivity of the breath releases the body's intelligence into fluidity; and the elemental sensitivity of fluidity brings everything into relationship with the still core of our being; then those relationships can be processed and clarified and brought into harmony only once we center ourselves in the pelvic bowl. And that brings us to grounding.

Earth: Rooted in the Present

In our Western industrialized culture the thinking of the body is nowhere more restricted than in the legs, the part of us that is farthest from the head. The natural flow of sensations through the thighs, the calves and the feet has been stifled to a dull stasis. Our language betrays our neglect: when we talk about our *bottoms,* we are not talking about "the soles of our feet"—as a cousin of the word meant in Old Irish; we are talking about the lower extremity of our trunk. What we experience as 'me' generally stops at the pelvis, and what lies below it is merely attached to 'me'. Naturally enough, we find that state reflected in our art: Western theater, for example, is an almost legless art form. The legs are used pretty much as stilts on which the actors perambulate across the stage when required to—typically, to move from one chair to another. The legs cannot anchor the actor's expressiveness, because their intelligence is stagnant. So the power of an actor's performance is concentrated from the waist up: in the flapping of the arms, the lean of the torso, the emphatic bobbing of the head, and of course, in the concentrated expressiveness of the face.

In oriental forms of theater, by contrast, the upper body is often kept open, relaxed and available—and it is below the waist that one finds the strength that really drives the performance, an exchange of power that flows through the legs from and into the earth itself. In the walk used in Noh theater, the feet never lose contact with the ground, and they slide along it with a sensitivity that attunes the whole actor to the world through which he moves. Kabuki, Kathakali, Chinese opera and Butoh are all similarly reliant on the power and sensitivity of the grounded intelligence below the waist.

As is the art, so is the culture. The Japanese return to the earth to sit and eat and sleep. A Westerner could spend months without 'returning to the earth', held apart from it by chairs and benches and sofas and beds and cars. More critical than all of that, our legs themselves separate us from the earth: by and large, we experience them as highly functional prosthetics. We perch on high in the hetabrain, and they sit at the bottom of the "vehicle," as Plato put it, moving us about. We experience neither what it is to live within them nor what it is to know ourselves through them. When we stand on them we habitually lock our knees, which desensitizes us to the earth and also locks our hips. When the hips are locked, the energy in the pelvis is restricted, the lower back is strained, and the responsiveness of the spine is compromised. In other words, our natural energy is stopped up. In traditional Chinese medicine the joints of the body are understood as gates for the body's energy. When the joint gates are open in the hips, knees and ankles, the hips are able to float, as a rowboat floats on water. That is something most adults in our culture simply never experience.

Experiencing the legs as prosthetics is so much the norm for us that it's become almost impossible to *tell* someone about knowing herself through her legs; there is barely the glimmer of a cultural memory left by which she could understand. Alexander Lowen, the founder of bioenergetics, relates an incident in which he was trying to help a woman inhabit the livingness of her legs—to help her experience them as embodied mind rather than mere matter. She came from a strenuously physical background: she had been a dancer, and when Lowen met her she was a T'ai Chi instructor. He took her through two intensive exercises, which deepened her breathing, and then he went straight into a third, during which her legs began to shake. When she finished, she stood up and said, **"I've been *on* my legs all my life. This is the first time I've been *in* them."**[336] Consciousness can only dwell within what is energetically sensitized, and this was the first time in her adult life she had been awakened to that sensitivity in her legs; and she had concentrated on her legs throughout her career in ways that most of us only dream about doing.

When Heracles was on number eleven of his twelve labors, a giant named Antaeus attacked him on the road. Heracles threw the giant down three times, but each time Antaeus hit the ground, he bounded back with renewed strength. The fourth time they tangled, Heracles hoisted Antaeus off the ground and strangled him. Antaeus, it turned out, was the son of Gaia, Mother Earth, who filled him with strength whenever he made contact with her. In a sense, **we are all Antaeus: children of the earth, we have been hoisted away from her by the male element of doing, and are suffocating for want of some meaningful connection with her.** As we have noted, the names we give to earth— "dirt" and "soil"—suggest something you would *want* to distance yourself from. But when we distance ourselves from the earth, we also distance ourselves from its ordinariness—just as Laius did in his carriage, the Kurgan on his horse, and the male gods in their sky. To distance yourself from the ordinary is to distance yourself from kinship; no longer a child of the world, you seek the altitude that resplendently asserts your independence from it. Living in such a rarefied orbit, we have become like astronauts who have departed from the Earth to gaze back at it from afar, but then have forgotten how to come back home.

Fifty years ago Dürckheim wrote, "Today the paramount problem is how, literally, 'to earth' people who are caught in the hypertrophy of the rational intellect."[337] If anything, that problem is more pronounced now than ever before. As the digital age infuses our lives with ever-increasing levels of abstraction, we increasingly rely on "the hypertrophy of the rational intellect" to navigate our way through them. Enthralled and fascinated with the abundance offered by the information glut, we stray farther and farther from the simple abundance of Being—and so too from our own sensational groundedness and presence. And despite the daily barrage of information bits to which we are subjected, we still hunger for more—certain that if given enough of them, we will eventually have all the bits necessary to make a whole. Our devotion to digital knowing is so focused that we neglect and even forget our analog intelligence. The head is in charge, and is doing its best to sort it all out. So much is that the case that our viscera are habitually clenched against the present, and we might live our entire adult lives without once exploring what it means to completely give up being 'in charge' of how we greet the moment—to give up all designs, expectations or ideas about it—and just release ourselves into its waiting arms, wherever that might lead us.

To come to rest in the present like that is also to come fully to rest on the ordinary earth. And the earth is, after all, *what we literally rest on;* consequently, as we lose our connection to it, *we lose our ability to rest*—to achieve the "quieted mind." When we do come to rest on the maternal earth—breathing from our heels, as Chuang Tzu put it— time rests too; as our sense of where we actually are is restored, the tyranny of time dissipates and we find that we are simply here, belonging to the place our senses have newly discovered. The word *place* is related to the Sanskrit word *prthuh,* which means "spacious"; and indeed, it is in the ordinary place to which you belong now that you encounter the spacious spirit of the present. The challenge, then, is to learn how to arrive where you are and pay attention to it; and to do that, it helps to have a clear understanding of what prevents us from being present: what makes it so difficult to 'be'? What in us obscures our sensitivity to place—to the vibratory intelligence of the here and now? What keeps us from being grounded?

Our very being is supported in its existence by all the universe: as we have seen, our lives are affected by the gravitational pull of a single electron at the remotest fringe of the remotest galaxy. The relationships that sustain us are not static, but are continuously expressed through exchanges of energy: where there is no exchange, there is no relationship; where there is a diminished exchange, there is diminished relationship—and so, too, a diminished sense of being. We diminish our being—our ability to be present—by locking up our energies, and we have at our disposal two primary means of achieving that: we can withdraw from sensation, retract into the head, and lock up our energy in *ideas and analysis*—what Dürckheim called "the hypertrophy of the rational intellect"; or we can lock up the energy of our *emotions,* and keep it bound in the body, unable to join the newness of the moment. Both methods belong to the diminished sensitivities of the 'known self'.

We have already looked at how ideas and analysis can promote *unintegrated perspectives* that lock up our energies. *Unintegrated emotions* create a similar effect: **like unintegrated perspectives, any unintegrated emotion will reduce the specificity of your response to the present, dulling you to it.** John Sarno, whom I mentioned earlier, has written about an epidemic of conditions that are commonly attributed to structural or systemic abnormalities in the body, but which he has often found to arise in order "to prevent the conscious brain from becoming aware of unconscious feelings like rage or emotional pain."[338] He has found that symptoms such as chronic pain in the back, neck, shoulder and limbs, fibromyalgia, carpal tunnel syndrome, eczema and arthritic pain are frequently our way of distracting the conscious mind from unintegrated emotions. Sarno writes about the ability of the mindbody to create "a reduction of blood flow to a specific part of the body, resulting in mild oxygen deprivation, which causes pain and other symptoms, depending on what tissues have been oxygen deprived."[339] He calls that effect TMS, short for tension myositis syndrome—and he and his colleagues have successfully treated a staggering range of conditions, often where medical interventions have failed, by helping patients acknowledge and integrate the emotions underlying their symptoms. To his credit, Sarno does not find any such psychosomatically based symptoms to be indicative of a defect in someone's personality: they are inextricably part of our very makeup—part of what makes us human. As he puts it, "Psychosomatic phenomena are not a form of illness. They must be seen as part of the human condition—to which everyone is susceptible."[340]

It is noteworthy that Sarno often finds rage at the root of TMS—for *rage is a concomitant of self-tyranny:* the inner tyrant feels rage at his own fear of Being, and at every instance in which his agenda is thwarted. Nor is he able to fully acknowledge his rage: such acknowledgment is either deemed superfluous to his objectives, or the rage represents an unacceptable contradiction of what he 'knows' of the self. I think it is no mere coincidence, then, that the epidemic of TMS disorders in our culture matches in its scope the epidemic of our self-tyranny—which itself expresses an epidemic mistrust of the female element of being. That brings to mind a harrowing observation by a veteran of the U.S. porn industry: "Nobody ever goes broke overestimating the rage and misogyny of the average American male."[341] And how, as a woman, could you not answer with rage?

Emotion literally means "to set in motion"; but an unintegrated emotion cannot move. Instead of helping to activate the self and bring the particulars of the world into focus, it binds up our energy and divides us from the world. By so doing it limits our responses to the fourth sphere of the mind's sensitivity—the Emotional Body. Some people hold on to emotions for weeks, years, or even decades. They can talk with fresh resentment about something that happened to them forty years earlier. And so we carry around unintegrated angers, fears, hatreds, jealousies, embarrassments, griefs—each of them fragmenting our relationships and stifling our being. Such unintegrated emotions wait beneath the surface, dissociated and invisible until triggered by some often fairly innocuous inconvenience or slight, unleashing a grossly disproportionate response that jerks us out of the present with a vengeance. ("Did you see that driver cut me off?") If you pay close attention to the events that trigger you, you will be peering into the vaults of your own frozen energies—your private cryonics bunker for emotions that periodically resurrect, and then go to sleep again, coiled within themselves, sapping your energy.

If our unintegrated emotions and perspectives are what keep our energies locked up—and keep us from a clarity of being, unable to join the all-liberating present—then how do we *unlock* them? First we should acknowledge that they are locked up in the mindful tissues of the body—so that liberating them actually means unlocking the body's consciousness in such a way that its energies might integrate with our being, and discharge into the world, much as the swarming energies of the sky course through a lightning rod to reconcile with the earth. The main issue facing us, then, as Dürckheim understood, is: how do we ground ourselves? Dürckheim was a master of grounding. His book *Hara: The Vital Center of Man* is a classic on the subject, and he left us eloquent testimony about the need for a paradigm shift to transform our entire relationship to the world around us—one that could be achieved only once we learned to return to the pelvic bowl and "earth" ourselves. Dürckheim died in 1988, but in our own day there is another master of grounding: Denis Chagnon. The strength of Chagnon's work lies not just in its proven ability to help countless individuals recover from illness and sustain well-being—occasionally in contradiction of what medical science deemed possible; its strength also resides in a technique Chagnon developed for grounding that is so simple that anyone can master and practice it. Tellingly, Chagnon's technique is not rooted in idea or imagination, but in the body's own intelligence.

Chagnon's story is known to many people: he developed cancer, and declined the treatments offered by conventional medicine. His condition deteriorated to the point that the cancer had spread through his body, he was barely able to walk, and was given three weeks to live. But he paid attention to the pain that was wracking him, paid attention to the energy of it, and slowly discovered he could alter that energy and alleviate the pain. With that, he began his slow recovery—during which he developed the specifics of his technique, as well as the ability to read and work with energy in others.

Chagnon's grounding technique is easy enough to learn. First, bring your awareness to the perineum—the very center of the pelvic floor. To find that spot it helps to slightly engage the perineum—something you do naturally when you keep yourself from urinating. Dropping your consciousness into that spot precipitates a number of changes. If you are patient with it, you will find that as your consciousness in that spot becomes increasingly clear, it will naturally extend out to connect with the exact spots where your ovaries are—or would be if you were a woman: a few inches below the navel, and to either side. *Those three spots—the perineum and the two ovaries—form what is called the pelvic triangle.* **The effect of its geometry within the body is to locate and harmonize the pelvic intelligence, that the corridor of our embodied consciousness might ground itself there and surrender to it, as Orpheus to Eurydice.** Once that happens, the analog axis can open the self to its potential for exchange with the world. And just as we find in the present a stillness that underlies all things, there is a stillness within the pelvic triangle that underlies the felt self: a deep center of present calm that supports and unifies all of its activities, a home in which the self continuously rests, even as it engages with the world and changes. It is in that borderless, still center of the felt self that present and self can meet in repose—newly sensitized.

An increase in the mind's sensitivity is also an increase in our vulnerability—and we can be at ease with such vulnerability only when there is a commensurate deepening of our stability. The heart cannot blossom with the world's sensitivities until the felt self is rooted in the triangle's dark stillness. In other words, our stability, our rootedness, comes about as we bring increasing consciousness to the geometry that locates and harmonizes our pelvic intelligence. The triangle is small enough in four dimensions, but in five it is bottomless. The easy dialectic of stability and sensitivity made possible by that triangle holds within it the creative tension of the felt self: as the fluid whole of the body's intelligence empties itself into the grounded stability of the pelvic bowl, it integrates into our being, imparting to the body a clarity of the utmost sensitivity. That clarity *is* "feeling the thing as a whole."

Our ability to consciously ground ourselves is made more challenging and more necessary by the historic journey from hub to head made by our ancient ancestors, and retraced by each of us as individuals in our early childhood. We were systematically taught to heed rules rather than our true being; and to separate our thinking from the inconveniences of sensation; and to so dull our youthful spontaneity and wakefulness to the world's calling that we could sit still for hours at a time, day after day, year after year within the four walls of a classroom; in short, we have all been taught since childhood to assert the male element and diminish the female. Evolving beyond the patterns of our upbringing requires intention rather than will; sensation rather than ideation; surrender rather than accomplishment; discovery rather than calculation. It involves the primordial, mythic ceremony of marriage by which the male genius for perspective devotes itself to being in an unreserved partnership. That ceremony never ends, but is played out ceaselessly within the crux of our consciousness as we fall more and more deeply into the spacious universe of the felt self.

The essence of that ceremony is played out in the exercise that closes Chapter Six—the Elevator Shaft—but with this difference: you begin by bringing your awareness to the pelvic triangle: first to the perineum, then to the ovaries. Once the base of the corridor within can be clearly felt, allow the center of your awareness to travel the length of its axis—from the head down through the body to the base. This is not an exercise of imagination: it is a journey of sensitivity and intention, and it will bring to the forefront of your attention any baffles, chambers or shadows that interrupt the seamless intelligence of the felt self and break it into the segmented multiplicities of the 'known self'. Those baffles and shadows emerge as you pay close attention to your descending center of awareness: if you find that it stalls, or becomes indistinct, you have encountered an interstice—a gap in the integration of your consciousness. The remedy is to just feel it: heighten your sensitivity to that consolidated energy so that you can thereby heighten its sensitivity—releasing its endarkened energy into consciousness. As you pay close and loving attention to that consolidation, it will soften and yield so that your center of awareness can chaperone it down through the corridor and into the welcoming receptivity of the pelvic intelligence—which can accept into its infinite womb all our unintegrated perspectives and emotions and bring them into relationship with being. Just as lightning clears the air, the mindful process of grounding clears the body; and such clarity in the body is no other than the clarity of our being.

As our self-divisions discharge, self-supervision gives way to self-awareness, and then to mutual awareness, as the unified self opens to the unified present. When we are grounded in the stillness of the living present, able to "feel the thing as a whole," the stability of our all-inclusive ease enables us to welcome the instability that is necessary to life itself. We can *remain* within the ever-shifting dialogue of exchange because we continue to *process* 'what is': nothing resisted, nothing frozen in a concept, everything assimilated and integrated and felt—the axes of our consciousness attuned to the exchanges that constitute our essential life. To process the present is to be grounded; to be grounded is to process the present. That is what the subtle dialogue is all about.

My mother, whose life of spiritual questing and service and honesty carries her into a profoundly grounded state, calls that state "Being at rest in the Spirit"—and I cannot think of a more apt description of it. Grounding centers us in the ease of 'being where we are', in the embrace of which union we welcome the unknown energies of the all-aware world, and submit to them, and exchange with them as intimately as a child with its mother. Understanding that provides us with some useful tools for reflection: *when you seek to move forward, do you tend to do so by consulting your own intelligence, or by joining it to the world's?* Does your attention reflexively dive back into the familiar paths of your own cognitive 'knowns', or do you discharge it into this place without design? Indeed, you might venture even further to ask: **what does your body's sensitivity understand, by belonging to this place, that you too might understand by belonging to its sensitivity?**

The primary function of grounding in the present is to clear your energy so that you can stand within *its* energy. That is implicit in Klein's suggestion of a relationship between *perineum* and a Sanskrit verb meaning "sets in motion, pours out, discharges." Once you recognize that the energy you experience in your body *is your intelligence,* it is easy to see that **when you clear the body's energy, you are clearing the mind.** In the early stages of learning how to ground, you just subtly lift the perineum, feel the ovaries answer, and let your awareness travel down through the corridor to merge with the pelvic triangle—a union that will carry you into the vibratory life of this newborn moment. Later, when you practice grounding consciously, it helps to begin elementally: first, allow your *breath* to drop into the pelvic floor, for until the pelvic floor is brought into consciousness, there can be no pelvic triangle; then consciously relax your body into *fluidity*—unlocking every cell into mindfulness; and then activate *the pelvic triangle,* and begin to process baffles and constrictions as you lovingly drop all of the body's consolidations into the infinite stillness that waits within it. I find it often takes five to ten minutes of grounding before I can clear the body's energy and come fully to rest in the present. A natural setting can make it easier: sitting by a lake, or on a large boulder, or standing by a tall tree with your hand resting on its bark, feeling its deep-rooted life—all of that will help you come to rest in the companionship of the here and now, and by doing so will help open the heart's gate to the light of the world.

With practice, the perineum becomes sensitized in your awareness without your needing to engage the muscles that help locate it. As the base of the pelvic triangle grows stronger, so does its sense of abiding stability. Eventually you may find that, in the way that a riverbed holds the coursing of the river, the corridor within holds the coursing of the present. As the sensational present flows down the corridor and out through the perineum—which "sets in motion, pours out, discharges"—the clear stillness within the triangle may feel to you like a glowing ember in a breeze, or the tranquility of the moon behind racing clouds, or a stone rooted in a rushing river. And so it is that the all-aware present courses through you as water through a whirlpool; or as the sun rises into the mouth of the Celestial, Two-Headed Serpent of Mayan mythology, travels through its body, and emerges from its other mouth to set; or as the setting sun enters the mouth of the goddess Nut of Egyptian mythology, travels through her body, and is birthed with morning to rise once more. When the life of the present travels through you, imparting the touch of its currents to the stillness in your core, you are not only grounding yourself—you begin to help the *world* to ground. That is, if you are grounded, those around you will tend to be calmer, more settled. If several people ground together, they can help each other ground more quickly and more deeply.

Chagnon's grounding technique is a powerful reality check, helping us shrug off the freight of our culture's self-absorption and the pull of its fantasies. It is the surest means I have found for escaping the bottled-up wasp trap of the head and liberating the self into the clarity of Being. I don't ground because I should, then, but because it is the easiest way I have found to simply 'be'. I ground in the course of my daily activities; but I also sit and ground as a practice—ideally in the morning, clearing my capacity for relationship in readiness for the adventure of the day. I sometimes imagine the circumstances of that coming adventure as I'm grounding, preparing an openness to each situation I foresee: I might imagine being grounded while helping my kids, or teaching a class, or at the outset of a meeting. This is not my way of planning what to do in the course of my day; it is my way of preparing to be present in it.

It is unusual for me to stay with any practice for very long: I typically go into a learning curve with a new technique for a while and then move on once I have integrated the learning, or if I run into a limitation I cannot navigate: either mine or that of the technique or both. My experience with Chagnon's method of grounding has been different—the wakefulness of the pelvic triangle has been unfailing in its support for my adventure of surrendering to 'what is', and I don't yet even sense a horizon: what it offers is as limitless as the energy of the present with which it unites you. The more deeply the marriage carries you into that energy—the more you can rest in its spirit—the more clearly you can process it; the more you can process it, the more deeply grounded you are. Many people come to Chagnon's technique to help them through an illness or injury—and as a tool for self-healing its potency is truly remarkable. I use it to heal myself into wholeness—for which its potency is just as remarkable.

The pelvic triangle locates an ancient place of relationship, one that has been referred to as the navel, the Mind Palace, the hub of Being, qosqo, hara and the root chakra. It is strikingly reminiscent of the pubic triangle so prominent in Ice Age Venuses, and turns up in other ways as well. Katsuko Azuma, a well-known performer of classical Japanese Buyo dance, speaks of a secret art that was passed down to her:

> My master used to say that every performer has to find his own power center. It could be imagined as a ball of steel in the center of a triangle whose apex is the anus and whose other two angles are the corners of the pelvis at the level of the navel.[342]

Azuma's triangle closely approximates Chagnon's—which holds a space of such power and grounded calm that I have come to think of it as the self's womb of stillness: within it the present gently rests, through it the present gently flows, rebirthing the self. That womb of stillness is not in itself a solution to anything, or a destination; it is just the primordial, physical, wordless, sacred base of the self which, centering you in the subtlety of your own wholeness, enables you to let go of your addictive *analysis* of 'what is' and the bound emotions that perpetuate that addiction, and come to rest in the *life* of 'what is'. It is the place in you that most fully answers to 'I' and most readily recognizes 'We'. It enables that perfect marriage in which you are utterly calm, and fully engaged. Once the present infiltrates your core and touches it, then you have succeeded in the heroic submission. In the simplest of terms, that's what being present is all about: as the present touches your core, it lives within you, even as you live in it—and then there really are no definitive divisions left in the world. In that porosity, in that self-achieved submission, you unite with the world's energy, strengthened by it—just as Antaeus was by his mother's.

Fire: The Phoenix of the World

Our elemental, five-dimensional sensitivity is what roots us in the world's. We have discussed air, water and earth; the final element is fire.

Fire is the most vivid and familiar display of the exchange of energies to which we all are born. For that reason it often and variously serves as a symbol of life: in our rituals (e.g., the menorah) and monuments ("the eternal flame"); in our literature ("Out, out brief candle"); our popular culture ("Like a candle in the wind"); and in common metaphors ("burning the candle at both ends"). To look closely at the brightness of a burning candlewick is to see a dancing shape which, like that of the whirlpool, is empty of anything permanent. But it also differs from the whirlpool: the particles that make up a candle flame are visibly transforming as they pass through it. Gases from wax, wick and air are being processed into light, heat and soot. In fact, those transformations *are* the candle flame, just as the energies that unite and transform through the crux of our consciousness *are* the life that burns in us.

The transformations that make up fire symbolized for Heraclitus not just life, but the way of the world: "Everything becomes fire, and from fire everything is born, as in the eternal exchange of money and merchandise."[343] Heraclitus saw all things participating in a worldwide conflagration of becoming and unbecoming. He observed,

> This world, which is always the same for all men, neither god nor man made: it has always been, it is, and always shall be: an everlasting fire rhythmically dying and flaming up again.[344]

The everlasting fire, dying and being reborn, is symbolized by the sacred, mythological Phoenix, which—as singular as the world—continually resurrects itself in a consuming fire: its old form burns away, releasing a burst of energy, and from the ashes a newborn Phoenix arises.

The Hindu god Shiva similarly shows us the world as transformation. Shiva—who like Orpheus was known as the "Player of the Lyre"—is the god of creation and destruction. In one hand he holds a drum, which calls the forms of the world into being; in another hand fire, which destroys all forms and names. The two actions are intimately connected: *you can hear the world call you into being only to the extent that you give the names and forms of your life over to the everlasting fire that sustains it.*

Heraclitus tells us, "Fire catches up with everything, in time";[345] but we nonetheless strive to preserve the names and forms we carry within us. Our commitment to their preservation can prove resilient even when challenged by the rigors of spiritual training and discipline; it sometimes yields only to a shock. Many shamans bear the scars of a traumatic injury that brought inner vision in its wake: Odin was blind in one eye; in some people, like Denis Chagnon, a reborn sensitivity was brought about by ravaging disease. I heard of a Zen monk who had trained diligently for years without achieving enlightenment and finally went to the abbot of the temple to express his discouragement. The abbot said that the monk was right to feel discouraged—in fact the abbot felt the same way, and if within three days the monk still hadn't found enlightenment, the abbot would have to kill him. The monk returned to his practices with a fevered determination. One day passed, without a breakthrough. Two days passed. Partway through the third day the abbot began preparing for the execution. Still nothing. The day ended. The monk was ceremoniously led to the courtyard to be put to death—and as he approached the gallows, he awoke.

Reality is always a thinly disguised fire: to awaken to the present is to see the world around you in flames, a Phoenix being burned and birthed even as you are. That vision throws open a doorway to the ordinary mind, a state in which you see neither abstraction nor permanence, but ephemera: the simple magic of newness and nowness in which we all share. You cannot awaken to that state of mind guided by the idea that you *should* see things that way; like the Phoenix, that state can only be born of a fiery transformation—whether it smolders slowly in the embers of the soul, or suddenly blazes forth as you are being escorted to the gallows. *What the transformation entails, specifically, is an incineration of the self-achieved discontinuities of the 'known self'.* Aoki experienced that on October 2, 1967, and speaks of reaching the "zero point of consciousness." As he tells it, he became literally nothing, and what he knew of the world became nothing; it was at first terrifying and confusing:

> Inside of me, the things I liked and disliked, virtue and vice, being and nothingness, truth and falsehood, light and dark, the world in which the system of order and symmetry is maintained completely disappeared.... Everything that does not pertain to the innermost self suddenly disappears and fuses with the original universe, as one gaseous element with another.[346]

Aoki also comments, tellingly, that the 'zero point of consciousness' enables you to see things "much more clearly than those who live in the 'systematic' world."[347] The systematic hetabrain, which insists on evicting mystery from the world, is in fact what keeps us from recognizing it. Western thought has historically devoted itself to refining its perspectives on reality—a proper undertaking for those who, as Genesis assures us, have been given dominion over it. The efforts we have put into that project have created an elaborate, sparkling framework of concepts and systems of knowledge—but they have done little to help us be alive to the world as it is, or to sensitize our broken hearts to its unbroken wholeness.

In medieval Europe, the first scholastic to argue for the unbroken wholeness of Being was the brilliant theologian Duns Scotus. His term for it was "the univocity of being." *Univocity* literally means "one voice," and Scotus argued that Being, as such, included things and creatures and God and their attributes, and was the primary object of the human intellect—much as David Bohm argued that the implicate order, as such, includes all the attributes of the explicate order and is the proper focus of study for physicists. And what became of Duns Scotus? In his day he was known as the Subtle Doctor; the cultural tide then turned against him with a vengeance. He is with us still, though, immortalized in our language: it is from his name that we get our word *dunce*.

We might think of the universe itself as the 'one voice' through which the limitless awareness of Being expresses itself. The history of thought in other cultures often shows a matter-of-fact acceptance of the univocity of Being and the contingency of all things on its mystery. The sixth Patriarch of Chinese Zen, Hui Neng, attained enlightenment when he overheard a stranger recite a verse from the Diamond Sutra: **"Let your mind function freely, without abiding anywhere or in anything."**[348] The verse, which describes the "zero point of consciousness," stands as a final abnegation of the authority of perspective. At the time, Hui Neng was an illiterate young peasant selling firewood— which, like perspectives, is continually gathered and burned away; but on hearing those words he suddenly experienced the true nature of his mind and was 'awakened'. We can glimpse the nature of that awakening by considering a description of mind that he later wrote:

> The capacity of mind is broad and huge, like the vast sky. Do not sit with a mind fixed on emptiness. If you do you will fall into a neutral kind of emptiness. Emptiness includes the sun, moon, stars and planets, the great earth, mountains and rivers, all trees and grasses, bad men and good men, bad things and good things, heaven and hell; they are all in the midst of emptiness. The emptiness of human nature is also like this.[349]

Your capacity for emptiness, as we have said, is also your capacity for relationship—and there is nothing neutral about it; it is fully sensitized, and wide open to the currents of Being.

Others have also found the dimension of mind to be "broad and huge." Gregory Bateson saw mind not just in the body, but in systems and matter at all levels of life. Physician Larry Dossey coined the term 'nonlocal mind' to describe the observed abilities of the human mind to function in ways that are confined by neither space nor time. Physicist Sir Arthur Eddington concluded that "the stuff of the world is mind stuff" and "the substratum of everything is of mental character."[350] Heraclitus stated that "No matter how many ways you try, you cannot find a boundary to consciousness, so deep in every direction does it extend."[351] Stanislav Grof, one of the twentieth century's foremost pioneers in the study of nonordinary states of consciousness, has noted that "under certain circumstances, human beings can also function as vast fields of consciousness, transcending the limitations of the physical body, of Newtonian time and space, and of linear causality."[352] Furthermore,

> each individual is an extension of all existence.... This means in the last analysis that the psyche of the individual is commensurate with the totality of creative energy.[353]

The mind of limitless sensitivity described by Hui Neng and others lies beyond the realm of the felt self: it belongs to the borderless final sphere of the mind's sensitivity—the felt One. We are born into it by a self-intentioned holocaust of the vanities of separation, and an abandonment to the sensitivities that attune to consciousness. When the fire of the world reaches your core and turns knowledge to ash, the fluidity of the logosmind undergoes a phase shift analogous to the change that water molecules undergo when heat breaks them from the confines of liquidity and releases them as vapor. When the energy of the world's fire ignites that phase shift in your Being, your consciousness opens beyond the fluidity of your discrete body into the limitless ether of the world. Aoki described it by saying that "everything that does not pertain to the innermost self suddenly disappears and fuses with the original universe, as one gaseous element with another, becoming one." Thomas Merton described it by saying that "one arrives at mind by 'having no mind': in fact, by 'being' mind instead of 'having' it."[354] Similarly, the Neoplatonic philosopher Plotinus wrote in the third century A.D. that when man "ceases to be an individual, he raises himself again and penetrates the whole world."

What does it mean, though, to 'be' mind rather than 'having' it? Or to cease being an individual? It is a sort of death, certainly, but it is a Phoenix death of resurrection. The discrete self dissolves, the margins all leaky, and the last vestiges of your self-consciousness vaporize. In the empty spaciousness of the present, foreground and background trade places: you become the background that contains your experience—you become the felt One that contains the felt self. You fuse with the kinship of the thinking world as "one gaseous element with another." Ancient Greeks believed that the cosmos was permeated by the gaseous element ether. It was from ether that the stars and planets were believed to have been made. In the late nineteenth century ether was postulated as the medium of space necessary for conveying waves of light. The word *ether* comes from the Greek word *aithein*, "to burn brightly," which itself comes from the Indo-European root *aidh-*, "to burn." It has cousins in the Sanskrit word *idhryas*, "of or like the brilliance of a clear sky"; *estuary*, "the mouth of a river"; and *edify*—and how often it is necessary to burn away a misconception in order to edify ourselves.

When the burning Phoenix of the world penetrates the loving logosmind and initiates a phase shift, your mind's sensitivity is born into the ninth sphere. No longer does that sensitivity just sustain a dialogue with the Logos—it joins it: it joins the bright-burning, spacious mind-ether of the world; and then the radiance of that burning becomes your radiance. If we wished to name the intelligence that sustains the felt One, we could look to the associations that cluster around the ancient Greek idea of the ether and speak of the **aithemind**. In that the word begins with the first letter of the alphabet, it helps us to remember that the aithemind is the alpha mind, the source of all thinking, the foundation of consciousness. In keeping to the Greek word, *aithein*, "to burn brightly," we are reminded that it is the bright-burning incineration of perseity and its tinderbox divisions that opens us to our true nature, which is part of and continuous with the mind-ether of the present.

And so it is that the Phoenix of the world, an elemental necessity to corational thinking, finally burns away corationality itself. Technically we cannot really call the thinking of the aithemind corational: because the specter of perseity is abandoned altogether, the sort of partnership on which corationality is based evolves into a merger. In respect of that, we might call its direct experience of the mind *holorational*—to mean "the thinking of the whole"; or even, in remembrance of the Indo-European root of *rational*, "joining the whole." When Morehei Uyeshiba recalled the occasion of his own enlightenment, he bequeathed to us a vivid description of the holorational experience. It came upon him in the aftermath of a training session in budo, which is the practice of a martial art for the purpose of self-knowledge:

Then in the spring of 1925, if I remember correctly, when I was taking a walk in the garden by myself, I felt that a golden spirit sprang up from the ground, veiled my body and changed my body into a golden one.

At the same time my mind and body turned into light. I was able to understand the whispering of the birds, and was clearly aware of the mind of God, the Creator of this universe.

At that moment I was enlightened: the source of budo is God's love—the spirit of loving protection for all beings. Endless tears of joy streamed down my cheeks. Since that time I have grown to feel that the whole earth is my house, and the sun, the moon and the stars are all my own things.

The training of budo is to take God's love, which correctly produces, protects and cultivates all things in Nature, and assimilate and use it in our own mind and body.[355]

If the logosmind is the realm discovered when you allow the present to touch your core—an act that we have identified as the true heroic submission—then the aithemind is the realm discovered when you recognize the light of the present, and allow it to touch your core, and live there. As Uyeshiba noted, we have come to call this state enlightenment. When he assimilated the light of God's love, his mind and body phased into the golden radiance of the bright-burning ether, and he was able to understand "the whispering of the birds." Indeed, with such a Phoenix-like revelation, the logosmind's sensations and vibrations turn into the harmonies of song; as the body becomes like air, the world becomes like an aria. It is song that enables Orpheus to call the world into harmony; Bateson found music in the morphology of the crab, "repetitive with modulation"[356]; Sammy, the hero of William Golding's novel, found that "the power of gravity, dimension and space, the movement of the earth and sun and unseen stars, these made what might be called music and I heard it." The music of Shiva's dance unifies all things by immersing them in its rhythm. Natalie Curtis in *The Indian's Book* observed, "In nearly every Indian myth the creator SINGS things into life."[357] And of course Rumi wrote of the bright reedsong that sustains us all.

The rhythms of song are the rhythms of life. We attend to rhythms all the time, often without being conscious of it. It is *rhythm*—from an Indo-European base meaning "to flow"—that constitutes the shape of any form: the replication of patterns, by contrast, bespeaks a mechanical beat. Rhythms arise from the present and tell us about it. The rhythm of a gesture reveals the present, as do the rhythms of branches in the breeze, clouds scudding across the horizon, birds wheeling in a flock, or ants scurrying. It is in the rhythm of an artwork that its deepest artistry resides, whether in the contours of sculpted marble or the undulations of an ink-brush painting. Rhythm is embodiment. When someone speaks it is the rhythm of her voice—its vibrational song—that reveals her life and mind, far more than the specific words she utters: within that rhythm are felt the implicit perplexities of the moment in a way that words, tied as they are to meaning, could not describe. Similarly, it is in the vibrational rhythm of the world's calling—its univocity, its song—that the life of the world is revealed. In the perplexing weave of reality, rhythm tells us about the living and dying of all its various currents: the ever-changing Phoenix—birthed, growing and perishing—over and over.

Fluidity is the medium of exchange: it is what the 'known self' guards against, what the felt self surrenders to, and what the felt One becomes. Technically, gases and liquids are both fluids—but the fluidity of a gas is finer and of a higher energy than that of a liquid. Similarly the exchange with the world in which the aithemind participates is finer and of a higher energy than that of the logosmind. And although hetabrain, logosmind and aithemind are discretely delineated only in our ideas about them, our perspectives on them may be sharpened by considering other differences:

- The thinking of the hetabrain is unipolar; the thinking of the logosmind is axial; and the thinking of the aithemind is the thinking of a field.

- The hetabrain is identified with ice, the solid state of water; the logosmind with its liquid state; and the aithemind with air, the gaseous state. The aithemind is the least substantial state—the least consolidated.

- In the hetabrain, the energies of consciousness—physical, emotional, spiritual and intellectual—are differentiated, divergent, and at odds; in the logosmind, they reconcile as one and come into relationship with the One Mind of the world; and in the aithemind, they are recognized *as* the One Mind of the world.

• The hetabrain looks at the world as though through a window; the logosmind opens a door onto the world; and the aithemind is without windows, doors or walls.

• Whereas the hetabrain maintains a tyranny of the self, and the logosmind is sustained by a self-achieved submission that allows the present to touch our core, the aithemind is sustained by a submission that allows the light of the present to touch our core. In its essence this is a self-union: the self with the Self.

• Whereas the hetabrain adheres to a consciousness of tyranny, and the logosmind dwells within a consciousness of being, the aithemind dwells within a consciousness of consciousness.

• Whereas the hetabrain is centered in the cranium; and the logosmind is centered in the crux of our consciousness—the interfusion of the two axes; the aithemind is centered in the consciousness of the world.

• Whereas the thinking of the hetabrain is segregated from Being, and the thinking of the logosmind is unified with Being, the thinking of the aithemind is unified with spirit.

• Whereas the hetabrain holds to the past and plans for the future, and the logosmind heeds the present, the aithemind merges with the present, replete as it is with past events and future potentialities.

• Whereas the hetabrain is characterized by *doing then*

here—reliving the past and anticipating the future; and the logosmind is characterized by *being here now*; the aithemind is characterized by *being here and there, now and then*. As Hui Neng understood, it functions freely, "without abiding anywhere or in anything."

• Whereas the unipolar hetabrain does not tolerate paradox, preferring to systemize phenomena into tidy schemes of duality; and the logosmind *lives* paradox in the union of complementary opposites that takes place along the axes of our consciousness; the aithemind is centered in a love that transcends paradox.

• Whereas the hetabrain lives in respect of its *duplicates of the world,* and the logosmind lives hand in hand with *the companionship of the world,* the aithemind merges with *the spirit of the world.*

• Whereas the hetabrain attends to only four dimensions, and the logosmind attends to five, the aithemind attends primarily to one—the fifth—finding it seamlessly expressed through the other five.

• Whereas the hetabrain experiences the body as mere *matter*—something to be known and controlled *from above* (i.e., from the head); and the logosmind *identifies with the body* as its fluid medium of thought; the aithemind identifies with *the light of love.*

• Whereas the hetabrain rules over a body of multiple parts in a world of multiple parts; and the logosmind discovers the wholeness of the self by surrendering to the wholeness of the world; the aithemind lives the world's wholeness through the wholeness of the self.

• In terms of the *search for wholeness*—the basic human activity—the hetabrain seeks wholeness by *analysis;* the logosmind seeks wholeness by *assimilation;* the aithemind finds wholeness in *a communion of spirit.*

• Finally, we can characterize what could be called the basic experience of each of the three realms of the self: whereas the basic experience of the barriered 'known self' is *This Is Me,* and that of the corational felt self is the mutual awareness expressed by *We Are,* the basic experience of the felt One is *I Am,* wherein one identifies seamlessly with all Being.

I have borrowed those last descriptive phrases from Jean Houston, who uses them to identify three realms of the psyche. *This Is Me* she describes as the mask we wear, the self we present in our everyday existence, which accords with the 'known self'. *We Are* she speaks of as the realm in which "psyche and cosmos gain access to each other"[358]: it is the state of corationality. Once the dark hood of perseity drops away, the living truth of *We Are,* of *I and Thou,* of self and present, is embraced as something the heart knows beyond all idea. The revelation of *We Are* is a full recognition of 'the human inseparability principle': it topples the barriers created by neglect; it dissolves the rules on which entitlement relies; it announces the continuum of Being to which we all belong. By honoring that continuum, *We Are* opens our hearts to the world's natural spaciousness—just as *This Is Me* is a slippery funnel that leads away from spaciousness. In fact, if we pay the slightest attention when we turn into that funnel and leave the reality of *We Are,* we can feel space contract and our sense of place ebb. And that makes me think of how different our experience would be if, like the Penan tribe of Borneo, we had, as Wade Davis observed, no words to distinguish between *he, she* or *it,* but many words for *we.* Finally, Jean Houston describes *I Am* as a realm of such union with the sacred ground of Being that "no longer do we persist in the pathos of the great divide between self and spirit."[359] The great *I Am* is the aithemind, the felt One.

We might also consider another, much older trinity: God the Father, God the Son and God the Holy Spirit. If, as is written, *we were created in God's image,* we should be able to look to God's threefold image to discover the basic modes of the self. And indeed, the trinity of God stands as a prototype for the trinity of the self. God the Father corresponds to the hetabrain. God was not immanent in the created universe: He did not come into Being with the world, the stars, the seas and land, but stood in Himself, independent of them, and made them—thereby at once modeling and sanctifying the hetabrain's basic division between thinking and Being. As the Pater watches the self from the perspective of the head, so the biblical Father watches over His children from above like a worried parent. He is rational and knows all of the answers, for which his children turn to Him for help. His Authority is absolute: He makes the rules by which they must live, and His entitlement in doing so is beyond dispute. His concern is with the laws that govern human lives rather than with the principles that animate them. He is also more concerned with the sins of the past and the building of the future than with the present, concerns that belong to the judicative hetabrain mode of 'doing then here'—the result-driven mode. By nature He is complete and fully mature—fixed and eternal—beyond any need for or possibility of growth. And just as the hetabrain self lives in a world of duplicates created by its willful concepts and answers and agendas, so too man lives in a world created by the will and agendas of God the Father.

God the Son corresponds to the loving logosmind. Unlike the Father, the Son is a child of this world. He doesn't watch it as from a window on high, but experiences it from within the sensations of flesh. Metaphorically, he is the doorway unto the world, "which no one is able to shut."[360] His life is driven by questions, with all of their attendant passions and doubts, and is in a continuous process of growth and discovery. What He offers to others is not answers, but parables and their attendant principles; not solutions, but the perplexing prick of reality: when the Pharisees brought the adulteress before Him and asked Him to uphold the law—which required that she be stoned—He replied, "Let him who is without sin among you be the first to throw a stone at her."[361] The living of the Son is rooted in the here and now; He doesn't take a shortcut around process for the sake of results; and His thinking is resolutely corational. Unlike the Father, who preaches law, the Son preaches love—the supreme intelligence.

The Holy Spirit doesn't preach. Like the aithemind, the Spirit is associated with light and is without a localized, individual identity. It is unseen and everywhere, without limit and without a center, like the field with which the aithemind is identified. True to its name, the Spirit is holy in both senses of the word: sacred beyond measure, and whole—inclusive beyond what we might imagine. It is the harmony that moves, and moves through, the five-dimensional world.

In thinking about the Holy Spirit, we might further consider that on a personal level, if our soul infuses flesh that is conscious rather than dispirited, then the more we can dissipate the consolidations of the 'known self' from within us, the more the light of the spirit, the burning, transforming love of the mindful world, might shine in and through us. The great Japanese novelist Yasunari Kawabata described how a Zen disciple leaves the isolated self and enters the world of spirit: the disciple

> departs from the self and enters the realm of nothingness. This is not the nothingness or the emptiness of the West. It is rather the reverse, a universe of the spirit in which everything communicates freely with everything, transcending bounds, limitless.[362]

This universe of spirit described by Kawabata is an experience of the felt One, and represents the direct experience of the mystic. It is a direct experience of reality. It is the experience that shows us, as Andrew Harvey put it, that

> at all moments, all manifested and separate things are secretly one with their source of Light—and so with each other.[363]

The three states of our Being—characterized as frozen, liquid and gas—are also represented mythologically: the frozen state is that of the consolidated tyrant, the liquid that of the hero, and the gaseous that of the hero reborn, Phoenix-like, from the ashes of the self. Krishnamurti once observed, "Enlightenment is an accident; but some activities make you accident prone."[364] The phase shift into the aithemind may indeed occur by accident; but our culture, infatuated with its own abstractions, probably makes us less accident prone than most. Opening through the spheres from hetabrain to logosmind, though, is not a matter of accident. Quite simply, once you recognize your own self-absorption, and recognize it as the product of self-tyranny; and once you realize that the world's sensitivity can only stir a heart that is not weighed down with self-directives, and that to willfully direct yourself is to bury yourself in fantasy—then you find yourself free to make a choice. Bluntly speaking, you can choose to side with fantasy—in all its flattering divisiveness—or you can side with Being. To choose Being requires the honesty and courage and submissiveness of the ordinary hero within you, who would rather risk the unknown terrain of aliveness than be stifled in the inadequacies of the normal. If you side with Being, you will change and be changed; but you will never again be alone. Be still, and know that you are known.

Elemental Hero, Elemental Mother

As we have seen, your elemental sensitivities consist of the *breath* that moves through you, the *fluidity* of your mindful body, your *groundedness* in the present, and the *fires of rebirth* that incinerate fantasies of division and sensitize you to a heartbeat that is not your own: the resting pulse of the present, which suffuses and supports all that is. As those elemental sensitivities awaken you to the sensitivities of the world, what you 'know yourself to be' is eventually felt as an anchor that holds you back from the sensational fluidity of the moment. In mythic terms, we might say that when the hero is reborn into Being, Phoenix-like, from the ashes of the 'known self', he allows the fullness of his own nature to be present. No part of him is censored; no isometrics are at work. He is fully at ease with all the perplexities that make up the present. Of course, the present knows no duality: it is neither male nor female, neither god nor goddess, but both. Similarly, the wholeness of the reborn hero is an androgyny that requires the sensitivities of female and male equally: it is transcendent and immanent, changing and resting, bold and gentle, light and dark, particle and wave, discerning and integrative, adventurous and receptive, wild and wholly at peace.

The androgyny of the felt self simply mirrors 'what is'. Until our culture deplores rather than celebrates the willfulness and arrogance of a male strength that disdains its roots in Being—until we recognize and fall in love with and attend to Being in all its corationality—we will continue to live out our impoverished ideas of 'what is', even as we remain stubbornly incapable of recognizing 'what is'. That the consciousness of patriarchy ruling most of humanity has left us addicted to perspective and incapable of integration is amply demonstrated in each of the major problems we face: the unsustainable and malignant values of the global economy, our crushing overpopulation, the insanity of our arms proliferation, the destructiveness perpetrated on our animals and environment by the practices of agribusiness, and the deep cultural crisis of meaning. What cannot integrate will disintegrate. Our culture, like Laius, stubbornly believes that whatever problems it faces are best solved through the exercise of power. But *no tyrannical measures, even the most sophisticated and best intentioned, can deliver us from the Four Horsemen we have summoned forth.* All our fundamental relationships are tyrannical ones, posited on division, mirroring the divisions within. Until we shake off that enclosed, acquisitive, self-serving tyranny, rescue the female element from the shadows, and heed her, we will never come into relationship with 'what is' or accord with our responsibility to it.

'First, Being: then doing' represents at the same time the path of the ordinary hero and the path of the mythic mother. As we have seen, the similarities between the mother and the hero reborn are striking. Both are resolutely on the side of life: both give birth to the new, and do so in love. Both undertake their labors with a self-achieved submission: they can fulfill their soul's journey in no other way. Both serve selflessly, and in that service move beyond self-consciousness into the consciousness of consciousness, which locates their spiritual center of gravity outside of the self: the mother's in the child, the hero's in unknown Being, calling. Furthermore, the mother and the hero do not insist on their own perspectives—they fulfill their work by loving and bending to 'what is'. We could comment, then, that the mother is a true hero; and similarly, that the hero's quest elevates him into motherhood. In fact, the whole journey of the soul is an evolution into cosmic motherhood—a state of grounded sensitivity that looks to the world with love, listens to its need and its calling with compassion, and acts, often heroically, always selflessly, on its behalf. Whether our own evolution shapes of us a heroic mother or a mothering hero is a matter of indifference. We can see that Christ on the cross was a mother, heroically giving birth to a new consciousness; and Mary stood by with the steadfastness of a hero, upholding his labor with peace and love. As a mother gives of herself to her child, wanting it to grow into its own strength and clarity, so too the reborn hero upholds with compassion the world around him and those with whom he shares it. Through his actions and inactions he births a deeper harmony.

As we learn to act from a mother's inclusive love, we also learn to extend it to our own bodies and souls. We learn to mother our own body as it seeks to birth itself into health and wholeness and grace and strength. We learn to mother our elemental sensitivities and help them grow into the world. And we learn to mother our own conscious innocence, to reclaim the spontaneous delight and curiosity and abandon and playfulness and fresh seeing that naturally belong to every child of this world. We can be summoned by the world only when that innocence is reclaimed; and only when we are summoned can we truly find ourselves—for what is true in us is, quite simply, whatever comes into relationship with the present and recognizes itself there. To do other than surrender to the present is always to retreat into fantasy. And that way tyranny lies.

Exercise Twelve: **The Hourglass**

As we have seen, the qualities of emptiness and fluidity and spaciousness are different perspectives on the same phenomenon: a receptivity to the present that allows it to move through us that we might move with it. "Form is no other than emptiness." Of course, it is one thing to theorize about emptiness; it is another to directly experience it.

In this exercise the body is imagined to be an hourglass filled with sand. If you stand in an alert, neutral position and close your eyes, you should be able to relax into the hourglass image and feel it clearly.

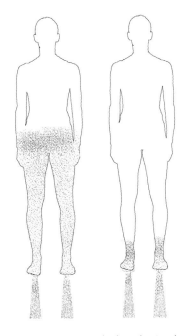

Imagine, too, that there is a little plug in the bottom of each foot that loosens and falls out, so that two streams of sand begin to pour down out of each sole. As that happens, the level of the sand in your body begins to slowly drop, leaving emptiness behind.

Feel the level of the sand drop as specifically as you can, from the top of the head, down past the eyes, nose and mouth, down past the chin into the neck, through the neck to the sternum, and so on down through the torso. If your fingertips are touching your thighs, you can imagine the sand in your arms running through your fingertips into the legs. As the sand drops through the chest, belly and pelvis, it leaves emptiness behind. And on it continues, through the thighs, past the knees, down through the calves, the ankles, to finally empty out through the feet.

Take a moment to scan the body for any grains left behind, and allow them to detach and drop through the emptiness and on out the bottoms of the feet. If you let yourself linger in this emptied state of spaciousness, you will have a chance to discover what it is to hear the world around you from essential emptiness. When you wish to, you can open your eyes and discover how the world looks from that emptiness. In emptiness, anything is possible. You may also wish to walk and discover what it is to step, empty, through the world. To get the most from the exercise, it helps to understand that this emptiness in the body matches the emptiness of pure Being, in which the isolated male element of doing has no place to stand. Whenever you feel the emptiness being compromised, dissociated 'doing' is simply trying to find a foothold.

13 | So as to Remain in Harmony

Keeping the One

Self-absorption diverts our gaze from the light of the world and mires us in our own crowded fantasies; and though those fantasies may proclaim our wealth, the soul—which belongs to the whole and yearns to know and be known through it—cannot be fooled: self-absorption is the truest form of poverty. How sobering, then, to recognize it as the tacit directive of our culture. In myriad ways, subtle and gross, our culture emphasizes 'I' rather than 'we'; it foments an addiction to mere analysis, which sabotages relationship; it presents metaphors for the self that invoke perseity, machinery, cybernetics, discontinuity and entitlement; it instructs us to 'keep our heads' even as it demeans sensation; and it provides a background of distractions and anxieties and incessant white noise, ensuring that we are unlikely ever to come to rest in the whole of the wide world's sensitivity. As a result, we are pretty much blind to our most fundamental relationship—our relationship to the mindful Thou; that blindness constitutes what we have called the "Mind-blindness" of our cultural autism. *And our Mind-blindness supports the modus operandi of our self-absorption: we habitually seek to move forward by consulting our own abstractions rather than the stillness of the all-informing present.* Only once you open to that stillness will you be able to feel the One Presence; and not until you can feel the One Presence will you have any compass to guide you other than the disembodied directives of the inner supervisor. As the Taoist mystic Chuang Tzu wrote, **"I keep the One so as to remain in harmony."** Andrew Harvey commented that Chuang Tzu's remark

> is the essence of the path of the sacred feminine, the
> clue to the sacred marriage, the fusion of masculine and
> feminine in the dark silent depths of the psyche.[365]

The fundamental choice we all face all the time, the choice this entire book has been at pains to clarify, can be stated in very simple terms: **you can keep the supervisor, or you can keep the One.** The first four spheres of the mind's sensitivity represent various efforts by the hetabrain to keep the supervisor: the authoritative thinker in the head who stands apart and 'knows'. The four spheres of the felt self, by contrast, are an awakening to the voluble fluidity of the world, and they culminate in the eighth sphere: the Thou of the Present—the sphere in which the mind's sensitivity thrives in an I-Thou relationship with the One.

The One, which is always here, *cannot be recognized or kept by any who choose to segregate their thinking from the consciousness of Being.* The "fusion of masculine and feminine," as Harvey points out, happens within the "dark silent depths of the psyche": thinking tumbles from the cranial brain and through the corridor within to ground itself in the pelvic intelligence, enabling it to unify with being and pass through the heart, joining the world in action. As we have said, that journey of unification expresses the journey of the ordinary hero. Campbell noted,

> Freedom to pass back and forth across the world
> division, from the perspective of the apparitions of
> time to that of causal deep and back ... is the talent of
> the master.[366]

The "world division" is not germane to the world itself: it is a construct of our thought and flesh. What is germane to the world is the set of foundational, complementary opposites that hold between them an energetic potential for exchange; we have recognized that energetic potential as the entelechy that shapes all life, as the axes of our consciousness, and as the source from which the creative energy of organic growth springs. As Chuang Tzu observed, those opposites "produce each other, depend on each other, and complement each other."[367] The master who keeps the One yields without resistance to the interplay between those poles, for she recognizes it as the weaving of the whole:

she keeps the still point, but holds nothing static—continuously integrating perspective and the "causal deep" of Being. The spacious, subtle, grounded corridor through which the poles of the self come into exchange is what enables the self to be felt as a unity; the spacious, subtle, corational corridor all around us through which the poles of self and world come into exchange is what enables the present to be felt as a unity. The crux of our interfusing axes is what enables us to keep the One.

No one can deny you the choice to ground yourself in stillness and awaken to the felt self; and that means no one can deny you the choice to be whole. But nor is your wholeness something you can keep for yourself or possess. In fact, it is clear by now that **your wholeness is something you offer to the world, as a gift.** Which is also to say that your freedom is something you offer to the world, as a gift. Whatever the world calls for, it is ultimately calling for the liberation of your desires, your energies, your caring and your heart's compass. It is calling for you to live fully, skipping along the cusp of the unknown, continually discovering your truth by living it. It is calling for you to find the peace of mind that can only be felt when you trust in your personal path and feel it in everything you do—a path that yields to and celebrates whatever the moment brings; a path that is never taken alone, because it always unfolds in the presence of the Thou.

Why then do we so often opt for the only alternative—keeping the supervisor? I think it comes down to the unseen 'normal' that lives in our bodies and governs our habits of thinking and seeing. For instance, we habitually believe that thinking is a head-centric phenomenon, and that our best bet in any situation—including our attempts to keep the One—is to take charge: to analyze the task before us so we know what to do. But as long as we are 'in charge', however subtly, we will be spectators—guided by our ideas of 'what is right' rather than by the loving touch of the empty present. Unintegrated ideas always lead to supervision, and serve as distractions from the One.

Similarly, our habits of seeing discover a world full of inconveniences and setbacks—a view that diminishes our capacity for relationship and tends to return us to our culture's belief that "where there's a will, there's a way." Often enough, that belief is proven to be true—but the way of the will is usually the dark opposite of the Way of the Tao or the Logos. When the world is understood to be alive and its sacredness is felt, there is but one Way and it belongs to no mortal;

and any event within the world is understood as a revelation of the Way. When your seeing is liberated from the habits of self-tyranny, you understand that **there are no obstacles; there is only guidance.** The world doesn't produce distractions from the One; it is the One. And the people and trials and frustrations around us are all agents of the One urging us towards wholeness, asking: Can you be whole in this conversation? Can you integrate this chaos? Can you keep the One in pain or injury or within the pressures of your work or your family? We would be nowhere without such trials: every new challenge you meet with wholeness deepens it.

Of course, it can be scary to sail into such encounters 'unsupervised', without the 'thinker in the head' taking care of you. The impulse to supervise is a reflex for most of us. The antidote, as the myths of the world teach us, is found in a self-achieved submission. Surrender, surrender, surrender. You spill the coffee? Surrender. You see your boss coming down the hall? Surrender. You turn a corner and a gust of cold rain hits you in the face? Surrender. The choice is always yours: supervise or surrender. And although stepping into the world 'unsupervised' is scary, stepping into the world in the tangible companionship of the One opens the heart and reveals what we call 'reality' to be an endless exchange of gifts.

Keeping the One is made more challenging, of course, by our culture's chronic Mind-blindness: how can you keep the One if you cannot even feel the One? Nor is it surprising that a culture that cannot "feel the thing as a whole," that is divorced from the body's intelligence and devoted to abstraction should, in turn, deny that there *is* a whole to feel, deny the body's analog genius, and abstract the One so fully with names and rules and institutions and an authoritarian insistence on mediating any experience of the One that it remains elusive and unreal for many. We are further confounded in our efforts to feel the One by the morass of our postmodern relativism—which claims that everything is relative, and denies the validity of any absolute. To say there is no absolute is to say there is no One. It is ironic that our outlook gained credibility from Einstein's theory of relativity, which lays out a view of reality in which measurements of length, time and mass lose their fixed values and instead transform according to relative velocity: an increase in that velocity contracts the length of an object, slows down its time and increases its mass relative to an observer. The concept of reality as a reliable, fixed framework—a framework epitomized by the unmoving ether through which all things move—suddenly crumbled. Losing the presence of the ether was a little like losing the stable, reassuring presence of the personified Deity. As the shock of that loss seeped into our consciousness, the phrase "everything's relative" gained currency and took on the patina of hard-won wisdom.

In fact, Einstein's theory could as accurately have been called the "Theory of the Absolute"—for everything within it serves to maintain the speed of light as an absolute constant for all observers. There is an analogy to be drawn: the more concerned we are with measuring right and wrong according to human laws; the more intent we are on nailing down verities; the more steadfastly we cling to fundamental laws or ideas as though they were absolute measures of value or truth; the more all of that happens, the farther we stray from our relationship with the true Absolute—which is universally associated with light—even when such laws or ideas purport to strengthen that relationship. An absolute is something that is free from any qualification or restriction—which the living, infinitely interrelated One of the cosmos to which we belong certainly is: to qualify it even by naming it is to risk diminishing it. The word *absolute* comes from the Latin word *absolvere,* which means **"to set free"**—and that is exactly what our relationship with the One effects: that primary relationship holds all others in its bosom, and liberates us into the grace of Being.

Yet another hurdle we face in trying to keep the One is our inculcated tendency to separate God from Being, just as we have separated our thinking from our being—and so he remains somewhere else, usually on high seated on his throne. To imagine him sitting there is to harbor a perspective that invites compliance rather than sensation. All such fractured hierarchies set up huge expectations about how we should behave and feel, and many people strive valiantly to fulfill those expectations, feeling any failure to do so as a sin. The irony, of course, is that the whole is actually the least abstract, most real phenomenon there is: it is what imparts reality to its every particular. Every person, every tree, every flower, every pebble is a visible and transitory sublimation of its aliveness; just as you yourself are. And every such instance of sublimation can be understood as an instance of thinking by the whole—the Divine Mind. To understand that is to experience not a diminution of the self, but a dilation. In fact, to see the world's aliveness sublimating through everything around you, and to feel it in yourself, is no less than to experience the sublime.

But the issue of keeping the One is actually even easier and more direct than that. Consider this: nothing exists outside of the present, nothing exists outside of the One; the present is all-aware, the One is all-aware; the present is the thinking of the whole, the One is the thinking of the whole. To come into an I-Thou relationship with the One, then, is to come into an I-Thou relationship with the present, for the present is what we feel as the living whole. It is what grants us the consciousness of being. If the One isn't what we tangibly feel as 'the present', I don't know what it is. The only thing abstract about the One is the names we accord it. So to someone who expresses difficulty feeling the Divine, or feeling the presence of God, I ask, "Can you feel the present?"; and when she stills herself enough to answer yes, I reply, "There, you are in touch with the Divine." Feeling the One is that ordinary. It is that simple. It is that transformative. It is that real. The One does not exist outside of the present—although, like the present, it contains all the resonances of the past (quantum mechanics reminds us that information cannot be destroyed) and all the potential flowerings of the future. We might also note that the present is omnipotent, omniscient and, of course, omnipresent—the attributes traditionally attributed to the Divine. For the purposes of our understanding, then, I think we would not be far wrong if we were to say that **the One _is_ the Present; and the Present—the all-aware, all-creating, eternal, all-remembering, spacious, all-encompassing, ever-renewing, unknowable, unthinkably sensitive, ordinary Present—_is_ the One.** It is the Thou. To feel the loving, singular Present, perfectly at rest and in perfect transformation where you stand right now, is to feel the One. "Be still, and know that I am Present." What all cultures have recognized as the Divine Presence might also be recognized as the Divine Present. The sense of that is beautifully captured by Wu-men, a thirteenth-century Chinese Zen master.

> One instant is eternity;
> eternity is the now.
> When you see through this one instant,
> you see through the one who sees.[368]

When you are continuous with the transforming Present, it lives within you. When the Present lives within you, the One lives within you. When the One lives within you, you are immutably bound cocreators—creating each other and being created in turn. By the same token, to turn away from the Present is to turn your back on the One.

Every culture feels and names the sublime, here-and-now One of the world differently. Discovering it for yourself, though, is something else: it is so much more subtle and vast than the ego that it can only be discovered with *the meek willingness to be carried into a newness that is not of your doing:* the newness of mutual awareness—I and Thou sensing each other here, now, uniquely; the newness of Being itself. What carries us into that mutual awareness is the grounded, loving gentleness of the logosmind, which acknowledges *We Are.* In the fluid coexistence of I and Thou, the logosmind offers itself to the Thou, like Odin crucified on the tree: "offered I was to Odin, myself to myself." And in the way that "the overall number of minds is just one," as Schrodinger observed, the overall number of stories is just one—a story that is infinitely richer than any fiction we might construct for ourselves. What the hero accomplishes in offering himself to the Present is the continuous creation of a new world, a revelation of its possibilities—even as his deeds recreate him. The Present is his shepherd, and everything he undertakes expresses that partnership, to which he contributes with his whole heart. And he understands that all the world is calling for his wholeness with every breeze and insult and drop of rain and twinkling star.

Like the hero, then, your challenge is to learn how to offer up your full participation in the one story; by doing so, you keep the One, and you experience the One keeping you. Newly awakened to yourself, you feel your heart's energy awakening to your necessity, your calling, your quest: a journey of ordinary, self-achieved submission to 'what is' that will not only ask for your fullest participation—it will give you the strength of heart and the joy to carry on long after your ego-strength would have flagged. In that journey—and only there—will you find the deepest harmony of your being: your passion, your intelligence, your sensitivity, your physical and psychic wakefulness to the world emerge as a single wakefulness, able to assimilate the Present and join it mindfully.

Harmony of the self is neither a possession to be attained nor a personal refuge to be created, any more than enlightenment is. Just as enlightenment belongs to the world, and you find it when you allow the light of the present to touch your core, so, too, you find harmony when you submit to the harmony that is. As Chuang Tzu wrote, "I keep the One *so as to remain in harmony.*" The work of the One is the work of harmonizing. To keep the One is to harmonize with the Present. The prairie dogs remind us that 'harmonizing with the Present' can be understood in two related but distinctly different ways. In the first sense, to harmonize with the Present means to receive its harmony into your emptiness and join it, yieldingly: *to come into harmony with it.* But remembering the prairie dogs that sustained the grasses, and Kukrit and Mati-i bringing rain to cool the jungle inferno, and Orpheus calling the world around him into harmony, we might begin to appreciate the second, more crucial sense. **The wild peace of the Present is a ceaseless harmonizing which renews all that is;** the Present does not exist apart from that harmonizing: that work of the Present *is* the Present. Its Being is its doing. You cannot truly join the Present by merely *observing* its work, however appreciative, however devoted your attention. *You cannot truly join the harmonizing Present until you join it in its work*—until you harmonize *with* it: I and Thou, together, deepening the harmony of the moment, carrying the world forward gently in both thought and deed. That, too, is the consciousness of Being.

As we have seen, whatever we do on this earth carries to the farthest shore of the universe, as a fish swimming in the sea sends its wake across oceans. You can move through your world in the ruinous disharmonies sown by the consciousness of tyranny, or you can join the harmonizing Present and help bring consciousness to its grace. You can insist that the guiding fulfillment of your life is to 'get your way' in all that you do, or you can join the Way and discover that your every faculty can contribute to the flowering of its revelatory love. You can hold on to your self, or you can open your heart to the possibility of **deepening the harmony of the Present in all that you do.** That's what keeping the One comes down to: harmonizing *with* the Present. In that work, that *dharma,* that responsibility, lies the most profound partnership of your life: to feel the caring, wild peace all around you infusing every mote of existence with its harmony, and to join the Present in gladness, to partner your caring with its caring and join its deepest, birthing currents in gentleness and companionship. However that work might manifest itself in your life, wherever it might carry you, it is the work to which you are called; it is the sacred adventure to which we are all born.

Of course, if it were easy to embrace the wild, loving wholeness of our humanity, or to live beyond our self-made borders, we wouldn't need the myths of the world to guide us. But we do: we need their vivid representations of the human adventure to countervail against our culture's stifling obsessions with control. *We need their help to clarify and encourage our work.* And because the Present is always here, our work is always here. Join it. Harmonize with it. Anytime, anywhere. So it begins. And you will know beyond question that that work is truly underway—that you are truly keeping the One—when the question that our culture instructs you to voice to yourself, "What should I do?" is increasingly realized as "What shall we do?" We Are, indeed.

The Soul's Hunger

The choice between keeping the supervisor or keeping the One is something you face hundreds of times on any given day, even in the most mundane of events. On a larger scale, that choice sets the bearing for the adventure of your life. On a larger scale still, it is the choice that will determine the evolving consciousness of our culture. We have already framed that choice from a number of perspectives; it is a choice, for instance, between forgetfulness and remembrance, between willfulness and gentleness, between self-absorption and service. We might also add that it is a choice between allowing the mind's sensitivity to accommodate the full reality of the self—in all its seeded entelechy and sacred responsibility—or retreating from that sensitivity into the havens of idea and hoarding. When we open the mind's sensitivities, of course, we open to the female element of being, which lives within us, 'massively connected' to all that is: indeed, to the analog universe itself.

The universe, as we have said, resembles a hologram in that the whole lives in each part of it. By extension, the whole lives in each of us. So just as the present rests in eternity; just as there is a plenum of silence within and around every atom of existence; just as the originating source of matter itself is the nothingness of the quantum vacuum—so, too, the felt self rests in eternity, rests in emptiness, rests in the nothingness that yields all. That is, when consciousness floods the deep within our core, we find there a stillness that is not self-achieved or peculiar to us or possessed by us; that eternal stillness abides there because it belongs to the nature of the world to which we belong.

Traditionally, the part of us that is rooted in the stillness of eternity is called the soul. Our head-centric culture views the soul as something that is trapped in the material body but remains properly detached from its senses. In fact, the opposite is true: our embodied sensitivities actually constitute our receptivity to the soul. When the body's genius opens to the crux of our consciousness, it awakens to the consciousness of the world and recognizes that part of us that is eternally one with the felt, unknowable, unbroken whole. Our deepest cultural assumption—that perseity is the underlying principle of reality—insists that the body contains the soul; but a long alternate tradition contends that *the soul is not in the body; rather the body is in the soul.* The soul is not an animating energy we harbor within us, but a field in which we stand. And like any field—whether gravitational or electromagnetic or morphogenetic—it has no outer limit: the reach of your soul belongs not just to the world around you, but to the heavenly bodies of the universe.

Because keeping the One requires a wholly embodied consciousness, it must be recognized as soul-work. The soul doesn't want to transcend flesh; it doesn't want to escape the 'temporary prison' of the body and reunite with the Eternal. In truth the soul neither wants nor needs to 'rejoin' the eternal—it is born of and remains ineradicably part of that dimension. What it wants and needs is something else entirely: it wants to inhabit the body and live its fully sensational wakefulness to the Present. The dialogue we enter with the living Present is a dialogue of the soul—*the soul knows only dialogue, never monologue*—and is also the world's window on itself. As Meister Eckhart put it, "The eye through which I see God is the same eye through which God sees me; my eye and God's are one eye, one seeing, one knowing, one love."[369] Through the dialogue of the soul we know the world that the world might know itself. Therein lies the true territory of the soul. The corational, present intelligence of the body is attuned to the subtlety of 'what is' with a five-dimensional sensitivity—and **what the soul wants, what it hungers for, what it is spending time on this earth to achieve, is a fully conscious, bodily experience of the Present.** It is through its hunger for, its love of, that bodily experience of 'what is' that the soul is most clearly felt: through the joy of being here, now, in the mutual awareness of the Present, and in love with the specifics of this ephemeral, sacred moment—which welcomes with a wide-open sensitivity all that courses through it. This is your life, and the eternity within you loves being present in all its sensational reality, whatever it brings, and however transient.

In the course of this book we have seen that the mind's sensitivity is brought into full consciousness only once we ground ourselves in the stillness of the Present, a stillness that waits for us at the base of the embodied axis, within the pelvic triangle. We can now understand that *by returning to the stillness of the Present, we return to the locus within us that knows eternity;* and it is in and through eternity that the soul resides. To relax into that bottomless stillness, then, is to relax into the soul's deep peace and into its hunger for the Present—its delight at all the world's phenomena. An agent of the fathomless harmony of the One Mind in which it is rooted, the soul seeks to know the Present as a way of knowing itself; and *it literally awakens to that task when the stillness within awakens us to the Present in which we stand*—when we open our hearts to the unique, never-to-be-revisited moment and experience it bodily, and experience the harmony of it experiencing us. That is what feeds the soul, and feeds its love of the One. And that eternal love of the Present is ultimately a love of Being, which sings to us through all of its particulars. The soul's love of the Present is the love that underpins all other loves that course through us and join us to the world. By that love the soul is nourished, and nourishes in turn all that falls within the compass of its awareness. **Let the soul be hungry. Its hunger is the source of your love.**

Soul awareness is as old as humanity itself, and crosses all cultural divides. In modern, postindustrial societies, though, the soul has become as estranged and distant from our lives as the remote, changeless God who dwells in heaven; as distant as the living Present from which our addiction to doing has exiled us. The soul, which longs to experience the Present in all its sensational specificity, is exiled from the body when consciousness is exiled from the body: until our consciousness deepens into our core of being, all of our pursuits will remain soulless.

The eternal Present, then, is what illuminates the transient moment and infuses it with meaning; and the soul provides our portal to the eternal Present. The soul connects to all that has been and all the potentialities to come: all information is shared information. To surrender to your soul's undeliberated wisdom is to surrender to a vastly sensitive, interrelated awareness that reveals truth without logic. When I surrender to that sensitivity, for instance, I can feel in the room with me now the presence and love of my grandmothers guiding me; I can feel the playful, precise challenge of one of my closest friends, Gilda, recently deceased and yet warmly present with me; and I can feel the presence, too, of the old weeping willow tree in which I spent so many hours as a child. These are not flights of fancy; they are sources of wordless, invaluable guidance.

It is within the soul that our entelechy is seeded, and it is to the soul that the world calls, urging it to step forth and grow. As Eckhart said, God is delighted when your soul grows bigger and bigger.[370] Naturally enough, for the embodied soul is our wakefulness to the mothering Present; and the soul grows bigger as its love opens it through the spheres of the mind's sensitivity. As the soul grows, its natural love of the One enables it to read the energy of the One expressing itself through the infinite diversity of the world's forms, and it cannot but answer. The soul finds joy in the particular smells of being here, now—in the particular colors of it, the taste of it, the passing music of it; it finds eternal kinship and eloquent wisdom in the transient beauty of blades of grass dancing in a breeze, in the tree's embrace of the sky, in a child's tears, in the easy, rhythmic surrendering of the sea along the shore.

Because the soul knows eternity, it knows such events for the miracles they are, and celebrates them—feels gratitude for being present with them in all their luminous specificity. The soul knows eternity, but we forget. We forget that transient marvels we so take for granted here on earth are likely unique in all the vast universe: our birdsong, our trickling brooks, the passage of clouds shaping and reshaping the day, our heaving seas, our quiet glades, our windswept mountaintops, our chirping insects, rainfall, conversation, the breeze stirring the leaves: we are surrounded by the celebratory transformations of a world that is attuned to the cosmos, and is attuned as well to each of us. But **the miracle and the mystery of 'what is' won't even exist for us until we have awakened to the soul's hunger to be present in all the wild chaos and beauty and rich transience that our life on this earth affords.** On the other hand, all of reality waits to sing to you *if you can but allow what is eternal in you to rest in and be ravished by the passing moment.*

Because the soul belongs irrevocably to the eternal dimension, it has no fear—it just has an infinite wonder and respect for life itself. Insofar as there is nothing in the Present that is not part of life's abundance, there is no experience in the Present that the soul fears. All experience is life, and it all potentially nourishes. The stumbling block for us, of course, lies in the word "potentially." As we have seen, although the hetabrain can't *access* the corational thinking of the soul, it can *disrupt* it. The hetabrain's stance is to say to the soul, "You can't rest in the nourishment of the Present now—I've got things to do." But any part of you that is not soul-suffused is uprooted from the eternal dimension—and without those roots, you are subject to all of Fear's grim companions: anxiety, unsteadiness, self-consciousness, isolation, tension and fantasy. In such companionship, you cannot but be doubtful of the harmony in which everything participates.

Ironically, when we come to doubt that sustaining harmony, *we invariably turn away from the needs of the soul to activities that deepen our self-absorption,* activities that might be broadly characterized by the phrase "the pursuit of happiness." That phrase covers a host of sins. When we devote our lives to the task of securing happiness for ourselves, we are too often anaesthetizing ourselves to the soul's true hunger for drinking in the specificity of the sensational, transforming Present; happiness is a dull stasis, a brief bulwark against transformation of any kind: either our own or that of the world through us. As such, it is pretty close to what Joseph Campbell called the unpardonable sin of being vaguely present. The idea that we somehow have an obligation to be happy, should expect happiness, or even have a right to be happy creates an invidious phantasm that people chase numbly through all their years, feeling cheated in the end not to have found it. The soul neither wants nor asks for you to be happy: the soul wants you to *live*—fully, bodily, open to passion and heartbreak and love and awakened to living vibrations of the One. The pursuit of happiness is a soulless enterprise.

The only true enterprise of the soul is in being ravished by the Present and answering its call. In doing so, though, we have to understand that our emotions are not somehow outside of the Present or irrelevant to it, or in some way an impediment to experiencing it; they are an integral part of the soul's "fully conscious, bodily experience of the Present." If you are not present with your emotions, you cannot be present. It's that simple. **Emotions are the energy that connects your humanity to the Present.** Of course, they can also take you the other way when they are feared and unintegrated. But when you are *present* with your emotions, they bring the moment and all its particulars into vivid focus. To feel the subtlety of your being is to feel what is present in your exchange with the world; more than that, it is to be *fully present* in that exchange, which is the ultimate affirmation of life. If you are able to be present with whatever emotion courses through you, a part of the soul will rejoice in the experience of being so feelingly alive to 'what is'. To open to your own emotions, to be at peace with them, subtle and wild though they are, is to open to your life and, by extension, to the energy of the Present; to open to your own emotions, then, is to feed the soul.

Of course, *we can open to our emotions only when we are secure in the eternity at our center.* Without that stability, the currents of the feeling Present tug us off balance and into abstraction. The queasy unsteadiness of that state persuades us to avoid certain feelings, or to hold on to others. The wiser course is to ground our hearts in the soul's bottomless serenity, which welcomes all life without fear. When the soul lives the emotions, it processes the Present. It is on the mutual awareness of the luminous ordinary that the soul feeds, and to which its true hunger returns us. In the kinship of that energy, the awakened soul can only grow in compassion and sensitivity and love. Eventually, a soul that is nourished day by day grows so great that it is beyond our control—it is beyond any kind of control. It is simply present.

The Principle of Grace

Keeping the supervisor binds your consciousness in rules; keeping the One opens your consciousness to the principled unruliness of life. Our transition from a supervised consciousness to one that enters the living awareness of the world doesn't happen merely because we want it to—that transition is your work, and that work depends on two primary skills: the skill of *paying close attention in a manner that is fully embodied,* which engages our female sensitivities; and the skill of *discerning and refining and understanding principles,* which engages our male sensitivities. Principles, as we said earlier, illuminate the dynamic at the heart of a harmonious relationship, and so open a door that helps bring us into harmonious relationship. In the course of this book we have drawn attention to some of the assumptions of our culture that live, often unnoticed, within the patterns of our responsiveness to the world; we have drawn attention to the elemental sensitivity of the body, which connects us to the world's; and we have also uncovered principles that shed light on the dynamic whole that is our intelligence, revealing possibilities by which it can enter more fully into its natural spaciousness. We might summarize those principles as follows:

- What you experience as the body's energies is an experience of mind. To experience the body as matter is to endarken those energies. An experience of the mind's sensitivities as a whole is the experience of the felt self, and can only occur through an abandoned passivity to them.

- Your mind's sensitivities are also the sensitivities of the world, and the mind's thinking is corational.

- The receptivity of gentleness reveals reciprocity in all you do, and so opens your sensitivities to corational thinking.

- The marriage within you of the male and female is made possible by a ceaseless surrendering of perspectives and will by the male to the integrating genius of the female. In other words, that marriage relies on the principle, "First being; then doing."

- The marriage ceremony takes place within the corridor of the embodied axis which, when emptied of its consolidations, allows you to rest in the pelvis and act from the heart.

- The analog axis is activated by the soul's hunger for a fully embodied experience of the Present, and it reveals to our mind's sensitivity the corational corridor in which we stand, and which consists of all that is. The soul's love in discerning the One through all the world's particulars is the source of all the love you experience.

- The more deeply you relax into the stillness of the body, the more spaciously your mind's sensitivity can open to and accommodate the Present.

- As you increasingly live in the Present, the Present increasingly lives in you. A true submission to the Present allows it to permeate your core.

- When the Present permeates your core, it initiates the dialogue of mutual awareness. To be in dialogue with Being is to join it in its work.

- The work of Being is to harmonize: changing, it rests. To join it in its work is to be called to rest and transform with it, deepening its harmony even as it deepens yours.

- The call of Being, once it is heard, births in you a necessity, a responsibility that brings your whole life into focus, even as it imperils your life by calling you into service on a journey into the unknown, in the companionship of the One.

It was pointed out in Chapter Five that the simpler a principle is, the more helpful it is likely to be. Only a principle you have sensationally integrated is able to open doors: to hold onto a principle without integrating it is to stare at the doorway, oblivious to the vista beyond. Any idea, once integrated, converts into a sensitivity; and of course, the simpler a principle is, the easier it is to integrate. It would help us, then, if we could distill the foregoing principles into their simplest expression—if we could articulate the inner dynamic "at the heart of a harmonious relationship": in this case, *the relationship between the self and its wholeness.*

It should be clear by now that there is nothing inert about the wholeness of the self, nor is it any sort of fenced-in haven. When the world calls for you to be whole, it is calling you to be activated: engaged, porous, cocreative, free, playful and present. If we try to activate ourselves, though, our cultural context, upbringing and patterns of thinking will all tend to lead us into mistaking 'action' for 'activation'—and that slight error will put the male element in charge. When we activate *ourselves,* we activate our power, our strength, our cleverness, our will and our solutions. By contrast, **when *the Present* activates you, when it calls you and summons you into wholeness, it is** activating you into your *full sensitivity*. That activation is your wholeness: it is what the soul hungers for; it is what liberates the exchanges of your deeply encoded entelechy; it is what illuminates and makes tangible the relationships that support the reality of your being; and it is what marries your being to your doing. If you are doing any task in the absence of your full sensitivity, however *active* you may be, you are not truly *activated*—because you will be active in the divided, enclosed and willful fashion typical of a unipolar consciousness. Only when the stuttering commands of the hetabrain fall silent and its unintegrated perspectives are brought home; only when our unintegrated emotions are acknowledged and lived and liberated—only then can we enter the clarity of being that is sensationally recognized as our experience of wholeness.

Clarity of being is not merely the polar opposite of self-absorption: it is the state that grants us our fullest sensitivity, and the state towards which all the great spiritual traditions guide us. It is also a state we recognize in ourselves and others by the quality of grace it gives rise to, imparting as it does a felt harmony to every action. We might speak of the grace of someone's gesture, or their grace of being, or of a state of grace that suddenly opens before us and brings peace and wonder to our hearts. We feel the whole through such grace because, like gentleness, it is fully at one with and informed by the Present; it rests in and arises from our clarity of being. **In seeking to articulate a principle of wholeness for ourselves, then, we might appreciate our goal as clarity of being; and we might understand that what would help us towards it is a tangible, bodily Principle of Grace.**

Our unipolar consciousness lacks grace because it intentionally *dampens* our sensitivity and our bodily experience of the world. The tyrant's belief is that the less activated your sensitivity, the less likely you are to feel pain. On the face of it, the assessment seems fair enough—but it neglects to take into account the pain of self-division, the pain of unintegrated emotions lived over and over, the pain of self-consciousness, the pain of a soul alienated from Being in all its comfort and sensational specificity, and the pain of an existence that can never know true peace. A fully awakened sensitivity, on the other hand, alerts your very core to the Present and rests on the foundation of Being itself; and that grants it a profound groundedness that is able to receive and integrate the hardships that inevitably greet any life that is fully expressed.

If to be whole is to be activated into the clarity of your full, vibrational sensitivity, and that sensitivity involves not just the outer senses, but your very core; and if the essential sensitivity of the core is an attunement to what we have called Being, the One or the Present—then bringing *the self and its wholeness* into a harmonious relationship would require that *our core be sensitized to Being.* The true goal, which is also the true starting point, is to realize the clarity of being that belongs not to the self, but to the moment. Understanding that dynamic is enough to suggest a Principle of Grace, a starting point for doing the work that will carry you into the state of grace we call wholeness: **allow the Present to live in your core.** What enables you to put that principle into practice is the heroic submission by which the thinking self comes to recognize its identity as the felt whole. We might further note that what signals that the principle has opened a doorway for you is the sense of *relaxing into the whole that guides you and joining it in its work of harmonizing*—the source of all true grace. If that principle represents the simplest expression of this book's central concern—the point to which its trail of perspectives and arguments has led us—then it might be useful to consider its effect.

Above all, the effect is one that switches what is normally the background of your field of experience to the foreground, and vice versa. That is, **your ideas about the world recede to the background, and what comes to the fore is your embodied experience of the Present, in all its companionship.** In that regard, the Principle of Grace prioritizes the analog sensitivities of being—when the Present lives in your core, so does its vibratory intelligence: the great wave phenomenon, singing through the cello string. The effect is tangible: it changes how the body pays attention, how it feels itself in the world, and how it feels the world in itself. To allow the Present to live in your core is at one and the same time a surrender, a softening, an abandonment of consolidations, a homecoming, an activation of the soul, an opening of the heart, a dilation of sensitivity, a marriage of male and female, a journey into the vibrant, felt unknown, a coming to rest in the moment, and a yielding to the One Harmony. "What is rooted is easy to nourish,"[371] Lao-tzu commented—and so it is with your being. When it is grounded in the fluid, vibrant Present within, and your male center of conscious thinking submits in passive, attentive receptivity to 'what is', your being is nourished by Being; and your pelvic intelligence acquires the foundation of stability that enables it to submit to the subtle, all-informing flux that is life.

The surrender that allows the Present to live in your core is as central to the harmony between the self and its wholeness as is the Golden Rule to the harmony of human relationships. If fact, we can understand its centrality to our wholeness by looking more specifically at its effect: **the Principle of Grace returns the self to the living relationships of its immediate reality and activates our core into the sensitivity and purpose of its foremost role, which is to attend to and integrate and clarify the mindful Present to which it belongs.** Once our core is activated into its true role, the self is activated into its living truth, and then all facets of the self naturally come into relationship with that truth—opening the analog axis to the coursing dialogue between self and world and birthing a necessity that summons each into newness.

The more spaciously the transient Present lives within your core, the more your soul's love will be liberated. As the fences of the hetabrain fall away and the fantasies that oxygenate the authoritative supervisor are left behind, the grace of the Present is revealed in every particular, and your eyes look upon the One. Recognizing the light of the Present, the soul's love dilates through the heart and into the world, where you discover the self. And therein lies a wondrous, golden and paradoxical truth that cannot really be understood, but only lived: **you don't open your heart to the Present so much as the Present opens your heart to yourself.** And when that occurs, you cannot but join the Present in the harmonizing that is its love and its work.

If "allowing the Present to live in your core" is the central principle by which the self ventures into its wholeness, we need to appreciate that the skill of putting that principle into practice—though supported by the sensitivities with which you were born, and by the soul's hunger that lives in you, and by the Present that calls to you—nonetheless constitutes a personal stand against the forces in our culture that espouse self-tyranny, deny the reality of mutual awareness, and shape our lives around a phenomenon that doesn't even exist: the phantasm of perseity. Enacting that personal revolution for yourself requires practice—as much as playing the cello or performing surgery or hitting a tennis ball requires practice. That is why I regularly sit and return to my elemental sensitivity: I ease into my *breath*, release my body into *fluidity*, and *ground*, burning away the baffles and consolidations that block up the interfusing axes. By doing so I find I can recover my clarity of being, that my sensitivity might never lose sight of the guidance of the whole, or of its own corational nature. Of course, like all true principles, this Principle of Grace is only a beginning; but it is a beginning that deflates all fantasies bred of the tyrant's isolation, unseats the tenacious supervisor, and brings you home to the fluid harmony of your true calling.

Love, Ignorance and Balance

It helps to recognize that when you allow the Present to live in your core, *the quality of grace you experience is your strength, your guide and your wholeness.* Of course, human nature being what it is, we occasionally need help to find our way back to it. In the course of this book we have met three qualities of female Being, three Graces, we might call them, who are ready to uphold you in your wholeness and facilitate the clarity of being that evinces it. Those three Graces are love, ignorance and balance.

The first of these Graces, **love**, has been recognized as our supreme intelligence, and is sustained by the soul's hunger to live every particular of our sensational, mundane existence. Aquinas said that the first effect of love is melting. Love literally delivers us from the frozen structures of the hetabrain into the sensational fluidity of Being. Its supreme intelligence, resting in stillness, welcomes the Present, and enables us to discover ourselves there. Given that thought is corational, it is not surprising to find that love suffuses all the traits of mutual awareness: gentleness, gratitude, fluidity, surrender, spaciousness, ease, playfulness, groundedness, our wakefulness to the ordinary, our sense of place, and the kinship of We Are: all are underpinned by love.

When the soul's love is liberated, it drinks in every detail of the manifest Present. That love allows your heart to flower, and it welcomes the vibratory world with grace, integrating whatever it may bring. That love grants you the sensitivity to stand gently, walk gently, sit gently, speak gently and harmonize gently, aware of the reciprocity of all relationships. That love dilates your awareness into the Present with devotion, and deepens it into the body. It restores consciousness to the world and enables it to talk to you. Rumi referred to the One Presence as The Beloved, and all the world spoke to him in ecstatic eloquence. If the One Presence is not beloved, it will remain mute. As the writer of the great medieval work *The Cloud of Unknowing* made clear in "The Epistle of Discretion," God is neither silence nor speaking, neither fasting nor eating, neither loneliness nor company, "nor yet any of all the other two contraries. He is hid between them, and may not be found by any work of thy soul, but *all only by love of thine heart*. He may not be known by reason, He may not be gotten by thought, nor concluded by understanding."[372] Similarly, the Present is hid between contrary poles, and cannot be known, gotten, concluded or found, but only loved. In loving the Present you offer it a gift that reveals *its* gifts. As we noted earlier, "If you don't love being here now, you will resist it—and such resistance is always successful." If you don't love being here now, you cannot root yourself in its eternal stillness, and your abstractions will tip the world into the coarseness of the 'known'.

Coming into partnership with the Present relies on love, but it also means giving up every temptation towards what is "fixed, solid and eternal"—the bastions of bound energy; and that means dispossessing your body of everything that does not belong to the Present, of everything that keeps it from fluidity, of everything that stifles its analog intelligence. As we have come to understand, that entails letting go of all your unintegrated perspectives and emotions and allowing them to join Being. And that means letting go of everything that is deliberately *forgetful* of the Present. Everything from which the fantasies of the hetabrain are constructed. Everything we have termed 'endarkenment'. Every anxiety-induced construct of the past or the future. Every duplicate of 'what is'. Every shadow in the body that obscures its subtlety with neglect. It entails a deliberate surrender of any thinking that might cut itself off from the grace of Being, and of any *wish* for such thinking. In short, living in partnership with the Present requires the fluid emptiness and honesty and courage of the second of our three Graces: **self-confessed ignorance.** Only ignorance enables you to say, "Guide me": when there is no knowing, there is simply nothing to talk to yourself about; there is just an energized clarity that lies open to the riches of the all-aware, vibratory Present and its tangible companionship. As Kakuzo Okakura wrote of the great masters in *The Book of Tea*, "Seeking always to be in harmony with the great rhythm of the universe, they were ever prepared to enter the unknown."[373]

Self-confessed ignorance is a vulnerable state: it topples the aegis of the supervisor and leaves you exposed to the world; but by making peace with your own ignorance you open to the fluid intelligence of Being. Indeed, as helpful as your ideas about what Being is and how to lean on it might seem, the unity of Being is of such paradoxical subtlety that any *authoritative idea* about it has the immediate effect of rendering it undetectable—staring at the doorway, you miss the world. But when the authority of the supervisor topples, so does the need for compliance—and you are left with the opportunity to grow into your kinship with the Mindful Present. If you enter the dialogue that constitutes Being, and heed its guidance, you risk the caring that will amplify that guidance; you risk discovering what Dietrich Bonhoeffer called "the loving obligations of the moment." For just as love and ignorance carry you into the Present, they carry you into responsibility. Life confronts life. You confront Thou. And in the exchange that passes between you, you will be summoned towards what the Book of John calls *having life, and having it more abundantly.* The felt Present calls for all the energies that the gift of your freedom liberates. As Frederick Buechner said, "God calls you to the place where your deep gladness and the world's deep hunger meet."[374]

And so we come to a question, born of self-confessed ignorance, that never elicits an answer but always elicits a response; one that welcomes the Living Thou in the fullness of its ability to guide us. It is a question that is grounded in the wild peace of the Present and is offered to the felt whole of its manifest grace: "*What do you ask of me?*" If you can let the supervisor fall like a painted backdrop and allow that question to permeate the roots of your core, **the Present will answer you by moving you.** If you offer no resistance to that movement, you will join the Present, join the flow and the certainty and the newness of it, exchanging gifts with every breath—keeping the One. Deepening the harmony of what is here, now.

> The Master is her own physician.
> She has healed herself of all knowing.
> Thus she is truly whole.[375]

To 'love' and 'self-confessed ignorance' we can add the third Grace that helps us harmonize with the Present: **balance.** Balance is fundamentally *a relationship of harmony between a felt whole and its still* *point*. The still point is not a static or fixed phenomenon, but a bottomless, dynamic place of rest that always answers to the whole. The more sensitively you balance yourself within it, the more sensitively you can "feel the thing as a whole". Maintaining that balance means you can't afford to hold on to anything else—not to an emotion, a preconception, or your own tiredness. The felt whole revealed by a still point might be the one that helps you balance on a tightrope, sing a song, play a tennis game, or pray; it is what sustains both the grace of the dancer and the grace of the moment. Relaxing into that whole and balancing within its specificity enables you to move with it and harmonize with it as no abstract idea ever could. Think of balancing on a bicycle: it requires above all a sensitivity to 'what is', which you can only achieve by dropping out of the tyranny of the head and into the subtle relationship between the whole of you on the bicycle and the whole of the earth on which you are poised. The relationship of your center to the whole is always changing—yet balance maintains that relationship, for **balance is a process of continuous integration.** In general, we might say *you are brought into balance—into the still point—by a remembrance of the whole, and are thrown off balance by the deliberate forgetfulness of neglect.*

Of course, if you rely on *ideas* to foster remembrance, you will only strengthen the stuttering chatter of the monologue. Ideas render the world static; they render the Present as a destination, as though we could arrive in it. As soon as we feel we've *arrived* in the Present, it passes us by. We don't *arrive* in the coursing intelligence of the Present—we balance there and feel it also balanced within us. That is, when the still, transforming grace of the Present touches your core, and you welcome its living companionship, *you allow the stillness of the world to live within you and speak to what is most personal in you;* and that stillness will show up the swarming, luminous specificity of the world around you in the way that a silence sensitizes you to a whisper, or a moonless night opens your eyes to the faintest starlight, or a fresh snowfall alerts you to the merest splash of color.

Our sense of balance gives us stability without fixity. It is a form of remembrance that rests in stillness, orients us to the One, and feels the birthing and dying of all that is as an inexhaustible dance coursing through your very bones. Once you partner the Present with the light-heartedness of the hero, the still point becomes the pivot that enables you to turn into the whirl and the ease of its wild peace, helping to usher the world forever into newness. To live that dance, grounded within it, is to become a conscious cocreator of it. Your soul's path—the one that is seeded in your heart—reciprocates the world's caring with caring of your own, and liberates your deep compassion as it unfolds. It is a path that twists and turns as it bends to each moment, balanced within love, balanced within the fluid honesty of ignorance, balanced within the stillness that is balanced within the swirl; and balanced ultimately in the grace of Being. The gifts that are exchanged along the way cannot be anticipated or planned, but only celebrated with an open heart.

Naturally, when you are off balance, you will tend to hold on to things to keep from falling—you hold on to what you 'know': to perspectives, ideas and 'shoulds', to structure, to status, to what is 'right', to the vanities and judgments of the ego, to past hurts and the armored tensions of your body. You bind up not just your energy, but the world's. Therein lies the seed of the tyrant in each of us. The inner supervisor.

If "allowing the Present to live in your core" is the Principle of Grace—the submission by which we relax into the guidance of the whole and discover our soul's work—then we might look again at the qualities of female being that, as they bless us, facilitate that submission: **love, ignorance** and **balance**, or the mnemonic LIB. It is worth noting that each of those Graces expresses a clarity of being and rests in grounded gentleness—the medium by which we open to the five-dimensional subtleties of the Present and remain in service to it. We could summarize those Graces as follows:

> Love of 'what is', which supports the world in consciousness and enables it to talk to us, even as it carries us into responsibility.

> Self-confessed ignorance, which topples all duplicates and the inner Authority who supervises them. In the absence of that supervisor, we enter the loving partnership of the sacred Present.

> Balance, which actively integrates the whole even as it centers us within its dance—summoning us along the path of our soul's eternal, wakeful hunger.

As the gentle Graces guide our surrender to the all-aware Present, its stillness descends more deeply into its our consciousness, and our mind's sensitivity opens more fully to the mutual awareness of its reality. In our partnership with the Present, our souls grow into the world, deepening its harmony: we deepen it in love, deepen it in ignorance, deepen it in balance. That is the beginning of the hero's journey: venturing into the unknown, you enter the subtle logosmind, even as the Logos enters you. The seed of the ordinary hero lies in each of us.

The Task Ahead

The historic journey our culture has made over the millennia from hub to head has been examined from many perspectives over the course of this book, as has the next journey that faces us: **from the head through the inner corridor to open our axial consciousness, and on through the summoning necessity of the analog axis into the mutual awareness of the living Present.** On a cosmic scale, it almost seems that humankind was charged with one task of heroic sacrifice, and now faces another of heroic integration. On the one hand, we have over the past millennia *sacrificed our own wholeness* that we might go forth and gather light-filled perspectives on every conceivable facet of the cosmic body—from the mathematics of the Big Bang to the double helix in our cells, to the six different flavors of quarks. Our achievements in that regard have been commensurate with our heroic sacrifice. But we are charged now with a second task: *enfolding those hard-won perspectives back into wholeness and achieving insight on ourselves.* A failure to do so will mean that our species might never find its way home from this particular journey.

We cannot turn the laden ship of our culture around for the homecoming without taking stock of the 'normal' that currently sets its course. The word *normal* comes from the Latin word *norma*, which means "rule, pattern" (reminding us that 'normal' is never 'principled'); and norma itself is related to a Greek word that literally means "one who knows." The 'normal' we have defined for ourselves makes it natural to inhabit the willful tensions of rules and knowing rather than lean on the companionship of the Unknown Present; it tells us to trust more in the empty promise of self-centeredness than in the living guidance of the One; it trains us to trust analysis, and neglect sensitivity.

Our 'normal' is the consciousness of the tyrant. Changing our course and setting a bearing for home—home to the Present that waits to greet us and guide us—is a kind of revolution that begins not on some grand scale, but on a deeply personal one. Quite simply, when you join the Present in its work of harmonizing—when you feel that work as a whole, in all its coursing specificity, and deepen it, and deepen with it—the ripple effect makes it easier for all those around you to recognize the grace of Being and join in as well. That personal work, as we have seen, begins with a loosening of the habits of seeing, judging, thinking and feeling that determinedly fracture your life, and it leads you on an ordinary, elemental, disorienting journey of submission that teaches you by degrees to relax into the infinitely subtle guidance of the whole. When you discover the stillness of the Present within you, feeling you even as you feel it, the spark of mutual awareness is ignited. Blazing in the tinder of your soul, it will activate your adventure and leave you fully sensitized to the mystery and corational grace of 'what is'. Wherever that adventure might lead, it will inevitably carry you into the wonder and wounding and serenity of belonging more and more deeply to this world—of living in it more fully even as it lives more fully in you. The alternative is clear. If we carry on with business as usual, hoarding ourselves within the painted scrim of our normality, life will suffer: our life, the life of those around us, and the life of the world on which we depend.

Whenever self-tyranny takes hold, the mystery that sustains our own wholeness starts to vanish from our sight—just as Eurydice did—and we are left with the 'known'. The known, of course, is abstract; it is therefore forgetful; it can therefore be turned into an object. That is what happens to the self. It becomes bound, like an object, in its fixed idea of itself. But the 'known self' is never here. Only the felt Present is here, and you a part of it. It holds who you are like a secret, ready to be discovered and burned away again. That's life. That's aliveness. That's the wondrous freedom of Being. Discovering it doesn't happen once, like finding your lost keys; your freedom is something you find anew each time you offer it to the Present. And doing so is as easy as forgetting who you know yourself to be, and remembering the world that holds your very life in its lap.

The real voyage of discovery consists not in seeking new landscapes, but in seeing with new eyes.

—Marcel Proust

Appendix

A Watched Photon Never Waves

Nobel Prize–winning physicist Richard Feynman had a remarkable knack for presenting complex issues in the simplest terms possible. He candidly admitted that nobody understands quantum mechanics and summed up its bizarre nature by singling out "a phenomenon which is impossible, *absolutely* impossible, to explain in any classical way, and which has in it the heart of quantum mechanics. In reality, it contains the *only* mystery."[376] The phenomenon of which he spoke is exemplified by the double-slit experiment. It not only baffles all attempts at logical explanation—it also raises fundamental questions regarding the relationship between consciousness and matter.

The story of the double-slit experiment spans more than two centuries; it has been called the most beautiful and most elegant experiment in the history of science. As new questions have been raised, it has been adapted to answer them—and in the process, the mystery it presents has only deepened. It seems fitting, then, to present the story of the double-slit experiment by framing it within a series of questions.

Is light made up of particles or waves?

Sir Isaac Newton studied light extensively and concluded in 1672 that light was a stream of particles, which he called corpuscles. But in 1801 another English scientist, Thomas Young, demonstrated that light was waves. The apparatus he used could not have been simpler: a light source was directed onto a curtain with two parallel slits in it, and beyond the curtain was a screen. If light were particles, it would pass through the narrow slits like bullets and show up on the screen as two broad bands. If light were waves, it would diffract at the slits and spread out; beyond the curtain the waves from each slit would cross each other and show up on the screen as an interference pattern: narrow bands of light separated by narrow bands of shadow. The explanation for that pattern is straightforward. Where two waves meet at the screen 'in phase' (meaning the crests precisely converge) they create superwaves and show up as bands of light; where they meet 'out of phase' (meaning the crests of one wave precisely converge with the troughs of the other) the waves cancel each other out, creating the bands of shadow. Such interference is similar to what is seen when ripples interact in a bathtub or on a puddle.

When Young tried his experiment and looked at the screen, he saw narrow bands of light separated by narrow bands of shadow—the interference pattern. Particles cannot create an interference pattern, so Young thought he had proved that light was waves.

But then, a hundred years later, Einstein's work on the photoelectric effect demonstrated that light consisted of particles. To solve the finding that the maximum energy of an electron ejected from a material by light was determined by the frequency rather than the intensity of the light, Einstein speculated that light consisted of little packets, which he named photons—and that the energy in a packet was determined by its frequency. So to the question "Is light particles or waves?" we would have to answer, "It is neither." It is rather something that under certain conditions demonstrates wavelike behavior, and under other conditions behaves like particles. As we now know, energy (such as light) and matter (such as atoms) are really two forms of the same thing. So that raises the question: if *light* exhibits a sort of dual nature, might the same be true of *matter*?

Do the particles that make up matter behave like individual objects, or like waves?

We can say a fair bit about electrons that makes them appear to be discrete, predictable objects: they have a well-defined mass, a specific electric charge, and something called spin angular momentum. If we had use of an electron gun similar to the ones in TV picture tubes, we could fire these 'objects' at randomized angles towards a barrier with two narrow slits in it, like Young's curtain. Beyond that barrier we could place a phosphor screen that would produce a tiny burst of light when hit by an electron. Once we set up our apparatus and started shooting, we would naturally expect the electrons to create a 'bullet pattern': two broad, overlapping bands. But they don't—we see the same interference pattern of narrow bands of light separated by bands of shadow that was produced by Young's light experiment. In fact we would see that same pattern were we shooting atoms or molecules. But how can two narrow streams of fast-moving particles interact to form an interference pattern? Quite simply, they can't. It's one thing to understand how light waves can meet 'in phase' or 'out of phase' to create alternating bands of light and shadow. But two particles that meet at the screen should simply hit it with twice as much matter. How are the shadows created, then? The law of conservation of mass/energy tells us that matter can't just disappear. We also know that to change the path of a particle (i.e., to deflect an electron from the band of shadow into the band of light), a force has to be applied to it from somewhere (Newton's second law of motion). None of it adds up: somehow the electrons leave the gun one by one like bullets, pass through the slits and arrive at the screen one by one like bullets—but interact like waves along the way to form bands of light and shadow.

Maybe something about passing through a narrow slit causes an electron to exhibit wavelike properties. Perhaps if we temporarily block slit two, we could study the electrons coming through slit one and figure out what's happening. But as soon as we block slit two, the interference pattern disappears and a single broad band appears on the screen. Areas that were in shadow before are suddenly illuminated, part of the bright band. But how does an electron passing through slit one know that slit two is blocked, so that it can carry on into an area that otherwise would have been in shadow?

Maybe we can get some answers if we try to fool the electrons. For instance, if slit two is closed when we fire the electron gun, but then we open it just before the electrons reach the barrier, then we might expect the ones that got through slit one to continue into the shadow area. This has been tried experimentally many times, though, and the electrons cannot be fooled. The behavior of an electron correlates exactly to the state of the other slit at the instant the electron passes through its own slit. We have to concede that each electron seems to 'know' whether the other slit is open or closed, and its knowledge seems to be infallible. This transfer of information over a distance is the aspect of quantum mechanics that most confounds scientists. As physicist Henry Stapp wrote:

> The central mystery of quantum theory is, "How does information get around so quick?" How does a particle know that there are two slits? How does the information about what is happening everywhere else get collected to determine what is likely to happen here?[377]

Perhaps we should take a closer look at how the electrons interact.

Is there some kind of interaction among the electrons that creates the interference pattern?

It may be that there is something about the shared presence of electrons that somehow changes or otherwise affects them. But we have a way around this. We can open both slits and set the electron gun to fire a single electron at a time. The solitary electron should logically travel like a bullet and, having no others to interfere with, fall into the wide-band pattern. If we were then to slowly increase the firing rate of the electron gun, at a certain point we should have enough electrons to create the interference pattern.

But no! When the experiment is set up, firing one solitary electron at a time, the ones that pass through the slits still build up an interference pattern—one electron at a time. In fact, as astrophysicist John Gribbin has noted,

> If we took a thousand identical experiments in a thousand different laboratories, and let one particle pass through each experiment, we could add up the thousand different results and still get an overall distribution pattern in line with diffraction.[378]

Even more confounding: if each time we fire a solitary electron we close slit two in the instant before the electron reaches the barrier, the electrons that pass through slit one will arrive on the screen in the wide-band pattern, somehow 'aware' of the state of the other slit. That is impossible according to any of our classical paradigms, and yet it happens infallibly. Reality apparently lies well outside the realm of those classical paradigms. Ripples in our bathtub interact with each other; an electron falls into an interference pattern even when it has nothing else to interact *with*. Unless it's interacting with itself. But an electron can only pass through one slit or the other. It can't be in two places at once, can it? Nor could it 'decide' at the last instant to split itself in two and send half of itself through each slit, to instantly re-constitute as one before it hits the screen. But if a single electron can only pass through one slit, there can be no diffraction from the other slit with which to interact. And yet the interference pattern tells us that two waves are interfering. Let's see if we can reduce our variables.

Does an electron pass through only one slit, or both slits, or—dare we ask—neither slit?

Suppose that, as we fire single electrons at the barrier with two slits, we were to shine a beam of light across the back of the barrier, so that an electron coming out of the slits would have to pass through it. When an electron crosses a light, it produces a flash. By watching the flashes we could answer our question, and we would also know by watching the screen where each electron went when. So we set up the experiment, firing electrons one at a time, and, lo and behold, we seem to be getting somewhere: the electrons are clearly passing through just one slit at a time, and are evenly distributed between the two slits. But then, when we turn our attention to the screen to find out which electron is going where, we see that the interference pattern has disappeared, replaced by the bullet pattern. How can that be? We switch off the light, and the interference pattern returns. We switch the light back on, and the bullet pattern comes back.

Okay, maybe the intensity of the light is affecting the electrons as they pass through it. What happens, then, if we slowly turn the light down? Nothing changes at first, so we keep turning it down until it is so faint that some of the electrons pass through it undetected. Now we start to notice something peculiar: the interference pattern starts to reappear faintly behind the bullet pattern. If we keep turning the light down until we are missing half the electrons, we have one-half of an interference pattern and one-half of a bullet pattern. Each electron seems to 'know' if it has been detected, and it reacts accordingly.

Let's switch tactics, then. We'll go back to the beginning, and instead of turning down the intensity of the light, we'll lower its energy by lengthening its wavelength (i.e., changing its color). Alas, this produces a similar result: at the exact point that the wavelength becomes so large that we can no longer tell which slit an electron has passed through, the interference pattern is restored. The light isn't missing any of the electrons; we just can't tell from their flashes which slit they passed through. In fact, however we modify the experiment, we find that the interference pattern returns at the exact moment that we lose information about the path of the electron: that is, its wave characteristics reappear when we can't determine its path. Can it really be that *the wavelike behavior of the electron* is contingent on whether or not *we can determine its path*? Just how closely connected are those two phenomena? What would happen, for instance, if we made the information about its path available for the first half of the electron's journey, and then erased it before the electron hit the screen? If the information were erased, would the particulate behavior of the electron be reversed?

Does an electron's behavior take into account an erasure of information?

Say we created an interference pattern using two streams of particles, and then devised a way of tagging the electrons in one stream so that we could discern their paths; but then before any particles hit the screen we erased the tags so that ultimately we would have no way of knowing which particle had come from which stream. If it was actually *our status as an observer*—whether or not we could discern the path of the particle—that made it behave like an object, and we have changed that status by eliminating the tag, then the question is: will the electron 'know' that and exhibit its wavelike properties?

This experiment was actually performed by a group at the University of California at Berkeley, led by Raymond Y. Chiao, and is known as the quantum eraser experiment. First the group crossed the paths of two identical beams of light at a half-silvered mirror. Such a mirror lets half the light pass straight through, the way plain glass does, and reflects half the light as a regular mirror would. When the identical beams of light met at the half-silvered mirror, it intermixed them into two new beams: one reflected beam and one that passed straight through. The photons in the new beams could not be traced back to either of the initial beams—and sure enough, when each of the new beams arrived at a detector, it created an interference pattern. Then the experimenters tagged one of the initial beams with a polarizer, so that the photons in the new beams could be sorted into polarized and not polarized, and their paths could be determined. Amazingly, the interference pattern disappeared. Then the experimenters took two additional devices that admitted only light polarized in one direction and inserted them just in front of the detectors, erasing the ability to distinguish the path of any of the photons. Instantly, the detectors showed that the interference pattern had been restored.

Strange as it may sound, then, it would seem that it is our status as an observer—whether or not we can determine the path of a particle—that makes it behave like a particle rather than a wave. Heisenberg himself suggested that the path of an electron does not even exist until we observe it. Many current physicists accept that a particle exists only potentially, as a mathematical wave function, until it can be observed, at which point the wave function 'collapses' into a real particle. Scientist David Darling sums up that view, known as the Copenhagen interpretation, by writing: "it is the mind—the mirror in which the object is reflected and becomes the subject—that serves as the essential link between mathematical possibility and physical actuality."[379] No one is able to explain how an electron can process whether or not its history could be ascertained, or how it can respond to that information infallibly; but if mind is distinguished by the ability to process information and respond to it, we can begin to understand why David Bohm came to the position that matter and mind cannot be understood as two. How can we be sure, though, that what is forcing a particle to change its behavior is actually our ability to gain information about its path, and not the intervention of our detection equipment? Yet another adaptation of the double-slit experiment addresses that.

Is the collapse of a particle's wavelike behavior actually precipitated by a change in the status of our information about it, or is it rather an effect of our physical intervention?

Leonard Mandel and coworkers at the University of Rochester devised an ingenious form of the double-slit experiment to answer this question. I offer a much-simplified explanation of it. To begin with, high-energy light from a laser hits a half-silvered mirror, which divides it into two beams: Beam A to the right and Beam B to the left. Each of those beams is then converted into two new low-energy beams. That is done with the use of two 'down-converters', specialized lenses that split a high-energy photon into two lower-energy photons. So high-energy Beam A hits the converter on the right, and out of it come two low-energy beams, a1 and a2; high-energy Beam B goes to the converter on the left, and out come low-energy beams b1 and b2.

Now it's time to intermix the low-energy beams. So a1 is directed to the left, where it intermixes with b1, and together they travel to detector number 1. They are being watched over by Mary, our experimenter on the left. At the same time, b2 is directed to Fred's detector on the right, where it intermixes with a2. Once b2 and a2 intermix at Fred's detector, he has no way of telling whether a photon landing there originally came from Beam A or Beam B. In other words, the photon paths can't be distinguished—and sure enough, Fred tells us that an interference pattern has been created at his detector.

So far, so good. But then Mary holds up a gloved hand and blocks a1 before it can intermix with b1 and travel with it to her detector. At the same time Fred, watching his detector over on the right, calls out that his interference pattern just disappeared, replaced by a bullet pattern. Mary then lets a1 through again; it intermixes with b1 and they travel on to her detector—and on Fred's side of the room the interference pattern immediately reappears. Mary blocks a1 again, and again Fred's interference pattern disappears. How can that be? How can what Mary does to one of her low-energy beams on the left side of the room affect the low-energy beams that create Fred's interference pattern on the other side of the room? Once they have left their converters, Fred's low-energy beams remain completely separate from Mary's low-energy beams.

We have to conclude that the wavelike behavior of the particles is not being destroyed by any *intervention* on our part: Fred's beams, a2 and b2, leave their converters and arrive at his detector in identical circumstances whether they behave as particles or waves. There is no added intervention. So their wavelike behavior is being altered by what Mary is doing on the other side of the room—and what she is doing, significantly, is changing the status of our *information* about Fred's beams. That change is a subtle one: when Mary blocks a1, it means that b1 arrives at her detector alone. In theory, that means Mary and Fred could now compare the arrival time of Mary's b1 photons with the arrival times of the photons at Fred's detector, and separate Fred's photons into two groups: those that matched the arrival time of Mary's b1 photons (which would have originated in Beam B), and those that didn't (which would have originated in Beam A). In other words, when Mary blocks a1, she inadvertently renders the paths of Fred's photons distinguishable, and the wave function collapses. Mary and Fred don't have to measure and match the arrival times; the mere fact that they theoretically *could* is enough to change their status as observers.

In considering that what causes the collapse of the wave function is spatially nonlocal (blocking some photons on Mary's side of the room changes what the photons on Fred's side of the room do) we might be tempted to call the phenomenon 'psychic'. Certainly it cannot be explained in the terms we have inherited from classical science. And it raises one further question: if a change of information on the left side of the room can change the behavior of photons on the right side of the room, might it also be possible to change information today, and thereby determine the way photons behaved yesterday? That question was addressed by John Wheeler in his *delayed choice experiment*.

Can a delayed change in the status of our information about a particle determine the outcome of an event that has already happened?

Mary could choose whether to make the paths of Fred's photons distinguishable or not, and her choice determined whether they behaved like objects or waves. So, then, what if Mary could delay her choice until after a photon had already gone through the slits on Fred's side of the room, but just before it hit the screen? Would the photon fall into the pattern that tallied with the initial state of the apparatus, or with the changed state? In other words, can the 'decision' of the photon to take one path as a particle or another as a wave be forced to work retroactively, backwards in time, in response to a delayed decision to observe its path?

John Wheeler proposed a thought experiment to test that question. It involves a removable screen. Light passing through two slits would hit the screen and produce the interference pattern typical of waves. Behind the screen, though, are two telescopes, each aimed directly at one of the two slits: the telescope on the left is tightly focused on the left slit, and the telescope on the right is focused on the right slit. The telescopes, then, would enable us to distinguish the paths of the photons, telling us which ones came through which slits.

The thought experiment works like this: a photon passes through the double slit unobserved, and travels, either as a wave or as a particle, towards the screen. As it travels from the slits, and before it hits the screen, we decide whether to leave the screen in place, or remove it and expose the telescopes. Wheeler predicted that *our choice* to leave the screen or remove it would determine whether the photon arrived as a wave or a bullet—even though that outcome should logically have been determined as the photon passed through the slit. Some critics called his prediction physically impossible. But five years later a version of the experiment using a specialized crystal called a Pockels cell was performed independently in two separate labs—one at the University of Maryland and one at the University of Munich—and Wheeler was proven correct: the behavior of a photon can be made to be wavelike or particulate even *after* it has passed through the slits, just by altering our method of detection from one that can distinguish its path to one that can't.

In physical terms, though, how can that possibly be? No one knows. John Wheeler has said that the deepest lesson of quantum mechanics may be that reality is defined by the questions we put to it. But we can note that even across boundaries of time and space, there seems to be no way to separate the behavior of a particle from our ability to distinguish its path. The two phenomena are somehow one. Consciousness looks less and less like a local phenomenon that is wholly explained by the material properties of the brain, and more like an integral part of a reality in which "every component of the universe—down to the level of each individual subatomic particle—is in some peculiar sense immediately 'aware' of what is going on around it,"[380] as David Darling put it.

And lest we imagine that the nonlocal properties of consciousness apply only on the quantum scale, I will conclude with an example taken from Larry Dossey's book *Healing Beyond the Body: Medicine and the Infinite Reach of the Mind*. The example is a small one chosen from among countless documented 'anomalies', but it is particularly apt since it mirrors the retroactive influence for which Wheeler's delayed choice experiment tested. Dossey refers to certain experiments reviewed by William Braud, professor and director of research at the Institute of Transpersonal Psychology in Palo Alto, California, and co-director of its William James Center for Consciousness Studies. Dossey explains,

> In five experiments involving inanimate objects, such as random-event generators, people were able to successfully influence their output *after* the machine had already run, if the earlier output of the machine had not actually been observed. There was less that 1 chance in 10,000 that the successful results could be explained by chance.[381]

It seems, then, that the double-slit experiment does not provide a view into some remote realm that barely intersects with our own. The strangeness of the subatomic realm underpins all we see around us: it courses through our bodies, it manifests in the events of our lives, and it shows itself to be ineradicably bound to the realm of consciousness. And as for consciousness itself: what could be more mysterious, more immediately felt or more sensitively experienced? And what could provide a more suitable terrain for the ordinary hero's journey of renewal? The only limit to such a journey is the one you place on your own sensitivity. As Heraclitus said 2,500 years ago, "No matter how many ways you try, you cannot find a boundary to consciousness, so deep in every direction does it extend."[382]

And Finally,
an Outpouring of Gratitude

So many people have helped to usher this book into the world with support and encouragement and provocation that the compass of these meager acknowledgments could not begin to equal that of my gratitude. I am reduced to naming only the most outstanding among those to whom the writing of the book owes a debt.

I will begin with Andrew Harvey who, one Sunday afternoon, accepted a manuscript from me—a complete stranger at the time—and not only read it, but took the time to contact me and discuss the book, and gently, graciously prod me to take it further. Subsequently he helped to usher it into the world. It is fitting, then, that Andrew, who is the book's true midwife, also gave it its title, *New Self, New World*.

There would have been no book to name at all if it hadn't been for the support of my family. In a way, I feel the book belongs as much to my wife, Allyson, as it does to me: not only does her design greet the world on the cover and on every page within; her generosity and her faith are what enabled me to sit at home, writing, while she kept our household going. More than that, though, what I have learned from her about integrity, patience, humor, service and clarity has informed the book's every phrase.

My daughters, Kate and Julia, though occasionally given to rolling their eyes at any mention of "Dad's Book," have actually been steadfast in their support—and at times, despite themselves, even a little proud of the accomplishment, I suspect. It was for their sakes, as much as anything else, that the book was written.

My siblings, too, were remarkable, always ready to lend a hand however they could. My mother upheld the journey of the book with daily prayer, and I felt the grace of those prayers daily. Rob Woodrooffe, among many acts of generosity, archived countless evolving versions of the manuscript over the years. Susan Shirriff helped out in a thousand acts of kindness. And Joe and Catherine Sepulchre inadvertently precipitated the whole adventure by inviting our family to join them for two weeks in the summer of 2001.

As it takes a village to raise a child, it has in my case taken a community to birth a book—and my community, gloriously quirky as it is, is an island of sanity in a resolutely depersonalized world. Many within it have played a special role in bringing the book to its fruition. Some of its ideas were first expressed or provoked over the course of several memorable lunches and conversations with Sam Mallin. Peter Newman, Jacquey Malcolm, Richard Baruch, Brad Harley and Michael Raby all read early versions of the book and reported back with helpful comments. Nancy Jackson organized my first lecture on the book at OISE. Marc Irman unknowingly helped me put the concepts of the book into practice on the tennis court with his patient coaching. Ella Webber helped me learn how the book wanted to be read aloud, by listening so attentively. Don Darroch generously came forward with support for the book at a critical juncture in its publication. Christoph Strube took the author's photo. Andrew McHaffe was an invaluable resource for the design aspect of the book. Ken McAuliffe helped plan a fundraiser and Matthew Ferguson helped make it happen, and so many community members performed and assisted and participated that the event was a success on every level. Those who bought advance copies of the book, more than a year and a half before it was published, expressed their faith in it in a way that tangibly made its publication possible.

Close friends from beyond my community have been extraordinary in their support. Leanne Dixon was my confidante during the evolution of the book, and graciously demonstrated the exercises for the photos that accompany them. Frank and Jean Hoff have supported me over my entire career with generosity and a remarkable sensitivity to sources of inspiration that might spark my own evolution. Fides Krucker, Alison Humphrey and Niloofar Hodjati all read early versions of the book and commented on it with insight and encouragement. Hector Bunyan has been a sort of comrade-in-arms. Erik Martinez graciously read the Appendix and vetted it for errors. Pete Patterson shot photos for an early version of the exercises. Marcie Flewelling has been remarkable in her belief in my work, and in her generous support of it.

And Jeff Brown could not have been more forthcoming with all kinds of encouragement and nuts-and-bolts practical advice on all aspects of getting a book out into the world.

I also owe a debt to people I've met only on the page—all of them literary heroes to me for one reason or another—who looked at early versions of the book and offered unstinting assistance. Larry Dossey, Jean Houston, Stephen Mitchell and Marion Woodman all displayed a generosity of spirit that could stand as a model for what this book seeks to write about. And the eminent J. P. Mallory somehow found the time to read my chapters on the Indo-Europeans and commented from the depth of his scholarship in ways that spared me displaying all too plainly the lack of such scholarship on my own part.

I consider myself something of an opsimath, one who has been blessed with remarkable teachers and friends to assist my slow journey towards the experiences and understanding I was so keen to realize. Among their number I count Gerald Lampert, John Herbert, Stephen Mezei, Jack Harris, Linda Mussmann, Claudia Bruce, David Smukler, Steven Rumbelow, Ho Ying Fung and Denis Chagnon. I would also be remiss not to acknowledge two friends from my teenage hood, David Hoyland and Gilda Mekler, in the crucible of whose companionship my sense of self and somewhat divergent sense of truth were first really tested and forged.

There are many to thank, too, for their help with the practical task of ushering the book into publication. Richard Grossinger, Jon Goodspeed, Elizabeth Kennedy, and Paul McCurdy of North Atlantic Books all offered invaluable assistance and support in guiding this first-time author into publication. Rusty Shelton, Megan Renart, Merritt Talbott and the crew at Phenix and Phenix came forth with invaluable expertise and energy in promoting the book. M. J. Bogatin provided skilled and uncommonly common sense in his assistance with the legals. Digital Won Imaging was generously helpful with the printing of some early publicity items. And finally, I was fortunate to have had the two best editors I could have hoped for to guide the manuscript into its final, polished form. Richard Kukan brought a scope of scholarship and a nose for clear truth to the manuscript that challenged my thinking in very important ways, and consistently sharpened and strengthened what I was trying to say. The time we spent together going over passages of the book was so engaging and enjoyable that it would have been over too soon at almost any duration. And Anne Barthel, with her preternatural sense of the music of a phrase and her impeccable sense of logic, saw so lucidly what I was attempting to achieve with the book and where I fell short that she was able to point me with precision and grace towards the clarity I sought, but could not always find on my own.

To all those mentioned above, and to the many who helped but remain unacknowledged here, I offer my gratitude, and my hope that, on reading the book, you will find your early faith in it to have been warranted.

Endnotes

A Note on Etymological Sources

In the course of this book there are quite a few occasions in which the etymology of certain words is considered. I have no training in this specialized field, and so have relied on the expertise of others. First and foremost among them is Ernest Klein, a scholar, rabbi and concentration camp survivor who was conversant in over forty languages. I have owned his remarkable work—*Klein's Comprehensive Etymological Dictionary of the English Language*—since the mid-1970s, and it is the most frequently opened book on my shelf. I still remember when I first discovered it in a library, and was lost for a couple of hours traveling along the crisscrossed paths of languages that it so lucidly illuminated.

If that sounds like a love affair, so too might my relationship with Eric Partridge's works. While in my early twenties I devoured his classic book, *Usage and Abusage: A Guide to Good English,* and later acquired his etymological dictionary, *Origins.* It is organized very differently from Klein's, and that makes them perfect complements for any etymological question.

My particular interest in the Proto-Indo-European roots of English has been well served by Robert Claiborne's book, *The Roots of English.* It is basically a dictionary of the reconstructed PIE roots that have led to English words, supplied with an ample index of the English words that have derived from them. Using the book gives one a better feel for the energy of each root, and for how that energy found its diverse paths into English.

Finally, I have made liberal use of John Ayto's *Dictionary of Word*

Origins—which, though not redolent of the scholarly depths displayed by the other volumes, has an engaging, relaxed and very informative approach that often delivers context missing from the somewhat drier tone of the other three. To all of these authors, and all of these books, I would like to express my gratitude.

The above-mentioned works are:

> Ernest Klein, *Klein's Comprehensive Etymological Dictionary of the English Language* (Amsterdam: Elsevier, 1971).

> Eric Partridge, *Origins: A Short Etymological Dictionary of Modern English* (New York: Greenwich House, 1983).

> Robert Claiborne, *The Roots of English* (New York: Random House, 1989).

> John Ayto, *Dictionary of Word Origins* (New York: Arcade Publishing, 1990).

1   Joseph Campbell, *The Hero with a Thousand Faces* (Princeton: Princeton University Press, 1973), p. 5.
2   Roberto Calasso, *The Marriage of Cadmus and Harmony* (New York: Knopf, 1993), p. v.
3   Ibid., p. 280.
4   Joseph Campbell, *The Hero with a Thousand Faces* (Princeton: Princeton University Press, 1973), p. 1.
5   Ibid., p. 391.
6   Ibid., p 20.
7   Joseph Campbell, *The Power of Myth* (New York: Doubleday, 1988), p. 174.
8   Joseph Campbell, *The Hero with a Thousand Faces* (Princeton: Princeton University Press, 1973), p. 11.
9   Joseph Campbell, *The Power of Myth* (New York: Doubleday, 1988), p. 70.
10   James Kullander, "Men Are from Earth, and So Are Women," *The Sun*, issue 368 (August 2006).
11   John Mansley Robinson, *An Introduction to Early Greek Philosophy* (Boston: Houghton Mifflin, 1968), p. 8.

12   Anne Marie Owens, "Boys' Brains Are from Mars," *The National Post,* May 10, 2003.

13   Ibid.

14   Ibid.

15   Louis MacNeice, *Collected Poems* (London: Faber and Faber, 1979), p. 30, from the poem "Snow."

16   John Mansley Robinson, *An Introduction to Early Greek Philosophy* (Boston: Houghton Mifflin, 1968), p. 94.

17   Rimer and Masakazu (translators), *On the Art of the No Drama* (Princeton: Princeton University Press, 1984), p. xii.

18   Joseph Campbell, *The Hero with a Thousand Faces* (Princeton: Princeton University Press, 1973), p. 16.

19   Ibid., p. 218.

20   Ibid., p. 111.

21   Christopher Alexander, *The Timeless Way of Building* (New York: Oxford University Press, 1979), p. 122.

22   Alan Alda, *Never Have Your Dog Stuffed* (New York: Random House, 2005), p. 160 (emphasis mine).

23   Simon Callow, *Being an Actor* (London: Methuen, 1984), p. 173.

24   Susan Sontag, *A Susan Sontag Reader* (New York: Farrar, Straus, Giroux, 1982), p. 98.

25   Joseph Campbell, *The Power of Myth* (New York: Doubleday, 1988), p. 5 (emphasis mine).

26   Ibid., p. 6 (emphasis mine).

27   Bohm, David, *The Essential David Bohm* (New York: Routledge, 2003), p. 264.

28   Ibid., p. 287.

29   Stephen Mitchell (translator), *Tao Te Ching* (New York: HarperCollins, 2000), p. 24.

30   Lancelot Law Whyte, *The Next Development in Mankind* (New Brunswick, NJ: Transaction Publishers, 2003), p. xv (emphasis mine).

31   Richard Tarnas, *The Passion of the Western Mind* (New York: Ballantine Books, 1993), p. 47.

32   Joseph Campbell, *The Hero with a Thousand Faces* (Princeton: Princeton University Press, 1973), p. 15 (emphasis mine).

33   Jared Diamond, "The Last Americans," *Harpers Magazine,* June 2003, p. 51.

34   *A Bit Rich* (December 14, 2009) can be downloaded as a PDF at neweconomics.org/publications/bit-rich.

35   Matthew Fox and Rupert Sheldrake, *Natural Grace* (New York: Doubleday, 1996), p. 41.

36   Larry Dossey, *Space, Time, and Medicine* (Boulder, CO: Shambhala, 1982), p. 82.

37   Wade Davis, *Light at the Edge of the World* (Vancouver: Douglas & McIntyre, 2007), text-only edition, p. 138.

38 Ibid., p. 139.
39 Barry Commoner, "Unraveling the DNA Myth" (Harper's Magazine, February 2002), p. 40.
40 Lancelot Law Whyte, *The Next Development in Mankind* (New Brunswick, NJ: Transaction Publishers, 2003), p. 36.
41 Taken from the Web site for the Alcor Life Extension Foundation *www. alcor.org* (emphasis mine).
42 Fritjof Capra, *The Tao of Physics* (Boston: Shambhala, 1985), p. 131.
43 Lee Smolin, *Three Roads to Quantum Gravity* (New York: Basic Books, 2001), p. 63.
44 Fritjof Capra, *The Tao of Physics* (Boston: Shambhala, 1985), p. 138.
45 David Ruelle, *Chance and Chaos* (Princeton: Princeton University Press, 1991), p. 76.
46 Barry Commoner, "Unraveling the DNA Myth" (*Harper's Magazine*, February 2002), p. 43.
47 Clive Cookson, "To Make a Person" (*Financial Times*, March 22/23, 2003), p. v.
48 Anne McIlroy, "Code 2" (*Globe and Mail*, March 11, 2006), p. A5.
49 Ernest Fenollosa and Ezra Pound, *The Chinese Written Character as a Medium for Poetry* (San Francisco: City Lights Books, 1968), p. 22.
50 I. A. Richards, *The Philosophy of Rhetoric* (London: Oxford University Press, 1971), p. 94.
51 Ibid., p. 72.
52 Ibid., p. 35.
53 Some of that research is available to download at prevnet.ca.
54 Lewis Mumford, *The Myth of the Machine* (New York: Harcourt Brace, 1966).
55 D. W. Winnicott, *Home Is Where We Start From* (New York: Norton, 1990), p. 63.
56 Samuel B. Mallin, *Art Line Thought* (Dordrecht: Kluwer Academic Publishers, 1996), p. 269.
57 Ernest Fenollosa and Ezra Pound, *The Chinese Written Character as a Medium for Poetry* (San Francisco: City Lights Books, 1968), p. 22.
58 Matthew Fox and Rupert Sheldrake, *Natural Grace* (New York: Doubleday, 1996), p. 116.
59 John Mansley Robinson, *An Introduction to Early Greek Philosophy* (Boston: Houghton Mifflin, 1968), p. 35.
60 Thomas King (editor), *All My Relations* (Toronto: McClelland & Stewart, 1990), p. ix.
61 *Selected Poetry and Prose of Blake,* edited by Northrop Frye (New York: Modern Library, 1953), p. 123.
62 Guy Davenport (translator), *Herakleitos and Diogenes* (San Francisco: Grey Fox Press, 1983), p. 22.
63 John Mansley Robinson, *An Introduction to Early Greek Philosophy* (Boston: Houghton Mifflin, 1968), p. 95.

64 I heard Alexander express this in an interview on CBC radio some years ago. I wrote it down and it stayed with me, although neither the date nor the show it appeared on managed to.

65 Jose M.R. Delgado, *Physical Control of the Mind* (New York: Harper & Row, 1969), p. 59.

66 Ibid., p. 62.

67 Joseph Campbell, *Transformations of Myth through Time* (New York: Harper & Row, 1990), p. 112.

68 Dalai Lama, *How to Practice* (New York: Simon & Schuster, 2002), p. 37.

69 John Mansley Robinson, *An Introduction to Early Greek Philosophy* (Boston: Houghton Mifflin, 1968), p. 104.

70 Ibid., p. 95.

71 Stephen Mitchell (translator), *Tao Te Ching* (New York: HarperCollins, 2000), p. 28.

72 David Papineau, *Thinking about Consciousness* (Oxford: Oxford University Press, 2004), p. 1.

73 Steven Pinker, "The Mystery of Consciousness" (*Time*, January 29, 2007), p. 48.

74 Eric R. Kandel, "The New Science of Mind" (*Scientific American Mind*, April/May 2006), p. 64.

75 Eric Steinhart, "Persons versus Brains: Biological Intelligence in Human Organisms" (Kluwer Academic Publishers, *Biology and Philosophy 16*, 2001), p. 19.

76 Ibid., p. 11.

77 Ibid., p. 14.

78 Ibid., p. 15.

79 Ibid., p. 15.

80 Ibid., p. 18.

81 Ibid., p. 21.

82 Byron Robinson, *The Abdominal and Pelvic Brain* (available online at *meridianinstitute.com/eamt/files/robinson/Rob1ch12.htm*), chapter 12, pp. 6–8.

83 Michael Gershon, *The Second Brain* (New York: Quill, 2003), p. 50.

84 Candace B. Pert, *The Molecules of Emotion* (New York: Touchstone, 1999), p. 27.

85 Ibid., p. 193.

86 Gyorgi Doczi, *The Power of Limits* (Boston: Shambhala, 1985), p. 3 et al.

87 Fritjof Capra, *Uncommon Wisdom* (New York: Bantam, 1989), p. 136 (emphasis mine).

88 Paul Canali, from his Web site *evolutionaryhealinginstitute.com*.

89 Eric Steinhart, "Persons versus Brains: Biological Intelligence in Human Organisms" (Kluwer Academic Publishers, *Biology and Philosophy 16*, 2001), p. 11.

90   Brian Stross, *The Mesoamerican Sacrum Bone: Doorway to the Otherworld* (retrieved from research.famsi.org/aztlan/uploads/papers/stross-sacrum.pdf), p. 4.

91   Oscar Sugar, "How the Sacrum Got Its Name," *Journal of the American Medical Association* 257, no. 15 (1987): 2061–63.

92   Stephen Mitchell (editor), *The Enlightened Mind* (New York: HarperCollins, 1991), p. 191.

93   Ezra Pound and Ernest Fenollosa, *The Classic Noh Theatre of Japan* (New York: New Directions Books, 1959), p. 31.

94   Stephen Mitchell (translator), *Tao Te Ching* (New York: Perennial Classics, 2000), p. 28.

95   Guy Davenport, *The Geography of the Imagination* (San Francisco: North Point Press, 1981), p. 270.

96   Marion Woodman and Elinor Dickson, *Dancing in the Flames* (Boston: Shambhala, 1997), p. 211.

97   Frankfort, Frankfort, Wilson, Jacobsen, and Irwin, *The Intellectual Adventure of Ancient Man* (Chicago: University of Chicago Press, 1977), p. 6.

98   Larry VandeCreek, *Scientific and Pastoral Perspectives on Intercessory Prayer* (Binghamton, NY: Haworth Press, 1998), p. 28.

99   Matthew Fox, *Sins of the Spirit, Blessings of the Flesh* (New York: Harmony Books, 1999), p. 67.

100 Ibid.

101 Andrew Harvey, *Light upon Light* (Berkeley: North Atlantic Books, 1996), p. 85.

102 Guy Davenport (translator), *Herakleitos and Diogenes* (San Francisco: Grey Fox Press, 1983), p. 21.

103 Charles L. Harper (editor), *Spiritual Information* (Philadelphia: Templeton Press, 2005), p. 237 (emphasis mine).

104 Guy Davenport (translator), *Herakleitos and Diogenes* (San Francisco: Grey Fox Press, 1983), p. 18 (emphasis mine).

105 Aldous Huxley, *The Perennial Philosophy* (New York: Harper and Row, 1970), p. 5.

106 Ibid., p. 12.

107 Thomas Merton, *Thomas Merton on Zen* (London: Sheldon Press, 1976), p. 7.

108 Stephen Mitchell (editor), *The Enlightened Heart* (New York: Harper & Row, 1989), p. 133.

109 Marion Woodman and Elinor Dickson, *Dancing in the Flames* (Boston: Shambhala, 1997), p. 191.

110 Thomas Merton, *Thomas Merton on Zen* (London: Sheldon Press, 1976), p. 15.

111 Stephen Mitchell (translator), *Tao Te Ching* (New York: Perennial Classics, 2000), p. 93.

112 Søren Kierkegaard, *Fear and Trembling, and the Sickness unto Death*, translated by Walter Lowrie (New York: Doubleday, 1954), p. 165.

113 Dylan Thomas, "The Force That Through the Green Fuse Drives the Flower," from *The Top Five Hundred Poems* (New York: Columbia University Press, 1992), p. 1056.

114 Richard Tarnas, *The Passion of the Western Mind* (New York: Ballantine Books, 1993), p. 47.

115 Pico Iyer, "Leonard Cohen: Several Lifetimes Already" (*Shambhala Sun*, September 1998).

116 Robert Graves, *The Greek Myths*, vol. 1 (Harmondsworth, UK: Penguin, 1983), p. 284.

117 Raymond Bernard Blakney, *Meister Eckhart: A Modern Translation* (New York: Harper & Row, 1941), p. 98.

118 Robert Pirsig, *Zen and the Art of Motorcycle Maintenance* (New York: William Morrow, 1984), p. 314.

119 Eugen Herrigel, *Zen in the Art of Archery* (New York: Vintage Books, 1971), p. 54.

120 Connie Barlow (editor), *From Gaia to Selfish Genes* (Cambridge, MA: MIT Press, 1998), p. 89.

121 Walter Wager (editor), *The Playwrights Speak* (New York: Dell, 1968), p. 152.

122 Guy Davenport (translator), *Herakleitos and Diogenes* (San Francisco: Grey Fox Press, 1983), p. 11.

123 John Tarrant, *Bring Me the Rhinoceros* (Boston: Shambhala, 2008), p. 173.

124 Marion Woodman and Elinor Dickson, *Dancing in the Flames* (Boston: Shambhala, 1997), p. 216.

125 Fritjof Capra, *The Tao of Physics* (Boston: Shambhala, 1985), p. 140.

126 Jonah Lehrer, "The Neuroscience of Screwing Up" (*Wired*, January 2010, vol. 18, no. 1).

127 John Bartlett (editor), *Bartlett's Familiar Quotations* (Boston: Little, Brown, 1968), p. 723.

128 Anand Giridharadas, "Are Metrics Blinding Our Perception?" (*New York Times*, November 21, 2009).

129 Anne McIlroy, "Inside the Search for the God Particle" (*Globe and Mail*, Toronto, September 10, 2008), p. A15.

130 Gregory Bateson, *Mind and Nature* (New York: Dutton, 1979), p. 30.

131 Edith Hamilton, Huntington Cairns, and Lane Cooper, *The Collected Dialogues of Plato* (Princeton: Princeton University Press, 1961), p. 49.

132 Joseph Campbell, *The Hero with a Thousand Faces*, (Princeton: Princeton University Press, 1973), p. 217.

133 Quoted in "Can This Black Box See into the Future" (RedOrbit News, *redorbit.com*).

134 James Jeans, *The Mysterious Universe* (Cambridge: Cambridge University Press, 1930), chapter 5.

135 Marion Woodman, *The Owl Was a Baker's Daughter* (Toronto: Inner City Books, 1980), p. 66.
136 Erwin Schrödinger, *What is Life? and Mind and Matter* (London: Cambridge University Press, 1969), p. 145 (emphasis mine).
137 Nick Herbert, *Elemental Mind* (New York: Penguin, 1994), p. 3.
138 Ibid., p. 5.
139 Ibid., p. 201 (emphasis mine).
140 Ibid., p. 230.
141 Joseph Campbell, *The Hero with a Thousand Faces* (Princeton: Princeton University Press, 1973), p. 217.
142 Luther Standing Bear, *Land of the Spotted Eagle* (Lincoln, NE: Bison Books, 2006), p. 193.
143 John Mansley Robinson, *An Introduction to Early Greek Philosophy* (Boston: Houghton Mifflin, 1968), p. 97.
144 Thomas Merton, *Thomas Merton on Zen* (London: Sheldon Press, 1976), p. 41.
145 Larry Dossey, *Healing Words* (New York: Harper San Francisco, 1993), p. 87.
146 Sogyal Rinpoche, *The Tibetan Book of Living and Dying* (New York: HarperCollins, 1992), p. 62.
147 Joseph Campbell, *The Masks of God: Occidental Mythology* (New York: Penguin, 1976), p. 44.
148 Andrew Harvey, *The Return of the Mother* (Berkeley: Frog Books, 1995), p. 353.
149 *The Bible,* Psalms 46:10.
150 T. S. Eliot, *Four Quartets* (Orlando, FL: Harcourt Books, 1971), p. 15.
151 Said by Marion at a workshop I attended in Guelph, Ontario, "Dancing in the Flames," organized by Barbara Susan Booth for the Sacred Wisdom Center, December 1–3, 2006.
152 Guy Davenport (translator), *Herakleitos and Diogenes* (San Francisco: Grey Fox Press, 1983), p. 18.
153 Hugh Brody, *The Other Side of Eden* (New York: North Point Press, 2000), p. 242.
154 Peter Payne, *Martial Arts* (London: Thames and Hudson, 1987), p. 47.
155 Alan Watts, *The Wisdom of Insecurity* (New York: Vintage, 1951), p. 46.
156 William Littler, "Dancing at 60—One Woman's Testimonial" (*Toronto Star,* September 30, 1976).
157 Guy Davenport (translator), *Herakleitos and Diogenes* (San Francisco: Grey Fox Press, 1983), p. 14.
158 Paul Reps, *Square Sun Square Moon* (Rutland, VT: Charles E. Tuttle, 1974), p. 59.
159 Stephen Mitchell (translator), *Tao Te Ching* (New York: Perennial Classics, 2000), p. 100.
160 Ibid., p. 76.

161 Larry Dossey, *Space, Time, and Medicine* (Boulder, CO: Shambhala, 1982), p. 84.

162 Paul Reps, *10 Ways to Meditate* (New York: Weatherhill, 1982), p. 11.

163 Plato, *The Last Days of Socrates*, translated by Hugh Tredennick (London: Penguin, 2003), p. 127.

164 Thomas Merton, *Thomas Merton on Zen* (London: Sheldon Press, 1976), p. 79.

165 Alan W. Watts, *The Wisdom of Insecurity* (New York: Vintage, 1951), p. 73.

166 Stephen Mitchell (translator), *Tao Te Ching* (New York: Perennial Classics, 2000), p. 93.

167 Ibid., p. ix.

168 Eugenio Barba and Nicola Savarese, *The Secret Art of the Performer* (London: Routledge, 1995), p. 237.

169 Ibid.

170 Eugenio Barba, *The Paper Canoe* (London: Routledge, 1995), p. 35.

171 D. Lyman (translator), *The Moral Sayings of Publius Syrus, a Roman Slave* (Cleveland, OH: L.E. Barnard, 1856), p. 16.

172 Joseph Campbell, *Transformations of Myth through Time* (New York: Harper & Row, 1990), p. 12.

173 Andrew Harvey (editor), *The Essential Mystics* (New York: HarperSanFrancisco, 1996), p. 155.

174 Thomas Merton, *Thomas Merton on Zen* (London: Sheldon Press, 1976), p. 80.

175 Yasunari Kawabata, *Japan the Beautiful and Myself* (Tokyo: Kodansha, 1969), p. 58.

176 Eugenio Barba, *The Paper Canoe* (London: Routledge, 1995), p. 9.

177 Joseph Campbell, *The Hero with a Thousand Faces* (Princeton: Princeton University Press, 1973), p. 388.

178 Matthew Fox, *Sins of the Spirit, Blessings of the Flesh* (New York: Harmony Books, 1999), p. 61.

179 Ibid., p. 60.

180 Retrieved from *planetproctor.com* (2001, vol. 9).

181 Matthew Fox, *Sins of the Spirit, Blessings of the Flesh* (New York: Harmony Books, 1999), p. 60.

182 Joseph Campbell, *The Hero with a Thousand Faces* (Princeton: Princeton University Press, 1973), p. 345.

183 Ibid., p. 267.

184 T. S. Eliot, *The Use of Poetry and the Use of Criticism* (1933), eight published lectures given at Harvard University. Eliot's original words were, "The chief use of the 'meaning' of a poem, in the ordinary sense, may be ... to satisfy one habit of the reader, to keep his mind diverted and quiet, while the poem does its work upon him: much as the imaginary burglar is always provided with a bit of nice meat for the house-dog."

185 Joseph Campbell, *The Hero with a Thousand Faces* (Princeton: Princeton University Press, 1973), p. 350.

186 Ibid., p. 237.

187 Ibid., p. 163.

188 Ibid., p. 389.

189 Stephen Mitchell (translator), *Tao Te Ching* (New York: Perennial Classics, 2000), p. 50.

190 *The Bible,* Luke 39–46.

191 Joseph Campbell quotes this passage in *The Hero with a Thousand Faces* (Princeton: Princeton University Press, 1973), p. 191. It is from a translation of *Poetic Edda,* "Hovamol," by Henry Adams Bellows (New York: American-Scandinavian Foundation, 1923), p. 139. For simplicity's sake, I altered the translation slightly, amending the original "Othin" to the more familiar "Odin."

192 Michael Murphy and Rhea A. White, *In the Zone* (New York: Penguin, 1995), p. 26.

193 This article is available at *gladwell.com.*

194 Marshall McLuhan, *Understanding Media* (New York: McGraw-Hill, 1964), p. 64.

195 This article is available at *gladwell.com.*

196 Nick Herbert, *Elemental Mind* (New York: Penguin, 1994), p. 185.

197 Ervin Laszlo, "Subtle Connections: Psi, Grof, Jung and the Quantum Vacuum," 1996. This article is available online at *goertzel.org/ dynapsych/1996/subtle.html.*

198 Stephen Mitchell (translator), *Tao Te Ching* (New York: Perennial Classics, 2000), p. 64.

199 From "Schrodinger's Surfboard" by Steve Hawk in *Harper's Magazine* (July 1994).

200 Larry Dossey, *Space, Time, and Medicine* (Boulder, CO: Shambhala, 1982), p. 74.

201 Alan Watts, *Does It Matter?* (New York: Vintage Books, 1971), p. 22.

202 Alan Watts, "The World as Emptiness," Part 2, p. 5, available online at *deoxy.org/w_world.htm.*

203 From an interview with David Jay Brown, May 27, 1994, available online at *mavericksofthemind.com/hou-int.htm.*

204 From an interview on CBC radio.

205 Lee Smolin, *The Life of the Cosmos* (New York: Oxford University Press, 1997), p. 221.

206 Charles Darwin, *The Descent of Man* (New York: D. Appleton, 1871), p. 44.

207 Rachel Carson, *The Sense of Wonder* (New York: Harper and Row, 1987), p. 45.

208 David Niven, *The Moon's a Balloon* (Philadelphia: Coronet Books, 1973), p. 283.

209 This popular quote appears at *sfheart.com/Einstein*.

210 J. Von Rintelen, *Beyond Existentialism* (London: George Allen & Unwin, 1961), p. 28.

211 Stephen Mitchell (translator), *Tao Te Ching* (New York: HarperPerennial, 2000), p. 94.

212 Peter Payne, *Martial Arts: The Spiritual Dimension* (London: Thames and Hudson, 1981), p. 36.

213 John Mansley Robinson, *An Introduction to Early Greek Philosophy* (Boston: Houghton Mifflin, 1968), p. 95.

214 This quote is excerpted on the Web site of the Institute of Noetic Sciences, which Mitchell helped to found: *noetic.org/about/history.cfm*.

215 Hiroyuki Aoki, *The Zero Point of Consciousness and the World of Ki* (San Francisco: Shintaido of America, 1989), p. 9.

216 Surendranath Dasgupta, *A History of Indian Philosophy*, vol. 1 (Cambridge: Cambridge University Press, 1973), p. 134.

217 Matthew Fox, *Sins of the Spirit, Blessings of the Flesh* (New York: Harmony Books, 1999), p. 20.

218 Brewster Ghiselin (editor), *The Creative Process* (New York: Mentor Books, 1957), p. 90.

219 Bash , *The Narrow Road to the Deep North and Other Travel Sketches* (Baltimore: Penguin Books, 1974), p. 105.

220 Kakuzo Okakura, *The Book of Tea* (available online at *everything2.com*), chapter 6.

221 Karlfried Graf von Dürckheim, *Hara: The Vital Centre of Man* (London: Unwin, 1971), p. 91 (emphasis mine).

222 Joseph Campbell, *The Hero with a Thousand Faces* (Princeton: Princeton University Press, 1973), p. 59.

223 James Hillman, *The Soul's Code* (New York: Random House, 1996), p. 87.

224 Moshe Feldenkrais, *Body and Mature Behavior* (New York: International Universities Press, 1981), p. 131.

225 Sophocles, *Sophocles 1* (Chicago: University of Chicago Press, 1965), p. 46.

226 Joseph Campbell, *The Hero with a Thousand Faces* (Princeton: Princeton University Press, 1973), p. 337.

227 Marion Woodman and Elinor Dickson, *Dancing in the Flames* (Boston: Shambhala, 1997), p. 159.

228 Charles Davis, *Body as Spirit* (New York: Seabury Press, 1976), p. 60 (emphasis mine).

229 Stephen Mitchell (translator), *Tao Te Ching* (New York: Perennial Classics, 2000), p. 71.

230 Joseph Campbell, *The Power of Myth* (New York: Doubleday, 1998), p. 41.

231 Stephen Mitchell (editor), *The Enlightened Heart* (New York: Harper & Row, 1989), p. 57.

232 Kevin Crossley-Holland, *The Seeing Stone* (New York: Scholastic, 2002), p. 164.

233 Dietrich Bonhoeffer, *The Cost of Discipleship* (London: SCM Press, 2001), p. 44.

234 Julius Lester, *The Pharaoh's Daughter* (San Diego: Harcourt, 2000), appendix.

235 Jean Houston, *Jump Time* (New York: Jeremy P. Tarcher, 2000), p. 38.

236 James Hillman, *The Soul's Code* (New York: Random House, 1996), p. 260.

237 Thomas Byrom (translator), *The Dhammapada*, "Section 12: Yourself." Available online at *thebigview.com*.

238 Alphonse Goettmann, *Dialogue on the Path of Initiation: The Life and Thought of Karlfried Graf Dürckheim* (electronically published by Nottingham Publishing), p. 27. Available online at: *tedn.hypermart.net/trans1.htm*.

239 The study was published in the March 2009 issue of the Public Library of Science (PLoS One). The quote is from GeorgiaDailyDigest.com, "Financial Advice Causes 'Off-Loading' in the Brain," March 25, 2009.

240 Sogyal Rinpoche, *The Tibetan Book of Living and Dying* (New York: HarperCollins, 1992), p. 36.

241 Russell Hoban, *The Medusa Frequency* (New York: Viking, 1987), p. 68 (emphasis mine).

242 Sogyal Rinpoche, *The Tibetan Book of Living and Dying* (New York: HarperCollins, 1992), p. 39.

243 Anne Applebaum, *Gulag: A History* (New York: Doubleday, 2003), p. 345.

244 Curtis White, "The Spirit of Disobedience," *Harper's Magazine* (April 2006).

245 Ovid, *The Metamorphoses* (New York: Mentor, 1960), p. 274.

246 Shinichi Suzuki, *Nurtured by Love* (Los Angeles: Alfred Publishing, 1983), p. 62.

247 Matthew Fox, *Sins of the Spirit, Blessings of the Flesh* (New York: Harmony Books, 1999), p. 200.

248 William Golding, *Free Fall* (London: Faber and Faber, 1979), p. 186.

249 Ibid., p. 187.

250 Alden Nowlan, *Selected Poems* (Toronto: House of Anansi, 1996), p. 145.

251 Arthur Miller, "The Shadow of the Gods," *Harper's Magazine* (August 1958).

252 Thich Nhat Hanh, *The Miracle of Mindfulness* (Boston: Beacon Press, 1987), p. 61.

253 Yamamoto Tsunetomo, *Hagakure* (Tokyo: Kodansha, 1983), p. 27.

254 Arthur Finley Scott (editor), *Modern Essays*, vol. 2 (London: Macmillan, 1947), p. 161, in the essay by Sir James Jeans, "Our Home in Space."

255 Sogyal Rinpoche, *The Tibetan Book of Living and Dying* (New York: HarperCollins, 1992), p. 63.

256 Malcolm Gladwell, "The Physical Genius," section 1, available at *gladwell.com*.

257 Donald Winnicott, *Playing and Reality* (New York: Routledge, 1999), p. 52.

258 Donald Winnicott, *Playing and Reality* (New York: Routledge Classics, 2005), p. 64.

259 Donald Winnicott, *Playing and Reality* (New York: Routledge, 1999), p. 65.

260 Terry Tempest Williams, "In the Shadow of Extinction," *New York Times*, February 2, 2003.

261 Elizabeth Marshall Thomas, *The Tribe of Tiger* (New York: Simon and Schuster, 1994), p. 119.

262 Stephen Kellert and Edward Wilson (editors), *The Biophilia Hypothesis* (Washington: Island Press, 1993), p. 210, from an essay, "Searching for the Lost Arrow: Physical and Spiritual Ecology in the Hunter's World" by Richard Nelson.

263 Hugh Brody, *The Other Side of Eden* (New York: North Point Press, 2000), p. 255.

264 Andrew Harvey, *Son of Man: The Mystical Path to Christ* (New York: Jeremy P. Tarcher/Putnam, 1998).

265 Jay Gluck, *Zen Combat* (New York: Ballantine Books, 1962), p. 178.

266 *The Bible*, Ecclesiasticus 3:19.

267 Ibid., Matthew 5:5.

268 Hiroyuki Aoki, *The Zero Point of Consciousness and the World of Ki* (San Francisco: Shintaido of America, 1989), p. 9.

269 Ibid., p. 8.

270 Frankfort et al., *The Intellectual Adventure of Ancient Man* (Chicago: University of Chicago Press, 1977), p. 6.

271 Zeami Motokiyo, *Fushikaden* (translation by Shidehara Michitaro and Wilfred Whitehouse in *Monumenta Nipponica* 4–5, 1941–42, p. 236).

272 *Concise Routledge Encyclopedia of Philosophy* (London: Routledge, 2000), p. 96.

273 Deitrich Bonhoeffer, *Letters and Papers from Prison* (New York: Macmillan, 1972), pp. 9–12.

274 Sogyal Rinpoche, *The Tibetan Book of Living and Dying* (New York: HarperCollins, 1992), p. 173.

275 Shirley Darcus Sullivan, *Psychological Activity in Homer: A Study of Phren* (Ottawa: Carlton University Press, 1988).

276 Richmond Lattimore (translator), *The Odyssey of Homer* (New York: Harper & Row, 1975), p. 307 (emphasis mine).

277 Ernest Fenollosa and Ezra Pound, *The Chinese Written Character as a Medium for Poetry* (San Francisco: City Lights Books, 1968), p. 19.

278 *Columbia Dictionary of Quotations* (New York: Columbia University Press, 1993).

279 William J. Mitchell, *The Reconfigured Eye: Visual Truth in the Post-Photographic Era* (Cambridge, MA: MIT Press, 1994), p. 59.

280 Paul Benedetti and Nancy DeHart (editors), *Forward through the Rearview Mirror: Reflections on and by Marshall McLuhan* (Toronto: Prentice-Hall, 1996), p. 116.

281 Frankfort et al., *The Intellectual Adventure of Ancient Man* (Chicago: University of Chicago Press, 1977), pp. 5–6.

282 Ibid., p. 6.

283 Ibid., p. 11 (emphasis mine).

284 Marija Gimbutas, *The Civilization of the Goddess* (New York: HarperCollins, 1991), p. viii.

285 Dr. Mallory graciously reviewed an early version of this chapter, and offered many invaluable corrections. In one of them, he used this provocative phrase.

286 Marija Gimbutas, *The Language of the Goddess* (San Francisco: Harper & Row, 1989), p. 321.

287 Marija Gimbutas, *The Civilization of the Goddess* (New York: HarperCollins, 1991), p. x.

288 Hodder's article "Women and Men at Catalhoyuk" appeared in *Mysteries of the Ancient Ones,* a special edition of *Scientific American.*

289 Ian Hodder, "Contextual Archaeology: An Interpretation of Catal Huyuk and a Discussion of the Origins of Agriculture" (London University Institute of Archaeology Bulletin, 1987), p. 43–56.

290 Marija Gimbutas, *The Civilization of the Goddess* (New York: HarperCollins, 1991), p. viii.

291 Margaret Ehrenberg, *Women in Prehistory* (London: British Museum Press, 1989), chapter 3.

292 Marija Gimbutas, *The Civilization of the Goddess* (New York: HarperCollins, 1991), p. 342.

293 David Anthony, Dimitri Y. Telegin, and Dorcas Brown, "The Origin of Horseback Riding," *Scientific American,* December 1991.

294 John Keegan, *A History of Warfare* (New York: Random House, 1994), p. 161.

295 Ibid., p. 189.

296 Marija Gimbutas, *The Civilization of the Goddess* (New York: HarperCollins, 1991), p. 352.

297 Ibid., p. 394.

298 Ibid., p. 401.

299 John Mansley Robinson, *An Introduction to Early Greek Philosophy* (Boston: Houghton Mifflin, 1968), p. 97.

300 Stephen Mitchell, *The Enlightened Mind* (New York: HarperCollins, 1991), p. 7.

301 Shakespeare, *Coriolanus*, act 2, scene 1.

302 J. P. Mallory, *In Search of the Indo-Europeans* (New York: Thames and Hudson, 1991), p. 12 (emphasis mine).

303 Ibid., p. 184.

304 David Anthony et al., "The Origin of Horseback Riding," *Scientific American*, December 1991.

305 J. P. Mallory, *In Search of the Indo-Europeans* (New York: Thames and Hudson, 1991), p. 141.

306 Thorkild Jacobsen, *The Treasures of Darkness* (New Haven, CT: Yale University Press, 1976), p. 11.

307 Marija Gimbutas, *The Civilization of the Goddess* (New York: HarperCollins, 1991), p. 399.

308 Ivan Illich and Barry Sanders, *A.B.C.: The Alphabetization of the Popular Mind* (New York: Random House, 1988), p. 13 (emphasis mine).

309 From "The End of the Wild," a documentary from the CBC radio series *Ideas*.

310 *The Bible,* John 1:1.

311 Karl Jaspers, *The Origin and Goal of History* (New Haven, CT: Yale University Press, 1953), p. 2.

312 Joseph Campbell, *The Inner Reaches of Outer Space* (New York: Harper & Row, 1988), p. 40.

313 Hugh Brody, *The Other Side of Eden* (New York: North Point Press, 2000), p. 293.

314 Stephen Mitchell (translator), *Tao Te Ching* (New York: Perennial Classics, 2000), p. 94.

315 John Mansley Robinson, *An Introduction to Early Greek Philosophy* (Boston: Houghton Mifflin, 1968), p. 228.

316 Plato, *Timaeus and Critias* (Harmondsworth, UK: Penguin Books, 1983), p. 61 (emphasis mine).

317 John Bartlett (editor), *Bartlett's Familiar Quotations* (Boston: Little, Brown, 1968), p. 115.

318 Jean-Paul Sartre, *Being and Nothingness,* quoted in "The Heart of Nothingness" by Harry Eyres, *Financial Times*, November 5–6, 2005, p. W7.

319 Jacques Monod, *Chance and Necessity* (New York: Knopf, 1971), p. 172.

320 Simon Baron-Cohen, "The Extreme Male Brain Theory of Autism," from *Trends in Cognitive Sciences* 6 (2002): 248–54. Available online at *vaccinationnews.com*.

321 Hugh Brody, *The Other Side of Eden* (New York: North Point Press, 2000), p. 242.

322 John Mansley Robinson, *An Introduction to Early Greek Philosophy* (Boston: Houghton Mifflin, 1968), p. 157.

323 Thomas Merton, *The Way of Chuang Tzu* (Boston: Shambhala, 2004), p. 63.
324 Kakuzo Okakura, cited in *Outlines of Chinese Symbolism and Art Motives* by C.A.S. Williams (New York: Dover, 1976), p. 132.
325 Jocobus de Voragine, *The Golden Legend: St. George,* available online at *fordham.edu/halsall/basis/goldenlegend/gl-vol3-george.html.*
326 Richard Tarnas, *Cosmos and Psyche* (New York: Penguin, 2006), p. 77.
327 Dalai Lama, *How to Practice* (New York: Pocket Books, 2002), p. 161.
328 Alan Watts, *Tao: The Watercourse Way* (New York: Pantheon Books, 1975), p. 25.
329 Dalai Lama, *How to Practice* (New York: Pocket Books, 2002), p. 165.
330 Stanislav Grof (editor), *Ancient Wisdom and Modern Science* (Albany: State University of New York Press, 1984), p. 138.
331 Alan Watts, "The World as Emptiness," part 3, p. 11, available online at *deoxy.org/w_world.htm.*
332 Lionel Giles, *Taoist Teachings: The Book of Lieh-Tzu* (published 1912, republished by *forgottenbooks.com* in 2008), p. 52.
333 Stephen Mitchell (editor), *The Enlightened Mind* (New York: HarperCollins, 1991), p. 111.
334 Stephen Mitchell (translator), *Tao Te Ching* (New York: Perennial Classics, 2000), p. 11.
335 Ludwig Wittgenstein, *Tractus Logico-Philosophicus* (London: Routledge, 2001), p. 87, proposition 6.4311.
336 Alexander Lowen, *Bioenergetics* (New York: Penguin Books, 1984), p. 194.
337 Karlfried Graf Von Dürckheim, *Hara: The Vital Centre of Man* (London: Unwin, 1971), p. 125.
338 John E. Sarno, *The Divided Mind: The Epidemic of Mindbody Disorders* (New York: Regan Books, 2006), p. 20.
339 Ibid., p. 11.
340 Ibid., p. 87.
341 David Foster Wallace, *Consider the Lobster* (New York: Little, Brown, 2006), p. 35.
342 Eugenio Barba and Nicola Savarese, *A Dictionary of Theatre Anthropology* (London: Routledge, 1995), p. 41.
343 Guy Davenport (translator), *Herakleitos and Diogenes* (San Francisco: Grey Fox Press, 1983), p. 16.
344 Ibid.
345 Ibid., p. 23.
346 Hiroyuki Aoki, *The Zero Point of Consciousness and the World of Ki* (San Francisco: Shintaido of America, 1989), p. 11.
347 Ibid., p. 13.
348 Mu Soeng, *The Diamond Sutra* (Somerville, MA: Wisdom Publications, 2000), p. 62.

349 Alan Watts, *Tao: The Watercourse Way* (New York: Pantheon Books, 1975), p. 25.

350 Thomas Ryckman, *The Reign of Relativity* (New York: Oxford University Press, 2005), p. 217.

351 Guy Davenport (translator), *Herakleitos and Diogenes* (San Francisco: Grey Fox Press, 1983), p. 18.

352 Stanislav Grof, *Beyond the Brain* (Albany: State University of New York Press, 1985), p. 73.

353 From an interview with Daniel Redwood, available online at *healthy. net/LIBRARY/interviews/redwood/grof.htm*.

354 Thomas Merton, *Thomas Merton on Zen* (London: Sheldon Press, 1976), p. 6.

355 Peter Payne, *Martial Arts: The Spiritual Dimension* (London: Thames and Hudson, 1981), p. 46.

356 Gregory Bateson, *Mind and Nature* (New York: Dutton, 1979), p. 10.

357 Natalie Curtis, *The Indian's Book* (New York: Dover, 1968), p. xxiv.

358 Jean Houston, *Jump Time* (New York: Jeremy P. Tarcher, 2000), p. 57.

359 Ibid., p. 59.

360 *The Bible*, Revelation 3:8.

361 Ibid., John 8:7.

362 Yasunari Kawabata, *Japan the Beautiful and Myself* (Tokyo: Kodansha, 1969), p. 56.

363 Andrew Harvey, *The Way of Passion* (New York: Jeremy P. Tarcher/ Putnam, 2001), p. 35.

364 Larry Chang (editor), *Wisdom for the Soul* (Washington, DC: Grosophia, 2006), p. 265.

365 Andrew Harvey, *The Return of the Mother* (Berkeley: Frog Books, 1995), p. 312.

366 Joseph Campbell, *The Hero with a Thousand Faces* (Princeton: Princeton University Press, 1973), p. 229.

367 Thomas Merton, *The Way of Chuang Tzu* (Boston: Shambhala, 2004), p. 40.

368 Stephen Mitchell (editor), *The Enlightened Heart* (New York: Harper and Row, 1989), p. 45.

369 Stephen Mitchell (editor), *The Enlightened Mind* (New York: HarperCollins, 1991), p. 114.

370 Matthew Fox and Rupert Sheldrake, *Natural Grace* (New York: Doubleday, 1996), p. 83.

371 Stephen Mitchell (translator), *Tao Te Ching* (New York: Perennial Classics, 2000), p. 64.

372 Evelyn Underhill (editor), *The Cloud of Unknowing* (Charleston, SC: BiblioBazaar *bibliobazaar.com*, 2007), p. 10.

373 Kakuzo Okakura, *The Book of Tea* (available online at *everything2. com*), chapter 7.

374 David M. Edwards, *Worship 365* (Nashville, TN: Broadman & Holman, 2006), p. 133.

375 Stephen Mitchell (translator), *Tao Te Ching* (New York: Perennial Classics, 2000), p. 71.

376 Richard Feynman, *Six Easy Pieces* (Reading, MA: Perseus Books, 1995), p 117.

377 Gary Zukav, *The Dancing Wu Li Masters* (New York: Bantam, 1980), p. 63.

378 John Gribbin, *In Search of Schrodinger's Cat* (New York: Bantam, 1984), p. 170.

379 David Darling, *Zen Physics* (New York: HarperCollins, 1996), p. 132.

380 Ibid., p. 134.

381 Larry Dossey, *Healing Beyond the Body* (Boston: Shambhala, 2001), p. 208.

382 Guy Davenport (translator), *Herakleitos and Diogenes* (San Francisco: Grey Fox Press, 1983), p. 18.

Credits

Index

Notes

Notes

About the Author

The course of Philip Shepherd's life has been shaped by questions. As a teenager he cycled alone through Europe, the Middle East, Iran and India on the way to Japan to study classical Noh theatre. Since then he has designed and built several houses; cofounded and written for an arts magazine, *Onion;* cofounded and directed an interdisciplinary theatre company; taught numerous workshops to help people discover increased presence and creativity; written two internationally produced plays and a documentary for CBC television; trained in Butoh dance and toured Canada with a show; edited a book of art criticism, *The Compleat Art Critic;* acted in several feature films opposite such talents as Mandy Patinkin and Delroy Lindo *(Strange Justice)* and Jon Voight *(Jasper Texas)*; earned a reputation as a corporate coach, helping business leaders hone their presentation skills; and played lead roles in theatre productions in Toronto, New York, Chicago, London and Hong Kong. He is currently a faculty member of The Institute for Sacred Activism, which is based in Chicago.

You can listen to Philip's reading of *New Self, New World* on CD. The set is available at philipshepherd.com, where an excerpt of the reading can be found, as well as further information about the book.